The End of the Future

The End of the Future

Trauma, Memory, and Reconciliation in Peruvian Amazonia

BARTHOLOMEW DEAN

VANDERBILT UNIVERSITY PRESS

Nashville, Tennessee

Library of Congress Cataloging-in-Publication Data

Names: Dean, Bartholomew, 1963– author.
Title: The end of the future : trauma, memory, and reconciliation in
    Peruvian Amazonia / Bartholomew Dean.
Other titles: Trauma, memory, and reconciliation in Peruvian Amazonia
Description: Nashville, Tennessee : Vanderbilt University Press, [2023] |
    Includes bibliographical references and index.
Identifiers: LCCN 2023034146 (print) | LCCN 2023034147 (ebook) | ISBN
    9780826506252 (paperback) | ISBN 9780826506269 (hardcover) | ISBN
    9780826506276 (Ebook/EPUB) | ISBN 9780826506283 (Ebook/Web PDF)
Subjects: LCSH: Movimiento Revolucionario Túpac Amaru—Interviews. |
    Collective memory—Peru—Huallaga River Valley. |
    Violence—Peru—Huallaga River Valley. | Psychic trauma—Peru—Huallaga
    River Valley. | Peasants—Peru—Huallaga River Valley—Interviews. |
    Mestizos—Peru—Huallaga River Valley—Interviews. |
    Insurgency—Peru—Huallaga River Valley. | Huallaga River Valley
    (Peru)—Rural conditions. | War and society—Peru—Huallaga River
    Valley. | Peru—Politics and government—1980-
Classification: LCC HV6433.P42 M68425 2020 (print) | LCC HV6433.P42
    (ebook) | DDC 362.880985—dc23/eng/20230830
LC record available at https://lccn.loc.gov/2023034146
LC ebook record available at https://lccn.loc.gov/2023034147

Front cover image: Former MRTA insurgent, contemporary paramilitary,
Caynarachi Basin. Photograph by Bartholomew Dean

Dedicated to the cherished memories
of Eric Edwin Dean and Jack William Keeper, and in
enduring remembrance of Nelson Standish Bathurst

Contents

Foreword by Manuel Burga   *ix*

Introduction. Narrative Renditions of Ugly Times:
  Memory, Violence, and Trauma in Peruvian Amazonia   I

Chapter 1. The Ugly Times of War   10

Chapter 2. In Search of the Rebel   23

Chapter 3. War Taxes   47

Chapter 4. Túpac Amaru Libertador   68

Chapter 5. Forest Encounters   97

Chapter 6. Discipline: Law and Disorder   121

Chapter 7. White Gold   141

Chapter 8. Attack on the "Pearl of the Huallaga"   152

Chapter 9. The End of the Future: El Porvenir   162

Chapter 10. Memory, Silence, and the Narration of Violence   180

Conclusion: Partisan Anthropology, Empathy, and Reconciliation   185

Notes 193
References   243
Acknowledgments 257
Index 261

Foreword

Manuel Burga

Passionate about understanding the "others" in Peru, Bartholomew Dean, an anthropologist by profession and practice, invited me to write a prologue for this book. I am a historian by trade and have a long-standing interest in learning about the "others," those who were defeated during the Spanish Conquest and came to be seen as "others." Bart might have asked me to write these introductory remarks because of our similarities, or it might have been because I am the director of the Lima-based Place of Memory, Tolerance, and Social Inclusion (Lugar de la Memoria, Tolerancia, y la Inclusión Social, LUM), where we are compiling a unique group of "memory storytellers." LUM has already published twelve volumes. Our narrators—women and men—are the family members of victims who perished or vanished between 1980 and 2000 because of the violence in Peru and whose names are listed in the Registro Único de Víctimas, or RUV (Single Registry of Victims). A list of individuals having the legal right to justice and reparations has been compiled in the RUV. Militants of the Sendero Luminoso (or Shining Path), and the Túpac Amaru Revolutionary Movement (MRTA) do not appear in the RUV; they are prohibited from being registered.

I consented to pen a few pages to evaluate the content and aim of this book for an essential reason. The Truth and Reconciliation Commission (TRC), whose work occurred between 2001 and 2003, began the grueling task of clarifying what happened from 1980 to 2000 in the confrontations among SL and MRTA subversives, the forces of order, the peasant self-defense committees, and countersubversive forces. In the twenty-five public hearings organized by the TRC between 2001 and 2003, at least four hundred testimonies were presented to induce Peruvian citizens to confront the horrendous tragedy that had occurred during the times of violence.[1] In the Upper Huallaga Valley alone, the TRC registered over 350 cases in Tocache (individual and collective) of victims affected by the period of violence.

This book includes multiple testimonies from the Central and Lower Huallaga regions, specifically collected from settlers who reside in the Caynarachi River basin. I am not sure whether the interviewees, men and women, appear in the RUV or whether they testified at any public hearing of the TRC in search of justice and reparations or whether, for the first time, in front of a singular interviewer, they recounted their traumas. They told their stories to Bartholomew Dean, an anthropologist who has dedicated more than thirty years of his life to the study of these "others," Amazonian natives, whether indigenous Urarina, Awajún, or Shawi peoples, or mestizo peasants, to see them, from the eyes of those "others," whom he knows and obviously loves. It is not frequent to find this approach in anthropological studies. Hence, I write these lines of introduction and admiration for someone who has put themselves squarely on the side of the "others."

Bartholomew Dean's interest in understanding the indigenous peoples of Amazonia, especially in northeastern Peru, has always struck me. With his books *At the Risk of Being Heard: Identity, Indigenous Rights, and Postcolonial States* (coedited, 2003), *Urarina Society, Cosmology, and History in Peruvian Amazonia* (2009), and *The State and the Awajún: Frontier Expansion in the Upper Amazon, 1541–1990* (2020), he has demonstrated the style of ethnography he employs, as other anthropologists logically do, to comprehend the historical and contemporary circumstances of Peru's indigenous peoples. But I should point out that I first met Bart in 1998 at the Universidad Nacional Mayor de San Marcos, where I was the director of graduate programs in the Faculty of Social Sciences. With funding from the John D. and Catherine MacArthur Foundation of Chicago, we established Peru's first master's degree in Amazonian studies. San Marcos's graduate program in Amazonian studies began with a special emphasis on the Awajún and Wampis communities of Condorcanqui Province, in the Amazonas region in northern Peru and bordering Ecuador.

Writing this book's foreword has given me the opportunity to learn more about the anthropologist I first met in 1998. Over the years, Bart

Dean has developed—particularly in his numerous recent investigations—a sensory anthropology that brings us closer to the political, cultural, and social dimensions of the actors who lived and took part, as perpetrators and victims, in the tragic years of violence that Peru endured. From their very particular memories, interviewees offer their testimonies to the anthropologist. In their efforts to understand the period from 1980 to 2000, also called the internal armed conflict, other anthropologists have used a similar method and hermeneutics, whereby they ask the actors for their reasons or motivations in the face of what happened. Three scholars in particular—the American Kimberly Theidon, the French woman Valérie Robin Azevedo, and the Peruvian María Eugenia Ulfe—have shown us a different way to look at the facts of that nightmarish time to explain how social actors participated in subversive and countersubversive actions and how those actions affected the mostly rural and indigenous high Andean peasant communities.

The studies of the aforementioned anthropologists focus on the highland regions of Ayacucho, Apurímac, Huancavelica, Huánuco, and Junín, where Sendero Luminoso flourished. They were written from the testimonials gathered during Peru's most recent post-conflict period. Through the memories that have been preserved of those trying times, from what is spoken and not said to what is told and silenced, these works have helped us come to a new understanding of what transpired. These works have allowed us to verify the existence in the initial years, 1980–1982, of radical new political discourses from Sendero Luminoso and the Túpac Amaru Revolutionary Movement (Movimiento Revolucionario Túpac Amaru, MRTA) pointing to the state and the economic elites as responsible for the country's misfortunes. During this short time, peasants had limited control over their own history or power to decide. Instead, the subversive or countersubversive forces decided their lives.

Bartholomew Dean takes us to the forgotten region of the middle and lower stretches of the Huallaga Valley, a vast area in which the colossal Huallaga River imposes its presence. The river originates in the lofty Andean heights of Cerro de Pasco, flows through two provinces in San Martín, eventually enters the region of Loreto via the town of Yurimaguas, where it meets the Marañón River and then empties into the Amazon River. During the internal war, the Sendero Luminoso held near-total control over the Upper Huallaga Valley, which includes the towns of Tocache and Uchiza. While the MRTA dominated the Lower Huallaga Valley, the Central Huallaga was a hotly contested area. Bart Dean's book focuses on what happened in the Caynarachi River basin of the Lower Huallaga region, a picturesque locale where small hamlets flourish along the banks of numerous waterways.

The author describes the accounts of twelve men and women, nine of whom were victims, residents, farmers, or merchants in the Caynarachi basin, and three of whom were MRTA militants. He worked closely with them between 2015 and 2022. Because of this, Dean's book is exceptional. Regarding the MRTA, the testimonies of Diego, known as Mando (Commander) Razor, are complimented by the writings of Sístero García Torres, alias Comrade Ricardo, the regional chief of the MRTA in San Martín, who wrote a singular text published in 2017. García Torres invoked the 1993 Law of Repentance. Sandra, a former MRTA militant and *comadre* (co-mother) of Commander Razor (Diego), who recruited her, and Fabiano, a fellow militant, also share their stories. This trio of eyewitnesses, with fascinating and very convincing stories, is what gives this book a charm and value all its own.

The testimonies in this book bring us closer to understanding the political consciousness that guided, justified, and gave meaning to the actions of the members of the MRTA in this region of the Central and Lower Huallaga Valley. According to these accounts, the MRTA received its funding and orders from Lima, and several of the San Martín–based insurgents were trained as guerrillas in Colombia. In the Huallaga Valley, the MRTA was part of disciplined detachments that obeyed orders and designed supply strategies through imposing quotas, or war taxes, on farmers and merchants. Some MRTA militants had already begun acting according to their own personal interests even before their years of military defeat, around 1996–1997. They undermined the confidence that the MRTA initially had enjoyed during its first years in the area by increasingly imposing war taxes and kidnapping farmers and merchants for their own gain.

The other interviewees in these pages are civil witnesses, merchants, farmers, and teachers who offered Bart Dean harrowing accounts of what happened in difficult times, such as the spouses Augustín and Regina, owners of a farm in the Caynarachi basin, or the Huicungo homesteaders Elena and Sebastián. They confessed they were more afraid of the armed forces than of the members of the MRTA. Many were well aware of the brutality of the MRTA, but also of the Sendero Luminoso, the armed forces, and the self-defense committees, or *ronderos*.

The people in the Caynarachi basin noticed variations in violence and expressed it through recounting impactful events. For instance, the story about the savagery of the Sendero Luminoso that Elena and Sebastián describe had a powerful impact on the community. According to them, Sendero Luminoso suspects hanged Huesito (Little Bone), a dog owned by a Huicungo local, at the door of a merchant whom the townspeople believed to be a snitch. This brings to mind several incidents in which Sendero Luminoso killed animals in the provinces of Ayacucho, including at the Alpachaca Experimental Farm of San Cristóbal de Huamanga National University, the Andean camelid research and experimentation center in La Raya (Cuzco), and the Fundo San Marcos in the Ucayali region, fifty-two kilometers from Pucallpa, on the Modesto Basadre highway. Sendero Luminoso killed different types of animals and massacred peasant communities. The army also practiced cruelty in its forced recruitment campaigns (*levas*) to fulfill the two years of compulsory military service, which were marked by fierce initial training. During basic training, referred to as the *perrada*, or "dog pack," new military recruits were treated like dogs. The fact that the young recruits, eighteen and nineteen years old, had to kill dogs to overcome their fear of blood had a terrible, lasting effect on many.

The MRTA began its armed actions in Lima in 1984. The insurgent group emerged as an offshoot of the American Popular Revolutionary Alliance, or APRA, a political party that came to power in 1985–1990. Its young president, Alan García Pérez, left the country bankrupt and deeply mired in corruption. Despite its best efforts, the MRTA could not take advantage of Luis Varese Scotto, alias Comrade Luis, and his rebel soldier's failed attempt to establish a base of guerrilla operations in the province of Sicuani, Cuzco. Varese moved to Lima after experiencing similar defeat in Satipo, the territory of the Asháninka.[2] The MRTA leadership then focused on establishing a front in the tropical forests of San Martín. MRTA rebels soon arrived in the Caynarachi basin, in the town of Lamas, in the city of Tarapoto, and throughout the regions of San Martín and Loreto, entering communities with their proselytizing in schools and other higher educational institutions. Just as Sendero Luminoso had Juan López Licera in Huanca Sancos (1982–1983), the MRTA had Sístero García Torres in the Central and Lower Huallaga, and many others like him, to do the same job of recruiting and training young militants.

What stands out as the most intriguing aspect of *The End of the Future*? Foremost, the articulation of a social anthropology that seeks explanations through dialogue and interviews with participants, whether former subversives or civilian victims, who intimately lived the years of violence between 1980 and 2000. It does not matter whether the testimonies convey half-truths or reinterpretations of what happened. They interest us because they transmit the participants' truths and thus bring us closer to the justifications for their actions. We are interested in what they say and in what they are silent about, what they regret, and what they admit to having done wrong. This can be a redemptive act, repentance by both individuals and collective groups by demonstrating an awareness of the errors made. This enables people to express desires for change, wishes for explanations, demands for justice and reparations, and aspirations for a common destiny, beyond the political, cultural, and social differences that all too often divide.

In addition, Dean's book seeks to go beyond ethnography and anthropology, to contribute to the understanding of the behaviors of the participants in any of the fronts of violent conflict. Be it the actions of MRTA terrorists, the Peruvian armed forces or self-defense committees, the memories of these events lead us to explore the way people remember that past and find explanations that help them understand their own behaviors in the context of violence, one without reference to the rule of law. The search for understanding the memories of what happened during those "terrible years" is what makes reading Bartholomew Dean's book a vital exercise in awareness that can help Peruvians and global citizens establish coexistence through acknowledging our differences. By so doing, we can ensure that circumstances such as social isolation, the lack of the state, and the catastrophic consequences of nefarious drug trafficking, remain things of the past, never to be repeated.

Lima, December 15, 2022

Narrative Renditions of Ugly Times

Memory, Violence, and Trauma in Peruvian Amazonia

These are men whose minds the Dead have ravished
Memory fingers in their hair of murders
Multitudinous murders they once witnessed.

WILFRED OWEN

This book expands the theoretical frameworks for comprehending the role that narrated memories of violence and trauma play in altering societal suffering and its different antidotes. It is based on substantial ethnographic fieldwork undertaken over seven years. Using the war-torn Huallaga Valley in the Peruvian Amazon as its point of reference, which served as a focal point for opposing leftist guerrillas and had a thriving shadow economy based in part on the production and distribution of cocaine during the 1980s and early 1990s—the text provides novel insights into the tangled web of connections between remembrance, trauma, and warfare violence.[1] The book investigates the various types of violence associated with guerrilla warfare and emphasizes that the internal war in the Huallaga Valley was not just about brute force. In so doing, the text emphasizes the importance of understanding the complexities of violent conflicts, their impact on memory and trauma, and the arduous journey toward reconciliation.

By examining narrativized memories of violence in the Huallaga Valley, it offers a comparative analysis of their individual, communal, and political effects on human well-being and the scars of trauma.

Trauma is a reaction to deeply distressing or disturbing events that overpower a person's ability to function; it induces feelings of powerlessness, corrodes one's dignity, and restricts one's ability to experience the entire range of emotions and moods. I accord here special attention to witness testimony and to elaborating techniques for documenting personal memory and joint commemoration. By doing this, I can identify sensory inputs and see how they shed light on the fluidity of trauma, dystopian sensibility, and social misery. However, the accounts of overwhelming fear, persistent depression, and profound grief examined in this book also offer valuable insights into resilience, endurance, and the reaffirmation of life in the aftermath of civil conflict.[2] In his 2008 book *Healing Invisible Wounds*, Richard Mollica reveals how trauma survivors can instruct us all on how to handle life's terrible situations by sharing their personal accounts.[3] An empathetic, therapeutic approach to social and personal trauma may turn humiliation and stigma—tools of violence, despair, and dispossession—into relief, redress, and reconciliation.

Foregrounding the points of view of the mestizo peasants of the Lower Huallaga's Caynarachi basin, this book chronicles the warfare violence associated with the Túpac Amaru rebels—that is, the Túpac Amaru Revolutionary Movement (Movimiento Revolucionario Túpac Amaru, or MRTA)—particularly the Northeastern Front (Frente Nororiental) and the Peruvian state's ruthless efforts to eradicate the Marxist-Leninist group.[4] Northeastern Peru's tropical Andes and lush lowland rainforests eventually saw violent contestation and guerrilla warfare because of decades of growing social polarization between the impoverished countryside and Lima, the capital city and the center of power ever since the country's colonial founding in 1535.[5] The Túpac Amaru rebels adopted "revolutionary violence" over the course of approximately ten years in order to bring about far-reaching social transformation in the Peruvian Amazon.[6] The MRTA held that history unfolds through a continuous sequence of forceful struggles. Embracing a Gramscian perspectives, the Túpac Amaru Revolutionary Movement tried to foment the most advantageous circumstances in Amazonia for the ultimate and decisive upheaval, social revolution.[7]

At its core, this book is not so much about what happened and with whom—although one can certainly read it that way with ample return— but it instead ponders what the violence meant to those who lived in what

FIGURE 1. Caynarachi Basin, Lower Huallaga Valley, photo by Bartholomew Dean

locals have dubbed the "ugly times" (*tiempos feos*). It reveals how individual lived experiences normalized petty brutalities and terror on a community level and created a common sense or ideology of collective violence. Analysis of the localized history of violence gives insight to several issues (political, legal, economic, religious, and symbolic) that control its very production and mobilization.[8]

Following Veena Das's illumination of how violence has entered "the recesses of the ordinary," this work explores people's narrative renditions of violent times.[9] Given that they integrate different cultural sign systems into one symbolic frame, narrative practices are of utmost significance. Repeated acts of violence (often attributed to culture) become visible through narratives and disrupt normalized gazes. Throughout the ugly times, systemic and systematic violence seeped into the pores of everyday life. Violence was not only expressed in dramatic events, acts, or behaviors but also became a quotidian occurrence. Violence distorted social interactions and interfered with daily living because it was both common and normalized. Visibly direct violence became conflated with opaque, structural violence during the ugly times of guerrilla war and army counterinsurgency campaigns in the Lower Huallaga's Caynarachi basin.[10]

As a key means for conveying standardized ideas about politics, social comportment, and individuals, personal and collective narratives have influenced symbolic violence by disseminating hegemonic notions of exclusion and inclusion, safety and harm, and justification and the logic of violence.[11] The exercise of power is always present in the articulation of narratives, giving sociocultural analysis a rich field to work in. Narratives also contain an ideological component. The individual wartime violence accounts I gathered during my fieldwork in the Huallaga Valley reflect conflicting experiences of trauma, spectatorship, testifying, guilt, pride, and eyewitnessing.

The lingering traces of violence associated with Peru's internal war are revealed in Valérie Robin Azevedo's ethnography *Los silencios de la guerra: Memorias y conflicto armado en Ayacucho-Perú* via the words and experiences of Quechua peasants from Ocros (Huamanga) and Huancapi (Ayacucho).[12] Azevedo adroitly recounts the peasants' untold stories of the conflict with Sendero Luminoso (Partido Comunista del Perú-Sendero Luminoso, or SL, the Communist Party of Peru–Shining Path), in which celebrations of patron saints, festivals, musical compositions, dance, nightmares, and the appearance of a miraculous saint conjure memories of the past. In so doing, Azevedo questions how memories of the conflict are created today and which aspects of the past are effectively muted. My book delves into the complex world of stories that recount histories of violence, shadow economies, and trauma. Through these narratives, I explore how they shape our understanding of violent conflict and reconciliation in Peruvian Amazonia. Stories can provide insight into social life, but they may also distort historical realities. The act of retelling events, for example, holds the potential to introduce subjectivity and deceptively selective memory, influencing our comprehension of past violent conflicts. In the realm of storytelling, certain narratives possess the ability to unveil weighty truths, while others have the potential to conceal vital aspects of the collective memory and the social reality we perceive.

Drawing on several contemporary accounts by indigenous peoples of southwestern Colombia, Mónica Espinosa Arango has explored the making of the discursive trope *lo indígena*, or "the indigenous," in terms of the genocidal impulses associated with the country's violent modernity.[13] Comparably, in Peruvian Amazonia's Huallaga Valley, the discursive practices of maintaining *cocaleros* (coca growers) and *terrucos* (terrorists—Sendero Luminoso and Túpac Amaru rebels) as co-constitutive categories are linked to embodied cultural memories and moral worlds in which narratives of trauma, appeals to justice, and actions of resistance and complicity all intermingle in the violent sociocultural topography of the region.[14]

This book offers an investigation of the individual and collective memories connected to the Túpac Amaru rebels or MRTA's bloody struggle to seize control of the Huallaga Valley's rainforest. Everyone who lives in this region of northern Peru knows well that during the armed conflict, known as the *lucha armada*, heinous acts of brutality that went beyond the bounds of acceptable daily behavior characterized the social landscape of the area. Like travel along the region's sinuous rivers, compromise was not always easy in this world of mistrust, shifting alliances, and violent encounters. It is precisely through the optics of fine-grained sensory ethnography that ineffable domains of monstrous brutality appear in the waiting rooms of Hades. During the war, the Huallaga Valley was a universe populated by *pishtacos* (vampiric boogeymen), *terrucos* (terrorists), *narcos* (drug traffickers), and *shapshicos* (forest demon).[15] In the sticky verdurous forests of this region, one should add *tunches* (malignant ghostlike spirits), Chullachaki (the clubfooted forest gremlin), as well as those who committed crimes against humanity—the *cumpas* (MRTA), Sendero Luminoso, merciless members of the state security forces, and *ronderos* (members of the civilian armed patrols)—to the list of volatile agents gnawing at the very fabric that once held together moral worlds, local or otherwise.

In times of conflict, Albert Camus argued, the intellectual's contribution cannot be to simply justify one side's violence while condemning the other.[16] Rather than an apology or condemnation of the actions of MRTA, or the state security forces that attempted to eradicate the members from the cultural and political fabric of society, this text is devoted to giving expression to the testimonies of those who lived during the internal war in the Caynarachi basin, a vast area that locals have long felt has been ignored by those in positions of regional or national power. The book delves into vicious memories that most informants want to erase through individual avoidance and collective forgetting.[17] Yet others can't seem ever to escape disturbing recollections of the violence associated with the Túpac Amaru guerrilla warfare and the state-backed counterinsurgency response. A number remain cast into a Conradian loneliness, marked by naked terror because of broken family ties; they exist in the postwar years as forlorn outcasts clinging to bitter memories. Indeed, from their facial expressions and bodily gestures, some informants seemed deeply troubled, if not haunted, by their harrowing experiences during the *lucha armada*, whereas others who had played major roles in the conflict (e.g., perpetrators, victims, bystanders) went on with their lives in a comparatively normal, even unfazed fashion.[18]

Methods for contemplating and deciphering the violent past's presences, silences, and enduring meanings are skillfully rendered in Elizabeth Jelin's *State Repression and the Labors of Memory*. Jelin's work explores how memory conflicts affect individual and group identities and societal and political divisions. It asks what those who have experienced "unbearable" circumstances might say or share about those traumas? What moral, governmental, and more broadly human issues are at stake?[19] Memory regimes use a variety of techniques, including narrating (creating a story that appears coherent), strategic silencing (concealing historical facts or events that diverge from one's own interpretation), performing (engaging in ritualized forms of reifying the narrative), and renaming or remapping (inscribing the narrative into the monumental and toponymic landscape).

Although Émile Durkheim did not invent the notion of collective memory, he explored how memories are handed down from one generation to the next as a result of historical education. Collective memory is one of the elementary forms of social life, according to Durkheim who thought that every society exhibited and needed a sense of continuity with the past and that it bestowed identity on people and groups.[20] Maurice Halbwachs, a philosopher and renowned sociology student of Durkheim, made significant contributions to the concept of collective memory.[21] He argued that our communal and cultural memories act as a filter through which we recall all of our personal experiences. By claiming that we can comprehend individual memories only in the context of the social group, Halbwachs underscored the centrality of collective memory, which unites the family, community, or nation across time and space.

In Peru's Huallaga Valley, memory regimes of past violence structure how people and social groups interpret trauma, fitfully render the present meaningful, and frame their future aspirations. While recognizing the constitutive, multifactorial nature of violence, the book reveals the extent to which narrativized memories of violent events and encounters are perceived as distressing or traumatic when they cannot be meaningfully integrated or recounted into autobiographical or collective memories. Violent encounters are socially and historically situated cultural events that expose people to the expression of aggressive and hostile attitudes, practices, and belief systems. The systematic study of such volatile events and encounters facilitates the elucidation of aggressor and victim perspectives, not to mention providing a framework for understanding the deeply ambiguous nature of such interactions. Guided by a phenomenological method, I assess the narrative accounts of the inhabitants of this poorly understood region within a reflective life-world approach.

This ethnography follows a constructivist approach to violence and trauma by considering the meaning-making process as an open-ended social dialogue in which strikingly different personal or socially collaborated testimonials vie for influence and hegemonic control. Explanations are unnecessary when we experience events we consider ordinary. In contrast, violence elicits distinctive narrative modes that allow people to recast chaotic experiences into causal stories to make them sensible, render them safe, and sometimes imprint memories that traumatize and restrain human well-being.

Besides autobiographical testimonials from inhabitants of the Lower Huallaga Valley's Caynarachi basin, the text is supplemented by many open-ended discussions and semistructured interviews I conducted (2015–2022) with former Túpac Amaru Revolutionary Movement rebels and militants, such as Diego, Fabiano and Sandra (pseudonyms). The comprehensive interviews I carried out with a diverse gamut of people hailing from rainforest towns (*caserío*) and cities in the Huallaga Valley, such as Sauce, Picota, Yumbatos, Tarapoto, Yurimaguas, El Pongo de Caynarachi, Pampa Hermosa, and Chazuta, offer substantial ethnographic context and depth.[22] To get explanations for the unbearable human cost of the internal war, the *lucha armada*, one must look into an underground world of secrets, social fissures, feuds, segregation, and interdependent solidarities. The number of young individuals who enthusiastically committed themselves to a radical cause they believed in is demonstrated in the personal stories I collected. They depict existential moral quandaries, everyday worries, selfless dedication, and invariable transformation. The narratives give a multidimensional richness to the narrow perspective of official Peruvian history, unveiling concealed and contradictory histories. They provide a human face to the officially sanctioned demons, heroes, and martyrs of the internal war. To give context to the causes and consequences of the presence of the *cumpas*— MRTA rebels—in this poorly understood, geographically isolated region of the country, the research drew on the methods of participant observation and interview-based oral history. From the outset, I was particularly impressed with how Diego, a.k.a. Mando (Commander) Razor, had built fibers of his tumultuous life into his narrative art; these in turn oriented the general direction of my account. I accumulated memories and comments about historical events through interviews, transcribed and summarized them, and analyzed them in relation to MRTA propaganda and written accounts by a prominent MRTA leader named Sístero García Torres, a.k.a. Commander Ricardo.

Besides oral accounts, the book draws from the final report of the Peruvian government's Truth and Reconciliation Commission's (Comisión de la

Verdad y Reconciliación, CVR), media representations, photographs, opinion journalism, and recent critical historical studies of this radical movement.[23] Analogous to the insurrection unleashed by the extremely violent Maoist group Sendero Luminoso in the Upper Huallaga, the participation of the Túpac Amaru Revolutionary Movement in the Lower and Central Huallaga Valley during the internal war (1980–2000) is poorly understood and virtually undocumented in the scholarly literature.[24] It was Túpac Amaru rebels, and not Sendero Luminoso, who challenged the Peruvian government along the lower course of the Huallaga River, yet no systematic study exists of this important aspect of the conflict that literally threatened to tear the country asunder.[25]

Dedicated to providing some semblance of order for understanding the diverse consequences of guerrilla warfare in Peruvian Amazonia, this book is deeply imbued with my own experiences of living with and studying violence. Ever since Sir Jon Peel pulled me from the heavens into Kings College Hospital in London, and sent me on my way to Virginia Waters, Surrey, warfare has long followed my wake. Born in the twilight of the baby boom, I am a child of parents who survived the London Blitz (1940–1941) and made a new life for themselves as immigrants in America.[26] Yet family stories of "the war(s)" have impressed deeply on my mind, invariably shaping the professional path that led me to become an ethnographer of conflict.[27] Unlike combat-tested soldiers, many children from war-torn families cope exceptionally well and may become more organized, empathetic, and independent than other kids not exposed to warfare.[28]

Notwithstanding, being an anthropologist passionately committed to understanding the lifeways of the peoples of Peruvian Amazonia has been profoundly stressful for me and my family. As a result of disease and psychic trauma, my kin have taken on a caretaking role during the many times I have been unwell. They have come to know a chronically ill son, brother, husband, and father—a person who has suffered from various diseases, medications, and surgical procedures, not to mention the psychic stress of witnessing violence in its various guises—symbolic, structural, and direct or bodily—and the moral outrage this has often provoked.[29] My loved ones have been unwittingly exposed to the negative effects of my maladies: cyclic vomiting, nightmares, migraines, malaria, and post-traumatic stress disorder. Yet I am convinced that my feeble body and ongoing bouts of illness invariably honed my focus on comprehending the complex interrelationship among trauma, collective memory, and the prospects for reconciliation following warfare.

Upon arriving in Peru in 1985, the year Alan García Pérez took power of a rapidly crumbling state, I witnessed some of the worst years of political violence, terrorism, and economic crisis that ever afflicted the country. In the shadows of guerrilla warfare and impending state collapse, I initiated my quest to understand social suffering and human resilience by conducting field research among the poor and working-class inhabitants of Lima's inner-city *tugurios* (slums).[30] However, by the late 1980s, increasing levels of urban, *everyday violence* made continued ethnographic study in Lima challenging at best.[31] Despite documenting the "meaning-making" capacity of Lima's inner-city poor, indiscriminate car bombs (*coche bombas*), electrical blackouts, rising levels of crime, and endless lines of underemployed workers and their families huddled outside of soup kitchens demoralized me. I found gray-skyed Lima dismal and gloomy, and I found little solace in the constant media coverage of the killings, kidnappings, and extensive damage to both public and private infrastructures caused by the Maoist Sendero Luminoso and the anti-imperialist MRTA, both of which espoused sanguineous class warfare.[32] Unable to acclimatize to the highlands and fearful of what I had seen during my field trips in 1985 and 1987 to the central Andean cities of Huancavelica and Ayacucho—Sendero Luminoso slogans painted everywhere—I turned my anthropological gaze to exploring the eastern slopes of the Andes and into Amazonia. This geographical pivot prompted the start of my scholarly career as an Amazonianist—that is, one who studies Amazonian regions, societies, and cultures over time and space. As a seasoned specialist in the indigenous and mestizo communities of northeastern Peruvian Amazonia, I have borne witness to numerous human rights violations.[33]

To wit, perched aloft a dusty filing cabinet in my University of Kansas office in Fraser Hall is a snapshot of a woman—Doña Luz Angélica—covered in blood from deep machete slashes to her scalp and head, wounds she received during a brutal attack by a Sendero Luminoso band in her Kokama-Kokamilla community on the Lower Huallaga.[34] The bloodied image serves as a painful yet moving reminder of a lesson that my doctoral mentor frequently emphasized: "states that make war on marginalized minorities are . . . states in which pluralism has either failed or has not been given a chance."[35] Unfortunately, Peru, the nation I have studied, fell in love with, and at times despised, is not an exception to this rule, where the powerful have long used commonplace violence to stifle the aspirations of those who long for a pluralistic, multiethnic nation-state.

CHAPTER I

The Ugly Times of War

The final two decades of the twentieth century are—to put it bluntly—
a stain of horror and dishonor on the Peruvian state and society.

TRUTH AND RECONCILIATION COMMISSION, Peru

An "internal war" between government forces, guerrillas, and paramilitar-
ies for control of the state resulted in the deaths of approximately seventy
thousand Peruvians between 1980 and 2000, the majority of whom were
campesinos, from indigenous and mestizo peasant.[1] All "sides" of Peru's
bloody internal war engaged in systematic human rights violations during
these obscene times, albeit to varying degrees and extents. The internal
conflict claimed more lives—dead and missing—than any other conflict
in modern Peruvian history according to statistics that are an important
part of the country's sociopolitical imagination. The political economics
of violence did not impact everyone equally; everyday violence had various consequences for people in different social groups. The government
or the armed opposition forcibly displaced nearly five hundred thousand
of the most vulnerable citizens of the nation.[2]

Peru's nightmarish internal war was not merely a binary clash of government forces opposing leftist rebel forces—the Sendero Luminoso and the
Túpac Amaru Revolutionary Movement.[3] Instead, many parties competed
with one another for dominance over rival discursive spheres of power, territorial control, and influence over various constituencies.

Political violence in the Amazonian rainforest took the form of asymmetric warfare because of the power disparity between the state and the

Túpac Amaru guerrillas. Because neither side could directly attack the other, they forced the rebels to rely on terrorism and guerrilla warfare. Many assaults on civilian targets and other noncombatants were part of this. Similar to the Sendero Luminoso, the MRTA had a history of stealing weaponry from soldiers and the police (*el tombo*). The MRTA targeted particular people in order to punish them for behaviors perceived as defying party rules or supporting the opposition, such as spying or offering assistance to the enemy. Túpac Amaru rebels targeted people collectively for their perceived affiliation with particular groups, including members of the LGBTQ community, sex workers, substance abusers, unfaithful partners, shamans, military personnel, and government agents. The militarization of social life gave rise to a variety of gendered forms of violence, as shown not only by direct political violence against women in particular but also by enabling the kidnapping, torture, sexual assault, and murder of women and gay and lesbian people as a warning to others who might consider asserting their legal rights, let alone their right to be culturally distinctive. Similarly, men were subjected to sexualized abuse within the armed forces and at the hands of the insurgents and paramilitary groups that emerged, such as the rural civil patrols, or *rondas campesinas*, organized to defend communities from outside incursions.

Although the vicious conflict and acts of systematic terror continued, Alberto Fujimori Inomoto's meteoric rise to power in 1990 signaled a significant change in the course of the internal war, which was mirrored by a stepped-up state offensive against the MRTA and the Sendero Luminoso.[4] While in office (1990–2000), Fujimori conducted a ferocious counterinsurgency war in the Huallaga Valley with full US support, which included restructuring the antiterrorist police forces and creating a Naval Special Forces unit (Fuerza de Operaciones Especiales) that later became highly effective in jungle warfare.[5] This eventually helped the Peruvian state turn the tide against the Túpac Amaru rebels, whose orbit of action ground to a low-intensity war in the country's tropical forests east of the Andes.[6]

In April 1992, Alberto Fujimori, who was becoming more authoritarian, executed a "self-coup" (*autogolpe*) that resulted in the constitution's suspension and the shutdown of Congress. As a result, he could establish his authority and implement dictatorial policies without the normal checks and balances of democratic governance. This occurred despite the significant progress made by Peruvian military personnel, police, and peasant civil patrols in their efforts to combat the MRTA and Sendero Luminoso insurgent groups.

When the leaders of both organizations—Víctor Alfredo Polay Campos of the MRTA and Manuel Rubén Abimael Guzmán Reynoso of Sendero Luminoso—were imprisoned in 1992, the Fujimori administration triumphantly declared that the Peruvian Armed Forces had crushed subversion. Fleeting was Fujimori's euphoric proclamation concerning the MRTA, swiftly overshadowed by subsequent events. Following their retrenchment, the MRTA launched a dramatic assault intending to free two hundred rebel captives and pulling off a publicity stunt to improve the rebels' standing and morale.

On December 17, 1996, fourteen Túpac Amaru Revolutionary Movement members carried out a raid on the residence of Morihisa Aoki, the Japanese ambassador to Peru, and kidnapped many prominent figures, including diplomats, government administrators, military personnel, and business moguls. The MRTA held seventy-two hostages for four months before the Peruvian Armed Forces stormed the ambassador's residence in April 1997, freeing all but one hostage. Two commandos from the Peruvian Army died during the rescue operation, and all fourteen MRTA militants were killed in a manifestation of state-directed genocide.[7] Subsequent investigations have indicated that at least three, and maybe as many as eight, of the *tupacamaristas* were summarily executed following their surrender to the armed forces, including the forty-three-year-old Túpac Amaru commander General Luis Néstor Fortunato Cerpa Cartolini.[8] The Túpac Amaru rebels' debacle during the hostage crisis marked the symbolic and literal collapse of the insurgent group's ability to challenge the Peruvian state as it had the decade before. The defeat effectively dissolved the militant group's leadership, and the death of Cerpa Cartolini dealt a major blow to the MRTA's organizational capacity, adding to the movement's problem of recruiting increasingly ill-prepared combatants.[9]

Following Alberto Fujimori's dramatic departure from dictatorial power in November 2000, the newly elected Perú Posible government (2001–2006),

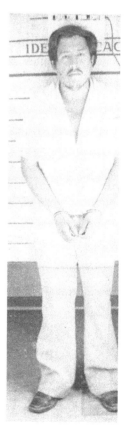

FIGURE 2. Luis Néstor Fortunato Cerpa Cartolini, photo by Yana-Colección Desco

of Alejandro Toledo Manrique, convened the official Truth and Reconciliation Commission, Comisión de la Verdad y Reconciliación (CVR) in July 2001 to investigate the human rights violations that had transpired between 1980 and 2000.[10] Based on some seventeen thousand testimonies, the Peruvian Truth and Reconciliation Commission's final report represented two years of work. Published in August 2003, the report estimated that some 69,280 Peruvians were killed as a result of the war that had raged for two decades.[11]

The Truth and Reconciliation Commission's report identified both institutional and individual accountability, as well as ethnic and sociocultural elements that became triggers for violent conflict. Within the context of extreme political violence, it demonstrated that all parties had, at various points and times during the war, committed widespread and/or systematic violations of human rights, infractions of which would have qualified as violent crimes against humanity under the standards of international humanitarian law.[12] Both state-sponsored and nonstate actors committed extrajudicial killing, kidnapping, forced disappearances, torture, wrongful detention, rape, servitude, mental torture, and other severe violations of human rights.

The CVR's report detailed a climate of everyday violence accompanied by gross human rights violations in the Huallaga Valley, noting that many of the victims and abuses occurred in endemic coca-growing areas.[13] According to the Truth and Reconciliation Commission's findings, human rights violations in the northern Huallaga region were characterized by selectivity. The perpetrators targeted specific individuals or groups, resulting in a higher proportion of victims who were subjected to enforced disappearances, extrajudicial killings, torture, or forced detention. In the Huallaga Valley, people were frequently abducted and separated from their families by state security forces, paramilitary groups, or other armed actors. The area likewise encountered extrajudicial executions, torture, and obligatory detention. These strategies were utilized to govern, frighten, and quell local opposition. They left victims and the community with lasting physical and psychological scars from these crimes.

The MRTA, Violence, and the People's Revolutionary War

In the Huallaga Valley, the MRTA and its state-supported enemies were powerful catalysts for igniting widespread and new sinister forms of violence.

As many eminent scholars do, I believe that violence is more than just an act or a string of events; it is a sociocultural condition.[14] As shown by Georges Sorel, violence is associated with capitalism as a manifestation of a normalized, total state of being. The concept of symbolic economics of violence is expanded on in William Pawlett's 2013 book *Violence, Society and Radical Theory* to highlight the instability and ambivalence of modern manifestations of hatred and violence.[15] Pawlett emphasizes the significance of the link between the structural or systemic violence of consumer capitalistic society and types of counterviolence that threaten this consumerist framework. The Túpac Amaru rebel leadership approached the interconnected phenomena of capitalism and neocolonialism as part of a mesmerizing spell that could be broken only by launching a violent revolutionary war, much like Sorel and his anticolonial heir, Frantz Fanon had advocated (2004).[16]

As Commander Andrés contended, the MRTA "developed as a military and political organization not to follow a specific ideology but because the Peruvian people's historic conditions have always been classified by the ruling classes' use of violence."[17] MRTA propaganda underscored Túpac Amaru II's proto-nationalism and the incomplete character of his 1780–1782 insurrection to overthrow Spanish colonial rule, positioning itself as the eighteenth-century revolutionary's legitimately destined successor.

Túpac Amaru II, the fervently charismatic social organizer who directed a major Andean rebellion against Spanish colonial control until his brutal death in 1781, is commemorated on roadway names, in the toponyms of new towns and urban settlements (*pueblos jóvenes* and *barriadas*), and in schools across Peru. In Cuzco, a significant monument honoring José Gabriel Condorcanqui Noguera Túpac Amaru II is found in the eponymous square.[18] Pregnant with diverse meanings derived from complex, contradictory historical genealogies, guerrillas and governments have long used the muleteer and trader, who claimed to be descended from neo-Inca royals, as a potent sociopolitical index for "rallying the people." Túpac Amaru II's life shows the iconic "power of imagery to resist censorship," as is illustrated in Charlene Black's thought-provoking research on the Catholic Church's efforts to censor the depiction of saints in art in New Spain.[19] In the modern epoch, they elevated Túpac Amaru II to the status of a national Peruvian icon under General Juan Velasco Alvarado's "revolutionary government" from 1968 to 1975, despite the deeply polarizing nature of him as a symbol. Among scholars and the public alike, Túpac Amaru II and his wife, Micaela Bastidas, are receiving a growing amount of praise for laying the foundations for Peru's 1821 war of independence from Spain.[20]

Having been demonized as ruthless terrorists by successive governments and national media outlets, the MRTA effectively reappropriated—primarily through print literature—Túpac Amaru II's iconic image from the clutches of state control.[21] Inspired by Túpac Amaru II's ethno-symbolism, the rebel insurgency was fortified by MRTA anthems, banners, slogans, and militarized marches.[22] The MRTA was increasingly armed with a cadre of dedicated supports, who found the party's message appealing and its recourse to a rich body of symbols referencing utopian liberation deeply alluring. Soon the MRTA launched the People's Revolutionary War (Guerra Revolucionaria del Pueblo) to overthrow Peru's neocolonial state, which the leadership argued was a lackey for the imperialism imposed by the United States and multinational financial institutions, such as the International Monetary Fund and the World Bank. From its outset, the fundamental aim of the Túpac Amaru rebels' revolutionary strategy was to capture state power and construct socialism in Peru, thus contributing to the defeat of world imperialism.[23] To do so, the MRTA tried to form a revolutionary party that provided political and military leadership to the masses, through all forms of struggle, aimed at the capture of state power.

MRTA apologists have emphasized how Peru underwent a historical shift from being a semifeudal society to an exploitative class-based society overly dependent on foreign capital. Túpac Amaru rebels worked to construct a national liberation front and promoted the creation of a revolutionary army as a regular structure, and popular militias as a mass structure, under the leadership of the party. Similar to "Che" Guevara, the MRTA leadership viewed guerrilla warfare as the central tactic of their armed struggle. Likewise, they thought that the strength of the Túpac Amaru rebel movement came from the collective power of the Peruvian masses.[24]

The Lima-based leadership viewed the Northeastern Front as the initial prerevolutionary stage of armed struggle through which the people's revolutionary army would be forged.[25] Over time, they believed it would incorporate more and more of the masses into the struggle for national liberation, and through armed struggle, those masses would become an invincible revolutionary army. Ultimately, the MRTA wanted to promote revolutionary war at the continental level under the principles of internationalism. In its political work, the MRTA underscored the bankruptcy and destructive character of the repressive apparatuses of the oligarchic ruling classes. The MRTA wanted to erase the system of ideological and cultural domination of the hegemonic groups that had marginalized indigenous and peasant communities and the working classes for centuries. Its leadership critiqued the fundamental seats of North Atlantic–based imperialist economic power and big-monopoly capital, arguing that the unfairly accumulated wealth should be recovered for revolutionary socialism.

Known colloquially as *cumpas*, from *compañeros* (or companions), as well as *tupachos* or *tupacamaristas*, members of the urban-based Túpac Amaru Revolutionary Movement launched their armed struggle in 1984. At midnight on September 28, 1984, Túpac Amaru guerrillas opened fire on the US embassy, causing minor damage but leaving no casualties.[26] During their first radio transmission, they proclaimed, "The war which [the MRTA] begin[s] today is a continuation of the open and clandestine war we Peruvians have waged against foreign and internal oppressors (for centuries)."[27] The *tupacamaristas*' initial acts of sabotage were limited to political propaganda and small-scale confrontations with Lima's ill-prepared police forces.[28] These confrontations eventually developed into a full-scale campaign of coordinated, urban guerrilla warfare. The MRTA staged terrorist bombings, conducted carefully orchestrated kidnappings of prominent industrialists and entrepreneurs, and held them in squalid "people's jails" for ransom, which was then used to finance their subversive actions.[29] Túpac Amaru insurgents engaged in strategic ambushes with the forces of the law, robbed banks, extorted individuals and businesses, and authored politically inspired assassinations, such as that of General Enrique López Albujar Trint, whom they gunned down.[30] On Tuesday, January 9, 1990, the former minister was driving himself to his offices in San Isidro from his upscale home on Sevilla Street in Higuereta, Santiago de Surco District. The driver and the escort had been late. López Albujar arrived at Central Street (now Avenida República de Colombia) at 9:20 a.m. to access a parking lot. Three MRTA attackers wielding submachine guns and 9 mm pistols then fired thirty bullets into the general's vehicle.[31]

Just as the urban-based MRTA was wreaking havoc with unbridled guerrilla warfare in the capital, the militant group's Lima-based National Directorate opted to simultaneously open an armed front in the rural rainforests of northeastern Peru.[32] Long marginalized in the national imagination while steeped in an endemic culture of everyday violence, the Huallaga Valley provided the MRTA with fertile grounds for widespread social revolt.[33] Largely forgotten by national politicians, the Amazonian region of San Martín had long been at the fringes of Lima-based policy decision-making, including the allocation of scarce state resources.[34] Young, well-disciplined militants willing to upend the symbolic violence dominating communal life were well received by many mestizo peasants tired of toiling

FIGURE 3. Terrorist attack of the Julio C. Tello branch of Banco de Credito
(Credit Bank) in Lince, Lima, photo by Nancy Arellano-Colección Desco

in the hot sun on another man's land for slave wages, or for those penniless parents unable to purchase a much-needed antibiotic for a sick child, or notebooks, pencils, and shoes for the school-age kids waiting expectantly in their barren homes. In contrast to this dystopian reality, the Túpac Amaru guerrillas' thunderous cries for the People's Revolutionary War were embraced among key sectors of the agrarian and city-based (peri-urban and otherwise) populace. Néstor Cerpa Cartolini, a leader of MRTA, gave hope to those who desired a new future of *popular power* with his words: "Yesterday we were a handful that had only our strength and morals as weapons, today we are thousands, organized in guerrilla fronts with militia and self-defense units spread throughout the country, but the most important thing is that our influence grows day by day. and the people join the struggle, and there in the field of the fusion of weapons and the masses, the embryo of the new and future popular power is taking shape."[35]

Forest and River: The Huallaga Valley

The Huallaga Valley, with its enduring remoteness, has forever beckoned to intrepid explorers and those bold enough to venture into the depths of its forests and rivers. For instance, Commander William Lewis Herndon of the United States Navy spearheaded an expedition to the region and authored a widely distributed report in 1854 titled *Exploration of the Valley of the Amazon*. Herndon's remarkable account effectively captures the irresistible allure of the region.[36] Located in the luxuriant tropical foothills of the Peruvian Andes, much of the Department of San Martín was relatively inaccessible until a herculean effort led to the construction of the Marginal Highway of the Jungle (Carretera Marginal de la Selva), linking the bustling city of Chiclayo on the Pacific coast with the then-remote northern rainforested regions of both Amazonas and San Martín.[37] For the first time, a road connected the settlements of the high-rainforest (*selva alta*) towns of Tingo María and Tocache along the fertile eastern flanks of the mighty Huallaga River.[38] Constructed during President Fernando Belaúnde Terry's first term in office (1963–1968) for the Popular Action (Acción Popular) party, the highway and its historical importance has received attention from various scholars. The roadway created a new and significant agricultural frontier in the Andean piedmont, linking the central Amazon to the highlands and coast. The trans-Andean highway transformed transport infrastructure, agricultural development—especially coca leaf production—accelerated in-migration and population expansion, increased urbanization, and hastened dramatic bio-cultural transformations, including the very nature of the region's population architecture.[39]

Travel from the San Martín's lowland Caynarachi basin, which was beyond the reach of the Carretera Marginal de la Selva, was still onerous until the recent, post-2000 construction of numerous penetration roads interconnecting the myriad villages and riverain hamlets in the humid and rainy basin. Previously, the passage across the Andean "Stair Mountain," or Cordillera Escalera, to reach San Martín's primary urban hubs of Tarapoto, Moyobamba, and Lamas, while scenic and replete with many waterfalls and dramatic vistas, could take days of strenuous walking up slick mountainside paths, not to mention fording tumultuous rivers. A faster, alternate route for residents of the Caynarachi basin to access markets and basic state services before the highway's construction over the Andes was to make their way down the Huallaga River to Yurimaguas, a well-established and thriving port town in the Department of Loreto's immense and sparsely populated lowland rainforest (*selva baja*).[40]

The Huallaga River originates in the high Andes and courses east, through abundant rainforests that flank the undulating slope toward the Amazon basin. On its way down the Andes, the Huallaga River passes through the *ceja de selva*, or "forest brow," the vernacular name given to the forests of the eastern Andes that extend between four hundred and one thousand meters of altitude in the region.[41] The Huallaga River, one of Peruvian Amazonia's most important waterways, is often described by hydrologists in terms of three sections—upper, central, and lower. The highland Upper Huallaga, also known as the Alto Huallaga, spans from the town of Tocache in San Martín, which boasted a population of approximately sixty thousand in 1990, to its Andean origin. The Central Huallaga courses from the town of Juanjuí in San Martín, and the Lower Huallaga flows from the historically important Kichwa-Lamista community of Chazuta, down to Yurimaguas in Loreto, where it eventually joins the vast Marañón River, a primary tributary of the Amazon.[42] The basin of the Lower Huallaga and the sub-basin of the Caynarachi cover approximately 5,971 square kilometers in the northeastern region of the *selva baja*—the lowland jungle—and includes the districts of Huimbayoc, Chipurana, Papaplaya, El Porvenir, Barranquita, Chazuta, and Caynarachi that correspond to the provinces of San Martín and Lamas, in the Department of San Martín.[43]

Located in the lower watershed of the Huallaga River basin, the Caynarachi River rapidly flows from the Motico Hill (Pongo de Caynarachi) on the eastern flanks of the Cordillera Escalera range (on the border with the Department of San Martín) and empties into the Department of Loreto as it passes the port city of Yurimaguas.[44] Following a southwest-northeast route, the Caynarachi River and its tributaries flow by several communities described (with pseudonyms) in this book.[45] All the streams and rivulets that empty into the Caynarachi River experience droughts from June through September (considered summer months) and have abundant water volume between October and May (considered the winter). The Caynarachi River is navigable by boats and canoes in the rainy season from the town called Pongo de Caynarachi, traveling about 104 kilometers from its source to its embouchure.

The Caynarachi basin has long been inhabited by mestizo campesinos, many of them with indigenous Kichwa-Lamista or Shawi heritage. At the outset of the MRTA's movement into the zone, the vast majority of the inhabitants were poor, many living in situations of extreme poverty. San Martín's illiteracy was estimated as the highest of the jungle departments, and approximately a third of children were chronically malnourished in the area.[46] Following the decline in the rubber boom, the new production cycle from 1920 into the 1960s was predicated on cultivating coffee, tobacco, cassava, and bananas, as well as cattle raising. These productive activities were served by transport networks for marketing goods downriver, bound for Amazonian cities such as Iquitos or Yurimaguas, or via land toward the northern coast, energizing the surrounding provinces and prompting a decentralized pattern of urbanization.[47]

During the epoch of the internal war, local inhabitants grew plantains, cacao, and other crops (e.g., corn, cotton, beans, sugar cane, peach-palm fruit, cassava, rice, oranges, coca leaves).[48] Some of the more fortunate and influential families had access to hundreds of hectares of pasture for feeding and fattening cattle or swine for the market.[49] Each district or town elected a mayor—or with villages or hamlets, the municipal agent— the lieutenant governor, and a justice of the peace, all representing the state-designated authorities characteristic of the hamlets and villages of Peruvian Amazonia.

By the early 1970s, Peru's nationalist military dictatorship under the command of General Juan Velasco Alvarado (1968–1975) began implementing agrarian reform and established state marketing organizations that guaranteed minimum prices for rice and maize. As a result, state-backed development policy in the Huallaga Valley turned away from its prior emphasis on Amazonian colonization through fomenting migration and toward the promotion of agricultural production and its commercialization in other parts of the country, especially the hungry city of Lima, whose urban poor clamored for cheap and readily available foodstuffs. Spurred by this new national policy, agricultural yields were to be increased to feed the booming coastal cities.[50] In the Huallaga Valley, local farmers reacted swiftly: within a decade, San Martín had become the largest corn-growing area in Peru. Annual production of corn rose from thirty thousand tons to over one hundred thousand tons between 1980 and 1989, and the trend for rice cultivation was similar. Yet the weak state apparatus in the Huallaga Valley ultimately failed to adequately sustain itself, and the state quickly abandoned intervention policies in the agricultural sector.

Beginning with General Velasco's leftist military government, state policies were implemented to promote and subsidize certain products, especially rice and corn, through the provision of credit and ensuring marketability. This generated a monoculture boom in the Huallaga Valley as small-scale farmers of cassava or cotton changed their production with the possibility of a less risky market for subsidized crops. However, this agrarian policy reinforced the vulnerability of producers, who became increasingly dependent on a weak state incapable of delivering on its promises. Low commodity prices, lack of credit, and the deterioration of road infrastructure, together with the state's breach of payments to producers, limited business liquidity, and chronic problems with transport, led to the loss of thousands of tons of production kept in warehouses of state-owned companies. Inflation and the devaluation of the national currency—the *inti*—gave the final blow to this model of regional development based on the cultivation of rice and corn, increasing social unrest, exacerbating confrontations, and unleashing a phase of unmatched political violence in the Huallaga Valley.[51]

During Alan García Pérez's calamitous first government in 1985–1990 (Alianza Popular Revolucionaria Americana), the state-financed subsidized system finally buckled as skyrocketing inflation ate up diminishing incomes.[52] Under García Pérez's watch, the mestizo and indigenous peasant farmers of the Huallaga Valley were largely abandoned to resolve their agrarian issues while the state turned to importing additional rice and maize to prevent growing popular unrest in Lima, thus compounding the growing agrarian crisis in San Martín.[53]

A realist understanding of the complex dynamics and causes of violence must go beyond the individual level and examine these cultural phenomena as part of broader social institutions, cultural fields, and contingent historical processes. The fierce and protracted conflicts that occurred in this area of northern Peruvian Amazonia emerged from simple questions: the state marketing policy for agricultural products from the Huallaga Valley, peasants' access to arable land, and freedom from the racialized violence and impunity of corrupt overlords and their brutal and dehumanizing sycophants. In the 1980s, people living in the Huallaga Valley increasingly demanded the right to live with basic human dignity—a rather tall order in a land where justice and equity were often in short supply.

While the traditional peasant movements in the Andes emphasized land reform, ownership of property in the Central and Lower Huallaga was less of an issue until the acceleration of widespread in-migration transformed the social and environmental topographies of the region, leading to unprecedented levels of violence beginning in the 1980s.[54] Lucas Cachay Huamán has identified historical causes for the outbreak of violence, underscoring specific past events that triggered the armed struggle, such as the 1982 peasant strike. In his estimation, "the violence did not start in 1987, [but] there [have been] five centuries of violence against the populations."[55] Once Túpac Amaru rebels brought insurrectionary politics to the Central and Lower Huallaga valleys, it was radicalized teacher-rebels, like

Commander Ricardo (Sístero García Torres), as well as students, impoverished smallholders, the landless poor, and marginalized urban workers and trade unionists, who were willing to take up arms for the right to live better than their ancestors by upending the racialized violence and neocolonial class system that oppressed them.

CHAPTER 2

In Search of the Rebel

With rebellion, awareness is born.

ALBERT CAMUS

Mando Razor

As I disembarked from the shallow bottomed canoe made from the hollowed trunk of a *caoba* tree (*Swietenia macrophylla*), I caught my first sighting of Diego*—a.k.a. Mando Razor—standing on the steep embankment of the Caynarachi River.[1] The outline of his body occupied a break in the verdant green tree cover and the azure sky above; he was near a rustic homestead, where chickens were plentiful and a horse was tied up to a calabash tree (*Crescentia cujete*) with a scraggly rope. The gangly limbed Diego is a man of humble means—part of the *gente humilde* (humble people) of Peruvian Amazonia's Lower Huallaga region. Like his *vecinos* (neighbors), Diego's homestead is modest. Rather than being built from "noble" materials (bricks and mortar) like those "well-to-do" residents of the town center, Diego's dwelling comprises a roughly hewn wooden frame and a series of cubicle-like living quarters constructed from plywood and adorned with fading and blotched magazine cutouts, with cardboard fringes of an assortment of popular media or advertisements. The home's floorboards are made from *pona* palm (*Iriartea deltoidei*), raised about a meter above the moist, dark earth below. The combination of thatched and aluminum roofing of the residence is characteristic of many campesinos' homes in the rainforest of the Central or Lower Huallaga, or in this case, the impressively luxuriant Caynarachi basin.

As I slowly approached Diego, who was wearing shorts, and a slightly torn and soiled red T-shirt adorned with the dual logos of Credi-Vargas

23

and Samsung, I was pleased to see his beckoning hand and to hear him call out, "How are you, *amigo*?" Smiling, I replied, "Good, my friend. And how about you? And how is your family? What news do you have to report?"

Having known Diego for several years, I always thought his gaunt face had the look of a tired cleric while his lanky body evoked the animation of a flimsy puppet. I told my droopy-shouldered mestizo buddy that I was looking for him. As a social anthropologist, I carefully explained how I was conducting an academic study about the times of violence in San Martín and Loreto, and in particular the Caynarachi basin. I was interested in learning about those whose lives had been affected by the MRTA during the peak of the armed struggle in the late 1980s and early 1990s.

Was Diego disposed to help me chronicle what it was like during the time he was a Túpac Amaru rebel combatant in the Caynarachi basin? "Several people have told me you know about this delicate subject and that you could help me in my work writing a book about it," I explained to Mando Razor, who by that point looked rather pleased, if not proud of himself. As a former commander with the Túpac Amaru Revolutionary Movement, a willing interlocutor like Diego could provide me with the opportunity to understand those *tiempos feos*, or the "ugly times," from the perspective of someone who had been on the front lines of the armed struggle. I told Diego that my project involved gathering oral accounts from a wide spectrum of people whose lives had been impacted by the internal war. My interest was in the points of view of MRTA rebels and those campesinos and others—teachers, shopkeepers, nurses, farmers—who were present in the Huallaga Valley during the internal war. I carefully explained to Diego, and to the many others I interviewed for this book, that it was through these narratives one could gain a more thoughtful understanding of those times of incredible terror marked by the disintegration of community. One could index not only the fragmentation of the social contours marking community but also its reinvigoration despite everyday violence, losing life, grief, and post-conflict trauma.

After I clarified the purpose of my study, Diego slowly turned in my direction, stopping to gaze at the chocolate-colored horse tied to the calabash tree, which was loaded with green fruit. Smiling like the Cheshire cat, he enthusiastically responded: "Yes, all right then, we have known each other for a long time. I'll talk about the ugly times. How can I forget the hardships and suffering? How can I? What more or less do you want to know?" Diego's gaze met mine, and his profusive smile melted into a pensive look while his arms flexed forward in my direction.

FIGURE 4. Bartholomew Dean in Peruvian Amazonia,
photo by Luz Angélica Gómez Mendoza de Dean

If anyone in the Caynarachi basin could tell me about the Túpac Amaru Revolutionary Movement's impact on local communities, surely Diego could. He had served as a regional *mando*, albeit at a mid-level in the guerrilla group's command structure.[2] He had spent six long years between 1988 and 1994 actively fighting in the steamy, disease-infested jungles of San Martín and Loreto as a *tupacamarista* insurgent. "Well, Diego, what I want to know is what your life was like then here in the Caynarachi, in the various villages, hamlets, and forest plantations that dot this massive river basin?" I carried on and told Diego that all the actual names of the people, places, and riverways would be disguised when the book was published. "You will hide everything? Like in cipher?" asked Diego.

No, out of security and privacy, I was going to conceal only the names of those who were not public figures, as well as the names of places that did not appear in published sources about the internal conflict. If individual people's names appeared in public sources—like the news or in texts or reports—that was another case. They were "fair game." I would mention their real identities, but for everyone else—those *gente humilde*, humble people—their names would be completely changed, as would the place-names, towns, and riverways in the Caynarachi basin. I made it clear to Diego that

I intended not to harm or to act as a judge, but to comprehend a time of incredible volatility, heartache, and death. I relayed how anonymity and obfuscation were part and parcel of ethically chronicling troubled times, especially ones that very much linger in the present.[3]

"Is there anyone else who could tell me about those times, perhaps a trusted friend?" I inquired. "Sure, what about asking my *comadre*, Sandra*, who lives on the other side of Don Xavier's* *fundo*. She knows all about the *cumpas* and what happened to us. Her household is not too far away. If we go now, we can get there within twenty minutes," Diego, informed me while pressing his sizable thumb against a somewhat antiquated Citizen wristwatch encircling his knobby wrist.[4]

"Yes, why not Diego?" I happily chirped. "Besides, the walk will give me time to learn a bit more about Sandra, a woman I have heard about before from some people in the village." As we strolled along the sinuous forest path, Diego told me that when Sandra was a student, she had several close friends who were leftist *dirigentes regionales* (regional leaders) and that she had "always taken a fierce interest in regional politics."

Both Diego and Sandra were not only lifelong acquaintances but also ritual coparents (*compadres*) who had forged a bond of friendship birthed from fictive kinship, common interests, and the hardships of armed conflict. Fortunately, Sandra was at home when we arrived after our jaunt through the thick secondary rainforest (*purma*). Sandra, who has a slender figure, was squatting in front of her doorstep busying herself by placing handfuls of redolent dark brown *frejolito* beans on a tarpaulin to dry them on the ground. As she crouched in that spot, meticulously dressed in a floral dress, immaculate lemon-colored nylon trousers, and white rubber boots, her face brightened with pure delight upon seeing her longtime friend Diego. He approached Sandra with confidence and a friendly demeanor, his arms outstretched and standing tall. With a beaming grin, Sandra stood upright and bolted to hug Diego without reserve. He introduced me to his amiable *comadre* and friend as "a person of great confidence" (*una persona de gran confianza*). Sandra has gentle facial features and piercing caramel-brown eyes that are deep set, which enhances her overall attractiveness. The daughter of campesinos from the community of Marupa*, Sandra has spent her entire life in the Caynarachi basin, except for a short period when she was a student teacher in Tarapoto. Diego's personal introduction facilitated Sandra's willingness to engage in conversation with me about her experience as a Túpac Amaru rebel sympathizer.

After she finished placing the rest of the kidney-shaped *frejolito* beans on the black tarp, Sandra beckoned us to take shade under the cover of her home. She offered us mildly fermented cassava beer (*masato*), and Sandra began telling us how in the 1980s she studied in Tarapoto at a pedagogical institute where a covert Túpac Amaru Revolutionary Movement cell emerged. Many students had arrived at the institute in Tarapoto from the rural sector, with little political experience. The fifty-five-year-old Sandra told us she soon became enamored of the MRTA. She proclaimed to Diego and me: "Yes, it was the professors who recruited the students who were just beginning their studies—those who were in their first semester. They were the most susceptible." For Sandra, a feisty and pragmatic woman, the ideas accompanying revolutionary change simply captivated many. Thanks to her teachers and their "progressive new ideas," she learned to believe that the "revolutionary war was a people's war." For Sandra, "the armed struggle was not simply a vanguard struggle." She insisted they did not isolate the armed struggle from the masses but that the masses were active participants in its development and execution. Sandra's sentiments resonate with the words expressed by Sístero García Torres, also known as Commander Ricardo, a prominent leader of the MRTA, who felt "the armed struggle was necessary, it put this land on the map."[5]

With self-assurance, Sandra told us that in the MRTA's meetings, student members, called *emerretistas*, discussed how the rich and the well-heeled bourgeoisie exploited the masses and how this would all change once the MRTA came to power. She believed at one time, "the [MRTA] Party would gain power through the armed struggle, and that they would divide the country's wealth into equal parts to be shared by all." Sandra thought the clandestine meetings directly motivated some students she knew in Tarapoto and Moyobamba to join the armed struggle. With a face of deep anguish, Sandra sadly contemplated how "many of [her] classmates who joined [the MRTA] died in conflicts with the armed forces convoys and the national police."

Even more so, Diego had many comrades who perished during the protracted internal war. "Sure, I remember my fallen comrades. It is miserable to dwell on this topic," he lugubriously confided. "But my dead *compañeros* are like 'passing clouds' [*nubes pasajeros*] for me now. Each day the clouds grow farther away, and with time, memory fades and even the darkest clouds float away," intoned Diego in a soft yet acute manner. From the narrow and tawny footpath leading toward the turbid river, I could hear the mellifluous voice of Paola María*, Sandra's daughter. Paola María was coming our way, singing a lilting tune in her thick, captivating voice that reverberated out to the dense green forests surrounding Sandra's modest home near the river. Like many in the region, Sandra's homestead was perched on a stretch of secondary rainforest—*purma*—methodically hacked from the jungle for planting food gardens (plantains, beans, and cassava) and cacao. As the fragrantly perfumed Paola María drew closer to where we huddled in conversation, the lyrics of her ominous tune became intelligible:

> They say that in the waters
> Of the Amazon River
> The anaconda hides
> Everyone watches everyone
> They say that in the waters
> Of the Amazon River
> The anaconda is hidden
> Everyone takes care.[6]

As soon as Paola María arrived, Sandra paused our conversation and told us she was in a hurry, because her granddaughter, Sandrita*, was in a school play that afternoon. She had just remembered she had yet to finish making Sandrita's costume, which comprised the folkloric costume of a Kichwa-Lamista girl. Sandra inquired, "Would you be willing to return when I am not so rushed?" and told us she was sorry not to have more time for us. "Of course, *comadre*. I wanted to see you and introduce you to my *amigo* Bartuco," responded Diego in a smooth and salubrious tone.[7] Sporting a radiant smile, Sandra spoke in a warm and welcoming manner, voicing: "Chévere" (cool). As we made our way down the winding and dimly lit trail through the forest, Sandra affectionately bade us farewell.

El Maestro: The Teacher

By the 1970s, migration into the northern Peruvian Amazon gathered speed from other regions of Peru, especially from the northern highlands and the center of the country, where land scarcity propelled the influx of newcomers.[8] Recently arrived colonists established hamlets (*caseríos*) in the Andean piedmont and tropical lowlands, where they built schools, which led to an increased demand for rural teachers. But those junior teachers who had just completed their certification rarely wanted to go off to distant and poorly equipped schools in the countryside, where they had little chance of professional advancement. Many licensed teachers were urbanites simply unwilling to spend months away from their families and homes. In regions like the Caynarachi basin, which remained a sleepy backwater, cut off from regional centers of commerce and power, it was difficult to recruit teachers from the city willing to spend long stretches of time enduring the rugged living conditions of the jungle, where boredom and culture shock were challenges. In response, the central government started recruiting high school graduates with decent grades to dispatch them to work as certified teachers in the remote rural schools mushrooming throughout San Martín. This is when Sístero García Torres, a poor and talented high school graduate from the small jungle town of Sauce, applied for a teaching post in a remote community in the Caynarachi basin. He worked at a school in Huicungo*, which was reachable only after several days of hiking down a forested path (*trocha*) across the humid Andes and into the hot, muggy basin. Accustomed to a rustic regimen, García Torres went into the city only to collect his pay every six months and during the fifteen days of break that the government allotted teachers posted to rural zones.[9]

When Sístero García Torres—the future Túpac Amaru Revolutionary Movement guerrilla commander of the Northeastern Front—was first employed in the small community school in the Caynarachi basin, he was only nineteen years old. He claims that even at that young age (*chibolo*) he was drawn to the radical left. García Torres spent his free time poring over left-wing or communist tomes and studying teacher professionalization. For García Torres, reading such texts provided him with the opportunity to respond intellectually to a national society that had systematically impoverished the region he loved and had spurned its people, leaving them social outcasts. History had shown him that the Peruvian elites considered Amazonia's rural poor "unworthy people." Rejecting such interpretations, García Torres eventually contacted maestros—teachers from Sauce who had already made careers in Peruvian leftist politics. For the admiring García Torres, these maestros thought themselves to be "heirs of José Carlos Mariátegui, 'Che' Guevara, Lenin, and Trotsky." Mariátegui believed that sterile teachers have to produce sterile disciples. García Torres and his fellow radicals drew inspiration from Mariátegui's perspective on how self-absorbed and domineering privileged educators could hinder the aspirations and goals of intermediate-level students. They aimed to cultivate a new generation of students capable of paving the path toward revolutionary change.

Lucas Cachay Huamán, a candidate for the Rebel Voice (Voz Rebelde, VR) of the Revolutionary Left Movement (Movimiento de Izquierda

FIGURE 5. Pilgrimage to the tomb of Amauta José Carlos Mariátegui in the
cemetery Presbiterio Maestro, Lima, photo by Alarse-Colección Desco

Revolucionaria, or MIR), and a number of other *mirista* comrades were
chosen leaders at the 1981 convention of the teacher's union in Sauce. The
Left's victory in the local teacher elections served as additional motiva-
tion for the young teacher Sístero García Torres to adopt revolutionary
politics. It was at the teacher's congress in Sauce where García Torres first
encountered MIR-VR supporters that his life as a skilled guerrilla combatant truly began.[10] Under their guidance, García Torres was soon tasked
with opening a clandestine MIR-VR cell. He also delved deeper into the
Marxist-Leninist literature that his friends Jacinto and Lucas had sent him
from Tarapoto, as well as volumes on the Vietnam War and Che Guevara's
manual on guerrilla warfare.[11] In terms of organization, García Torres created three militant cells, each with fifteen members, and integrated them
into the MIR within six months. With a proven record of success, García
Torres was soon promoted to leader of the Sauce zone and served as a departmental representative in the 1982 MIR congress held in Juan Guerra, a
little rural community around fifteen kilometers from the bustling urban
center of Tarapoto. For the young rebel, the MIR meeting was crucial because it made his own commitment to Marxism clear.[12]

    During the departmental congress in Juan Guerra, supporters of the
MIR decided to begin preparing for combat by establishing the first military

school in Upper Shanusi. They also chose members of the MIR partisan steering committee at this time, with Lucas Cachay Huamán as policy secretary for the masses, Osler Panduro as secretary of the MIR organization, and Sístero García Torres as head of the Central Huallaga Regional Military Committee.[13]

The teacher-rebel, then, had become a member of a group of young revolutionary intellectuals discussing issues at the national and worldwide levels, far beyond the grasp of the average Amazonian teacher of the day, much less the local farmer, store owner, or transport worker. They read and debated texts written by Marx and Lenin as well as Adam Smith's works on political economy; their analyses were Marxist. They referenced ancient Peruvian history books and researched José Carlos Mariátegui, the man who founded the country's Communist Party and wrote the deeply influential collection *Seven Interpretative Essays on Peruvian Reality*.[14] In brief, they devoured a variety of left-wing texts and debated ideas that were in fashion at that time. Combining an appreciation for Peru's indigenous history through the optic of Marx, Lenin, and Trotsky, they concluded that the "poverty and the abandonment of our peoples was the fault of the Peruvian bourgeoisie—the richest of Peru. They, in reality, were the ones who ruled, with the help of Yankee imperialism."[15] In contrast to orthodox Marxists, García Torres and his comrades represent the tradition of Peruvian leftists who have long valorized the potential of nonindustrial workers, whom they see as politically conscious agents capable of popular rebellion.[16]

Politically motivated, Sístero García Torres and his companions began proselytizing among like-minded colleagues in the rainforest villages of Pilluana, Tres Unidos, and Buenos Aires. This included attempts to recruit teachers, students, farmers, and others who attended the union meetings for educators and peasants (Sindicato de Profesores y del Campesinado). They also engaged with those sympathizers or active militants of the Sendero Luminoso to persuade them to join the MIR-VR's cause.[17]

MIR-VR and Colombia

Sístero García Torres's path to political radicalization is linked to his professional experiences as a teacher in a historically "resource-poor" sector of national society. Teachers' collective labor bargaining, marches, and strikes have been potent instruments to defend the embattled public education sector of Peruvian national society. In 1979 the Unitary Union of Education Workers of Peru (Sindicato Unitario de Trabajadores en la Educación del Perú, or SUTEP) staged several large strikes by Peruvian educators, pressing the government for a wage increase and recognition of SUTEP as the only legitimate teacher's union.[18]

By then fully radicalized, García Torres joined five fellow teachers in a hunger strike. As a result, he lost his school job for a year, restarting work in 1980. Nonplussed, García Torres attended the following SUTEP union assembly, where he became acquainted with several militant comrades (*camaradas*), including "Marcos" and "Azul," both from the Revolutionary Left Movement, or MIR. They extended an invitation to García Torres to travel abroad to a political-military academy where he might enroll in hands-on guerrilla warfare training. Enthused, he accepted without hesitation; in his mind, he had images of travel outside the country, perhaps to Cuba or even to distant Russia. However, his subsequent experience did not pan out the way he had imagined his future to be. In 1985, as a member of the MIR-VR detachment, García Torres traveled from Amazonia to Lima and then made his way to Colombia to join a group of thirty insurgents; they were the so-called America Battalion.[19] The America Battalion comprised young rebels from Ecuador, Peru, and Bolivia, as well as seasoned Colombian guerrillas from the 19th of April Movement (Movimiento 19 de Abril), or M-19, the Quintín Lame Armed Movement (Movimiento Armado Quintin Lame, MAQL), the National Liberation Army (Ejército de Liberación Nacional, ELN), and fighters from the Farabundo Martí Popular Liberation Forces (Fuerzas Populares de Liberación Farabundo Martí, FPL).[20] García Torres agreed in Lima with the MIR-VR that he would stay in Colombia for only six months before returning to Peru to train his fellow militants, who were waiting for him there. After arriving in Colombia, García Torres spent roughly two years traveling through the mountains of the Cauca Valley, Cali, and Popayán on his way to becoming an experienced guerrilla.[21]

Following his eventual capture by the Colombian authorities, Sístero García Torres and a Peruvian compatriot, Marco Burga, were unceremoniously deported from Colombia to Ecuador, where they both escaped from police custody.[22] The youthful guerrilla fighters crossed the border in the hot and dry Peruvian town of Tumbes and moved toward Chiclayo, Peru's fourth-largest city, located in the northern region of Lambayeque. While his comrade Marco decided to turn away from life as an engaged revolutionary, García Torres opted to contact MRTA operatives from Chiclayo. García Torres was handed a counterfeit identification document by the commandos after providing them with a thorough account of his time spent with the Colombian rebels. This allowed him to fly to Lima and then on to the city of Tarapoto in the Amazon rainforest. Having returned to the jungle, García Torres was committed to taking up armed action in the name of the MIR-VR in San Martín's Sisa Valley.[23]

During Sístero García Torres' time in Colombia, the MIR-VR made a decision to establish its inaugural military school. This decision was reached during the departmental congress held in 1982 in Juan Guerra, the tranquil village known for cultivating tobacco (*Nicotiana tabacum*). Created that year in the Upper Shanusi, San Martín, the combat school trained fifteen men in preparation for the formation of what was to be later known as the Frente Nor Oriental (FNO), or Northeastern Front.[24] The basecamp was under the leadership of the veteran Comrade Dario, a rebel who had fought in Nicaragua in the successful battle of the Sandinista National Liberation Front (Frente Sandinista de Liberación Nacional, FSLN) to topple Anastasio "Tachito" Somoza Debayle's dictatorial regime in 1979. Among the fifteen *miristas* who enrolled at the Upper Shanusi military school, only Javier Tuanama, Alberto Gálvez Olaechea, and García Torres were alive at the time of the Truth and Reconciliation Commission's 2003 final report publication, the others having been killed in clashes, arrested, or disappeared or having died of natural causes. The *miristas*' military training lasted for thirty days and included instruction in using Argentina-made FN FAL light automatic rifles and SIG Pro pistols, training in explosives, and reviews of the basics of guerrilla warfare.[25]

According to Sístero García Torres, the first *mirista* contingent to leave Colombia entered the Peruvian rainforest in 1986 to train soldiers for combat both politically and militarily. The group was split into two platoons. One was sent to Shanusi (along the Lower Huallaga River) and the other was based near Sauce (along the Central Huallaga River). Ten rebel fighters made up the first detachment, and twenty-seven rebels made up Sauce's second platoon. They trained and made reconnoiters in the region, but they lacked modern firearms. They were armed only with shotguns that they had acquired from the local subsistence farmers. At that time, the Regional Military Committee (Comité Regional Militar) was organized in the Central Huallaga Valley under the command of the former teacher from the Caynarachi—García Torres, a.k.a. Comrade Ricardo.[26] A few months later, the regional MIR held a convention in Shapaja, a small town near the commercial hub of Tarapoto, promoting the Defense Front of San Martín, which included peasants, workers, and popular organizations.[27]

The Birth of the Túpac Amaru Revolutionary Movement

Akin to many other Latin American leftist insurgent groups, the Túpac Amaru Revolutionary Movement was part of the New Left. It comprised what has aptly been described as a "patchwork of organizations" that reflected its distinctive origins.[28] The emergence of the MRTA goes back to the MIR's formation in 1962 as a breakaway faction of the APRA political party called APRA Rebelde.[29] In 1964, under Fernando Belaúnde Terry's first government, MIR guerrilla forces took up arms on three national fronts: in the country's north (Piura and Cajamarca), in the center (Junín and Cerro de Pasco), and in the Cuzco region of the Andes (Mesa Pelada, Ocobamba District, and La Convención Province).[30] Luis Felipe de la Puente Uceda's "Party of the Peruvian Revolution" was, from his point of view, "an insurrectional process" that would birth a revolutionary cadre from the struggle itself.[31]

The MIR leader De La Puente Uceda divided Peru into three political and military influence zones to spark the "people's revolution." In the country's north, Gonzalo Fernández Gasca was in charge of the Manco Cápac faction; in the south, Rubén Tupayachi Solórzano led the Pachacutec group; Guillermo Lobatón Milla, an Afro-Peruvian intellectual educated at San Marcos University in Lima and the Sorbonne in Paris, and Máximo Velando were in charge of the faction in Peru's central jungle. The MIR's attempts to incite revolutionary insurrection through the creation of *focos* ("focuses" or "centers") fell completely flat among residents.[32] The Revolutionary Left Front (Frente de Izquierda Revolucionaria), led by former Peruvian ELN commander Hugo Blanco Galdós, and the MIR remained at odds, preventing any coordinated action from the Left. An army convoy captured and killed Luis Felipe de la Puente Uceda in 1965 and shortly afterward completely annihilated the remaining MIR column—including Lobatón and Velando.[33] Guillermo Lobatón was killed in September 1965 near Obenteni, and Máximo Velando was captured in Puerto Bermúdez a few weeks later.[34]

It was not until the end of the 1960s that the MIR began reappearing in numerous guises in Peru.[35] The MIR eventually split into various factions, one of which was the Movement of the Revolutionary Left—The Militant (or MIR-EM, for "El Militante"). A group of radical army officers who had taken part in the putative "first phase of the revolution" under the rule of General Velasco Alvarado founded the Partido Socialista Revolucionario (PSR) in November 1976. General Leónidas Rodríguez Figueroa (the former head of the Sistema Nacional de Apoyo a la Mobilización Nacional, or the National Social Mobilization Support System, SINAMOS), General Jorge Fernandez Maldonado, Enrique Bernales Ballesteros, and Alfredo Filomeno were among the PSR's founders. After the 1978 election, the PSR split into two factions, the Partido Socialista Revolucionario Marxista-Leninista (Marxist-Leninist Revolutionary Socialist Party, PSR-ML) and the Partido Socialista Revolucionario-Leónidas Rodríguez Figueroa (the Revolutionary Socialist Party-Leónidas Rodríguez Figueroa). Established in 1978 after the Revolutionary Socialist Party split, Antonio Aragón, Carlos Urrutia, and Andrés Avelino Mar were some of the PSR-ML leaders. It ran on the Popular Democratic Unity lists in the general elections of 1980.[36] In reaction, the radical leadership of MIR-EM—Antonio Meza Bravo, Elio Portacerrero, Víctor Polay Campos, Peter Cárdenas, and Hugo Avellaneda—reactivated the armed struggle and united forces with the Revolutionary Vanguard (Vanguardia Revolucionaria) group, headed by Manuel Rincón Rincón, and a Sendero Luminoso cell, directed by Néstor Cerpa Cartolini.

On March 1, 1982, the leaders of the two guerrilla groups—the PSR-ML and the MIR-EM—agreed to join forces and to call themselves the Movimiento Revolucionario Túpac Amaru, or the Túpac Amaru Revolutionary Movement.[37] The new insurgent organization declared the necessity of renouncing electoral-based legal reforms in favor of violent revolution to establish a democratic socialist state.[38] The Túpac Amaru's armed struggle, or *lucha armada*, began that year with an attack on a bank in Lima so they could get cash to finance "revolutionary actions" (e.g., political graffiti, propaganda, distribution of pamphlets and leaflets, the takeover of radio stations).[39] After 1984 the Túpac Amaru Revolutionary Movement entered the rainforest areas of central Peru, including Oxapampa (Pasco), inhabited by the Yánesha and by Andean settlers. They also began incursions into the Perené and Pichanaki (Chanchamayo) areas of central Peru, with deadly consequences.[40]

The former leader of the Orga, a clandestine wing of the Socialist Revolutionary Party (PSR), Luis Varese Scotto, alias Comrade Louis, directed a thwarted effort to open the MRTA rebels' first armed front near the community of Tinta (Cuzco Region).[41] The MRTA's endeavor from 1984 to 1986 to establish a presence in the jungles of Cusco resulted in the apprehension of the majority of their fighters.[42] This led the Túpac Amaru Revolutionary Movement's national leadership to shift its focus of attention to the San Martín region, where previous political work would facilitate their armed military actions. Between July and September 1987, the *tupacamaristas* concentrated their forces in the north of San Martín, near the border with Loreto, to conduct brief forays into Sendero Luminoso territory and to abscond with enemy supplies. In July and August 1987, the Túpac Amaru rebels, led by Comandante Rolando—Víctor Polay Campos—made several brief incursions into the towns of Campanilla and Pajarillo, starting a pattern that would become the modus operandi of the MRTA's campaign of guerrilla warfare.

The Tupacamarista Popular Army (Ejército Popular Tupacamarista, EPT) eventually grew to a military force of 150 uniformed troops, with rank, insignia, and hierarchies that constituted detachments, platoons, and squads under the authority of a general command and a general staff. The EPT had leaders for political and mass mobilization, press and propaganda, communications, logistics, and finance—all dependent on a National Executive Committee (Comité Ejecutivo Nacional, CEN), as decided by the First Central Unification Committee in December 1986.[43]

On December 9, 1986—the date commemorating the anniversary of the Battle of Ayacucho—the MIR-VR and the MRTA created a single organization to continue together with the armed insurrection.[44] Based on shared socialist principles and political objectives, as well as their affirmation of the inevitability of class struggle, they integrated their organizations' command structures and combatants. They agreed that the military organization would also bear the name Túpac Amaru Revolutionary Movement and approved that the political association or legal arm would be called the Popular Democratic Unity (Unidad Popular Democrática, or UDP). Akin to Colombia's National Liberation Army (Ejército Nacional de Liberación, or ELN), the MRTA had a Cuban-style command structure. The Lima-based National Executive Committee, which directed the guerrilla forces in coordination with a high command controlled it. The high command supervised military operations and comprised five separate committees: political (the Popular Democratic Union), intelligence and security, support and logistics, communications, and members' issues.

At its establishment, the leadership of the Túpac Amaru Revolutionary Movement comprised the commander in chief (*comandante general*) Víctor Polay Campos (a.k.a. Comrade Rolando), Miguel Rincón Rincón (a.k.a. Comrade Francisco), Néstor Cerpa Cartolini (a.k.a. Comrade Evaristo), and Peter David Peabody Cárdenas Schulte (a.k.a. Comrade Alejandro or "El Siciliano"), who would travel with around thirty guerrillas to the jungle. Thirty-five insurgents joined them from the MIR-VR and their military

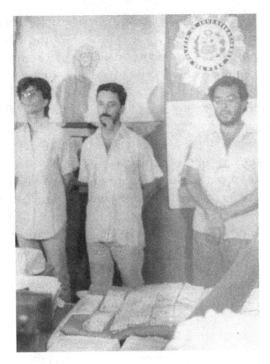

FIGURE 6. Peter David Peabody Cárdenas Schulte, photo by Luis Jiménez-Colección Desco

leaders: Rodolfo Klein Samanez (a.k.a. Comrade Dimas), Alberto Gálvez Olaechea (a.k.a. Comrade Guillermo), and Cecilia Oviedo Huapaya (a.k.a. Comrade Tía). The merger of MRTA and MIR-VR never overcame the different ideological approaches, political visions, individual interests, and personalities of its leaders, creating ongoing conflicts that ultimately undermined the organization's operational capacity and in due course helped give way to its collapse.[45] While the rural Túpac Amaru guerrilla columns comprised primarily mestizo and some indigenous peasants, the well-educated leaders, like Víctor Polay Campos and Peter Cárdenas Schulte, came largely from the middle and upper-middle classes or had access to a university education.

With the help of their MIR-VR rebel partners, the Túpac Amaru Revolutionary Movement was well positioned to continue an active armed front in the northeastern Amazon basin. Since the late 1970s, the MIR-VR had promoted the mobilization of regionalist claims and demands for better living conditions, trade and industry opportunities, communication routes, and increased access to markets for local farmers' products.[46]

Teachers from the North Coast city of Chiclayo and a Lima-trained engineer from San Martín oversaw the expansion of the MIR-VR in the Central Huallaga valley. They focused their energies on establishing militant MIR-VR politico-military cells in the communities where they had worked—Shapaja, Shanao, and Pucacaca—and subsequently in the town of Juanjuí and in the city of Moyobamba, all in the San Martín Region. These cells promoted the study of Marxist-Leninist texts and the history of Luis de la Puente and the MIR's earlier, albeit futile, efforts to foment revolutionary uprisings in the countryside.[47]

The MIR-VR gained legitimacy by incorporating well-established campesino leaders into its ranks, such as those linked to the Committee of the Producers of Corn and Sorghum (Comité de Productores de Maíz y Sorgo), among whom Velarde Ríos and Marcial Cumapa, an indigenous Kichwa-Lamista leader who was originally a supporter of Velasquism. Under their direction, particularly Cumapa, who was beloved and well respected by the population, the MIR-VR gained a foothold in the Middle Mayo Valley.[48]

Previously, Alberto Gálvez Olaechea had spent a decade with the MIR to bolster support among teachers and agricultural farmworkers throughout San Martín. As MIR's general secretary Gálvez Olaechea visited the mountainous and dense forests (*monte*) of the region, promoting the party, he began recruiting teachers in Tarapoto for the MIR. But in 1982, several MIR followers broke away to form the MRTA. In a similar vein, Gálvez Olaechea changed his path and became a member of the MRTA after witnessing the growing influence of the United Left, a coalition of progressive national political parties that had been gaining significant traction in electoral politics.[49] Given its growing force and political orientation that he admired, Gálvez Olaechea began conversations with Víctor Polay Campos in 1986 to integrate his forces into the MRTA ranks. Yet according to Gálvez Olaechea, this unification caused debates and bitter divisions among the *miristas* because of the conditions of incorporation imposed by the Túpac Amaru Revolutionary Movement.[50]

Víctor Polay Campos and his associates would be the ones who would assume direction, ultimately relegating the *miristas* to second fiddle. Because the Peruvian authorities caught Alberto Gálvez Olaechea before the *tupacamaristas'* planned jungle insurgency, Polay Campos—Comandante Rolando—assumed leadership of the Túpac Amaru Revolutionary Movement's Northeastern Front in the Amazon.[51] According to Polay Campos, the chief intellect and leader of the movement, the fundamental political aim of the MRTA was to replace so-called representative democracy with

FIGURE 7. Police raid at San Marcos University, Lima, photo from Colección Desco

the "power of the people." The insurgent group had a tripartite organizational structure: the full-time revolutionary forces; the part-time militia; and the grassroots village bases, including self-defense committees committed to overseeing a wide range of issues (e.g., military, sociopolitical, legal). Rather than creating "liberated zones," the MRTA, in Comandante Rolando's estimation, militarily "organized bases of popular power."[52] The Caynarachi basin became a significant base of general local support for the Túpac Amaru rebels, as is described by Diego, a former MRTA logistics commander who has lived much of his life in the Huallaga Valley.

El Mando: The Commander

My many stays in the Caynarachi basin between 2015 and 2022 were compelled in part by a desire to understand the allure of becoming a rebel commander, a *mando*, much like Diego. The day I went back to see the leggy campesino, I told him more about my life. In sum, I spoke to him about how I first arrived in Lima in 1985, as a youngish (*chibolo*) backpacker (*mochilero*) with romantic visions of Che Guevara and ended up fifteen years later living in Lima teaching anthropology at the National University of San Marcos, a bastion of radicalism during Peru's internal war. In those years, I had worked among the Urarina of Loreto's *selva baja* and written a book describing their history, culture, and cosmology.[53] Also, Diego knew about my human rights work in the Loreto, so I had "street credibility"—at least according to him.

Clad in saggy soccer shorts, budget-friendly flip-flops, and a loose-fitting blue polyester long-sleeve shirt, Diego pulled up two roughly cut stools to provide us seating under the palm-thatched veranda. He gave two handfuls of feed corn to a group of chickens that had unexpectedly arrived from his backyard garden (*huerta*) while I waited for him in the shade. He turned away from me and started speaking in a melodious and charming singsong voice. "Well, *bróder*, there was a group of *cumpas* that took up arms.[54] I'm not talking about Sendero Luminoso, but the MRTA that we spoke about last week, the Movimiento Revolucionario de Túpac Amaru. The country's ongoing economic crisis served as its catalyst. That coward . . . son of a bitch Alan García was the president, and his government wasn't doing anything for the people like it is at least trying to do now."

I paused for Diego to finish reliving his version of the events before my eyes met his slightly pursed lips. There was a light breeze blowing, and frogs, crickets, and forest birds could be heard everywhere. He continued: "One factor to consider in all of this was that the people of San Martín were willing to fight for their demands to be heard. They were willing to take up arms to fight for their rights. The group I joined, the Túpac Amaru Revolutionary Movement, was part of that larger fight for regional autonomy, for the defense of the people [*el pueblo*]. We were part of the *lucha armada*. And of course, Bartuco, I think we must consider the status quo at that time. It was a case of severe social injustice caused by an economic system that only benefited a select few people."[55]

When the Túpac Amaru Revolutionary Movement rebels first appeared in San Martín, the Caynarachi basin, like the rest of Peru, was going through a profound political and economic crisis. San Martín's society increasingly demanded from Lima's central government solutions to its agricultural problems, more investment in infrastructure, and basic services such as education and health care.[56] These demands were amplified in the second half of the 1980s with growing assertions for political and administrative autonomy of decentralized government that had been inaugurated by the Acción Popular administration of President Fernando Belaúnde Terry (1980–1985), and that Alan García Pérez's APRA government was to steadfastly follow (1985–1990).[57]

The sun broke through the palm thatching only to illuminate Diego's rugged countenance, casting a crisscross maze of light against his bent frame. He had seen much in his life. Diego's voice erupted with a booming resonance in my direction, not only reaching me but also capturing the attention of the horse and the squawking hens. Leo Tolstoy viewed government as an "association of men who do violence to the rest of us"; similarly, Diego expressed little faith in the benevolence of the Peruvian state apparatus, which he saw as a bulwark in the country's political and economic inequality. Instead, he saw government as an organized system of oppression that relied on coercion to maintain the status quo. "The corrupt model still holds true today: money comes before people rather than the other way around. Consumerism and egoism have destroyed community," Diego's booming voice reverberated as he fervently professed. "Yeah," I responded in agreement. "The economic model of the big cartels and the multinational corporations, they are the monopolies. For them, it's the ones with the money that always win. You know what I mean? They are shameless scoundrels [*conchudos*]," howled Diego.

His leftist sympathies remained intact despite the defeat of his dream of socialist rebellion, cultural autonomy, and national liberation. Diego was more than prepared to speak his mind freely in the comfort of his own house. The afternoon was becoming hot and sultry. Large, billowing clouds were gathering in the distance. The buzz of botflies had replaced the croaks, trills, and chirping sounds of the swamp frogs and forest birds.[58] I began feeling the sweat slowly dripping down the back of my neck, prompting me to proclaim: "Sorry, Diego, I brought nothing with me. Would you like me to get us some *chelas* [beer]? A soda [*gaseosa*] perhaps?"

"No, *amigo*, I have some *jugo de maracuyá* inside the house that I want you to try. It's delicious." Soon we were swigging down gulps of refreshing and vibrantly aromatic passionfruit juice. Diego then imparted how the pleasing passionfruit juice reminded him of his childhood, particularly visiting his *tío* and *tía* (uncle and aunt), who were briefly part of his life before they moved to Yurimaguas, the old port along the Lower Huallaga. After all these years, Diego recounted, he had lost contact with them.

Sipping passionfruit juice amid the rainforest with a former rebel commander was strangely relaxing. The Caynarachi River beyond was sparkling with reflections from the clouds and sunshine, and I was finally making progress in my project with someone who had fought as a *tupac-amarista*. While many had suffered and some had surely died at the hands of this former Túpac Amaru insurgent, I still felt at ease when I was with Diego. I couldn't help but believe that our meeting that hazy afternoon in the Caynarachi basin was meant to be, back in the early 2000s when I first started going there. Did I want to rest in the hammock? Was I tired?, asked Diego. "No, I am good," I quickly retorted.

Diego then changed the tone of his speech and his mannerisms. Gone was the jocular lilt in his singsong voice It had become serious and linear, and his posture had become more formal and somewhat stiff, as if he were ironing the wrinkles from his creased body. With shoulders arched back and his head at attention, Diego began recounting how things, "as an *emerretista* were very good at the start of his times with the Movimiento Revolucionario de Túpac Amaru. I was glad and proud to have been part of the movement or party [*partido*]." Resting against the home's external plywood wall embellished with a weathered calendar and a few provocative images from glossy magazines, Diego proclaimed, "Some people only think of the *tupacamaristas* as *terrucos* [terrorists], but it began in a very different way." He acknowledged that "terrible things occurred in those times," yet he asserted that the MRTA "tried to defend the people by striking against the heart of imperialism." Catching his breath, Diego pulled from his shirt pocket a *mapacho* (*Nicotiana rustica*) cigar and said, "Thanks to those wise ones [*los sabios*], the teachers, some around here began to realize that things could change if we fought the system that made so many of our *compañeros* enslaved peons. Our chances in life were so limited. With little education what could we hope for?"

With the *mapacho* cigar dangling somewhat precariously from his puckered lips, Diego remarked that he "wasn't a *platasapa* [wealthy one]" and that he had learned how to skillfully manipulate a razor-sharp machete in the forest (*monte*) long before he was wearing shoes or learning how to write his name. He insisted: "It is the political structures that have kept us impoverished and ignorant, just like our ancestors were enslaved for centuries. We lived in a virtual system of feudalism in the Caynarachi basin when the MRTA began the armed insurrection. We still suffer from the oppression of multinationals, along with the Lima elites [*pitucos y platasapas*].[59] They have always been the vampires [*vampiros*] of our economy. During the *lucha armada*, we fought to violently remove them from power."

I took special note when Diego shared with me how the MRTA taught him the key concepts of political science and the importance of history. "That's interesting," I responded. "Yes, Bartuco, understanding our [Peruvians'] history and political science changed me." Diego began a lengthy discussion of the basic tenets of the *tupacamaristas*, in which he again thanked his teachers for opening his eyes to "the historical reality of Peru's domination." As an active member of the MRTA's Northeastern Front under the command of various *mandos*, such as Professor Sístero García Torres, or "Comandante Ricardo," Diego said their political and military actions detected the true enemies of "the people" and to establish a socialist state based "on the will of the people." While Diego realized they were militarily crushed, he was still an adherent of essential aspects of the platform.[60] "The system must be changed," Diego insisted again, gesturing with his open hands toward the massive *lupuna* tree (*Ceiba pentandra*) sheltering the side of his home. Diego believed that even during conflicts, the local population should not be seen as the enemy and that the lives of subordinate personnel in the armed forces should always be valued and respected. He verbally reaffirmed the virtues of the Túpac Amaru Revolutionary Movement's rebel actions, especially against those objectives considered anti-popular and anti-national, the "repressive apparatuses of the state, transnationals, and the high bourgeoisie."

Diego suddenly stood up and motioned with a pistol-shaped hand gesture that I enter his humble abode. I gladly obliged, and we walked toward the door frame that was blanketed in the long shadow of the nearby towering *lupuna*. As I ascended the three wooden planks to the interior of the raised house, I uttered, "Permiso," the standard greeting before entering a stranger's home in Peruvian Amazonia. We were alone, besides the clucking chickens beneath the *pona* floorboards. Diego's blue-sheathed arm reached for his makeshift book stand and rummaged about for something. From underneath a stack of old newspapers and another faded calendar from 2015 advertising a *chifa* (Chinese-Peruvian) restaurant in Tarapoto, I saw Diego empty a large discolored manila envelope with a bundle of limp photocopied papers inside. "Here it is!" exclaimed Diego. "This is the *tupac-amarista* book I was telling you about the other day at Don Wilder's* *fundo* [farm] in Huicungo." As Diego perused the weathered and dog-eared photocopies, his thick fingers paused upon a MRTA slogan that stood out. The slogan—which boldly declared "For the cause of the poor! With the masses and the weapons! Overcome!"—had been underlined on the photocopied text, showing its significance.[61] "We thought of the enemy all the time," Diego told me, "but we treated them well." Drawing closer to me, Diego crouched in my direction and compellingly stated, "Look here, *bróder*, as the Party clearly states, 'The enemy, was to be allowed to surrender and be treated correctly if they had not committed crimes against the people.'"[62]

"But Diego," I cut in abruptly as he earnestly read from the guerrilla document, "how does this explain all the bloodshed, the trauma, and the violence experienced by so many at the hands of Túpac Amaru rebels? Don't you think that's just propaganda? According to many I have spoken to around here, a lot of what you just read is nothing but *flores* [lies, or literally flowers]?"[63] With his head bowed to the palmwood floorboards and nervous chickens below, Diego went silent. He lit his pungently aromatic *mapacho* cigar again and took a big draw before slowly exhaling and beginning to speak. "At first, everything was fine for me and for my other comrades with the *tupacamaristas*," recounted Diego. It seemed eerily still outside; the anxious chickens had even become inaudible. Besides my interlocutor, all I could hear was the sound of the breeze gently rustling through the forest trees that majestically bordered the homestead. Diego told me their lives as innocent young *tupacamaristas* eventually changed, much to their despair. They became "fugitives, constantly running away from the justice meted out by the state." Diego, like several of his *compañeros* I came to know, felt traumatized by being caught up in Peru's internal war. "Those were horrible situations we went through. Hunger, thirst, fatigue, sleeplessness, everything," Diego said, lamenting: "I never thought it would turn out like it did, that we would lose so much and gain so little. So many sacrifices for nothing in the end."

"How did it begin, Diego? The armed struggle, the *lucha armada*? I mean, how did it start here in the Caynarachi basin?" Judging by Diego's pensive visage and engaged body language, I knew the answer to this question was bound to be involved. "Well, that's an endless story: but it began in the schools with the teachers, with people like Sístero García Torres, who eventually became my comandante," replied Diego. "But we also had an important base of rebel operations here." The rainy, hot, and humid Caynarachi basin has dense jungles and many rivers, "which provide better protection than in the high Andes. And it's not like on the coast, where the deserts don't protect you at all. I know that the [MRTA's] Central Committee sent a group of seven people. A certain Comrade Abel and Comrade Persi led them. They were the first who arrived here in town," Diego disclosed.

Always curious, I inquired where these commanders were from; were they from Lima (*limeños*), or the Andes (*serranos*), or from the jungle (*selváticos*)? "No, Bartuco, there weren't any *cholos* [Andean peoples], they were all *selváticos*, people from the jungle.[64] They were in charge of first scouting the area," commented Diego. Evidently, the National Directorate in Lima wanted to position a detachment in the lower Huallaga area. Túpac Amaru rebel scouts were instructed "to survey the Caynarachi and make a detailed blueprint of the region," explained Diego. "Do you know where the first Túpac Amaru Revolutionary Movement *camaradas* like Persi and Abdel came from? Were they locals?" I asked, hoping to map out the organizational structure of the MRTA in the Lower Huallaga.

"I suppose so, Bartuco; Comrade Persi and Comrade Abel were from Yumbatos and Pampa Hermosa, both of which are in our territory," Diego continued.[65] "As the platoon expanded, Comrade Miguel* from the district of Chirimayo* eventually joined us," he said.[66] The rebels looked for a suitable location to establish a military basecamp and evaluated which areas could accommodate an armed guerrilla detachment.[67] With the help of the *milicianos*, El Porvenir* on the Huituyacu River* was selected. "In El Porvenir, there was a forest path to the highway near the bridge at the Pongo de Caynarachi. There were outlets for the community of Caspi-Yacu*, as well as a direct trail to town—the *caserío*—that we could easily patrol with our rebel forces. And walking by the forest trail (*trocha*), there were vital forest exits leading toward El Pongo, the town along the dirt roadway to Tarapoto across the Andes. So, from a strategic point of view, El Porvenir was an excellent locale to set up a MRTA detachment. From El Porvenir, we didn't have any problems moving to escape the ever-threatening armed forces. If the military or the police (*el tombo*) were in the *caserío*, it was often best for us to escape toward the Pongo del Caynarachi," Diego told me. "After the Túpac Amaru scouts conducted a comprehensive survey of the area, a platoon eventually arrived in the Caynarachi. Forty armed men and five women appeared one day to establish the detachment. I wasn't in the Túpac Amaru Revolutionary Movement yet. Then I was just observing the *emerretistas* from afar," he said.[68]

Diego's description of El Porvenir matches Jeremy Bigwood's 1992 journalistic account of his time in an MRTA encampment in San Martín. At El Porvenir, basic amenities were provided, as in other Túpac Amaru rebel encampments. Likewise, when Bigwood visited the rebel camp of Commander Francisco (Miguel Rincón Rincón), he noted it had basic furnishings—chairs and tables—that were meticulously fashioned from tree limbs bound together with forest vines, while a line of handmade hammocks draped in plastic tarps hung from the dense tree cover.[69] The thick rainforest canopy and the ambient heat shielded Commander Francisco's jungle camp from satellite surveillance, and there were no nearby clearings for putting down helicopter-borne commandos. This was also the case in the Caynarachi basin, where anyone resolved on attacking El Porvenir would have to march for more than a day from the Huituyacu River to reach the heavily guarded forest encampment.[70]

Diego had given me a key name—Sístero García Torres—who was linked to how the conflict all began in the Caynarachi basin, but I feared my questioning bordered on interrogation, a topic common to the personal accounts I collected, not to mention the discipline I practice. "Diego, let's talk again if you like. It would help me. Could you tell me about how you joined the Túpac Amaru Revolutionary Movement and became an

FIGURE 8. Víctor Polay Campos at the Ministry of Justice
(Palacio de Justicia), photo from Colección Desco

emerretista rebel? Would you be willing to do that?" Smiling, Diego's gaze met mine as his head bobbed. He said, "*Sí, por supuesto. Bróder*, we are both in this together."[71] I tucked the blotched and stained manila envelope with Víctor Polay Campos's Túpac Amaru Revolutionary Movement's photocopied text under my arm and made my way from Diego's veranda toward the riverbank.[72] I waved goodbye to my host and departed in a dugout canoe across the glistening river back into the bustling town port, teeming with activity and late afternoon energy.

CHAPTER 3

War Taxes

The MRTA dominated us. We were no longer the owners of our *chacras* [food gardens] or of
what we produced with the sweat of our hard work. They would show up without warning and
have assemblies to explain to the people what the Party's political platform was. The MRTA used
their AKM assault rifles and fear to oblige the villagers to attend the meetings and to support
them with cash, livestock, and food. If the people disobeyed, they were punished, or worse yet,
disappeared

DOÑA REGINA*

By happenstance, I maneuvered my canoe into the noisy port just as Doña
Regina* and her husband, Don Augustín*, were heading up a muddy ra-
vine toward the *caserío*. To determine how the presence of the Túpac Amaru
Revolutionary Movement had changed lives among the peasants of the
Caynarachi basin, I had sought the counsel of Regina and Augustín some
days before. They had agreed to my interviewing them the next time we
saw one another.

"Don Augustín, Doña Regina," I exclaimed, "It is me, Bartuco." The
wizened, owl-eyed Augustín, is an eighty-year-old rancher (*ganadero*) who
lives halfway between the bucolic village of Marupa* and town, near the
confluence of the Chirimoto* and Caynarachi rivers. The couple have more
than one hundred hectares of some of the region's prime pasturelands, reflecting the wealth they have accumulated over many years of hard work
and personal sacrifice. While they represent the middle socioeconomic
strata in the Caynarachi basin, Regina and Augustín's family life has been
difficult. They had three sons, two of whom were involved in killing a man
in Yurimaguas and served lengthy periods of incarceration. Their other
son, José Eduardo*, drowned when he was thirteen in a boating accident on
the Huallaga River. Don Augustín's doting wife, Doña Regina, is at least

two decades his junior. Slender and graceful, Doña Regina seemed always to be at her husband's side, steadying his faltering gait as he made his way through the forest trails to their *fundo* on the banks of the Chirimoto River.

As I quickly made my way up the footpath, I asked if I could follow them home and talk with them about the past, when the Túpac Amaru Revolutionary Movement was thriving in the *caserío*. Don Augustín agreed, and then Doña Regina nodded in the affirmative: "Yes, Gringo Bartuco. Please come and have *merienda* [afternoon meal] with us. We are all alone and we would enjoy your company." "*Bacán* [great]," I exclaimed with enthusiasm, "I'll be by your home in town soon, let me bathe first," then departed. On my return to their house, which overlooks the river's paved boulevard, I stopped by a bodega and purchased some salted biscuits (*galletas de soda*) and hard candies (*caramelos*)—favorite foods of Don Augustín and the gregarious Doña Regina. I made my way to the boulevard and walked toward the old couple's home. Upon arrival, I announced, "*Permiso*, it's Bartuco," and then made my way into their orderly home. Don Augustín greeted me as he was adjusting the shortwave transistor radio, trying to tune it to Radio Oriente, and then motioned toward the *tushpa* (cooking fire).

As I turned my head around to view my host's spacious living quarters, images began to match the piquant smell of fresh cilantro, boiling cassava, and burning firewood logs. In sight was a bubbling cooking pot of *caldo de gallina* (chicken stew) precariously perched over three smoldering logs—the *tushpa*. I could also see a large vessel of boiled grayish-green plantains nearby. "That's our *merienda*," said Doña Regina as she fussed with her loosely fitting apron that concealed her wafer-thin torso. She had birthed five children, three of whom never made it to adulthood. Their home was spartan. The couple did have a faded photograph of José Eduardo—their beloved dead son—on the wall. Dressed in his school uniform, José Eduardo's creased image was encased in a sooty gilded frame and illuminated from below by a small yellow light, replete with plastic flowers. Resembling the sacred icons adorning the revered halls of the Roman Catholic Cathedral of the Virgin of the Snows in Yurimaguas (Templo de la Virgen de las Nieves), the photograph of the departed schoolboy held an irresistible allure, making it impossible to look away.[1] The fusion of José Eduardo's portrait and the decorated frame created a captivating juxtaposition—a convergence of themes that intertwine the realm of the divine and the fragility of profane existence.

Wasting no time, I pulled out my trusted tape recorder and wondered aloud to the couple, "What did the MRTA do when they showed up at your *fundo* or here at your home in the *caserío* of Yana Puma*?" Augustín turned off his Sanyo radio, which was emitting a staticky signal from Ecuador, and we began to converse. While known to be fun loving, the couple has always tried to stray from any local trouble, they assured me. This non-conflictual strategy of adaptation was wise considering the appearance of the Túpac Amaru Revolutionary Movement and the state's counterinsurgency forces.

"When the *cumpas* showed up, they terrorized the local population with their weapons. We were fearful because they were always heavily armed," Doña Regina told me, directing her keen gaze toward the nearby animal pen (*corral*). She said: "They had automatic weapons and grenade launchers. We were simply defenseless. They came to our modest homes, and we had no access to heavy armaments like they did. They demanded that we give them our pigs, chickens, and cattle, and since we had livestock, we had to give them [to the MRTA]."

Augustín's watchful eyes turned slowly toward mine, and he bolstered his wife's account: "They ate in our homes; they took away our food to their basecamp upriver. They would return in a month and ask for *cupos* [war taxes] again."[2] The Túpac Amaru Revolutionary Movement sequestered people and returned them once their family paid a ransom, "like the time Ángel* was kidnapped," related Don Augustín.[3] He said they asked only him and his wife to collaborate (*colaborar*) in providing food, not to pay the MRTA *cupos*. When demanding the payment of *cupos*, the Túpac Amaru rebels typically told villagers they were voluntary (*a su voluntad*) "collaborations" or payments. Sometimes, the MRTA would ask for *cupos* with stipulated time frames for their payments. Túpac Amaru rebel cells would put letters under the doors of merchants asking for their demands to be ready the following day. Augustín laughed cynically and told me about their requests: "*Compañero*, sell me a chicken. Can you collaborate with a pig or even a chicken? But how could we charge [*cobrar*] them [the MRTA]? No one did that without fearing lethal retribution!"

Like many who were keen to distance themselves from any association with the leftist rebels, Don Augustín was quite adamant in denying that the MRTA ever camped overnight at his home. In an impassioned yet straightforward rendition, Augustín said, "The *emerretistas* were constantly on the run from the military and *el tombo*—the police—who were always in their hot pursuit." He recalled the Túpac Amaru Revolutionary Movement first appearing in the Caynarachi basin, originally from the Upper Huallaga, specifically Uchiza and Palmeras in San Martín. Don Augustín relayed: "The first time that professional revolutionaries arrived in our village was in the mid- to late 1980s. I had never seen them before. People like Professor Sístero García Torres, or as he was later known, 'Comandante Ricardo,' reappeared in our midst, having gone away to be trained as guerrillas in Colombia."

To identify themselves and garner popular support, "the armed rebels called everybody *compañeros* [companions].They wanted the villagers and local campesinos to help them create the Peasant Vanguard [Vanguardia Campesina]," Doña Regina told me in a whispered voice.[4] She said: "According to the *cumpas*, they defended us, to free us from subjugation. But it was all propaganda. How could they defend us when they came to Yana Puma only to ask us to collaborate with food or pay *cupos*? It was all a lie!" Doña Regina pondered as she continued to stir the simmering pot of *caldo de gallina* on the billowing, woody cooking fire.

The Northeastern Front's *mando*, Sístero García Torres, claims that the Túpac Amaru Revolutionary Movement's Regional Directorate had people dedicated to managing the *cupo* funds. These members typically lived in the urban centers as they supplied the guerrilla platoons with provisions: food, clothing, boots, medicine. Each detachment chief had reserve money that was ostensibly for the purchases on behalf of their fighters, as well as for food, including the purchase of cattle, pigs, chickens, and fish. But like most accounts I collected from residents of the Lower and Central Huallaga, García Torres accurately admits, "Sometimes in the area, the MRTA *asked* for donations."[5]

When Diego was the Túpac Amaru rebel's commander of logistics (*mando logístico*) for the Caynarachi basin, he told me he was typically given a stipend of one thousand *intis* and a detailed list of provisions to buy for the rebel detachment stationed at El Porvenir.[6] MRTA commanders held the role of quartermasters, granting them full authority over financial matters. Diego maintained he did not ask residents for food but bought his own; he went around with sufficient amounts of cash, and thus it was unnecessary to ask for *cupos*. But he conceded that some Túpac Amaru Revolutionary Movement detachments did not use the money allocated by the Regional Directorate but relied on *cupos* to not only sustain but also enrich themselves. Diego readily disclosed: "We eventually had lots of claims by the people against us for indiscriminately taking livestock to eat. This was the behavior of some of the Túpac Amaru *cumpas*, but please remember Bartuco, not all of us acted this way. In our encampment we were well-stocked thanks to the *cupos* paid by the *traqueteros* [drug dealers]." Túpac Amaru rebels protected the *traqueteros*' secret airstrips and guarded their economic interests. As Diego put it, "It was *choba choba* [reciprocal labor]: The *narcos* had obligations to us as well."[7] The *firmas*, or cartels, are transnational organizations created by a group of producers of coca leaf and its narcotics derivatives to regulate supply and manipulate prices. They were intimately involved in the syndicate of the terrorist organization Sendero Luminoso and the MRTA in the Huallaga Valley.

A well-circulated rumor in the Caynarachi basin about Don Augustín's prior association with the Túpac Amaru Revolutionary Movement had originally prompted me to ask if he would be interviewed. According to many reputable sources, the local priest had accused Augustín of being connected with the region's Túpac Amaru column. As a result, the police arrived from Tarapoto to investigate Augustín. With the help of members of the self-defense committee, or *ronderos*, the police captured him in his *chacra* and take him prisoner. When I asked Don Augustín about this one early evening, he was calm, given what I had heard had happened to him and several other teachers in the village.

Against the audioscape of billions of buzzing bugs and screeching crickets, Augustín declared confidently: "I had a clean conscience. I had nothing to hide from, Bartolomé. That's why I turned myself in when the fucking police convoy came looking for me that rainy Sunday. Isn't that right, Regina? Yes, I presented myself to the police stationed here in Yana Puma and gave my testimony to the police captain and his men. I assured my interrogators that I was not a terrorist [*terruco*]. I was no *emerretista*! The captain, a big bellied man—*buchisapa*—was a nasty bastard. Yes, the corpulent *tombo* treated me like shit. He repeatedly threatened to have his men hog-tie me and toss me from a helicopter to my death. After hours of questioning, and me assuring them I was not a *tupacho* [MRTA militant or rebel], they finally released me from their custody."[8] As I absorbed the details of Don Augustín's harrowing encounter with the police, Doña Regina called us to the table and benches in the central room where we were to eat.

While she served the steaming hot *caldo de gallina* into the shallow metal bowls set before us on the rustic wooden table, Augustín handed me some boiled cassava and plantains—standard fare in Peruvian Amazonia. After the meal was served, Don Augustín transitioned from talking about the police in the Caynarachi basin and started providing a detailed account of the abuses committed by the armed forces. When the drab-green-clad soldiers arrived, they numbered as many as one hundred. The villagers had to provide them with food, as they had done for the MRTA. "The *terrucos* moved about in small groups, ten, fifteen," Augustín added. In contrast, the military had larger assemblages of up to one hundred soldiers at a time camping in the village. Like the Túpac Amaru Revolutionary Movement, Don Augustín felt that "the army forced us to provide for them as well. They trapped us on all sides. They all abused us—the *tupachos*, the army, *el tombo*—the police, and the *narcos*."

Augustín's and Regina's accounts were familiar ones. They had some access to agrarian wealth (land, cattle, and crop production) but would have gained little from an open confrontation with followers of the Túpac Amaru Revolutionary Movement, let alone with a direct alliance with the state security forces, whose presence in the area was intermittent. They lived within a social realm that was characterized by ambiguity, a murky world of apprehension common to many inhabitants of the Caynarachi basin. Taking part in collaboration with the rebels, informants, the military, local law enforcement, or individuals involved in drug trafficking entailed grave repercussions, including the possibility of enduring torture, facing death, or disappearing without a trace. Perhaps Regina and Augustín were blessed with luck (*bendecido con suerte*), or maybe they were sympathizers (*milicianos*)?

Over time, I found out patterns whereby entire communities in the Caynarachi basin had been polarized by the violent conflict that had lasted decades. Some people I spoke with were deeply distressed by the actions of the Túpac Amaru Revolutionary Movement, whereas others expressed painful memories associated with the state's counterinsurgency campaigns. This is readily clear from my interviews with other long-term residents of the basin, such as fifty-five-year-old Elena*, who had no apparent connection with the Túpac Amaru Revolutionary Movement.[9] Of mixed mestizo and Kichwa-Lamista background, Elena was born in the Pongo de Caynarachi but moved to Huicungo when she married her husband, Sebastián*, whose family had been farmers in the area for decades. Identifying as a "housewife" (*ama de casa*), the stout and meticulously groomed Elena claimed she knew "very a little of the history of the ugly times."

Fortunately for me, Elena is an easygoing woman of even temperament, and my persistence in recording her point of view paid off. One day, after offering to buy Elena a fruit popsicle (*chupetín*) from the village vendor, I struck up a lengthy conversation with her in the market square about the MRTA and the state's efforts to combat the insurgents. Elena told me that, compared to the *emerretistas*, she was much more terrified of the military during the ugly times because of their bald impunity and their indiscriminate use of lethal force. In Elena's rendition, "The military accused everyone here of being accomplices of the *emerretistas*." She realized, as well as to "everyone in the community," that it was only the young men and teenagers in Huicungo who would attend the MRTA meetings. At the outset, these meetings were always held at night, often in the soccer field bordering the sinuous Caynarachi. Elena recalled the time Túpac Amaru *cumpas* stormed into Huicungo one afternoon and obliged all the villagers to attend a political meeting in front of the municipal office. Those who refused to join were forced from their homes and obliged to listen "to some guy rattle on about their political party. They talked about all of the great things associated with their political movement." Her neighbor and stalwart friend Doña Lucinda* said to her: "Let's go Elena, because if we don't, they could do us real harm. The *emerretistas* might even come and rape or kill us."

Camped out in front of the municipality, the villagers had to listen to a series of lengthy speeches that met with general agreement from the gathered crowd. Eventually, all those in attendance were asked by the Túpac Amaru Revolutionary Movement to collaborate with money. Elena said, "We had to give something—two, five *intis*, whatever we had." Intrigued, I asked Elena if these were *cupos*, to which she responded, "Oh no, these payments were a way to show our collaboration with the MRTA; they charged *cupos* for those who had wealth." Elena was told the money would treat the MRTA's wounded and to pay for food and supplies. This differed greatly from what happened to Joaquín*, Huicungo's mayor. Elena remembered how the former high school teacher, "without thinking, handed over a large *cupo* from the municipal treasury to the MRTA. But who could blame him?" As the town mayor, Joaquín was petrified. He didn't want to be kidnapped like his brother-in-law Ángel or, worse, killed, Elena explained. It did not surprise Elena, or to others in the community, that Joaquín ended up doing just as the Túpac Amaru Revolutionary Movement demanded and gave them a large amount of money from the Municipal coffers. For Elena, all the Túpac Amaru Revolutionary Movement wanted was money— "*plata, plata, plata*" (literally, "silver"). Like many in the region, Elena felt that followers of the MRTA were motivated by financial self-interest rather than community well-being, not to mention social justice. She expressed how young coca growers, known as *cocaleros*, would voice their frustrations to the MRTA about their lack of funds to carry out necessary tasks such as fumigating their fields and providing fertilizer for their coca plants. As their crops suffered and faced the risk of dying, the disillusioned *cocaleros* would become willing recruits for the Túpac Amaru rebels, prepared to engage in tropical forest warfare.

Twirling her long, jet-black hair, Elena's delicate facial expressions changed as she began describing the arrival of the army, which was the time "when the innocent people began to die." With a grimace, she described how the military would use whomever they found and make them go first into the *monte* in search of the MRTA rebels. She recounted stories of young men from El Porvenir who had vanished without a trace, and described the homes in her community that the army, and sometimes the police, had forcefully raided. After momentarily pausing, Elena told me she thought the armed forces killed or disappeared entire families. Elena, like so many peasants of her generation, had harrowing experiences during the Caynarachi basin's ugly times.

Likewise, Rosa María*, Elena's cousin, had a dreadful experience during the armed struggle. The military burned her house to the ground after they heard reports that Túpac Amaru rebels were using it as a way station. "We were innocent. The MRTA ate from our *chacra* but we didn't give them food," Rosa María told me the day I met her by chance in Yurimaguas. From her house there was a small path to the hills of Cachiruna* and then on to El Porvenir, so many rebels were often passing by her home. One night, in the ominous glow of the full moon, she vividly recalled the haunting sight of shadowy lurking silhouettes. Emerging from the depths of the forest, the figures of MRTA rebels emerged, their presence shrouded in darkness. With an unsettling air of determination, they steadily closed in on her humble homestead. Little did Rosa María know that the encounter would mark the fateful moment her home would mercilessly be razed to the ground. She hurriedly boarded a dugout canoe to get to the safety of the nearby town as she sought refuge from the impending danger.

In the embrace of her older sister and brother-in-law's family, Rosa María sought refuge and a momentary respite from the overwhelming challenges that beset her. In their protective presence, she found solace and a sanctuary where she could momentarily escape the weight of her burdens. As the night unfolded, she said her "restless mind" (*mente inquieta*) conjured visions of the devastation that awaited her return.

Rosa María reminisced about how she returned to what was once her home at daybreak, only to find the remnants of her life scattered and burned, a cruel testament to the ruthless forces ravaging the Caynarachi basin during the ugly times. After experiencing an unspeakable loss, Rosa María stood near the embers, struggling with feelings of both sadness and determination. Despite losing everything to the fire attack, she realized: "The flames may have taken my belongings, but they could never extinguish my inner strength." She resolved to start anew, collecting the charred fragments of her life and finding courage in her own resilience.

How It All Started

Mateo*, a willing informant, grew up in a small *caserío* called Nuevo Libertad* nestled along a small tributary of the Caynarachi River.[10] Roughly in his midfifties, Mateo—or "Pelechón" (Baldy), as his buddies call him—is a stocky electrician living in Lima. Having spent his youth in the Caynarachi region, Mateo eventually went to live in Yurimaguas, where he attended high school in preparation to become a cleric. This plan never materialized because of Mateo's exposure to what he says was "rational science and the inexplicable suffering of humanity." He opted for a practical life and eventually migrated from the Caynarachi basin to the Pacific coast, where he had been living at the time I interviewed him for a decade and a half.

According to Mateo, indications of the ugly times that were to come in the Caynarachi basin started in 1984 or 1985. This is when "the terrorists had their first meetings in my village—Nuevo Libertad—thanks to the rotund Professor Núñez*." Mateo recalled the snug fit of Núñez's shirt around his ample midsection, with the buttons appearing strained under the weight of his many layers of adipose tissue. Flabby Núñez apparently arrived with several Sendero Luminoso insurgents and started recruiting high school students in the village and nearby agrarian communities, like Yana Puma. One of Mateo's *primos*, or cousins, went to the clandestine gatherings and told Mateo that some militants were not from the Caynarachi basin. They had their secret meetings far from Nuevo Libertad so no one could find out about them. Pseudonyms were used to obfuscate their identities, a practice that mirrored that of the armed forces.[11] Within a short time, students from the third, fourth, and fifth years of high school had slain a dog, Huesito, owned by a *chibolo*, a young boy named Roger*, the nephew of Mateo's Tía Claudia*.

The *senderistas*, or followers of Sendero Luminoso, hung poor Huesito from the doorway of Don Ignacio Romero's* shop with thin cordage and tied a placard around its neck that read "So die the snitches."[12] The dog's killing caused a considerable stir in the hamlet. According to Mateo, people in the village claimed they placed the ominous sign at the entrance of Ignacio's place because he allegedly was a "big mouth" (*bocón*), always talking about what was going on in Nuevo Libertad. Several of Mateo's descriptions confirmed what many told me; Don Ignacio "had a loose tongue" (*tenia la lengua suelta*) and was known as the village gossiper (*chismoso*).[13] The local story is that the *terrucos* were upset that Romero was talking about the militant outsiders and their clandestine meetings. Poor Huesito's death and the placard ostensibly were warnings for Don Ignacio not to speak. While there are conflicting reports regarding the event and the timeline involved, Huesito's death seems to have been the work of Sendero Luminoso.[14]

The daughter of Don Ignacio, who claimed it was a threat perpetrated by Sendero Luminoso corroborated Mateo's rendering of the events surrounding Huesito's demise. Ignacio Romero's daughter told me that's why she was sent off to a coastal city to take refuge with her aunt during the incursion of Sendero Luminoso. Likewise, José*, the slender and athletic proprietor of a river taxi (*colectivo*) in the Caynarachi basin, insisted that Professor Núñez was associated with the Sendero Luminoso and killed the dog: "That is why we forced the professor from the community. He fled after we threatened him. I don't know where he is today."[15] Don Augustín also recalled "professional revolutionaries" in 1984 or 1985. When I asked Diego about the fate of the unfortunate Huesito, he, too, confirmed my hunch that the Túpac Amaru Revolutionary Movement had not yet arrived in the area: "Yeah! Sendero Luminoso strung that poor scrawny black dog up. The Túpac Amaru Revolutionary Movement didn't do it. That was done by a teacher, *el Gordo*, the chubby Professor Núñez. He was a militant member of Sendero Luminoso. I was still a schoolboy. That was in 1985. The MRTA didn't do that sort of thing." Diego confirmed that Sendero Luminoso was briefly in the basin. It had platoons in the area, but "they were like a quick flash, just like an alarm to alert the people of our miserable conditions."

I asked Diego, "Why was Sendero Luminoso never successful in the Caynarachi basin, and the MRTA, at least at the outset, seems to have had the support of some people?" Diego was quick to respond, telling me it was "because we respected our territories [with Sendero Luminoso]." He said by the time he was active in the Túpac Amaru Revolutionary Movement in 1988, both groups—the MRTA and the Sendero Luminoso—had already dominated a certain amount of territory "supposedly conquered to fight capitalist neoliberalism."[16] The Sendero Luminoso controlled the Upper Huallaga in areas such as Uchiza, Aucayacu, and Tocache, and the MRTA dominated the Lower Huallaga. The Túpac Amaru Revolutionary

Movement fought Sendero Luminoso in the Central Huallaga. As Diego put it, "We were enemies with different strategies, though most think of us simply as *terrucos*, as terrorists."[17] Sendero Luminoso the older, larger, and more violently ferocious of the two rebel groups, adhered to a hard-line Maoist ideology.[18] In contrast, the numerically smaller and militarily weaker Túpac Amaru insurgents espoused a *guevarista* revolutionary platform, more akin to that of the Castro-inspired insurgent groups that flourished in the 1970s and 1980s throughout Latin America.[19] The Túpac Amaru rebel's approval grew among some elements of the populace, especially as peasants left the violence of Sendero-controlled areas and sought refuge in MRTA-controlled districts north of Juanjuí in the Huallaga Valley's center and its lower reaches. In some instances, entire villages had turned to the MRTA for protection from not only Sendero Luminoso but also the army.

San Martín

Mikhail Bakunin asserted that rebellion is an inherent trait in all human beings. He astutely noted that even worms strive to avoid danger by wriggling away from the looming threat of a human's foot. Bakunin firmly believed that the intensity of one's rebellious spirit is a measure of vitality and dignity.[20] The MRTA attempted to reshape society within this framework by enacting rebellious change. While the Túpac Amaru Revolutionary Movement had shown itself as an effective urban guerrilla force; it had yet to gain traction in the countryside, and Víctor Polay Campos thought it was time to do so.[21] He felt the conditions were favorable: the farmers in the countryside were extremely well organized, and the area had one of the country's most stable bases of the Campesino Confederation of Peru (Confederación Campesina del Perú, or CCP). In the cities, there were the "popular fronts" (*frentes de defensa*) that provided strategic and logistical assistance to the guerrilla fighters.[22]

Rejecting Pariahuanca, a district in the province of Huarochirí within the Lima Region, and the Tocache region, known as a stronghold of the Sendero Luminoso, the leaders of the Tupac Amaru Revolutionary Movement established their initial guerrilla front in the Central and Lower Huallaga regions of San Martín. Per the theory of *foquismo*, the MRTA selected the northern rainforest, a region of Peru marked by political mobilizations, as its primary theater of guerrilla operations.[23] They believed that by creating polarizing conditions and acquiring popular support for its cause, the rebels would be joined by the masses in San Martín and elsewhere in a general revolt to overthrow the Peruvian state.

The Central Huallaga was chosen in part because of the existence of robust left-wing organizations, like the Forest Teachers Agrarian Federation (Federación Agraria Selva Maestra, or FASMA), the Popular Democratic Unity (UDP), and a MIR-VR guerrilla base with thirty-five combatants. These leftist networks fostered mass mobilization in San Martín, which the new alliance between the MRTA and MIR-VR could take advantage of. FASMA, comprising rural and urban instructors and peasant leagues, guided the principal social movements of the area. In the 1970s, many of San Martín cooperatives and agrarian leagues were centralized under the direction of FASMA, which was affiliated with the leftist pro-*velasquista* National Agrarian Confederation. However, with the ascension of right-wing General Morales Bermúdez to power, FASMA and many other peasant organizations throughout Peru moved away from the orbit of influence of the National System for Support to Social Mobilization (Sistema Nacional de Apoyo a la Movilización Social, SINAMOS), achieving greater autonomy while increasing their proximity to left-wing parties, the teacher's union, regional guilds and union workers from companies like Inka Kola, and workers from the state-owned tourist hotel and water and sewage services.[24]

From 1975 to 1984, there was a notable involvement of radical leftist political alliances, like SUTEP, and influential figures such as Segundo Centurión Pérez, who led the Forest Teachers–San Martín Agrarian Federation, and Lucas Cachay Huamán from MIR-VR, who headed the Unitary Fighting Command (Comando Unitario de Lucha, CUL). These individuals played a significant role in organizing and advocating for peasant strikes that effectively paralyzed the region. Having operated in the zone for more than a decade, FASMA controlled the peasant and labor organizations that engaged in strikes and roadblocks.[25] During the twenty-day general campesino strike of 1982, the Carretera Marginal was blocked in the south toward Juanjuí, with picket lines in Juan Guerra, Puerto Lopez, Pucacaca, Picota, and Bellavista, closing 130 kilometers of roadway. To the north, the highway was obstructed in Morales (Tarapoto), Cacatachi, Tabalosos, Moyobamba, and Rioja. The unpaved road to Yurimaguas was made impassable at the intersections of the Pongo de Caynarachi, Alianza, and Pampa Hermosa. Eventually, the police violently intervened in the road blockages and wounded scores and killed five civilians in the towns of Juan Guerra and Tabalosos.[26] In taking control over the roadway, local protesters were seeking the best price for their products, namely maize and rice. Likewise, the Defense Front of the Department of San Martín (FEDIPSM), led by Lucas Cachay Huamán, a former MIR-VR cadre who established the left-wing UDP to replace the defunct MIR-VR, aided in drumming up popular support and promoting regional autonomy.[27]

The CUL fostered the first strike of rural and urban workers in 1984. Two years later, it successfully staged another regional strike that forced the *aprista* government to send an official commission, led by Armando Villanueva and other ministers, to seek a peaceful resolution to the regional crisis. Negotiations with the CUL and two hundred delegates from the peasant base lasted sixteen hours. The CUL transformed into the Front for the Defense of the Interests of the Province of San Martín (Frente de Defensa de los Intereses de la Provincia de San Martín, or FEDIPSM) in 1986.[28]

In the following decade, San Martín's political Left supported the creation of a regime of local, autonomous, and independent self-governance for the region within the general process of regionalization that the *aprista* government had been promoting since 1986. In the struggle for San Martín's autonomy, FEDIPSM came to count on the active support of the Túpac Amaru Revolutionary Movement. Still, there was strong resistance from the San Martín elites to accept the decentralization of the APRA regime, whose intention was to separate some provinces of the region and incorporate them into other regions.[29] In 1987, the MRTA appeared publicly in the Huallaga Valley, leading to regional militarization, a state of emergency, and a nightly curfew.[30] During that tumultuous period, many social organizations found themselves in a state of paralysis because of the heightened repression they faced and the pervasive fear of further exacerbating the existing conflict. The dread of reprisals and escalating violence created a stifling atmosphere, inhibiting the mobilization and collective action that had been vital to their work. For almost two years, the actions of FEDIPSM were minimal; only in 1989, with the debates on regional autonomy raging, had the front recovered its potential and strength as a strategic organization capable of responding to the demands of the region.

By refusing to ease the agrarian crisis and denying resources to San Martín, the leftist leadership saw nonaction by the government as a form of induced political violence. The campaign for the San Martín Autonomous Region, led by the FEDIPSM and supported by the MRTA, organized an indefinite regional strike. Beginning on February 15, 1990, they staged the strike amid a political milieu convulsed by the national electoral process and the growing indignation of San Martín's mestizo peasantry over the state's noncompliance with promises following previous mobilizations, demonstrations, and strikes. The twenty-four-day work stoppage achieved state commitments to increase prices for rice and to pay debts to rice and corn producers deposited in the country's agrarian bank. It also included the government's commitment to complete the pavement of the *carretera* between the highland forested city of Tarapoto and the lowland Amazonian port city of Yurimaguas, a long-awaited promise that unfolded over the course of more than fifteen years.[31]

The Return of the Native

Playing off the mounting demands of San Martín's increasingly vociferous, sociopolitical movements, several columns of the Túpac Amaru Revolutionary Movement were reconstituted from the end of 1988 to early 1990. One of them was under the leadership of Sístero García Torres, or "Commander Ricardo," who rose to become *comandante general* of the entire Northeastern Front.[32] Returning to his natal home from his time abroad, García Torres "assumed a double life of being with family and being with an organization of guerrilla fighters in the San Martín area." He was in disrepute because of reports about his involvement in the guerrilla wars in Colombia. He had lost his state teaching job, and his family longed for him to not leave them again. Meanwhile, the Túpac Amaru Revolutionary Movement was putting pressure on him to continue his revolutionary work in the Peruvian Amazon. Confused and anxious, García Torres was at a personal crossroads.[33]

Despite any misgivings, Sístero García Torres forged forward along the path of armed revolutionary struggle. And on this issue, he was not alone in his efforts to radicalize San Martín's populace over long-standing socioeconomic demands. In San Martín, the *miristas*, under Gálvez Olaechea's direction, relied on their network of teachers to drum up partisan support for their cause. They had the backing of students, workers, and peasants, such as Diego, Sandra, and Fabiano, along the Lower Huallaga River, and the MIR-VR commander believed they could be organized swiftly and successfully to launch a guerrilla front in the region.[34]

Sístero García Torres arrived in the rainforest of San Martín with the mission of organizing and directing a guerrilla column. A student of *foco* theory, García Torres thought the area was "a breeding ground for the rebellion to break out." His *camaradas* urged him to establish and lead a guerrilla training camp in the solitude of the lush rainforest. The timing was thought ideal to open a rebel column in the territory. The region had many young and enthusiastic people who were waiting for that moment, especially students from local pedagogical and technological institutes whose anti-capitalist politics made them perfect for building a revolutionary movement among the masses. From García Torres's perspective, it would not be difficult to recruit roughly sixty young people and take them into the rainforest—*la selva*—to train them for the initiation of the armed insurrection to topple the corrupt and dependent capitalist state.[35]

To accomplish his goal, Sístero García Torres contacted comrades in the area for their help, including Migdoño Silva, a.k.a. "The Puma," who had also been in Colombia training to be a revolutionary soldier and had almost the same experience as his *compañero*-in-arms. Puma had escaped to Cali, Colombia, where he was provided with bogus documents and returned to Peru without problems. The first rebel contingent García Torres led was near the town of Sauce. It comprised a group of *miristas* who marched about twelve hours into the jungle to set up their first forward operating basecamps. García Torres was determined to recruit combatants and prepare them politically and militarily. In the beginning, his group comprised only fifteen fighters. They trained day and night for six months. No one suspected anything odd about their presence in the *monte,* or forest. It was a remote area where only peasants came hunting for wild animals: deer, peccary, and capybara. By the time of their arrival, news of the terror of the Sendero Luminoso in the Upper Huallaga was reaping great fear in the Central and Lower Huallaga.[36]

The *mirista* encampment's presence was passed off initially as part of the activities of drug trafficking (*narcos*) or coca growers (*cocaleros*). Local peasant farmers were usually more afraid of insurgents than of the *traqueteros* (low- to mid-level drug traffickers) or *firmas* (drug cartels) who operated independently with their *sicarios* (hitmen) and own moral economies. Within six months, more combatants arrived at Sístero García Torres's forward operating base. Subsequently, twenty-five showed up who had guerrilla warfare experience from their time in Colombia. They were well versed in target practice and in using rifles, pistols, bazookas, and explosives. Nevertheless, García Torres's training facility had few weapons at that point, only an AKM rifle and FAL semiautomatic rifle, some six grenades, and six .16-caliber weapons. Despite the lack of weapons and munitions, the morale and courage of the *compañeros* stood firm: "In the future [the MRTA] had access to excellent weapons, like Russian AKM assault rifles."[37]

Depending on whom you talk to and where, people's opinions of García

Torres vary drastically in the Huallaga Valley. The former schoolteacher's reemergence as Commander Ricardo, the rebel leader of the MRTA's Northeastern Front, fomented a mixture of fear, awe, and admiration among inhabitants of the Caynarachi basin. For the disillusioned, of which there were many—especially among the youth—Commander Ricardo represented the charismatic allure of a new path forward, a break from the old ideas and political structures that had kept Peru impoverished for centuries. For others, his reappearance triggered a spiral of abuse, accompanied by times of fear. Commander Ricardo represented foreign ideas associated with the literate Left and was seen with great suspicion. Many associated his name with all the dangers of an unknown that ended in years of violent conflict. I captured this in several conversations with the mother of a good friend, Hilda*, and her soft-spoken husband, Juan Manuel*, who had various encounters with Sístero García Torres in Sauce, albeit unbeknownst perhaps to the rebel commander.[38]

Sauce

Sauce is located on the slopes of the Eastern Cordillera, about fifty kilometers south of Tarapoto. Hilda had never heard of the *terrucos* before Sístero García Torres returned to his town in the fertile forested hills across from the Central Huallaga River. She told me how that all changed the day she went a few blocks down a dusty street to the corner shop to buy some eggs and bread to cook the family breakfast. Hilda was in her late twenties back then, and like many women from her area, she had married a local farmer from an adjoining hamlet. Looking at her gnarled and weathered hands, I tried to imagine how Hilda was many years ago before hard work had broken her now-gaunt, arthritic body. She told me she had trouble toiling the long hours in the family's food gardens (*chacras*), nor could she make much of a living in Sauce, given the limited employment opportunities open to a woman with no formal education or access to capital, political connections, or social status.

In various respects, Hilda's upbringing was not too unlike that of García Torres. Although their life paths diverged sharply, they came from similar socioeconomic backgrounds. Like Sístero García Torres, Hilda complained of the dearth of educational opportunities when she was a young *chibola*, and of the countless "lost opportunities" that passed her by as a teenager. Regrettably, her unintended pregnancy at seventeen forced her to abandon her aspirations of pursuing a career in health care, extinguishing her dreams of becoming a nurse or medical lab technician. Unlike García Torres, she never went to Lima, let alone abroad.

While García Torres was off learning how to become a leftist rebel fighter, Hilda continued her agrarian life much like her ancestors had, working in the verdant fields that flank the Huallaga Valley. After marriage, Hilda settled with her husband in the village of Sauce but devoted much time to the family's *chacra*. They grew subsistence crops, and Hilda helped her husband in marketing their produce in Sauce, or on a rare occasion, they went to the "big city" of Tarapoto to sell their food crops. Her family's gardens had plantains, cassava, beans, corn, peppers, and a wide variety of medicinal plants that Hilda once loved to show off to anyone in the community willing to listen.

In the 1980s, Hilda and her husband, Juan Manuel, had a growing family, yet they were barely getting by, as money was always tight. The national political and economic conditions were going from bad to worse to unbearable. Under Alan García's faltering APRA government, hyperinflation, road blockages, and mounting food shortages were common. Pointing to an old black radio dangling from a rusty nail in the adobe wall, Hilda recalled that the battery-operated shortwave radio was usually broadcasting depressing news of the growing threat of Abimael Guzmán's Sendero Luminoso, or about the power outages (*apagones*), car bombs (*coche bombas*), political assassinations, and Túpac Amaru rebel attacks on government targets in Lima.[39] The fiscal situation of the country reflected the family's domestic economy. Hilda told me that the couple constantly fretted about putting enough food on the table, even if it was only beans, rice, and *ají* (chili peppers), supplemented by dry salted fish (*pescado seco*) or a chicken or two each week. Beef and pork were rare indulgences, eaten only on special occasions—a birthday, baptism, or marriage. They rarely had enough money to spend on a luxury item—like shoes, ice cream, or building materials to fix their ramshackle home. Feverishly gesturing toward the home's naked rebars and unfinished second floor, the barrel-chested Juan Manuel became animated and began nodding his head while his wife Hilda continued narrating her experience.

On that ill-fated day when she learned about the Túpac Amaru Revolutionary Movement, Hilda recalled walking toward Don Héctor Silva's* corner bodega. In the distance, Hilda heard one of her neighbors (*vecinos*) impatiently bellowing: "The *terrucos* are in the *monte*. Here they come. Neighbors, take cover!" Hilda did not know what her *vecino* was rattling on about. "Why was my neighbor so worried?" she pondered. "Maybe it was some sort of *shapshico* [forest spirit] that has appeared!" Hilda declared with a toothy smile on her rumpled face. She said that when she turned to the soccer field, she saw a long line of uniformed armed soldiers marching single-file out of the jungle along the main path (*trocha*) toward town. This made Hilda "dizzy" (*mareada*), and "her stomach churned with fear" (*se le revolvió el estómago de miedo*). She rushed off to the bodega to take cover in the well-stocked shop just as the mysterious soldiers began entering the local school. Amid the store's neatly lined rows of canned goods, well-arranged vegetables, bottles of beer, plastic tarps, shoes, and sundry hardware, Hilda hid behind two enormous sacks of rice and a bag of dried *haba* beans in the entranceway. She quietly inquired, "What's going on?" to Don Héctor, who watched Hilda from beneath the shop's front counter as she took cover behind the sacks of food. "They are *terrucos*, rebel soldiers who have come to invade the town. Be careful, it's the MRTA!" Don Héctor forewarned.

Recalling her panic, Hilda waited until she saw the strange-looking soldiers heading in the opposite direction. She then furtively scurried home as fast as she could to tell her husband and their two children about the masked armed fighters. Soon, word was out among Sauce's townspeople that the armed outsiders were a detachment from the Túpac Amaru Revolutionary Movement. The abrupt appearance of rebels who emerged and vanished in a logical and ordered manner, as well as in military formation, elicited sympathy and alarm among the fazed public. From their temporary base in Sauce's school, the *tupacamaristas* began entering the empty streets, thumping on doors and cajoling the populace to attend a communal meeting (*mitin*) in the Plaza de Armas, the town's primary square. As had become customary, the Túpac Amaru invaders went from house to house and solicited cash from each family, calling the people to their political assembly. "No matter what we thought, we all had to go listen to the meetings even if we didn't want to. I was nervous about what they could do to my family," recalled Hilda. "No one in their houses," shouted the *cumpas*.

At the gathering, Sístero García Torres introduced all of his Túpac Amaru *compañeros*-in-arms to the community. He talked to the gathered crowd about the *lucha armada* and told them the revolution would happen, bringing them to power under Comandante Rolando, or Polay Campos. During their political meeting, the *emerretistas* obliged the townsfolk to salute the Túpac Amaru flag as it was raised before them. Underscoring its links to its revolutionary credentials, the MRTA flag was the triple-striped red-and-white Peruvian flag emblazoned with the mace and assault rifle, which formed a *V* around the dark image of the eighteenth-century revolutionary hero—José Gabriel Condorcanqui—popularly known as Túpac Amaru II. The stylized *V* is formed by a star and a gun—the firearm (similar to a Kalashnikov AK-47) indexing the MRTA's belief in an armed struggle to achieve their objectives. The *V* denotes the Spanish word *venceremos*, "We will win!" Túpac Amaru flag adulation was complemented by rebel singing of dirgelike anthems to Túpac Amaru II and to the "Victory of the People's Revolutionary Struggle."[40]

During the singing of the militaristic tunes, "some of Sauce's children and young men began sniggering along with the *cumpas*, or at least they were trying to mouth the words," ruminated Hilda. For Juan Manuel, "it was a fiesta-like atmosphere while the MRTA was in town. Chaotic, but it was something we had never seen before. It seemed truly electrifying and important all at the same time." Hilda cut off her partner's description of the events, "Yes, Juanico, but don't forget from the Plaza de Armas, Sístero García Torres ordered everyone as if he were our *patrón* [boss], and the town had to provide him with what livestock we could." As Hilda detailed, in the main square, García Torres told the residents of Sauce, "From now on, we are going to be part of the community. We are going to be the owners of the *caserío*."

The Túpac Amaru Revolutionary Movement detachment had shown up in Sauce with ten well-armed insurgents flaunting AKMs, grenades, and pistols to collect war taxes. While the sight of AKM rifles was intimidating to her, Hilda seemed more impressed with how Túpac Amaru rebels went about the *caserío* with big aluminum cooking pots and mountains of provisions (*carga*). The *tupacamaristas* went from shop to shop asking merchants in Sauce for *cupos*, provisions, and food. Over time, Juan Manuel said they all became "accustomed to the *terrucos* and, on their insistence, we support them."

The day Commander Ricardo and his rebels first showed up in Sauce, the villagers were petrified. As the Túpac Amaru Revolutionary Movement's political assembly unfolded, a crowd had congregated in anticipation. Suddenly, they heard the distinct sound of an approaching army gunship helicopter, growing louder with each passing moment. The expectation heightened as the helicopter drew nearer, and eventually, the crowd could see it emerging on the horizon, descending toward the main square. The combat helicopter added a dramatic element to the atmosphere, capturing the attention of everyone present and setting the stage for what was to come. "Shit, if there were going to be a gun battle, where would we have run off to? Where would we have hidden with so many bullets flying around?" contemplated Juan Manuel. Yet Hilda recalled that there were no battles in Sauce, but in the *chacras* and surrounding hamlets, "the echoing sound of nightly gunfire was pervasive." While engaging in conversation with Hilda and her husband in Sauce, a picturesque town nestled along the shores of the celebrated Laguna Azul (Blue Lagoon), Hilda shared a thought-provoking reflection on their personal experiences during what she referred to as "the times of terrorism" (*los tiempos del terrorismo*). She conveyed that their lives were deeply affected, burdened by a constant state of affliction. Hilda further emphasized the profound impact of living in perpetual fear, which emanated from both the MRTA and the army. The magnitude of this fear was so immense that death itself seemed to loom over the crystalline indigo waters of Laguna Azul, its presence unwavering and undeniable.[41]

The couple knew shootouts and ambushes were occurring in the *monte* that skirted the irregular perimeter of the town, and they endured personal loss at the hands of the movement. Hilda's favorite uncle, a respected community figure, had publicly scorned Sístero García Torres. She told me her uncle had no trouble speaking his mind to anyone about his disdain regarding the transformation of Sauce after the MRTA rebels. Unfortunately, one day, on a routine trip to Tarapoto to purchase kerosene, Hilda's uncle was pulled over along the road by masked Túpac Amaru guerrillas who, she says, robbed him, bound his hands and feet, and shot him in the back. Although his death was never officially solved, Hilda remains convinced it was in retribution for her uncle's ill-placed words against García Torres, coupled with his refusal to "provide any *cupos* or give any cattle to the *tupacamaristas*, even though he had a large herd in Sauce."

Comandante Ricardo and the Caynarachi Basin

Comandante Ricardo's reputation in the Lower Huallaga's Caynarachi basin preceded his return to Peru from Colombia to take up arms in the name of the revolutionary struggle to establish a socialist state. For those who knew him from his days as a schoolteacher in the area, Sístero García Torres's reemergence as a rebel commander came with much astonishment and a dose of pride. "The children's parents [*padres de familia*] found him to be especially respectful," said crotchety Alberto*, who knew García Torres as a young teacher in Huicungo.[42] Considering the fraught relationships that teachers often have with the communities they are assigned to work in, Alberto's words represented rare compliments.

"With us, he was noble," recounted those who knew García Torres as a school teacher in the area. He was a respected professor, along with his colleague Don Wilder in Huicungo, said Wagner*, the convivial owner of a local bodega, as he described his time with the future *tupacamarista* rebel.[43] "I remember the day he just disappeared. We never knew where he went to. Had he died? Had he gone off to the city and found work? Or maybe he had gotten into trouble, as some rumored it. Did he go to Lima? Pucallpa? Iquitos? I'm not sure. But when he came back to the Caynarachi, he was one leader of the MRTA. It all surprised us since he was well respected. He was always cordial with us," slender-nosed Wagner told me.

As a former Túpac Amaru Revolutionary Movement rebel, Diego worked under Sístero García Torres's direction while he was the commander of the Northeastern Front. As the Caynarachi's logistics commander, Diego "coordinated" with Commander Ricardo on multiple occasions. They shared food (*rancho*) in the MRTA's forward operating base at El Porvenir. They were both involved in several MRTA armed assaults, like the daring seizure of Yurimaguas, the capture of Lamas, and various river attacks. Diego knew García Torres through his affiliation with the party. All of Diego's *tupacamarista compañeros* were well aware that Commander Ricardo had been trained in Colombia with the 19th of April Movement and was well respected for his courage and proven experience on the battlefield. His recognition of the rebel leader's charisma marked Diego's impression of García Torres. Whenever García Torres surfaced in a tiny community—like Yumbatos or Pampa Hermosa—the populace galvanized to support the rebel commander.[44] Diego would interact with García Torres for thirty minutes on several occasions. The brevity of their encounters was not surprising for Diego, given that Comandante Ricardo "was a very busy guy. Though he spent time with us in the field [*campo*], he did not direct a platoon but was in the national leadership with people like Comandante Rolando—Polay Campos."[45] Like his rebel *compañeros*, Diego came to know the character of his leaders by being a member of the Túpac Amaru's armed forces and participating in their military actions, such as the Túpac Amaru Liberator campaign of 1987.

CHAPTER 4

Túpac Amaru Libertador

Con las masas y las armas, patria o muerte.

MRTA POLITICAL SLOGAN

By 1987, a throng of *tupacamaristas* had been assembled in the San Martín region, combining MIR-VR insurgents and MRTA militants who came from Tocache, a community along the upper portions of the Huallaga Valley. Both armed groups united in the Pongo of Caynarachi–Shanusi area.[1] According to Lucas Cachay Huamán, members of San Martín's insurgent movements, like the MRTA, included students, peasants, trade unionists, and teachers.[2] The uniforms for all the Túpac Amaru guerrilla combatants eventually arrived, and each recruit received two sets of olive-green clothing fashioned after the Russian military.[3] Knee-high rubber boots, special backpacks for supplies, food, and water-resistant bedding were handed out to each member of the Tupacamarista Popular Army (Ejército Popular Tupacamarista, or EPT).

As detailed by Diego, training in the EPT ranks was strict—taking place every day in full sun or torrential downpour. The EPT organized two companies with thirty combatants each. Commander Ricardo—Sístero García Torres—was commissioned to direct one company. All the National Directorate eventually arrived at the training camp, among them Polay Campos (a.k.a. Comrade Rolando), Néstor Cerpa Cartolini (a.k.a. Comrade Evaristo), Miguel Rincón Rincón (a.k.a. Comrade Francisco), Rodolfo Klein Samanez (a.k.a. Comrade Dimas), and Alberto Gálvez Olaechea (a.k.a.

FIGURE 9. Military uniforms seized from MRTA rebels in San
Martín, photo by Alarse-Colección Desco

Comrade Guillermo) who together agreed to officially initiate the armed
insurrection in Amazonia.[4]

Following their initial inroads in training and establishing a viable rebel
fighting force, the Túpac Amaru Revolutionary Movement launched a new
political-military campaign in 1987 dubbed Túpac Amaru Libertador in
direct homage to the insurrection of Túpac Amaru II.[5] The EPT's Comandante Rolando—Víctor Polay Campos—directed the guerrilla column's
first armed campaign in the rainforest.[6] The MRTA embraced the calendar
as a battleground, mounting attacks to commemorate significant milestones
in the history of Peruvian and Latin American revolutionary politics, as is
clear from its assault on the jungle towns of Tabalosos and Juanjuí. Such
events involved symbolic acts recollecting the Túpac Amaru Revolutionary
Movement's founders' deaths and paying honor to the people's struggle.
For instance, the rebel command decided to conduct the raid on Tabalosos
on October 8, a date of historical import marking the naval Battle of Angamos during the War of the Pacific (1879–1884), in which the great Peruvian national hero Miguel Grau Seminario was immortalized. Moreover,
Tabalosos is located in a district where police responded on that day in 1982
to a farmworkers' strike and road blockade by killing four campesinos.[7]

From their forest encampment, the Tupacamarista People's Army
marched for several days toward their objective, the town of Tabalosos,

which they took without any police resistance. For the final approach, they used trucks and vans they had commandeered. The village police station and a section of the Carretera Marginal were quickly seized. The residents were assembled and food contained in the two commandeered trucks was distributed among the expectant throng, gaining the trust and sympathy of the local populace. In the main square of Tabalosos, the MRTA held its customary popular assembly or meeting with the participation of most villagers, which culminated in political speeches and the raising of the *tupacamarista* banner. As was to become common during the attacks on the towns and villages of the Lower and Central Huallaga, the withdrawal of the Túpac Amaru rebel detachment from Tabalosos was accompanied by an animated and enthusiastic crowd that followed the insurgents to the road out of town.[8] Ten days later, the second EPT platoon went to take the small settlement of Soritor, located about twenty-five miles from Moyobamba, the historically important capital of San Martín. The takeover in Soritor was intended to mislead the enemy by causing confusion about the MRTA's movements in the region.[9]

On November 21, in the vicinity of Soritor, a Túpac Amaru rebel detachment of the Northeastern Front ambushed the army's advance forces, leaving four soldiers killed and six wounded. The strikes on Tabalosos and Soritor were considered a decisive success by the Túpac Amaru Revolutionary Movement. The MRTA saw no casualties, nor a single wounded rebel, and managed to seize twenty weapons from the police stations, along with abundant ammunition, bullets, and grenades.[10]

On the basis of its putative respect for human rights, compliance with the Geneva Conventions, and proper treatment of civilians, the Túpac Amaru Revolutionary Movement's leadership was determined to draw the government and civil society's attention to the active existence of an armed group that distinguished itself from the brutality of its rivals, the Sendero Luminoso.[11] Faced with the populace's initial terror upon seeing the Ejército Popular Tupacamarista arrive in their midst in full uniform, and the surprise of the few police officers who surrendered and relinquished their weapons without much resistance, the MRTA rebels took pains to explain their armed actions to the people assembled in each town's major square.[12] In their assaults on Tabalosos and Soritor, for instance, the *tupacamaristas* summoned the community in order to explain to them the reasons behind their insurgency. They told the villagers the MRTA had arrived in their midst to assess the behavior of the local authorities (mayors and governors) in light of possible corruption or abuse of authority. They had also come

FIGURE 10. Civil Guard Police post in Cuñumbuque, San Martín with
MRTA graffiti, photo by Francisco Rivero-Colección Desco

into town to invite all able-bodied inhabitants to join their ranks. Despite
the capture of Tabalosos and Soritor, news of the MRTA's actions failed
to make much of an impression on the rest of the country. Always seeking
the media limelight, this prompted the MRTA leadership to plan an even
loftier military action that would jolt not only the region of San Martín,
but also the country—the capture of Juanjuí, and the Northeastern Front's
takeover of all the towns in the Sisa Valley over the course of a week.[13]

This military-political effort culminated on November 6, 1987, in the
assault on Juanjuí (Mariscal Cáceres Province) by a Túpac Amaru rebel column of sixty men. From their basecamp, the *tupacamaristas* hiked several
days toward Juanjuí, a town of roughly twenty-five thousand people. For
the final approach to the provincial township, they boarded previously captured trucks and vans, as they had in their capture of Tabalosos. The slow-
paced entry of the MRTA combatants to Juanjuí occurred at 5:00 a.m., and
the rebels managed to remain until 10:00 a.m.[14] During this time, a section
of the Carretera Marginal was quickly taken while a MRTA column simultaneously attacked the town's three police posts (Policía de Investigaciones,
Guardia Civil, and Guardia Republicana). Although the province was in a
state of emergency, the police were not in the detachments, many having
been out partying that night. The remaining police fled, leaving three of
their *compañeros* to surrender to the MRTA.[15] Lieutenant Cieza Lacho, of

the Civil Guard, was killed by Túpac Amaru forces. During the relatively short time its members spent in Juanjuí, the MRTA succeeded in taking control of the town's small airport, the telephone company, the subprefecture, the prosecutor's office, the electoral registry, the post office, banks, and the church, as well as the primary thoroughfares leading into town.[16]

The people of Juanjuí were then summoned to the town center, and again food from trucks seized by the MRTA was distributed among the gathering crowd. In the Plaza de Armas, the MRTA, with Víctor Polay Campos taking charge, conducted a rally with the participation of "almost all of the people."[17] Before withdrawing from Juanjuí, the *tupacamaristas* ceremoniously hoisted their flag. Many residents reportedly expressed their identification and sympathy with the MRTA's incursion into town, which reflected, among other things, the rejection of the legitimacy of the police, whom many locals considered corrupt and abusive criminals.[18]

The Túpac Amaru Revolutionary Movement, unlike the Sendero Luminoso, was "publicity driven" and willing to negotiate with the Peruvian state. It went to lengths to publicize the successes of the Túpac Amaru Libertador campaign, which included two ambushes with the Peruvian Army, three encounters with patrols, and numerous days of combat in retreat against seven helicopters and troops that left a score of dead army soldiers, including two officers, a captain, a lieutenant, and a large number of wounded.[19]

At daylight, the MRTA left Juanjuí and made its way through the El Dorado province via the *caserío* of Bellavista to San José de Sisa, a smaller community with a population of about five thousand.[20] Arriving in the afternoon on November 7, the Túpac Amaru rebels entered the town in a motorcade of trucks.[21] They encountered no resistance from the police, who had been warned of what had happened in Juanjuí, so had departed shortly before, allowing the rebels to seize their weapons. While in San José de Sisa, the MRTA fraternized with the local inhabitants, who at first were panic stricken by the guerrilla's presence in their midst. After resting, the rebels held another communal meeting at night in the Plaza de Armas, where several residents gave folkloric performances. The next day, when the Túpac Amaru rebel column was preparing to continue to a retreat camp set up in Los Aguanos, Francisco Rivero of *Caretas* and Alejandro Guerrero, a reporter for Panamericana's Channel 5, arrived and requested a television interview with the Túpac Amaru Revolutionary Movement's Comandante Rolando, or Víctor Polay Campos.[22] The interview broadcast would change the course of the internal war. President Alan García, Víctor Polay

Campos's former roommate in Paris, recognized the rebel leader after he gave the TV press conference.[23]

Shortly thereafter, on November 10, 1987, García's government declared a curfew and a state of emergency in the region of San Martín, handing control over the area to the armed forces.[24] From that moment on, residents, particularly mestizos and indigenous campesinos, were subjected to countless abuses by state authorities, and the ghastly phenomenon of forced disappearances, already common in other areas, spread to the region.[25] Lima swiftly deployed a large number of troops to locate and annihilate the MRTA rebel columns in the area's luxuriantly forested hills and thick rainforest. The declaration of the state of emergency turned life topsy-turvy for *tupacamaristas*, peasants, and urban dwellers alike.[26]

The number of government soldiers sent to the San Martín region during the state of emergency is unclear.[27] Airborne troops were dispatched from Iquitos, Trujillo, and Lima, as were specialized personnel from the police forces. According to the MRTA, the government's counterinsurgency plan greatly increased the armed forces presence in the region to include 3,000 army personnel, 1,500 police, and 300 intelligence service agents, as well as twelve helicopters (for cargo, gunships, surveillance, and transport)—all these committed a wide array of atrocities against the civilian population, particularly peasants, in the scorched-earth campaign to crush the *tupacamaristas*.[28]

A meeting took place on November 21, 1987, in Tarapoto aimed at coordinating government responses to the mounting threat posed by the Túpac Amaru Revolutionary Movement. Prominent figures in attendance at the event included General Enrique López Albújar, Peru's minister of defense; Admiral Juan Soria Díaz, president of the joint command of the Armed Forces; General Rafael Moral Rengifo, head of the political-military command of the Huallaga Front; Guillermo Larco Cox, president of the Council of Ministers; and retired general Germán Parra Herrera, minister of transport and communication. They also convened in an effort to respond to the forty-eight-hour strike that the people of San Martín had just concluded in support of regionalist demands.[29] The Military-Political Command of the Huallaga Front had its headquarters in the Morales barracks in Tarapoto. In addition, the armed forces established multiple countersubversive military bases in districts throughout the Department of San Martín, including in Tabalosos, Lamas, Soritor, Uchiza, and Tocache.

The rebels' initial plan after taking Juanjuí was to strike Tarapoto, the mercantile center and principal city of San Martín, which had a population of roughly fifty thousand.[30] Despite its importance, Tarapoto was only thinly protected by a military garrison manned by only thirty soldiers. The MRTA wanted to assault Tarapoto in order to hold a press conference to defend the armed insurgency, explain the party's objectives, and lay out its overall plan of national governance by the Vanguardia Campesina—the Peasants' Vanguard. Two days later, Túpac Amaru Revolutionary Movement fighters raided the nearby community of Senami. On November 19, they took the district of Chazuta, and the following month they assaulted Shanao (December 11) and then the community of Yorongos (December 16). The final confrontation of the Túpac Amaru Libertador campaign took place in Agua Blanca two days before Christmas.[31] Triumphant following a series of military victories, the MRTA's Northeastern Front began its retreat to the Alto Sisa Valley, where the *tupacamaristas* had been concentrated before initiating their successful raid on the town of Juanjuí.[32]

In response, the Peruvian Army began attacking the MRTA detachments with full force following the declaration of a state of emergency in the Department of San Martín. General Moral Rengifo commanded his two thousand soldiers to surround the Túpac Amaru rebels who had tried fleeing to the Porotongo Valley, between the villages of Saposoa and Sisa. For more than twenty days, the MRTA rebels were immobilized by the encircling government forces, who controlled a significant area of the Sisa Valley.[33] The Túpac Amaru contingent fought hard to retreat to the Alto Porotongo region, eventually managing to circumvent the military's encirclement.[34] The military hounded the MRTA on the ground and from the sky. The armed forces' counterinsurgency campaign included the aerial bombing of mestizo and indigenous peasant communities of San Miguel del Río Mayo, Panjui, and La Shinao in the province of Lamas, for allegedly harboring Túpac Amaru insurgents. According to Roberto Lay, the residents of La Shinao were indigenous, including families such as the Cumapas, Fasabis, and Pizangos. Many of them reportedly became guerrillas and were subsequently imprisoned, killed, or went missing during the internal war.[35]

As the government forces relentlessly pursued them, Sístero García Torres's guerrilla column began to fall apart. The Peruvian Army, with the support of its awe-inspiring helicopter firepower, demoralized the *tupacamarista* forces. Many of García Torres's peasant commandos wanted to desert and never return to combat. The army's counterinsurgency strategy was working as anticipated. The military wanted to root out the insurgent enemies with hunger and thirst, or to shoot them if they looked for something to eat or drink in the forest or rivers. The Túpac Amaru Revolutionary Movement guerrilla column was decimated, and there were several sick combatants in need of immediate medical attention. Two *tupacamaristas* risked their lives by daring to cross enemy lines in search of much-needed medicine for wounded and sick combatants. The MRTA comrades who left looking for medical aid encountered the army in the Sisa Valley in the area of Shanusi, where they fought to their death. While the column was in the withdrawal encampment, various exploratory groups were sent to detect the movement of the enemy and proceed to deconcentrate their forces. At this time the first clash with the army occurred, and Comrades Alcides Reátegui, Roger López and Lainz "Comrade Melvin" fell fighting the enemy forces. As Sístero García Torres noted, this marked "the fall of the first martyrs of the Northeastern Front."[36]

Surrounded by the ever-encroaching armed forces, García Torres and his comrades struggled for fifteen more days to open a trail to Saposoa Valley, toward Pasaraya in the province of Huallaga, where there was an airfield. Upon reaching Pasaraya, the rebels' national leaders—Cerpa, Polay, Rincón, and Klein—successfully escaped in a small airplane (*avioneta*).[37] Comandante Rolando and his rebel entourage boarded the *avioneta* on their way to a town on the border of Peru and Colombia. Aboard the aircraft were numerous weapons seized from police stations the MRTA had attacked, which they planned to use for the formation of other guerrilla fronts. García Torres did not see the MRTA national leaders again in the Northeastern Front columns for a long time. About twenty-five *tupacamaristas* destined for Junín to organize a guerrilla front also departed by airplane. However, these Túpac Amaru rebels were discovered by an army battalion convoy and they killed most in Juanjuí. In revenge, the MRTA's National Directorate sentenced Defense Minister General Enrique López Albújar Trint to death.[38]

For MRTA commanders, like Víctor Polay Campos and Sístero García Torres, the Túpac Amaru Libertador campaign was a triumph, both politically and militarily, despite the battles with the Peruvian Armed Forces that led to the rebels' retreat into the forested hill country of San Martín in the Central Huallaga Valley. Most importantly, the leaders believed they had won the regard and respect of key sectors of the local populace. The appropriate behavior of the Túpac Amaru combatants, their discipline, their use of uniforms, their humanitarian treatment of the wounded police, and the public community meetings to explain party objectives and why the rebels had taken up arms all instilled confidence among their commanders.

An emphasis on rooting out criminality, corruption, and enforcing the accountability of the authorities (e.g., mayors, governors, judges, prosecutors) before constituents was central to the rebels' popular support.[39] The MRTA propaganda emphasized that the goal was not "executions or physical liquidation," but engaging in attacks to force the enemy to abandon positions and capture prisoners, as in the incidents of Tabalosos, Soritor, Juanjuí, and San José de Sisa. A considerable amount of weaponry was "recovered" during all these operations.[40]

On December 9, 1987, the MRTA's national leaders ended the Túpac Amaru Liberator campaign and restructured forces. One group of militants was sent to the eastern region and another went off to the central region. The remaining thirty-seven *tupacamaristas* stayed in the Department of San Martín under the responsibility of the members of the Regional Directorate.[41] Sístero García Torres notes that the Northeastern Front had three platoons, one of which had fourteen men that he was commissioned to command. Comrade Lucho directed a platoon sent to Huayabamba with twelve fighters, and Comrade Puma and a platoon of eight were dispatched to the Shanusi Valley.[42]

Rearticulation

The temporary dismantling of the Northeastern Front occurred in early 1988 with the capture of some of its middle-ranking leaders, such as Sístero García, and the untimely deaths of the Túpac Amaru rebel martyrs Roger López (Comrade Cabezón), Alcides Reátegui (Comrade Tananta), and Roger López y Lainz (Comrade Melvin).[43] This forced some of the *tupacamaristas* who did not have much ideological training but had accumulated military experience to try to rearticulate forces by building off the enthusiasm the rebels had instilled among the young people of San Martín. However, the biggest difficulty was in filling the void of cadres who were migrating to Lima and other regions to open the new Túpac Amaru Revolutionary Movement fronts of armed action.[44]

Meanwhile, Defense Minister Enrique López Albújar Trint was pursuing a ferocious, yearlong scorched-earth policy to eradicate the MRTA in San Martín. This was evident in January 1988, when a flock of buzzards alerted travelers in the Sisa Valley to the decomposing remains of fifty camouflaged Túpac Amaru rebels who had succumbed in combat with the army. By taking the offensive, the armed forces inflicted heavy *tupacamarista* losses, recuperated weaponry, and uncovered several MRTA bases.[45]

Nonetheless, with the aid of the Defense Front of the Department of San Martín (FEDIPSM), led by veteran leftist activist Lucas Cachay Huamán, the Northeastern Front's rearticulation was deliberately carried out by MIR-VR cadres under the command of Rodrigo Gálvez—Comrade Roberto.[46] Efforts to reconstitute the MRTA column meant that Rodrigo Gálvez had to resolve bitter internal disputes. As a result, Pedro Ojeda Zavaleta, also known as Comrade Darío, a former member of the MIR-VR, was put to death for his attempt to break away the MIR-VR faction from the central leadership of the MRTA and establish a new, autonomous front.[47] By 1989, several detachments were fully reconstituted, and in 1990, the MRTA had between three hundred and four hundred uniformed and armed soldiers in the Huallaga Valley.[48] In 1989, a MRTA column attacked the Picota police station, ambushed Pilluana and Shapaja, and conducted raids on the police stations of San José de Sisa, Papaplaya, and Rioja.[49] The Northeastern Front's guerrilla column Alcides Reategui occupied the town of Pacayzapa, took control of the police post, and recovered a large amount of weaponry and war matériel.

Rearmed thanks to these assaults, the Northeastern Front continued to carry out military incursions, such as the February 9, 1990, attack on the town of Picota. This resulted in the death of the Northeastern Front's Commander Rodrigo Gálvez, but it did not stop the Túpac Amaru's guerrilla war in the Central and Lower Huallaga Valley. Sístero García Torres, who had been released by the state justice system in January 1990, was called back by the MRTA's new commander in chief, Comrade Evaristo—Néstor Cerpa Cartolini—to take charge of the three detachments of the Northeastern Font that had been reconstituted in April 1990.[50] According to García Torres's testimony, the MRTA's security zones grew to five at that time (one was created in 1987, another in 1988, and another in 1989), adding up to five hundred armed militants in 1990 spread across the region.[51] These detachments were responsible for a series of guerrilla assaults on Saposoa, Bellavista, Pacayzapa, and Yurimaguas that netted the MRTA some three hundred weapons.[52]

Training

One resplendently bright Sunday morning in 2017, Diego and I decided to take a stroll along the river so we could talk about his becoming an active *tupacamarista* who would spend months on end in the *monte* in search of "enemies of the people." Why exactly had Diego, like Sístero García

Torres, decided to take up arms and mobilize the masses to topple the Peruvian state? What recollections did he have that could shed light on the ways warfare and everyday violence shaped the contours of social life in the Caynarachi basin? Before leaving his homestead for our stroll, we sat on an uneven timber bench overlooking the river and Diego pulled out a *mapacho*, a traditional uncured tobacco (*Nicotiana rustica*) cigar. Just as he was about to light it, I offered him instead a Hamilton cigarette ("a fine cigarette"). "*Gracias, bróder*. I got in [to the MRTA] because of family problems."

Diego grew up primarily with his grandmother in the *chacra* after his father abandoned his mother when he was a year old. Without a close paternal relationship, Diego felt he "was raised with social resentment." He would see other children eating and playing with their fathers. "You can't ask someone who is not your father, say your uncle who is providing for his sons," said Diego. "And if you grow up filled with that resentment, in the long run it brings violence," he continued. Diego had lived in a rented room in the village of Huicungo when he was fifteen and had to support himself by working odd jobs. He recalls always suffering from hunger and never having it easy when it came to buying school supplies or getting new shoes. Diego said that fortunately he was good at math, which enabled him to complete his friend's math homework for much-needed food (*juane* or *arroz chaufa*).[53] He got by with his brother's old clothes and shoes while supplementing his income for school supplies by working in his neighbors' *chacras*.

Diego had always wanted to be an agronomist. Nearing completion of high school, he began working for his eldest brother on his plot of land so he could earn enough to pay the fees to apply to the university in Tarapoto. Diego was an excellent student, graduating second in his high school class. Diego soon realized his brother did not want him to apply until the following year because he planned on getting married and was unwilling to support Diego's university studies until after the wedding. "Like Cain and Abel, we fought over my future," recalled Diego. In the meantime, his other brother unfairly accused him of having an affair with his wife from Chazuta. "Intense family problems began; I just simply couldn't take it. All the anger, the violence, and poison [*ampi*] words in my brother's home. So, when I was seventeen, I just left Huicungo one morning. All depressed with nowhere to go, I joined up with the Túpac Amaru Revolutionary Movement."[54]

Diego's mom always lamented the fact that he had become a *tupacho*— and it was difficult for her to fully understand the barriers preventing Diego from simply leaving active participation with the MRTA. Many people, friends and family alike, asked Diego why he was involved. "Why don't you get out?" they would question him. Diego told them he could not leave the MRTA once he had joined, despite his desire to do so. As a novice recruit, Diego was surveilled by the Túpac Amaru commanders and subcommanders. Gone was his freedom of movement. If Diego left camp and went into a *caserío* or hamlet, he was expected to be collaborating with MRTA militants, the *milicianos*, in creating flags, painting walls and vehicles, or distributing posters and pamphlets as his commanders had instructed.

The Túpac Amaru commanders and older cadre would say to the young recruits, "Go away if you like." But in the long run, the same comrades-in-arms who said this would disappear or annihilate those who left the guerrilla group. "Hey, you see that guy's a traitor," Diego told me, and he then moved to cut his neck, showing they killed him for renouncing membership. "They would say things like, 'We will kill the traitor for betraying the party.' I wanted to remain alive, so I did not leave the MRTA," remembered Diego. Those who tried to leave the MRTA were taken deep into the forest and made to dig their own graves. Diego went on saying: "That's how many were disappeared . . . dozens of human beings," he recounted, while slowly swaying his head back and forth. Looking in my direction, Diego sighed, "Well, in every conflict and every internal war, there's always a loser and a winner."

I nodded in agreement and waited for Diego to resume our conversation. Instead, he quickly stood up from the crooked bench and made his way to the narrow path leading to the pasture abutting the far corner of the land that has been in his family's possession for at least two generations. Seeing Diego bouncing forward, I said, "Yeah, let's go, *amigo*, the river looks beautiful today. It's just a bit low, but beautiful. I am going to have a great time swimming later this afternoon." Diego glanced out toward the iridescent river and counseled me to be careful of falling victim to the toxic barb of a stingray while out bathing.

After walking for an hour down a long—and surprisingly dusty—path toward a colossal bend in the watercourse, we came to a sandy beach (*playa*) littered with tangled tree roots and wooden flotsam. It was the height of the dry season in the Caynarachi basin; the river was low and people were frolicking in the cool water or net fishing in the distance. The beach was bordered by a thin fringe of *caña brava* (*Gynerium sagittatum*), a grass that grows up to six meters tall that locals use to weave hats. Behind sunglasses, my eyes fixed on the *caña brava*, which began swaying. Moments later, a rather lanky man with a scruffy beard and a red baseball cap emerged from the riverbank's thick overgrowth.

"Diego, who is that guy coming in our direction?" I asked my companion.

"That's Fabiano*, my 'soul pal' [*pata de alma*]. My *compadre* knows about you, and he is a trustworthy person [*persona de confianza*]. I am sure he will be pleased to tell you about our times with the MRTA. Fabiano endured much misery, just like me. But he got out of the Túpac Amaru Revolutionary Movement early. He understands torment and affliction. *Trust me!*" said Diego in an animated voice that faded to silence.

The muscular Fabiano, or "Fabi," as his acquaintances called him, was soon shaking my hand and bear hugging Diego. Without skipping a beat, Fabiano dove into telling us about his beliefs on climate change, the ecological destruction wrought by the palm-oil plantations encroaching on the valley lands, and the sustainable development potential of cacao beans for organic chocolate production.[55] Fabiano was illiterate, like many of his generation and social standing, but full of complex ideas and nuanced opinions.[56] "Fabi, let's go back to my house. Carmen* is making fish soup [*chilicano de Boquichico*], and we can talk about all that stuff on the way." Fabiano hesitated for a moment, and then said to his *compadre*: "Well, Diego, I am going to town, and your house isn't too far out of the way. Sure, let's go. It will be like the old days when you were in charge and told me what to do!"

I instantly took a liking to the affable Fabiano, who was full of all sorts of questions. As we walked, he wanted to know about the differences between the US Republican Party and Democratic Party, and whether the Central Intelligence Agency controlled the *traqueteros*. "Hmm, I'm not sure about the last question, Fabiano, but I know it is a complicated subject full of many murky characters and their dubious intentions," I responded. After taking an alternate path through the *purma* (secondary forest) and food gardens, we finally arrived back under the shade of Diego's veranda. His diminutive niece, Carmen*, was inside, helping fix the afternoon's lunch. Upon entering his house, I could hear Diego saying to his niece, "Carmucha, bring us some lemonade, *por favor, hija*."

Served graciously by Carmen's willowy hands, the lemonade quickly sated my thirst and afforded me with an opportunity to answer Fabiano's questions. I could also catch my breath after what I thought would be only a short stroll along the Caynarachi River—not a three-hour trek through the forest. Fabi began asking what I thought about President Trump and the "war in Iraq." From a distance, Carmen, in her lilting San Martín intonation, commented, "Tío Fabi, you're always talking about politics."

"*Hija*, let Fabi talk. You know this is important for us, and you should learn," retorted Diego. "Besides, Don Bartuco teaches university classes in Tarapoto and Lima and the USA. He is our guest, and we have a lot to talk about. Why not leave us alone? Finish making the *chilicano*, damn it!" Carmen departed as abruptly as she appeared, leaving three middle-aged men to chat. I pressed Fabiano or Diego to relax in the hammock while I took field notes, using a stool to sit on and the wobbly table for my pen and notepad. "Would it be all right with you both if I took notes?" I asked. I heard one of them say, "Yeah, sure, go ahead. We trust you."

After joining the Túpac Amaru Revolutionary Movement, Fabiano and Diego told me they were trained rigorously by committed *compañeros*, many of whom were no longer alive. They attended political sessions together, which were held in a camp at the break of the day. Diego mentioned that it was during that time he encountered Eudoxio Ortega's 1968 *Manual de historia general del Perú; historia crítica*, alongside philosophy texts penned by Mariátegui. Moreover, he expressed that his fondness for reading dictionaries developed during that period of rebel training.[57] He, like Sístero García Torres, came to his own conclusions about inequality, and he always sought the counsel of well-educated friends. He told Fabi and me how "the great teacher" Manuel González Prada said that Peru is like a great wound: "You squeeze the wound and the pus comes out everywhere." Besides conversations with his former Túpac Amaru rebel *compañeros*, Diego said that whenever he talked politics or philosophy to his acquaintances in the Caynarachi Valley, he felt as if he were talking "in an empty box" (*un cajón vacío*).

While in rebel training, they studied key principles and the history of the Túpac Amaru Revolutionary Movement, which Fabi disliked immensely. "*It made no sense because I couldn't read, so I always felt out of place, like a burro,*" Fabi humbly confessed. This a point worthy of mention given that most MRTA recruits in the Caynarachi basin had limited education and many were illiterate. All recruits learned basic medical instruction and honed their marksmanship skills. They taught the ablest sharpshooting with semiautomatic Dragunov sniper rifles. Forty minutes of free time (*recreo*) were followed by physical conditioning. After lunch, recruits engaged in combat instruction, testing their skills of endurance. This involved learning about the theory and praxis of guerrilla warfare from military trainers from El Salvador, Nicaragua, Mexico, and Chile. Diego and Fabiano became friends with several of them, especially those who treated them well, like Orlando*, who was a member of the Farabundo Martí National Liberation Front and had fought in El Salvador.[58] The men were not sure if they paid the foreign insurgent instructors like Orlando, and Diego knew only that the Regional Command in Tarapoto coordinated their presence in San

Martín. Diego received guerrilla warfare instruction in Huitoyacu*, Sauce, and Juanjuí, whereas Fabiano was prepared to be a *tupacamarista* fighter in training "schools" convened in Huitoyacu and Shanusi.

Acting as military advisers, the foreign instructors would stay with each Túpac Amaru column for fifteen-thirty days at a time. Advisers rotated among rebel camps and trained in all aspects of combat, whether grenade launching or physical conditioning. All the instructors were men and, according to my interlocutors, "were respectful and practical in their methods." Diego learned how to effectively assault police stations, and eventually became a specialist in this activity whenever he took part in MRTA incursions into towns.

During their guerrilla warfare combat training, the Túpac Amaru rebels would rest in their hammocks, either in improvised forest encampments or within the dwellings of local campesinos. These brave individuals, at great personal peril, offered temporary refuge and provisions to the insurgents. In the thick jungles of San Martín and Loreto, the Túpac Amaru Revolutionary Movement columns often elected to split into multiple platoons to disorient and better deconcentrate the police guards and army lines. When the MRTA attacked a town, this strategy of decisive dispersal caused the army or police to pursue one rebel detachment while allowing another detachment to conduct a successful assault.[59] In this way, the MRTA attacked with ease the important city of Yurimaguas in July 1990. Diego told me that after the efficacious taking (*tomada*) of Yurimaguas, his *compañeros* left the town to regroup: "We had different MRTA detachments. They ordered us to come together to meet at a predetermined spot. We were organized and well disciplined at that point."[60] In the El Porvenir encampment, the Túpac Amaru platoon comprised combatants from the Caynarachi basin, as well as regional towns like Moyobamba, Lamas, Yumbatos, and Rioja. Each platoon comprised various rebel soldiers. In the detachment of El Porvenir, there were at least fifty Tupacamarista People's Army olivaceous-clad troops flaunting heavy armaments.

As logistics commander and MRTA quartermaster, Diego allocated equipment for every detachment so they could all be prepared for combat. In determining how to get supplies to the detachments, Diego had three routes, via Chazuta, the Pongo de Caynarachi, and Yurimaguas. The preferred route for the MRTA rebels was to Chazuta, as there was a limited police presence, so it was a less risky option, albeit an arduous one. From Chazuta, provisions were sent to Achinamiza and then on to the basecamp at El Porvenir. The route via the Huallaga was much riskier, as the police were on the lookout for Túpac Amaru insurgents and militants, while the MRTA risked having informants in Yurimaguas.

In a solemn manner, Diego confided in me he had to gain the skills of combat within the untamed Amazonian wilderness, known as the *selva*. This entailed mastering the art of weaponry and conducting stealthy ambushes and surprise assaults on enemy targets, particularly agents or institutions of the state. Unfortunately, Diego's rebel leaders failed to teach them how to withstand physical pain. This became readily clear when Diego and his comrades were thrust into battle, faced attacks from the enemy, endured prolonged periods without nourishment, and witnessed the injury or death of their fellow MRTA companions. The harsh and merciless surroundings demanded their utmost effort.[61]

An avowed adrenaline junky, Diego said he was often part of the first wave of diversionary attacks before a planned assault on a targeted town or hamlet, such as during the surprise strikes on Juanjuí and Huayabamba, situated nearby to the localities Lupuna and Huacamayo. Somewhat immodestly, he described the number of "successful attacks" (*asaltos exitosos*) and "ambushes" (*emboscados*) he was part of while serving as a *mando* for the MRTA. He interwove these recollections with elaborate sounds simulating battles and police garrison attacks. A masterful orator, Diego used his facial and bodily gestures to convey sensory context for his narratives. "Each MRTA insurgent had their assigned task—we were all very well organized," said Diego. Motioning with his elongated arms like the wings of a bird, Diego revealed that his *nom de guerre* was "Razor." The guerrillas also used numbers—everything was in cipher, Diego said in a slightly jumbled manner. For example, "It's red" meant "Proceed forward," Diego said. Before any of the attacks, various detachments were brought together to review and carefully rehearse the planned military actions.

While fighting with the MRTA, Commander Razor had bodily strength, resolve, and a great deal of good fortune on his side. Pointing toward a scrawny, hunchbacked man standing fifty meters away, Diego interjected, "Bartuco, you couldn't be *poshaco* [anemic] or a *potolomo* [hunchback] like that ill-fated guy over there, Jorjito*. You needed to be physically fit, a vigorous person ready for the armed fight. If we had anemic recruits, we would send them for treatment to the MRTA nurses or medical technicians to get them in shape to join our ranks."

While a civilian, Diego said he felt "normal," but that all changed during the assaults when he became Mando Razor and felt the adrenaline coursing through his system, "like strong alcohol" (*como trago fuerte*). During the various MRTA attacks on the *caseríos* and villages of the Huallaga Valley he recalled "the flashing lights and strange sulfuric odors, reminiscent of aromas of burning engine oil, battlefield burn and metallic smelling gunpowder" As a logistics commander, Diego said that when he went into battle, he became fully animated, as if he were merely "part of a film on TV," yet it seemed authentically real. He described the duality of his warfare experiences: on the one hand, he felt alive to the world; on the other hand, he was numb to the surrounding horrors. He recounted that during the heat of the battle, "all of your energy changes knowing you can do mortal harm and all the time you need to defend yourself. To shoot at someone seemed like nothing." In the Caynarachi basin, killing had become normalized in this nebulous space of death. But eventually, Diego became disturbed by all the carnage and endless suffering.

Someone originally tasked Fabiano with learning about ammunition and the deadly arts of explosive combat. He was called "Bolsacho," or "Baggy Trousers" by his comrades because he was quite scraggly and wore loose-fitting clothes in those days. After witnessing a botched rocket-propelled grenade drill that left a *compañero* gravely wounded, he transferred to studying the general principles of combat and MRTA iconography. Fabiano used this knowledge of MRTA symbology in his role as a rebel militant, effectively spreading the party's message of revolutionary change throughout the area's villages and tiny hamlets. Extroverted Bolsacho also worked as a go-between with the Túpac Amaru militants of the Caynarachi basin and the surrounding valleys of the tropical Andes in San Martín and downriver communities of the lowland Amazon (*selva baja*) of Loreto.

While the *tupacamaristas* began with a few well-trained rebels, they had many *miliciano* supporters, like Bolsacho, who were residents of the region and provided vital help to the EPT. Militants were distinct from the guerrillas, who were part of the military structure of the MRTA's mobile Northeastern Front, composed of the EPT. The *milicianos* were committed not to the military structure of the MRTA, but to its broader ideological and political objectives. They used sabotage tactics in the cities and the countryside to advance the goals of the MRTA. Militants collaborated in the city, towns, and hamlets by providing essential intelligence, recruiting, and gaining and transporting provisions for the rebel columns via trusted go-betweens, such as Fabiano. His community was a hotbed of sympathizers and militants who provided the MRTA with logistical support. They would alert their comrades of the army's movements. They acted as snoops, letting the rebels know who was speaking ill of the MRTA. Some of the

FIGURE 11. Communications equipment seized from MRTA forces
in San Martín, photo by Alarse-Colección Desco

village's teachers collaborated with the MRTA in the logistics of food acqui-
sition and distribution, the collection of information, the hiding of seized
armaments and provisions, and the distribution of MRTA pamphlets and
propaganda throughout the region.

Much of the provisions, particularly weapons and ammunition, were
hidden in well-secreted stashes in the *monte*. Maps or sketches were later
used to locate the caches. But *tupacamarista* leaders, such as Sístero García
Torres, as well as militants like Fabi and Diego, think they lost a lot of
weapons and ammo by hiding them in this way.[62] "We didn't have GPS
in those days," mirthfully chuckled Diego. While in the forest and on the
run, they would eat *rancho frío* (cold food), such as soda crackers, *chifles* (fried
plantain chips), *rosquillas* (donut-shaped cassava bread), and canned goods
like tuna, sardines, and *salchichas* (sausages). They were constantly obliged to
move about at night for security reasons. They would rest during the day,
taking cover from army convoys, which they feared more than the police
forces. "We only respected the army who could quickly call on their lethal
attack helicopters, which would arrive hovering over us in ten to twenty
minutes. These flying machines of death would unexpectedly arrive, and
we could do nothing but try to escape into the dense forest cover," surmised Diego.

The Túpac Amaru rebels had two radios that were given to them by a Colombian drug cartel. It housed them in the basecamp in the *comandancia* (the command center), a separate fortified shelter accessed exclusively by the radio operator, the commander, and his most trusted *mandos*, like Diego. Fabiano recalled that many of their walkie-talkies were eventually obtained from the drug traffickers, who had access to them on the black market. The radios were used to coordinate flights between Peru and Colombia. In each rebel camp, such as El Porvenir, Túpac Amaru *cumpas* had one or two designated communications specialists who had privileged access to the radios and, most importantly, the messaging codes.

Diego and Fabiano's military leader in the Caynarachi was Commander "Grillo" (the Cricket), a former military man experienced in using firearms who had deserted the Peruvian Armed Forces.[63] El Grillo was sent by the MRTA's Regional Directorate to El Porvenir to command the base. While El Grillo was his boss, Mando Razor, or Diego, was one of his trusted men. For Diego, El Grillo was a wonderful person during "regular times," but he changed into an "authoritarian leader during our assaults or when we were being attacked by the Peruvian Armed Forces."

Fabiano said he was dispatched twice by El Grillo to bury weapons; "they were concealed, well oiled, very well greased, and tightly wrapped in plastic tarps. Many of those who were sent to bury the weapons died in clashes." Diego commented: "Our deceased *compañeros* know where the firearms are stashed. But today there'd be no one to guide you to where those weapons and ammunition are, they're buried deep in the *monte*." The location of the underground armament stashes remains a popular topic of conversation, particularly among those who were alive during the *lucha armada* (1980–2000).

Fabi confirmed, mentioning that they sometimes cached weapons to sell later on the black market to drug traffickers and other criminal elements. Both Fabiano and Diego confirmed Sístero García Torres's assertion that at the beginning of the formation of the Northeastern Front, its military equipment comprised Soviet-made folding metal stock AKM assault rifles and ammunition from the National Directorate supplied from Lima. The detachments subsequently began seizing weapons and bullets from multiple raids on police stations and soon started gaining autonomy from the Lima-based National Directorate.[64] The social mobilization of San Martín's populace in the late 1980s, combined with President García's failing national government, prompted the MRTA to affirm that "conditions were ready [in San Martín] for the initiation of the *lucha armada* against the enemy of the people."[65]

Elvira of Picota

After his release from prison in 1990, Sístero García Torres would have gotten used to being a city dweller, but that all changed when he caught the news on the local radio stations and daily paper about MRTA's February 9, 1990, attack on the city of Picota, a town on the Central Huallaga some sixty kilometers from Tarapoto. Diego told me that the MRTA's objectives were to steal weapons, conduct a public meeting, and educate the Picota community about the rebel's ideology. However, for Diego, who took part in the attack as a veteran *tupacamarista* (as in three other efforts to take the town), the attack was a disaster from the start. Local inhabitants of Picota, like Elvira*, were equally horror-struck by the raid; it was actual combat, something this mild-mannered, woman had never experienced.[66]

Elvira, a sixty-four-year-old former schoolteacher and lifelong resident of Picota, was an eyewitness to the attack. She told me the MRTA assault on her community left her deeply distressed, " after all these years, it's as if I keep observing it over and over. Where has my cheer gone? I'm anxious and fearful all the time."[67] When I asked this kind middle-aged woman if she was willing to give me her version of what occurred in 1990, she agreed without hesitation. Elvira's fashion style mirrors her melancholic personality and may even reflect the traumatic challenges she has faced. Elvira looked stylish in her pastel clothing, which struck a perfect balance between sophistication and individuality. However, she is distinctive from the others of Picota because of her cerise, dapple-dyed hair. Each one of Elvira's hair strands is an artistic brushstroke, weaving hues of crimson, shell-pink, amber, and mahogany as if her very essence had been painted on them.[68]

"Were they *tiempos feos* here in Picota?" I asked, thinking about what I had been told by those in the Caynarachi basin. "Yes, they were ugly, fearful times, and I will tell you why," replied Elvira in a cogent and resolute voice. Sitting in her ornamented parlor, or *sala*, Elvira started by telling me that the MRTA attacked Picota in February 1990. In her account, the *emerretistas'* assault began at roughly 6 p.m. and lasted until about 5 a.m. the next morning. With great detail, Elvira vividly described the events to me while we drank savory *chicha morada* and ate *queso fresco* with *rosquillas de maíz*.[69]

Elvira told me she was in her mother-in-law's house on the fifth block of Jirón Miguel Grau, next to the town's principal police station (*comisaría*), when the *tupacamaristas* entered town. She thought the MRTA had arrived in town that night on a mission to liberate some of their comrades who were imprisoned in Picota. The number of fully armed *tupacamaristas* she saw in town did not bode well, she recalled. Taking cover inside an interior room in the house, Elvira remembered hearing the sounds of a shootout coming from all directions surrounding the home. "I dare not risk going outside," Elvira said. Nor could she sleep, she told me, with the "ferocious battle raging outside." Elvira said that during the attack, "all you could hear were *balazos* [gunshots]." Fortunately, her family was together, and they waited until the light of the morning to leave the interior room of the home.

At daybreak, Elvira discovered that the police had slain three MRTA members the previous night, including Jaime Trigoso García, who she claimed had been incarcerated in Picota's prison. "They killed him on his return to Pucacaca. The police [*el tombo*] detained him about two-three kilometers just before he arrived back at his home in Pucacaca. So, the MRTA freed their leader, Trigoso García, but the *terruco* was later killed," remembered Elvira.[70]

During the first violent confrontation in town, there were no police fatalities—only the *tupacamaristas* lost their lives, Elvira told me. Picota and the surrounding vicinity became a deadly battlefield as the rebels confronted the police. In Elvira's words, "It was a horrible time. From then on, we would always hear gunshots piercing the night's silence. We couldn't travel to the cities of Tarapoto or Moyobamba because the MRTA would detain us on the highway. The MRTA made us wait until nightfall when they would charge us a toll. Yeah, they forced us all to travel when it was dark." Hundreds of armed Túpac Amaru rebels from various platoons began arriving during those years, all trying to capture Picota.

The peril of unexpected warfare violence and omnipresent fear is remembered and sequestered in the bodies of those who lived through the ugly times.[71] With all she experienced during those tumultuous years, Elvira says she doubts she could live through those times of perpetual fear again. "When the Túpac Amaru Revolutionary Movement existed, we didn't know if we would ever return home at night or not. That is how bad things were for us. I worry things will get bad again. You never know when violence will strike again. It was calm once, and then we had all of these problems. Now I have *susto* [fright] and *nervios* [nerves]. That is why I still have nightmares of all that happened," she said in a voice marked by despair.[72] During the MRTA's armed assaults on urban centers—such as Picota, Tarapoto, and Yurimaguas—local civilians, like Elvira, were caught in the crossfire.

While Elvira highlighted the conflictual and chilling nature of her community's encounters with the MRTA, she also speaks of the compassion shown for the "enemy" during the unprecedented bloodshed. Elvira's account of an act of empathy followed her chronicle of the terror in Picota. Elvira remembers a young *tupacamarista* hiding in her house the day following that second incursion into her sleepy town. He was just a boy of fifteen or sixteen, and he was squatting precariously beneath the house's *tushpa* with his AKM rifle projecting out toward Elvira's unsuspecting family members. Startled after discovering him, Elvira's father-in-law grabbed the boy by the broad collar of his green uniform, "but he did nothing to him. My *suegro* was a man of kindness. He understood that the *terruco* was only a boy who also had a family, just like ours. He simply took away his firearm and later gave it to the police," recalls Elvira. "The MRTA *chibolo* was younger than my little brother, Pepe*. My *suegro*, Don Óscar* let the MRTA *terruco* escape into the forest through our *huerta*. The entire time, the frightened kid was trembling like he was cold from taking an early morning swim in the Huallaga River. Rather than telling *el tombo* which direction the young *tupacamarista* had escaped, my *suegro* told them the boy fled toward the road to Tarapoto," Elvira proclaimed.

Corroborating Elvira's description of the February 9, 1990, attack on Picota, Diego told me that the Túpac Amaru's raid lasted the entire night and concluded around daybreak, "just as the roosters were stirring." Picota remains a potent emotional space in Mando Razor's ongoing ruminations about Peru's internal war. In his recollections, it signifies military defeat and personal hurt. "We lost because the fighting lasted until sunrise and then the Mil Mi-24 army helicopters arrived—so we were always forced to retreat," Diego recalled when describing the details of the clash in Picota.[73] By daylight, large numbers of police reinforcements from Tarapoto would show up, making it suicidal for them to continue fighting. "They controlled the battlefield, we did not. El Tombo held their ground, and we simply lost," he said. This matches Elvira's narrative of the rebels' assault on the town, which emphasizes how "all the police posts in Picota were surrounded by reinforced cement barricades and sandbags. Our police were well prepared and trained. They defended us and were able to get help from Tarapoto."

Unlike Elvira's description of the lethal attack, Diego denies the MRTA was attempting to liberate rebel prisoners. "Our mission for that assault on Picota was to get weapons and not to liberate *compañeros*. We wanted to get the police station's large stock of bullets and guns—pistols, revolvers, assault rifles, machine guns. Whatever we could get! Of course, if we could, we would have released prisoners, as was done in Yurimaguas," cried Diego. He said in all four attempts to capture Picota, the MRTA commanders, like

Ricardo and El Grillo, always ordered them to fall back and retreat because of military failure, mounting Túpac Amaru fatalities, and wounded rebel fighters. He recalled the difficulty of escaping army counterassaults, remembering the episode when he was tasked by his comrades of convincing comandante El Grillo that the planned escape path was a cul-de-sac. "It's locked! I can't open this [jungle] trail. There are many army soldiers blocking the way through the forest [path]" he frantically said to his commander, El Grillo.[74] Mando Razor dolefully recounted, "*Pucha madre* [holy mother], in one attempt to take Picota we lost our Commander Roberto [Rodrigo Gálvez]. That's when Commander Ricardo [Sístero García Torres] took over the leadership of the MRTA's Northeastern Front. And our heroic fight went on."

In Sístero García Torres's rendition of the MRTA's incursion into Picota, Commander Roberto, along with his comrade Jaime Trigoso García, had taken a motorcycle to check on the attack on Picota. However, within a kilometer of reaching town, they were ambushed by the army or police and gunned down. The death of the commander of the Northeastern Front was blamed on Comrade Pablo, the Túpac Amaru fighter designated to prevent the police from interfering with their incursion. Pablo, deemed a coward by his fellow comrades, was shot by them after he failed to stop the police from killing Rodrigo Gálvez. Rodrigo's lifeless body, covered in blood, was then soaked in gasoline and set on fire.[75]

Marisol and the Police

Elvira's younger cousin, the loquacious and thin-lipped fifty-nine-year-old Marisol*, also remembers the MRTA assault on Picota.[76] Exhibiting a refined complexion and commanding an impressive stature, Marisol told me she was working in the community's health post and noticed something was amiss one night when the rebels attacked. Known for her independence, Marisol had been working the late afternoon shift and was returning home to breastfeed her four-month-old daughter, Lizbeth*. That is when she saw a large throng of police gathering in the center of town. The erratic movement of the police forces made people anxious. "It felt as if something was going to happen," said Marisol. By the time she arrived home, it was about 7:00 p.m., but her babysitter and husband were nowhere to be found. Marisol went outside in front of her house on the third block of Jirón Túpac Amaru to see if her spouse was on his way back home. Outside, she saw a teacher she knew hysterically running by hollering: "Marisol, Marisol, quick . . . get inside your house . . . turn off your lights . . . the *emerretistas* are now entering Picota!" She could make out the sound "*thud, thud, thud, thud, thud,*" as all of her neighbors were scurrying out in the recently paved street, trying to find secure cover before the impending attack.

Marisol ducked inside her house and hurriedly slammed shut her front door and fastened the dead bolt her husband had recently attached for added security, which he thought necessary given his new accountancy job in Picota's municipality. Within ten minutes of being warned by her teacher friend, Marisol was crouched underneath a mattress with her infant daughter and young son, tormented by the sounds of bombardment and fearing for her missing spouse. For Marisol, "It was a very desperate situation. It felt as if I were in a movie, you know, the sort you see on television that is full of explosions." Like her cousin Elvira, Marisol was spellbound by dread during the MRTA's battles with her town's police force. She vividly recalls thanking God for the safety of her two brothers, who were both police. She said they fortunately had not been stationed in Picota that ill-fated night. Marisol remembers the volleys of gunfire continuing well into the night. She heard all sorts of activity and clamor outside of her centrally located house that had once served as a fashionable rendezvous point for the young wives of Picota's commercial and bureaucratic elite.

While in Picota, the Túpac Amaru combatants would communicate with walkie-talkie radios and use various codes. Marisol told me they would yell out numbers or nicknames. The rebels would shout "number two" or "*Cumpa,* Chato está de baja" ("compadre, Chato is down"), meaning that Chato (Shorty) was wounded or had been killed. "This was going on at 9 and 10 p.m. It was complete chaos, a disgrace," said Marisol. She remembered her neighbor, Jason*, who lived only fifteen meters from her, had had his dwelling looted by Túpac Amaru bandits. Marisol was convinced they were killing her neighbor, Jason, as they ransacked his home. Jason had graduated from high school in the same class as Marisol. She told me she wept, thinking the MRTA was killing her lifelong friend. But Jason was not home. The rebels destroyed all his household goods instead. By 11:00 that night, the shooting and shelling had subsided. Marisol recounted it was then that her brother-in-law arrived in town, announcing, "*Cuñada,* you are alive!" In the tense darkness, they both wondered how many police and Túpac Amaru insurgents had been wounded or killed.

Marisol could not sleep after her encounter with her brother-in-law. "How could I sleep if my husband still hadn't arrived back home?" she remarked.[77] The battle lasted four or five hours, and then, Marisol said, "a haunting calm descended over Picota." Marisol felt the rebels attacked her town because of their anger with the police. She did not associate the incursion with the rebels' goal of obtaining weapons and political or military capital. Marisol knew that the *emerretistas* wanted to have a popular meeting in the town's Plaza de Armas, but the guerrillas' efforts to do so were frustrated.

Marisol's brother was a police officer stationed in Saposoa who, by happenstance, was in Picota visiting family on the night of the *emerretista* assault. Dressed in civilian clothing, he detected the red armbands with the MRTA logo on the left side of the rebels' uniforms. Without hesitation, he ran to warn the Picota Police of the impending MRTA incursion. Forewarned, the security forces were well prepared and thwarted the insurgents' frontal attack on the police garrison. Marisol recalled how a terrified Picota police officer hid in his outdoor latrine while the *tupacamarista* troops ransacked his home. He escaped in the shadow of darkness by furtively slipping through the neighbor's fence into the *chacra*. While hiding in the garden, the police officer lay pinned down—surrounded by Túpac Amaru rebel fighters. He was "unable to help his police colleagues who were being attacked," recollected Marisol.

In the morning's light, Marisol remembered waking to the gruesome news of the killings in the town. Meanwhile, sensational reports of the MRTA attack on Picota had been broadcast on Radio Tropical, alerting the citizens of Tarapoto to what was happening in the neighboring town.[78] "All the population was crying. Some were even weeping. We were all desperate," remarked Marisol. She said that her extended family and many friends in Tarapoto had visions that the community of Picota had been completely wiped out by the MRTA's attack. Marisol said that at 4:30 or 5:00 a.m., she "saw numerous police reinforcements arriving into town." That is when she was reunited with her older brother, Pablito*, who had been dispatched to Picota as part of the police reinforcements sent in from Tarapoto. Never had Marisol imagined that her brother would be in a gunfight in her hometown. She said it was simply beyond belief.

"Mari, Marisol! How are you? Is everything all right," extolled her brother Pablito, the police officer from Tarapoto. Her older sibling was visibly shaken—Marisol remembers—"he thought I was among the dead. Yeah, he told me how he had dreamt the night before of hearing a sharp whistle . . . *wee . . . wee . . . wee . . . wee.* In Pablito's dream, I was falling from a bicycle, and he took that as a premonition of my impending demise." Marisol recounted that when her brother was at her side, near the neatly swept stoop of her expansive house, she hugged him with all her might and assured Pablito she "was not a *tunche* [a malignant spirit]."

During the commotion, Pablito and his detachment apprehended three guerrilla fighters. The unfortunate *emerretistas* were just changing out of their uniforms so they could escape into the cover of the jungle's thick vegetation when they were caught by Pablito and the others from Tarapoto. It was after that, recalled Marisol, "when the police began stopping all the vehicles coming and going from Picota in search of members of the Túpac Amaru Revolutionary Movement." She recalled seeing groups of *emerretistas* and young militia members go off to block the road (called a *toma de carretera*), stopping traffic to hand out political leaflets and paint MRTA slogans like *¡Venceremos!* on the cabs of pickup trucks and the sides of cars.

This was the start of the fearful time of checkpoints (*garitas policiales*), danger, and death in Marisol's narrative. With a haunting resonance, Marisol confided that her "mind unearths the past for the purpose of naming the victims."[79] To underscore the impending threat of violent killings, all too common during the Huallaga Valley's ugly times, Marisol relayed what Pablito told her about what had happened in Villa Nueva at a *garita policial*—a police security checkpoint. Pablito's company saw a group of red-arm-banded rebel soldiers, which forced all the police officers to hide in the forest overgrowth for fear of being attacked. A gunfight ensued, leaving several of Pablito's police companions severely wounded. In discussing traumatic times, Marisol launched into additional descriptions of the chaos ensuing from the MRTA attack on Picota.

She told me about two horses owned by her police officer neighbor that were slain by the MRTA, their inert bodies unceremoniously dumped in the middle of the highway. Marisol described how the MRTA incursion into Picota had blinded a local police officer. Proudly, she discussed how every year there are announcements on TV marking the anniversary of the Picota police officer becoming a sightless national hero. Another police officer, who went by the moniker Rambo, was not so fortunate, said Marisol. She recounted how Rambo was also injured in an MRTA attack on Picota and evacuated for treatment in Lima with the man who lost his vision. Rambo recovered in Lima, and he later returned to working in the Huallaga Valley, but he was slain in an MRTA attack on the town of Bellavista. Likewise, another police officer who was injured in an attack on Picota subsequently perished in an assault on the Central Huallaga town of Juanjuí.

On my return car trip to Tarapoto following my interviews with Elvira and Marisol, I spent the time contemplating the suffering the MRTA visited on Picota during the internal war. I thought about how Elvira and Marisol had endured these troubled times, but I wondered, at what psychological cost? My ruminations were drawn to Marisol, the statuesque woman whose countenance bore the weight of profound suffering. Like Elvira, she was a bystander caught in the middle of political violence that profoundly scarred her community. With her lopsided smile and stony countenance, Marisol expressed the pain of vicious memories perhaps best forgotten.

Mateo and the Stranger

By the time the MRTA had established a firm hold in the Lower Huallaga, Mateo was studying to become a Catholic priest. Years before, he had fled to Yurimaguas at the height of the violence in the Caynarachi basin, returning to his village of Nuevo Libertad only to do his pastoral work and on vacations. This was in 1992 or 1993. His mother always told him not to go out at night because the MRTA passed through the village in search of recruits.[80] Thanks to the brooding nature of his severe father, Mateo's early years were structured by precautions, which felt too cautious to him as a youngster growing up on a small farm in the Peruvian rainforest. Yet Mateo said these deterrents accompanied recollections of the real danger of death looming outside the door of his parents' modest home.

When Mateo was in Yana Puma, he lived in the same hostel as a stranger by the name of Ramírez*, a social activist who was slaughtered by the military. He was from the Andean highlands (*sierra*) and had his *chacra* in the village near the Pangayacu River*. Mateo at the time was proselytizing for the Catholic Church as part of his studies to become a priest. Ramírez would show up at Mateo's religious meetings, but he never confronted him, although he was an alleged member of the MRTA. Mateo recalled: "One night I went off to the Church to conduct Bible study for the youth around seven or eight o'clock in the evening. The children knew the stranger was a fellow called Ramírez, and according to them, he was a leader of the Túpac Amaru Revolutionary Movement. They shouted to me, '*Hermano, hermano,* the *cumpas* are outside, be careful!'"[81]

"Mateo, were you worried about the appearance of the stranger?" I asked. Mateo said he was indeed terrified but nevertheless continued with the Bible study, as he did not want to frighten the people in attendance, particularly the young. Mateo told me he acted as if all were normal to avoid alarming those who had gathered. Mateo's work was celebrating the liturgy. "Did anything ever happen with Ramírez and the Túpac Amaru *cumpas?*" I asked. "No, I was never confronted by the *cumpas* even though I counseled the student catechists not to get involved with the movement," said Mateo. He assured me he "never had a negative encounter with the MRTA, and Ramírez always treated [him] with great respect."

Mateo, the *limeño* electrician, by no means is a supporter of the MRTA, and he told me of their excesses during the internal war. But he is a greater critic of the armed forces' counterinsurgency campaign in the Caynarachi. Mateo recounted the various times that army convoys would arrive in villages like Nuevo Libertad, Marupa, and Yana Puma, and the soldiers would shout at the campesinos: "Are there any terrorists here? Have they passed through here? Have you given food or shelter to the terrorist *tupacamaristas?*" Unannounced and in the dead of night, camouflaged army troops would show up to startle the locals. Some campesinos would say to the military, "Yes, the *cumpas* have passed through [Nuevo Libertad]," recalled Mateo. This, he remarked, "frequently led to the military punishing the entire village. Hanging many innocents who were accused of being accomplices. People were dangled from house beams [*vigas*] or tree branches. Worse, soldiers raped the village's young women. They would separate mothers and daughters in order to rape them. Yes, the military abused women." Over time, Mateo described how people dreaded the military more than the MRTA. He stated, "When the Túpac Amaru Revolutionary Movement arrived, they only asked for food or for the locals to prepare their food; they never came to rape the women."[82]

In Mateo's version of the ugly times, villagers were much more apprehensive when the military arrived; they would accuse innocent people of being terrorists (*terroristas*) with no proof. Soldiers took some blameless people away to punish them and some were tortured. The purpose of torture and the practice of leaving mutilated corpses on the side of the road or in rivers was to deter the living. The military abused local women and villagers who could not respond. It often prevented them from denouncing any human rights violations because of the state of emergency and martial law imposed by the government, which gave the armed forces freedom of action with no oversight. "The military could do whatever they wanted during the state of emergency. They didn't respect human rights. They shot people and livestock with impunity. They committed all sorts of atrocities," asserted Mateo, with bitter resentment in his declaration.

With bent forehead furrows, he told me, "This is very clear in the CVR [Truth and Reconciliation Commission] report. The armed forces hurt many innocent people. The *fujimoristas* deny that the military committed abuses." Like the Peruvian Army, the MRTA would show up and accuse locals of being traitors. They, too, were abusive. With his head cradled in his open palms, Mateo forlornly shared how his "family suffered from the abuses of the MRTA, but we suffered from the military. I think even more so." Mateo's memories of familial pain shape and flavor his present. He credits the trauma he experienced in the Caynarachi basin in part to his decision to migrate over the Andes and live in what Mateo refers to as "the gray city of ten million faces—Lima."

Although some could escape the fear and insecurity of the Caynarachi basin, many did not, because of economic, community, and personal constraints. As the war raged on in the late 1980s and early 1990s, violent clashes became all too common in the Caynarachi basin. "I stopped going home for years because it was simply too dangerous," Mateo said, bitterly recounting how he could not attend his mother's funeral because of an MRTA blockade preventing access to the community. "Had I never left the Caynarachi basin, the course of my life would have been very different. It's possible that I would still have a place to call home. . . . Not like now, when everything that I once knew has vanished completely," he observed. When I asked Mateo if he had any regrets about moving to Lima, he reflected despondently on the fact that his family had all passed away and that their lands were now in the possession of a third party. In 2017, during our conversation in Lima, Mateo ended things poignantly by telling me his "future was once in the Caynarachi, but the war put an end to that hope, extinguishing it like water on a blazing fire."[83]

CHAPTER 5

Forest Encounters

In times of war, life becomes cheap and nothing is funny anymore.

NELLY

In the ugly times, there was one primary path from the Pongo de Caynara-chi to the community of Yana Puma. That meant Túpac Amaru rebels were often passing by Camilla's*¹ home at night. Of petite build, Camilla is a middle-aged woman and a longtime resident of Yana Puma. To this day, Camilla still remembers her observations on the distinct sound of rubber boots that she shared with me. When I quizzed her on the "boot acoustics," the high-cheeked Camila made the sound "*tran, tran, tran, tran, tran,*" and she told me that was the noise she recalled hearing as the Túpac Amaru guerril-las marched by her family while they slept. Camila, a perceptive observer, mentioned that she could differentiate the "chomping" noise produced by the rubber boots worn by the MRTA from the "crunching" sound made by the soldier's more professional leather footwear.

The day I spent with her, Camila told me that once, around 2 a.m., her dog Oso (Bear) began woofing uncontrollably. With Oso barking, Camila reported she was now compelled to warn her young children, and she re-called saying in her most commanding tone, "Kids wake up. Here come the *cumpas*. Hide!" The most upsetting incident Camila said she ever recalls having with MRTA insurgents was the time she went downstream with her family to work in their *chacra*. Her husband, Rolando*, and their children were accompanying her. She said that the events in question occurred in

1989 or 1990, during the most intense phase of the conflict. She explained that "it was simply too dangerous to leave your kids at home by themselves. It was much safer for a family to be together."

On their way along the jungle path to their *chacra*, Camila said they were startled by muffled sounds. Soon they encountered the entire Gálvez* family, tied up with rough cordage. Camila declared that her neighbors' mouths had been completely bound, and they also had their hands and feet tied. The MRTA had hog-tied the entire family, apparently because the army had recently eaten in their home. "It was completely shocking to see the whole Gálvez family there, including small children, bound and gagged," Camila said. She told me that all of them were hunching over on their sides like "wild forest animals" that had been captured and tied up for slaughter.

Camila and Rolando liberated the family, who informed them they believed a snitch had told the MRTA that they were providing false aid and information to the army. Just as Camila and her family were untying the family, an army convoy arrived and took them all into custody for questioning. The army soldiers threatened and punished both families, making them perform physical exercises (*ranear*).[2] Camila said to me in a sour and indignant tone: "No one has condemned these atrocities, and there has never been a reckoning. It was prohibited to criticize the army, as doing so was equivalent to a death sentence."

Camila and Ronaldo's experiences of ugly forest encounters are akin to Nelly's* renditions of living in the region during the internal war.[3] A resourceful, middle-aged widow of Shawi ancestry, Nelly confided to me that the *tupacamaristas* frequently visited her residence wearing drenched olive-drab uniforms. She said this happened "whenever they couldn't find dugout canoes to cross the Pangayacu, Pumayacu*, or Caynarachi rivers." Nelly said she will never forget the time she was cooking *pijuayo* (peach-palm fruit; *Bactris gasipaes*) and a detachment of rebels surprised her. She recalled it was about 10 a.m., and she was out working in her forest garden. While she busied herself hacking a bundle (*racimo*) of plantains for the family's meal, Nelly recalls hearing her young sons, Pedro*, Raúl*, and Martín*, call out to her. She said Pedro, her eldest son, began yelling, "Mom! Please come over here, quick!" Nelly described how she briskly returned to her *chacra* to see what her son was screaming about. Arriving at her forest *tambo*, or lean-to, Nelly encountered many MRTA *cumpas* with their faces shielded by balaclavas.

Nelly said they asked her, "Señora, what are you cooking?" She told them *pijuayo.* "There was a huge number all around us, like a descending group of *curinsi* [leaf-cutter ants]," she remembered. Nelly relayed how the MRTA *mando* said to her, "Señora, take the *pijuayo* and share it among us all." Petrified, Nelly recounted how she placed all the fruits on the *emponado* (palm floor) of her *tambo.* could hear the as the boat approached. Upon hearing water splashing and the propeller spinning of a fast-approaching boat coming upriver, the Túpac Amaru insurgents placed a gun to Nelly's head and told her not to reveal anything about what she had seen. Nelly told me how they ordered her children into their mosquito nets (*mosquiteros*) and some *tupacamaristas* ran off into the surrounding forest cover while others scrambled to hide near the lean-to.

In the boat was the Civil Guard (Guardia Civil), which stopped at Nelly's *tambo* and asked whether any "subversives" had been through the area. Nelly said she had to tell them no because "the *cumpas* were within earshot," hiding with their guns ready; two rebels had even taken refuge inside her children's mosquito nets. Nelly recalled how she and her children were fortunate. None of them made any commotion, and the Civil Guard eventually went on their way, thus allowing the insurgents to evade detection. A trim woman of great fortitude, Nelly calmly described the toll on the family of filling the bellies of those who had nothing to do with the household. The MRTA rebels would often arrive at 1:00 or 2:00 a.m. at her meager homestead and ask Nelly to slaughter one or two of her plumpest chickens for them to eat. Just as soon as she had served them, they were rushing off, "always on the run," Nelly recalled, saying, "They left my family with nothing to eat." While her family went hungry, Nelly told me how the *tupacamaristas* would eat in her house. She was still stunned: "Sometimes their food wouldn't be fully cooked, but the *cumpas* still ate it because of their hunger. They were always ravished and in a hurry."

Unlike Mateo, Nelly felt that the police and army behaved better with the locals than the MRTA. She told me she thought the MRTA was much more unyielding and authoritarian than the armed forces, with whom she could reason. She recalled, for instance, the time during the *pijuayo* episode when she nervously smiled at her aggressors and was chastised by female members of the MRTA. Nelly recounted how one particular *cumpa* with a balaclava, an AKM rifle, and a gold-capped tooth told her, in a grainy and guttural voice, "to stop smiling." She described how the "*terruca* shouted, '*Basta* [enough]! There is no joking or laughing allowed here!'" Yes, Nelly concluded, "nothing is funny when you are at war." Perhaps this is no more apparent than in the cat-and-mouse fight the MRTA performed to topple the neocolonial government and the state's ferocious efforts to eradicate the armed opposition.

Cat and Mouse

Many older, longtime residents in the Caynarachi basin told me that the MRTA always seemed to know precisely when the army convoys were in hot pursuit. I asked ex-combatants like Mando Razor, as well as Sandra and her brother Fidel*, about this veritable "cat-and-mouse game."[4] They all came to the same conclusion: the efforts of the MRTA's Northeastern Front to reduce innocent casualties in the Caynarachi basin led to a symbiotic relationship between rebels and villagers. The toll of innocent lives lost and the harshness of armed confrontations deeply affected communities. This somber reality weighed heavily upon villagers' hearts, as they grappled with the sharp truth articulated by Fabiano's stark observation: "There were innocent victims. Sometimes in despair, people became fatalities in the armed confrontations."[5] Judging by what I was told, most locals were acutely conscious of this cruel reality, as it cast a penumbra of sorrow and unease over their community, reminding them of the fragility and vulnerability that permeated their daily lives. For Diego, "the people would protect the MRTA. Some would purposefully misdirect and tell the army that we had gone in the opposite direction to throw them off our track."

Likewise, in Sandra's estimation, it was a question of community interdependence. She related: "The local townspeople helped us. They would give us a hand [*dános la mano*]." She declared that in the *caseríos* where the MRTA made incursions, they never abused people. Sandra insisted: "We had to be gracious and respectful. To live well, you have to be reasonable and on good terms with your neighbor. We helped them." In the countryside, when peasants were working communally (*peonada*), the MRTA would show up, rest, and then go on their way. For Sandra, a long-standing left-wing activist and former Túpac Amaru rebel, "A good neighbor (*vecino*) that is close by you is much better than one hundred siblings far away." *Hmm*, I thought, *Sandra is articulating her vision of community*. "Why do you think neighbors can be more important than family?" I asked Sandra. "The nearby respectful neighbor can assist you. It doesn't matter how much money you have. A humble neighbor can support you in an emergency," Sandra told me.

Sandra's older brother Fidel, the village's well-regarded cobbler, broke into the dialogue: "Your neighbor has to save you, this gives you independence and true freedom. With a loyal neighbor, you can say, 'Take me to such-and-such a place,' and he's going to take me [in his canoe or auto]. Money will not take you across the river or over the mountains." Villagers such as Fidel and Sandra said that MRTA rebels had to be respectful of the community and its customary practices, otherwise community members would alert the army when insurgents arrived. Typically, villagers would mount their horses and gallop off to warn Túpac Amaru soldiers who were eating or resting that the army was on its way. Militants and sympathizers operated a veritable relay system, traveling through hamlets, villages, and towns to alert MRTA members of imminent danger and ambushes.

The symbiotic relationship between the community and the Túpac Amaru guerrillas minimized episodes of explosive violence: I was told frequently—by both ex-combatants and civilians—that everyone wanted to avoid confrontation because civilians invariably experienced the tragic consequences. This was confirmed by Sandra, who said the villagers were unequivocally clear that they did not want armed conflicts in their community. "Our children would have died if we allowed the army to enter our village," she commented while motioning her head toward a group of young boys carelessly playing in a fresh mound of ocher-colored dirt and a small pile of smooth stones, designated for a forthcoming public infrastructure project.

I broached how the MRTA was always escaping from the clutches of the army with my friend, the good-natured and vociferous Marcos*.[6] A river-taxi owner with a twisted gait, square jaw and contorted fingers, Marcos had innumerable acquaintances and a large extended family living throughout the Caynarachi. According to his compadre Diego, the pug-nosed Marcos, who many call "Shorty," or Chato, weathered the internal war relatively unscathed because "he has an uncanny knack for knowing when to talk and when to be silent." Ever since the Túpac Amaru rebels' emergence in the zone, Marcos owned at least one or two cargo and passenger boats (*colectivos*) that made regular trips between the Caynarachi basin and Yurimaguas (as well as the surrounding villages along the Lower Huallaga). An excellent conversationalist, Marcos is someone I have known for many years. Marcos—as so many other longtime inhabitants of the basin—would continuously talk to me about the arduous journey crossing the tropical Andes to reach high-jungle (*selva alta*) cities like Tarapoto, Lamas, and Moyobamba, which could be made only on foot or horseback. As a result, various locals from the Caynarachi preferred traveling "in the ancient times" (*en los tiempos antiguos*) by boat to the steamy rainforest town of Yurimaguas along the Huallaga River. This enabled them to access markets for their products, health care, and state services.

While aboard his timber-crafted river taxi, propelled by a forty-horsepower, long-necked outboard motor, Marcos would surreptitiously entertain me with accounts of the MRTA's presence in the forests and sinuous waterways and vast lagoons of the Caynarachi basin. According to Marcos, "it was no one's land; we had no confidence; it was a moment of total terror." Amid one of our conversations, he recounted a noteworthy encounter he had while traveling alongside fellow passengers—a moment that left him scared (*asustada*). At the confluence of the Caynarachi and Pangayacu rivers, they unexpectedly stumbled upon a group of armed Túpac Amaru rebels, resplendent in their uniform attire. Similarly, he regaled me with his fabulous accounts of late-night travels upriver to El Porvenir, where he said he had various encounters with MRTA rebels at their encampment. Always fast in pursuit was the army, which, according to Marcos, was abusive and seemed anomalous in the Caynarachi backwaters, where people had historically settled their disputes among themselves, without the interdiction of the meddling state. This all changed with the arrival of the MRTA and then the Peruvian Army and Police, which imposed a new rhythm to daily existence. As Marcos said to me: "That was our life. One day it was the *tupachos*, the next day we had to deal with the army or *el tombo*. We had to collaborate with the army, the police, and the MRTA; they forced us to give them both food and assistance."

Frequently, Marcos said he had to transport Túpac Amaru members in his boat to the mouth of the Huallaga River, or from the Huallaga to the communities of Marupa or Bellavista. He was not remunerated, having instead been asked to "collaborate" with the rebels' requests and demands. "If you refused their demands," Marcos said, "later on, you would be accosted or abused by an MRTA sympathizer." If you collaborated, they would not harass you when they encountered you again. "Collaboration provided us with protection," recalled Marcos.

I gleaned similar versions of life on the river from Zacarías*, also a river *colectivo* operator who made a living transporting people and small loads of cargo and livestock throughout the zone while the MRTA came to dominate portions of the Caynarachi basin.[7] Similar to Marcos, Zacarías is *chato*, a short man with a jovial temperament and a strong inclination for drinking *aguardiente* (cane alcohol). Zacarías was also asked to transport the Túpac Amaru Revolutionary Movement rebels to various villages and small hamlets in the immense basin. When the rebels first demanded "transport collaborations," Zacarías told them he had no fuel and could not take them where they wanted to go. He recalled that this made the rebels visibly upset and the contingent left in a huff.

A few days later, Zacarías said, "masked [*encapuchados*] Túpac Amaru members came looking for me." The *tupacamaristas* showed up during the daytime and dragged Zacarías from his home. In the struggle, Zacarías could wrestle the balaclava of one of his assailants. He said he recognized Professor Tomás, and the others then revealed who they were—including Professor Wilbert*. They detained Zacarías in Huicungo—the village where Sístero García Torres had his first teaching post. His passengers were made to disembark. Meanwhile, the Túpac Amaru rebel soldiers hopped aboard his vessel and then made Zacarías take them to Nuevo Libertad. He returned later that afternoon to Huicungo after the MRTA warned him he would do as they ordered and sleep the night on the concrete floor of the village's one-room schoolhouse. Zacarías said he had literally learned his lesson and was fortunate to be alive, unlike the fate of other villagers, like Ramírez, who eventually meet their demise in a gruesome fashion.

Decapitation

Many in the Caynarachi basin, like Alejandro* identified Ramírez as the supreme leader of the *tupacamarista* base in the Caynarachi and one of the most dangerous MRTA leaders to boot.[8] Alejandro has a thoughtful gaze and an infectious smile that seems to allay the fear people in the basin have for him. Although he looks withered beyond his years, the sixty-year-old, curly-haired peasant was willing to talk to me about a prominent individual in the collective memory of the Caynarachi—Ramírez. This paper-thin, wizened farmer, known to his friends as El Flaco, or "Slim" in English, previously served as brigadier for Nuevo Libertad's autonomous civil peasant patrol (*ronda campesina*).[9]

Alejandro, looking bony and fatigued, confided in me, "We know [Ramírez] wasn't from around here and claimed he couldn't read and write." Similarly, Don Augustín had relayed that "Ramírez would play himself off as an illiterate campesino from the highlands." Alejandro said Ramírez had spent five years in the Peruvian Army and, after his discharge, had helped strengthen El Porvenir's military encampment.[10] As I had been told numerous times, Alejandro recounted how during the internal war, the population turned to the MRTA to ensure popular justice (*justicia popular*). Ramírez would send off his soldiers from the base at El Porvenir to capture and punish those who had been denounced by villagers in the Caynarachi basin.

According to Alejandro, during the late 1980s, he had a major run-in with Ramírez at a community festival in Nuevo Libertad. As the head of the rural self-defense watchman—*los ronderos*—Alejandro was called in to break up a fight with the help of twenty-five designated guards, or *varayocs*, who also served as *ronderos*.[11] That is when Alejandro got into verbal fisticuffs with Ramírez, who asked if he would work as his bodyguard. Alejandro said no to Ramírez because he was an employee of the state charged with maintaining village security. He said: "You have your people, the *tupachos*. Why don't they serve you as your bodyguard?" Ramírez retorted in an arrogant and threatening fashion, warning Alejandro to watch his back and stating that "he was going to look for him in his house." Alejandro said Ramírez shouted out, "I know who you are and I will get you, you motherfucker!"

Alejandro responded: "'All right, come and look for me.' I told him I would wait for him. And if Ramírez wasn't lucky in slaying me first, I would kill him." After about a month, Ramírez and his people appeared around midnight at the homestead of Alejandro's family; they had not forgotten about Alejandro and had come seeking revenge. Ramírez told Alejandro's father they had come to take away his son. But Alejandro had fortunately gone to the *chacra*, where he slept the night. Shortly thereafter, the military captured Ramírez. This was a blessing for Alejandro, who said it allowed him "to escape from death. It all ended [*se terminó*] with the killing of that bastard Ramírez." According to bony Alejandro, "Ramírez was a *Cumpa*, he was a terrorist [*terrucos*], and that is why they killed him." He told me that in the ugly times, Ramírez would regularly go off and work deep in the center of the jungle. The military began tracking his movements and finally captured him.

After earning his trust through the exchange of cigarettes and a lukewarm bottle of Cristal beer, Benito*, a taciturn neighbor of Alejandro, became willing to help his friend recount his version of the life and brutal demise of Ramírez.[12] Being a farmer who owned lands in the region, Benito was well aware of Ramírez's residence close to Yana Puma, and knew that Ramírez had a reputation for frequently evading law enforcement. Yet Benito said the army and the police never captured him. Benito took note of Ramírez's hidden abode, situated deep within the forest, approximately an hour's distance from the *caserío* (hamlet) of Yana Puma. It required a forty-minute walk from Benito's own forest plot in Nuevo Libertad to reach Ramírez's secluded residence. Ramírez built his house next to a lagoon frequented by *shansho* (*Opisthocomus hoazin*) birds. *Shanshos* are notorious for loudly chirping when people approach. Locals claim the birds provided Ramírez with an intelligent, natural "personal security system." Despite his elusiveness, Ramírez was eventually captured after extensive investigations by the Peruvian intelligence services. The military located Ramírez's secret hideout and sent in camouflaged troops to apprehend him.

In gut-wrenching detail, Benito recounted the gruesome fate that awaited Ramírez. He disclosed that Ramírez would suffer a slow and agonizing demise, as his tormentors intended to inflict a methodical dismemberment upon him, "killing him slowly by cutting him into parts . . . bit by bit." Ramírez was first hog-tied and then mercilessly beaten by the troops and some bystanders who had gathered to gaze and gawk at the violent spectacle in each community. Together, they punched and pummeled his torso and kicked his bruised head, bloodying his ears and nose. In each locale they paraded him about, and the army would further mutilate Ramírez's body in a sadistic effort to make the suspected insurgent reveal the whereabouts of weapons, collaborators, and most importantly, the Túpac Amaru's primary encampment in the area, El Porvenir. The military cut off one of Ramírez's ears, and then one of his fingers in Yana Puma, Benito remembered. He said Ramírez let out an ear-piercing scream to his captors: "Kill me! When are you going to kill me? Do it, captain, you motherfucker!" Benito told me the army captain responded to Ramírez's pleas for compassion cruelly: "Don't worry, *terruco*. We will soon put you to sleep forever!" Ramírez was then dragged off to Nuevo Libertad, "as if he were a wounded animal," reflected Benito, who was shaking his head in disbelief. Benito finished his miserable account by encouraging me to talk to his cousin, Carmen*, who was a witness to the barbarism visited on Ramírez.[13]

Carmen, the loquacious owner of a bodega in Nuevo Libertad, recalled that when the army brigade apprehended Ramírez, they paraded him about in many of the villages in the Caynarachi. Coupled with Benito's commentary, her account illustrates the extent to which violence can quickly become a spectacle. She told me the military wanted him to divulge where the MRTA bases and arms caches were located, as well as who his accomplices were. "Where are the damn terrorists [*los maldito terrucos*]?" they screeched at Ramírez, Carmen said. But Ramírez did not utter a word. The image of the military brutalizing Ramírez by inhumanely inserting sewing needles into his fingernails will linger with her forever, Carmen declared. She was particularly disturbed by Ramírez's refusal to speak to his tormentors. "Why didn't he simply confess? Things would have turned out differently if he had only spoken to the army," Carmen mused. George Orwell noted that in the presence of pain, heroism ceases to exist, yet Carmen's words shift the blame from persecutor to victim.[14]

Mute to his torturer's interrogations, Ramírez writhed in pain as another digit was severed from his bent and disfigured hand, leaving bloodied fascicles. Mutilation seemed to harden Ramírez's resolve; Carmen said he became even more resolute in resisting efforts to interrogate him. Despite the ruthless torture they meted out, "he refused to confess to anything. The army then stripped Ramírez's shorts down and cut off one of his testicles. They kept torturing him, and eventually, they cut his tongue from his mouth and someone smashed his face. We all watched as they sliced off more of his fingers. In the end, he had no more fingers," Carmen gloomily remarked as we stood outside her tiny shop, where a flickering light cast its beckoning radiance, drawing in a fluttering congregation of nocturnal moths. The torture and extrajudicial murder of Ramírez is seared in the personal and shared memories of countless people who lived during the years when the MRTA and the Peruvian state were locked in a clash for control over the Central and Lower Huallaga Valley.

Recollections of Ramírez's life and demise differ, as is clear from former rebel Diego's version of the death of a man he characterized in terms of honor. While Fabiano used the label of "show-off" (*figureti*) for Ramírez, Diego firmly refuted this characterization. Diego assured that not only was Ramírez tortured and his body wickedly disfigured; he was also decapitated for refusing to reveal to the army the location of Túpac Amaru detachments and weapons. "He was innocently murdered" (*fue inocentemente asesinado*), Diego indignantly proclaimed—thus refuting what others conveyed about Ramírez's "shadowy" activities in the Caynarachi basin. I told Diego what I had heard from others about Ramírez, and he wrinkled his brow. "No, Bartuco! Ramírez was a social activist, not an MRTA member," he firmly asserted. According to Diego, Ramírez led the Liga Agraria Juan Velasco Alvarado, an agrarian league, a fact later confirmed by others I spoke to in the region.[15] Diego maintained Ramírez was involved in trying to get the agrarian bank to loan to the campesinos.[16] From Diego's point of view, the parish priest had unfairly accused Ramírez of being closely associated with the Túpac Amaru Revolutionary Movement.

It was true that Ramírez had asked the MRTA to provide him with

FIGURE 12. MRTA guns decommissioned in San Martín, photo by Alarse-Colección Desco

personal security, Diego recalled. He surmised that this is why the army and the priest had most likely suspected Ramírez was a *cumpa*. For his part, Ramírez appeared apprehensive and would fidget whenever Diego and his *compañeros* came to visit him in the last months of his short life. "We made the mistake of accompanying Ramírez one day, and in that way, the army mistook him for being part of our MRTA column," Diego recounted. From Diego's perspective as a former rebel, Ramírez did not want to be a turncoat, so he refused to talk while being viciously beaten and dismembered. Diego felt Ramírez decided intentionally not to divulge the locale of the rebel camps, weapons, or MRTA members. "If he revealed any vital information, the following day the party would have liquidated him," said Diego, who believed "the poor guy had no way out from sure death at the hands of either the army or the MRTA." Diego recalled the army gave orders for no one to move Ramírez's headless body from where it had been unceremoniously dumped on the forest floor. Rather solemnly, Diego said, "and so Ramírez's headless corpse remained in the jungle, only to be eaten by buzzards."[17] The ruthless demise of Ramírez shows the extent that violent spectacle and surveillance became two sides of the same hideous coin.

Lucky Innocence

Luciano*, a dedicated father known for his clever acumen and sardonic humor, became a willing informant sometime after he learned of my book project.[18] At first, he was hesitant with me, speaking obliquely in metaphors about the ugly times. Luciano would engage in friendly banter, asking me, the "Gringo," if I had taped ghost (*tunche*) stories from the village's overgrown, bramble-infested graveyard. Filled with grit and a determination to "tell what happened," Luciano approached me one morning near the port. I was watching a group of men unload bundles of plantains from a *balsa* (raft) softly bobbing up and down on the tranquil river—its crystal-clear waters originating from the snowcapped Andes.

"Gringo, I hear you are writing a history of the Caynarachi basin and the *terrucos*, and that you are interviewing people. Is that true, Don Bartuco?" A voice spoke out from behind me. I turned to face the person who had made the inquiry, and there was bowlegged Luciano, dressed in jeans, a yellow- and blue-striped sports shirt, and an old black baseball cap embossed with the Umbro logo. "Yes, that's true, Luciano. Would you be willing to speak to me anonymously? In other words, what you tell me will never be connected to your identity—say your DNI [Documento Nacional de Identidad, the national ID card], for example, or your real name or actual identity. I do know these are difficult topics to discuss." After a brief pause, Luciano removed his worn baseball cap, stroked his balding pate, and nodded in agreement. Luciano consented to my request, and so I learned about his life over the course of numerous meetings. Speaking with him revealed the turbulent conflict pitting *tupacamarista* forces against the military in its counterinsurgency campaign in the Caynarachi.

The first day I recorded Luciano's narrative, I learned about his son, Edgar*, who had been whisked away in an army combat copter from the village during the state's counterinsurgency campaign to eradicate the MRTA from the Huallaga Valley. In 1992, Edgar, who lived in Tingo María, was on vacation when the army apprehended him as a possible Sendero Luminoso member. To complicate matters, Luciano recalled Edgar had been unfairly accused by the Túpac Amaru Revolutionary Movement of being a Sendero Luminoso partisan. The MRTA had threatened his son with eviction from the Caynarachi basin just as he arrived in town to visit his family.

"The army took my son away with the help of the MRTA. Most of those captured with him were from San Rafael del Río Mayo* and the Pongo de Caynarachi," Luciano recounted. He described how they tortured his son and four other young men at the decrepit police station by repeatedly submerging their heads in buckets of filthy water. Luciano's wife, Sonia*, wept when she heard what had happened with Edgar. She dispatched her husband to the garrison to see what might be done to save her precious boy. Edgar is the eldest child and "has always been his mother's favorite," according to Luciano. He claimed he asked "a squinty-eyed major" why they were torturing his son. The military *jefe* shouted that Luciano's son was a *senderista* and had most likely participated in various acts of terror that had sown fear in the nearby countryside.[19] "The foul-mouthed army major was a very, very bad guy. Major Brando* was his name," recalled Luciano in a forceful voice. He explained how he attempted to hand over a hefty bribe of two thousand *intis* for Edgar's release.

The violence of war becomes banal when its horror and trauma are understood in terms of the everyday lives and social spaces shaped by oppressive structures and ideologies. Notwithstanding his courageous effort, Luciano told me that his offer to bribe the "*pendejo* major" fell on deaf ears.[20] After listening to the father's impassioned pleas and offers of money for his son Edgar's release, the tall *serrano* major obscenely told Luciano he could not use the bribe to buy more ammunition for his troops. Luciano said the major sternly told him: "Releasing your son would liberate 'the shitty enemy' (*el enemigo de mierda*), who then would ambush my soldiers. Señor, you must go now, or we will take you prisoner and kill you as well as your damn son!"

Luciano's eyes exhibited a striking appearance as his coffee-colored pupils, coupled with the whites of his eyes, protruded noticeably. This visual resemblance was akin to porcelain saucers, evoking a sense of fear and anguish. It conveyed the harrowing memory of the atrocities committed by the army against his son. As he continued to recount the history of Edgar's arbitrary detention, I could tell he was distraught by verbalizing the past; his feet began to tap apprehensively as he obliquely leaned his head against the wall, and he started gazing aimlessly into the air. His former vibrant expression was gone, as was the twinkle in his eye. "Edgar's hands and feet were bound with thick nylon cords, his face was bruised and bloodied, as was his shirt and football shorts, which his mother had given him as a present for his birthday. His left eye was swollen, and his lip was split open from being struck in the face. His sandals had droplets of dried blood on them, too," Luciano continued to meticulously recount. Summarily found guilty by the military outpost's officer, Edgar was then hoisted into a large black sack and taken away, left dangling from the side rail of an army helicopter gunship that disappeared into the hazy puffs of clouds above the *caserío*. Edgar and three others were whisked off over the mountains to the military base in Tarapoto. Upon arrival, Edgar was told he had only two days to live; on Thursday he was scheduled to be summarily executed. Luciano pondered for a moment and said to me wistfully, "My son's fate was totally in the hands of God—dear God, the generous one who protects from above."

According to Luciano, his son told him that while incarcerated, ten prisoners were selected to be summarily executed on the upcoming Thursday. "At some point, a sergeant who is a family member—who I didn't know personally—but he knew of us in our small hamlet, the family Pinedo*—had to read out a list of the captives to be executed that day," Luciano explained. Edgar told his father that while the sergeant recited the names of the ten people who would be killed, he noticed the surname Pinedo from Luciano's settlement. "Miraculously," Luciano recalled, "the sergeant commanded Edgar to step aside and replaced him with someone else who was to have their throat cut." Edgar was fortunate to be saved from death because of his surname and family connections. Luciano recounted that despite "having been tortured and abandoned to die, our family name saved Edgar from imminent death." [21]

Following the arbitrary deaths, the army sergeant approached Edgar and inquired about his family, namely his father. Edgar identified his father as Luciano Pinedo Quispe*. The sergeant asked whether Doña Marta Pinedo* was a family relation, to which Luciano's son responded she was his aunt, that she could vouch for him. He emphasized to the military interrogators that she would undoubtedly tell the soldiers that Edgar was no *senderista*. The sergeant in command appears to have taken pity on Edgar after learning that he was a member of the Pinedo family. "Miserable army bastards finally liberated my son after four days of detention," Luciano remarked. Edgar made it back home, but he was never the same, according to his father, who noted how his son had severed his physical ties with the site of his birth and upbringing.

Traumatized but lucky to be alive, Edgar left the Caynarachi for good, returning to Tingo María and eventually migrating to Tarapoto, where he was working as a day laborer in the construction trade. Edgar kept in touch with his family by sending them cash and packages (*encomiendas*) of food, clothing, and vitamins, and by calling them regularly on WhatsApp. Moreover, Edgar was always an eager host to family members, who visited him periodically in his cramped living quarters in Tarapoto, where he lives with his wife from Sauce and their two teenage children. With his parents' permission, I contacted Edgar in Tarapoto and asked if he would meet to discuss his near-death experience at the hands of the military inquisitors.

Through a series of phone calls and text messages, I arranged a meeting with the eager and amiable Edgar for an upcoming visit to Tarapoto in 2019.[22] Over cold *chelas* (bottled Pilsen beers) and salty *canchitas* (roasted corn kernels), Edgar reviewed his troubled past in the Caynarachi basin, which included a jilted romance and frustrated plans to work in the municipal office following a fight he had with the mayor and his loyalists. Fractured by geographical displacement, lingering memories of victimhood, and a nostalgic longing for the peaceful times before the arrival of the MRTA, Edgar told me he had struggled to disregard what happened to him and to create a new life in the city. Despite his resilience, Edgar mentioned being plagued by night terrors. Unable to silence the past, he was avoiding contact with those in charge of securing order: the police and armed forces. Many during the ugly times were not as fortunate as Edgar, instead becoming victims of untold crimes.

Massacre at Yumbatos

The armed incursion of the Túpac Amaru Revolutionary Movement into hamlets and villages, such as Yumbatos, Grau, Pampa Hermosa, and Dos de Mayo, were frequent, according to the accounts I recorded from the inhabitants of the area and testimonies assembled by the Truth and Reconciliation Commission (CVR).[23] To wit, one person declared to the commission that, "in each raid, the MRTA ordered the authorities and residents to take part in its meetings. Everyone who did not go was threatened."[24] The MRTA's April 1, 1989, armed strike on Yumbatos seemed no different from any of the other various ambushes in the Lower Huallaga on the face of it. However, a review of testimonies from those involved in the massacre calls into question the official version recounted in the CVR's final report. From Yumbatos, the view of the fertile valley on the eastern slopes of the Andes is a beautiful landscape of gently rolling, forested hills. Frequent rain showers and highland winds cool the heat before it gets oppressive, and the abundant soils of the region make it agriculturally productive.

During my first trips to this idyllic community, I did not know Yumbatos had been the site of a horrific slaughter some years before. Speaking with Ronner*, a brawny and athletic fifty-three-year-old resident of the modest farming village hidden at the base of the lush Cordillera Escalera, I learned about the MRTA and the massacre in Yumbatos.[25] The wavy, oily-haired Ronner took a liking to me after our first meeting. This laid-back resident said he had been awaiting someone from a human rights nongovernmental organization to tell the truth (*la verdad*) about what had occurred all those years ago in his natal community. From the shade of a massive mango tree, Ronner told me how a group of Túpac Amaru commandos arrived in town one day and stationed themselves in the local school, the Colegio de Yumbatos, where they camped for the evening. Ronner recalled that the following day the MRTA rebels held a large public assembly in the town's plaza, after which army soldiers arrived in pursuit of the insurgents. This, he said, eventually led to a battle between the MRTA and armed forces. Ronner remembered how his mother hid beneath her bed. "We don't want a stray bullet [*bala perdida*] to kill us," she said to her adolescent son, who crouched alongside her. Ronner told me that there had been at least five casualties during the battle. He recalled the names Jackson and Ricardo Púa among the victims. According to his version, the MRTA eventually retreated to Nuevo Lucumayo*.[26]

Ronner's neighbor, Silvia*, a middle-aged market vendor, also from the region, joined our conversation about personal recollections of the MRTA in Yumbatos. Pondering Ronner's words, Silvia began her narrative with a firm proclamation: "There hasn't been justice."[27] From the marketplace, she said she saw "the *terrucos* walking the streets very well-armed. They came whenever they wanted and respected nothing. We lived in a difficult place at a worrisome time." Ronner and Silvia, both told me about attending multiple MRTA political rallies in the Plaza, and how the *cumpas* were always trying to recruit new followers to their ranks.

Silvia and Ronner said there would always be a throng of people, including children, at these gatherings where the MRTA enthusiastically conscripted not just young men but women as well.[28] I was told that people in Yumbatos were threatened if they did not join the insurrectionary soldiers, or a family member would fall victim to an "unfortunate" accident or, worse, be disappeared. Like Ronner, Silvia remembers how the MRTA would come into town and offer the youth cash, explaining that they would earn a high wage if they joined the ranks of the MRTA. "But it was all a lie," she said emphatically, pounding her clenched fist against the tabletop upon which I was scribbling my notes.

Surveying the commercial bustle in Yumbatos's market, Silvia recalled the time when she witnessed the killing of a *tupacamarista* by an army salvo. One day, while she was preparing fish to sell in the market, she spotted a group of rebels buying food in a bodega. They had not realized an army convoy was fast approaching in well-camouflaged trucks. The army ambushed the MRTA from the corner of the plaza. Complete mayhem ensued, as panicked villagers ran in all directions. In Silvia's words, "We felt despair [*desesperación*] as the *terrucos* ran off with the army following them into the *monte* . . . they went off like peccaries to hide in their *chacras*." Silvia said the military commander shouted, "No one can be here [in the central square]!" The villagers had to obey the army and return to their homes. Silvia remembers one person perishing in the confrontation and many more being wounded.

Ronner, who had turned especially quiet and seemingly motionless while Silvia was talking, began to speak in a quiet and measured voice. Using his weather-beaten hands as a performative aid, he recounted how "others died in the *monte*." For personal reasons, he said the MRTA still has a very negative place in his memory. Ronner felt it might be pointless to talk about the troubled times, despite his longing to hold accountable those responsible for the death and destruction associated with the internal war. With his left index finger pointing to the firmament, Ronner emphatically broadcasted, "There was no justice in the past, so why should there be any in the future?" (*No hubo justicia en el pasado, ¿por qué debería haberla en el futuro?*). The lack of investigative follow-up and ongoing impunity associated with the massacre haunts Ronner.

"They wouldn't leave us alone; we couldn't move about freely. They thought they were the owners of the village," said Silvia, as she detailed how the MRTA stole from two traveling merchants (*mercachifle*) while she watched them being brutally killed in public. Villagers had to be in their homes by nightfall, and if the MRTA saw anyone not from the community, they were taken to the fields (*campo*), and some disappeared, never to be seen again. "Silvia, do you recall what Ronner just told me about the killings here?" I pensively asked.

"Yes, how can I forget that? One morning, I awoke to learn that five people had been slaughtered. Near the plaza was a house where the villagers found the lifeless bodies—three men and two women. It was horrible. That putrid, cadaverous scent of death that came forth from the house still lingers with me . . . the scent of death, and the villager's weeping still troubles me," Silvia dolefully intoned. Like Ronner, Silvia was unequivocal when declaring that "there has not been justice" (*no ha habido justicia*) for the victims of the Yumbatos massacre.

According to the CVR, on the night of April 1, 1989, a group of approximately fifteen MRTA members raided the small community of Yumbatos. They entered Felipe Tapullima Amasifuen's home at 11:00 p.m. while his wife and two children slept. The Túpac Amaru members berated Felipe for refusing to join their armed organization. Claiming that he was a *soplón*—a snitch, they threatened to assassinate him extrajudicially. In his defense, Felipe replied he did not want to join any rebel group. He had a wife and two children whom he wanted to raise, and he was afraid that if something happened to him, his family would have no one to fend for them.[29]

Despite his pleas, the Túpac Amaru insurgents flung Felipe to the ground and struck him on the head with the butts of their rifles. Felipe's wife was also hit in the face and beaten by the insurgents. Felipe was then taken away by his MRTA assailants. They assured Felipe he would be detained for only an hour. Meanwhile, his wife stayed inside their house, guarded by two Túpac Amaru rebels. An hour later, MRTA insurgents returned to the Tapullima household and threatened Felipe's wife again. They reportedly told her: "If you move from here and ask for help, you are dead. You must wait here." About half an hour later, Felipe's wife heard gunshots from the main square. She then left her home with her two children in tow, seeking refuge at her mother-in-law's house. She was forced to hide in the *chacra* for fear that the *tupacamaristas* would find them. Armed young Túpac Amaru fighters began looking for Felipe's wife at her mother-in-law's house but without success. Meanwhile, Felipe's parents remained in their house during the tense ordeal; they were too frightened to venture out to look for their son until daybreak.

Upon approaching the village's main square, Felipe's parents saw a group of people peering inside a house. When they entered, they found their dead son with four other corpses in one room. He had been killed with one gunshot to the head and two to his body. A sign was left on Felipe's body that read: "This is how snitches die." The other corpses belonged to the house's owner Wilder Flores Jumpo, Julio Huasi Huasi, Ricardo Púa Paima, and Nilo Tapullima Romero. The last victim also had been kidnapped from his home at midnight. The MRTA insurgents threatened his parents while they held a gun to their nineteen-year-old son's neck and took him captive: "'If he lets us know where Brosvin [Huasi Tapullima] is, you will see your son again soon. Close your door, don't yell, and don't come out.' They took him by his hair. We waited that night, and at 1:00 a.m. we heard ten gunshots."[30]

Fearing Túpac Amaru reprisals, Wilder Flores Jumpo's parents waited until 5:00 the next morning before going out to search for their missing son. Soon they heard from villagers that there were five victims of a massacre in Wilder Flores's house, including their son. They assumed he had been murdered because "he was always with his cousins Brosvin and Cléber Huasi Tapullima." Both young men were killed that morning in the Caynarachi basin in a place known as Naranjal. They were intercepted by Túpac Amaru insurgents when they returned to Yumbatos. Hours earlier, three-armed people had raided Brosvin's home and threatened his mother, Aurora Tapullima Amasifuen, with a shotgun. When they did not find the men, they abducted Raquel Pashanasi Sangama, blindfolding her and shackling her hands. Raquel was a witness to the extrajudicial executions in the home of the Flores Sangamas. She begged her captors not to kill her because she was pregnant. Raquel's MRTA kidnappers transported her to Tarapoto, where she was eventually released in an area known as Laguna Venecia.[31]

When Raquel returned to Yumbatos, she said that MRTA would release Felipe Tapullima Amasifuen with the warning that he had an hour to leave town and never to return. One of the *tupacamaristas*, however, said that he had seen everything, and if they let him go, he could speak—so he was also killed. "Raquel recognizes the criminals; she doesn't know their names. She saw them three times in Tarapoto market number two. In the last encounter, Raquel was told that she must disappear from Tarapoto if she didn't want to be killed. She went to Lima and made no complaint."[32]

In the early morning of that fateful April 1, the parents of Brosvin and Cléber Huasi Tapullima learned their children had been murdered between the hamlets of Pinto Yacu and Nuevo Lomas. Their limp bodies were thrown in to "a hole in the jungle," but they did not look for their corpses out of fear of violent retribution. The parents say that "they killed their sons because they didn't want to join the Túpac Amaru Revolutionary Movement, even though they were offered money and they didn't accept it."[33] The same MRTA group also murdered Emilda Sangama Cahuaza and her fifteen-year-old daughter, Teresa Flores Sangama, that morning. According to the testimony of Angélica Cahuaza Huasi, Emilda's mother was intercepted as they were returning to Yumbatos from Nuevo Lamas and Pintoyacu. "They were shot. It was said that they were raped. They told Teresa that they were going to release her. She said to them: 'If my mother dies, I will die with her too!' They buried them in the stump of a tree and covered them with leaves."[34]

Although the perpetrators of these gross human rights violations were never identified, the CVR implicated members of the Túpac Amaru Revolutionary Movement as responsible for the murders in Yumbatos. Residents reported that the MRTA regularly raided Yumbatos, forcing the authorities and residents to meet and subjecting them to their propaganda performances. "Anyone who did not attend the meeting was threatened," noted one witness for the CVR.[35] When I returned to the Caynarachi basin after talking to Ronner and Silvia, I made a special point of asking Diego, Sandra, and Fabiano about the torturous history of the MRTA and Yumbatos.

The day I brought up the subject of the Yumbatos massacre, Fabiano was constructing a dugout canoe in the forest, and Sandra and Diego had stopped by the worksite on their way to town to meet with a friend from Yana Puma. After exchanging pleasantries, I asked them all about the Túpac Amaru rebels' massacre of the Yumbatos villagers. Sandra, leaning toward a majestic Sangre de Grado tree (*Croton lechleri*) that provided us with the cover of a natural awning in the bright and hot midmorning, was the first to respond. She said she remembered "several clashes in Yumbatos" and then, counting on her stubby fingers, held up four digits. Sandra went on to say she knew about the massacre and had knowledge of the "violent fights" (*broncas violentas*) that transpired in Yumbatos when the MRTA controlled the Caynarachi basin. When I prodded former militants Fabi and Diego on their experiences in Yumbatos, I learned they had firsthand information that seems to counter the "official" CVR account of the massacre.[36]

Fabiano confirmed that in Yumbatos there had been an "annihilation" (*aniquilación*) of villagers by the MRTA that was authorized by party officials in Tarapoto. In his rendition of the gruesome events in Yumbatos, Diego discussed how a motley group of young people from the *caserío* of Yumbatos were robbing, illicitly charging *cupos*, and raping women in the name of the Túpac Amaru Revolutionary Movement.[37] "When we learned about these bad elements, they were disappeared. . . . The party made us annihilate them. We killed them. Why? Because they were stealing in the party's name and for the MRTA, they were nothing," Diego coldly observed. He seemed noticeably annoyed by this line of conversation. With a steely gaze, he declared that there were airstrips in Yumbatos, Pampa Hermosa in the Lower Huallaga, and Bellavista in the Central Huallaga. He told me that a small group of residents who were not Túpac Amaru *cumpas* had been taking advantage of the *traqueteros* by charging them *cupos* in the party's name.

The theft of the *cupos* destined for the MRTA tripped a ferocious response from the Regional Committee in Tarapoto. A *tupacamarista* commander "went to speak with the cartel's paymaster to see why the *cupos* [taxes] were not being received," said Fabiano. The *narcos* maintained they had been paying and revealed to the MRTA *mando* that the *cupos* were being collected by a Yumbatos-based group posing as rebels. The MRTA regional leadership investigated and determined that nine or ten people were involved in siphoning off precious funds from the local drug traffickers. "Yes," Diego said, "in the name of the Túpac Amaru Revolutionary Movement, those who were annihilated were responsible for atrocities. That's exactly what happened in Yumbatos. There were no clashes with the army while I was there with *compañero* Persi or with Commander Cricket."

In Sandra's opinion, the "liquidations" were conducted in Yumbatos because the community "was in moral disarray; the town's youth had become involved with crime. No one in Yumbatos respected or listened to the governors, the local authorities, or even the parents. The people had become extremely lazy [*bastante haragán*], and criminals had taken over the village." For Sandra, like so many I interviewed from the Huallaga Valley's rural communities, "justice did not exist." She described to me how those who wanted justice in the 1980s and 1990s "turned to the MRTA" for its application of it—one that was grossly imperfect. This sentiment was echoed by Diego, who divulged that "the roles changed as people preferred to denounce thieves and the corrupt in front of the *cumpas*."[38] Perhaps given the weak state presence, some Lower Huallaga communities considered the Túpac Amaru Revolutionary Movement as enforcers of customary morality and traditional authority, rather than their own elected community officials. For example, when discussing law and order at the height of their presence in the Caynarachi basin, Fabiano remarked how a person could utter: "Oh look, so and so is an adulterer [*runamula*] . . . and they weren't taken to the town's governor or the justice of the peace [*juez de paz*].[39] No, no, no! Instead, the adulterer was taken to the *tupachos* for judgment. Yes, they brought them directly to us to be judged. No, Bartuco, they stopped going to court, they didn't go anymore. We were the law here in the Caynarachi."

Various factors were considered when the MRTA meted out "popular justice" to Caynarachi villagers. Contrasting the MRTA's selective application of punishments with the Sendero Luminoso's reputation as merciless enforcers of draconian social mores, Sandra told me a spouse could be abandoned by his or her partner for alcoholism or drug addiction and then legitimately form another conjugal partnership. This was considered when the MRTA was deliberating over the fate of fornicators, adulterers, or philanderers. "There were various factors that led to this extreme. Some said their partners would not have sex with them, so they took up a paramour," commented Sandra. "Yes, for popular justice, we considered each case on its own merits," chimed Fabi, who frequently portrayed his involvement with the Movimiento Revolucionario Túpac Amaru favorably.

Diego asserted that the people "followed our law because of the fear they had of our threats of violent retribution." Villagers were typically given ultimatums, and the MRTA forced them to submit. With civil judges, one would often be expected to offer bribes to oil the judicial machinery or be forced to wait months for "justice," which often never came in the Caynarachi basin. Sandra, Diego, and Fabiano admired the MRTA's efforts in challenging the conventional power structure, promoting voluntary cooperation, and seeking to reorganize society. My MRTA interlocutors concurred with Pyotr Kropotkin's evaluation of the law, perceiving it as a skillful amalgamation of societal-benefiting customs that could be observed even in the absence of formal legal systems. Similar to Kropotkin, they also acknowledged the existence of regulations and conventions meant to benefit a ruling minority, which required the use of coercive measures to enforce them.[40]

Fabiano put it bluntly: "The MRTA was not like the weak and corrupt authorities of the past. If people didn't obey the MRTA's justice, we would simply kill them. We had the will, the weapons, and the ammunition to do so."[41] During the MRTA assemblies, the rights and duties of the villagers were defined. Minor offenses were negotiated by a hastily convened people's court: whoever pilfered a chicken, item of clothing, or plantains, for example, had to return the goods and weed the soccer field, clean the plaza, or do physical exercises as a punishment. The Túpac Amaru Revolutionary Movement also had public trials of allegedly "crooked" *tombos*—police officers—or elected municipal officials as performative "educational" occasions. The MRTA were pro-social in several ways. They garnered important backing from key sectors of the community by enforcing fair wages, adjudicating the resolution of petty crime and violent domestic disputes, and successfully managing disagreements among rival families, social groupings, and adversarial communities.

The Túpac Amaru rebels' right to pass judgment was a common theme in Diego's, Sandra's, and Fabi's narrative accounts of their interactions as *tupacamaristas* with the Central and Lower Huallaga communities. In their conversations with me, they presented the Túpac Amaru Revolutionary Movement as a legitimate provider of communal justice in a land where no laws were respected unless down the barrel of a gun. As Diego poignantly said: "Once there was a man who killed his brother in Huicungo. We had to liquidate him because the authorities were doing nothing about his crime, so we enforced order and punished him." In Sandra's words, "the local judges or prosecutors had no backing anymore, they were corrupt and had lost their authority [*habían perdido los papeles*]." Likewise, Diego told me, "The governors of that time even came to us for justice." He remarked that when they controlled the Caynarachi basin, the local judges lodged their complaints with the MRTA and relied on MRTA to sanction criminals and those who had violated community standards of comportment.

Highlighting the interplay between individual agency, communal knowledge, and the influence of the MRTA in shaping relationships and societal expectations, Fabiano recounted a troubling incident involving paternity fraud. He shared the story of how his Túpac Amaru comrades pressured a young man from the Yana Puma community to accept legal responsibility for a child, although the entire community was aware that the youngster was not biologically his. This instance sheds light on the complex dynamics and power exerted by the MRTA within the community, showcasing the social and cultural implications of such actions.

Predicated on threats of violent retribution for those who disobeyed their decisions, the MRTA became an important adjudicator of local morality. As Fabiano self-confidently observed, "The people feared those with the guns—the Túpac Amaru Revolutionary Movement." If the *cumpas* had not reestablished order, Fabiano thought "the delinquents would have laughed at the judges; they would have ridiculed the official authorities. We would have no law."[42] Asserting the law provided the MRTA with a monopoly over violence and guaranteed its continued existence among the local populace, as well as existential foes like the rival and more powerful Sendero Luminoso insurgency.[43]

In 1990, the MRTA was involved in a grisly confrontation in Yumbatos with members of the Sendero Luminoso. Campesinos from the Shanusi area had informed Túpac Amaru rebels that there was another armed group operating in the zone. This prompted Sístero García Torres to dispatch a reconnaissance patrol to a house where the region's residents had told them *senderistas* were hiding out. Following a pitched gunfight, the MRTA insurgents captured eight combatants, all of whom declared they were members of Sendero Luminoso.[44]

Víctor Polay Campos, the supreme rebel commander, questioned his subordinate, García Torres, "When they were taken captive, why did you not convince them to stay in the column and fight with us for the MRTA?" García Torres, replied by commenting "No, *compañero*, on the contrary, they insulted us. 'Long live Chairman Gonzalo!' they screamed. When we questioned them, they said they were opening up a new Sendero column, and they knew that if we captured them, we were going to shoot them, just as they said they would have done to us," said García Torres.[45] "Sístero, we are not for that," retorted Polay Campos. "No, *compañero*, they did not want to know anything. They told us that in the Ponaza Valley they killed five of our *compañeros*, including Carlos Arango, without giving them the same opportunity," rejoined García Torres. Polay Campos reportedly told García Torres, "You should have taken their weapons and let them go under the condition that if you saw them again, they would be shot." "No, *cumpa*, we decided to shoot them," said García Torres. Polay Campos inquired, "Where are they, so you can tell their mothers and tell them everything that happened to their children?" To which García Torres answered: "They are buried in a common gravesite near the Yumbatos cemetery, the eight are buried there. It is said that war has its costs. Thus, we declared war also with the Sendero Luminoso."[46]

There was no collaboration between the MRTA and the Sendero Luminoso; the *senderistas* saw the *tupacamaristas* as fierce rivals profoundly corrupted by "revisionism."[47] As insurgent movements, the more elusive Sendero Luminoso had various advantages over the smaller, weaker Túpac Amaru Revolutionary Movement. The Sendero Luminoso had enlisted the logistical and financial support of drug traffickers earlier than the MRTA. This relatively more violent group recruited members and obtained weapons through the collection of *cupos* from those involved in the narcotics trade considerably earlier than the MRTA. The Túpac Amaru Revolutionary Movement was decidedly not clandestine; its followers sported balaclavas, military garb, and red armbands emblazoned with their partisan logo, which made them more discernible to the general populace, to the state security forces, to the *rondas campesinas*, and to their Sendero Luminoso foes.[48]

The decisive battle in the Huallaga Valley pitting the MRTA against Sendero Luminoso ended in a symphony of gunfire in Tocache in March 1987, resulting in the death of between forty and sixty Túpac Amaru rebels. Because of this routing, the Túpac Amaru Revolutionary Movement forces had no choice but to concentrate their efforts toward the north, specifically targeting the Central and Lower Huallaga Valley.[49] Upon arrival in the regions of San Martín and Loreto, the Túpac Amaru Revolutionary Movement sought to replace the state presence and install zones of security to ensure their sovereignty. This was readily evident in MRTA efforts to mediate local conflicts, enforce novel codes of morality, and respond to criminality and corruption in the Caynarachi basin.

CHAPTER 6

Discipline

Law and Disorder

¡Sin justicia, no habrá paz! Without justice, there will be no peace!
MRTA REBEL SLOGAN

In the Caynarachi, it was common for thieves (*rateros*) to be denounced by residents to members of the Túpac Amaru Revolutionary Movement, who meted out punishments according to the dictates of their codes of conduct. One of the more symbolically potent disciplinary acts that all my informants mentioned was the MRTA's practice of shaving the hair (*rapar*) of the person found guilty of a violation of sanctioned modes of behavior. I was told it was common practice for the *tupacamaristas* to discharge their weapons next to the ears of those found "guilty," impairing their hearing. Disobedience to the MRTA or community wishes could be fatal.

As Doña Regina recounted to me, the Túpac Amaru Revolutionary Movement would say: "Get out of town to the fortunate ones. Others were just killed on the spot!" Some endured harrowing cascades of merciless and savage beatings, but not killed, despite the gravity of their transgression. For instance, a mother in Yana Puma denounced her daughter's nineteen-year-old boyfriend, and he was detained and systematically tortured by the MRTA. Doña Regina, like most I spoke to, was deeply ambivalent about the coercive imposition of codes of honor. She described several episodes of how the MRTA shaved the hair of those who stole livestock or of common house thieves. Repeat offenders were disciplined with obligatory collective work as a second warning, and the third offense was punished by execution. In more extreme cases, some were strung up (*colgado*) in the plaza for all to see. As recounted in Regina's words: "The law for all those who misbehaved was the same. In those times, there weren't any rumors, no adulterers, or thieves and that became the norm for us while the *tupachos* were here in the Caynarachi. In this way, life was easier."[1]

During my encounters with various individuals in the Lower Huallaga region, a collective narrative began to emerge regarding the disciplinary measures enforced by the *tupacamaristas*. Among those who shared their experiences was Benito, a skilled farmer and dedicated angler of river fish, who also happened to be Regina's cousin.[2] He told me that one evening; the MRTA showed up unannounced at his home in Zungracocha*, which borders the town's soccer field and agrarian cooperative. The jovial Benito described how he was always on good terms with the *tupacamaristas* and the state security forces. However, his best friend in those days, Pepe*, was well known as a pilferer. Given the strict mandate prohibiting theft, the MRTA came seeking Pepe to punish him for his constant robbery. Having not found him, they left Benito's house after a few hours, during which the Túpac Amaru rebels played soccer. Benito told me the Túpac Amaru Revolutionary Movement scouts eventually encountered his friend hiding later that day and then savagely beat him for stealing from the market in Nuevo Libertad.

Benito remembered how "they shaved the poor bastard's hair and prepared to kill him with a single gunshot to the forehead. But Pepe was blessed that day." According to Benito, some of Pepe's captors were uttering: "Kill Pepe, the stupid guy [*huevón*]. Kill the fucking thief [*choro*] once and for all. Let's do it now!" Yet somebody in the group who knew Pepe blurted out: "No, we can't kill him. He has five children to support." That is how Pepe was saved, recalled Benito—"someone knew him and prevented his death." His friend never stole from that day forth. Benito said he "counseled Pepe against doing 'stupid things' [*cojudeces*] or you are going to get yourself killed." Pepe used to steal *pijuayo* fruit at night and sell the seeds during the day. "Imagine that!" chuckled Benito in a booming voice, which reverberated across his spacious *huerta*, chock full of plantains, papaya trees, corn, and cassava.

At a work party—a *minga*—Benito introduced me to his cousin Magdalena*, an acerbic thin woman with prematurely gray hair in her early fifties.[3] She, too, had potent memories of the past and, when prodded by Benito, provided me with her testimonial of what had happened to her brother Eduardo* at the hands of the Túpac Amaru Revolutionary Movement. Apparently, Eduardo had shown up in Magdalena's *huerta* one rainy afternoon, having just been disciplined by the MRTA. Eduardo had all his hair shaved off, with his head completely bald and bruised and covered in welts and hematomas. When discussing the details of Eduardo's fatal run-in with the MRTA, Magdalena went to some pains to explain her brother's fate, remarking how she thought he was a good-natured person, albeit a poor *cojudo*, an "emptyheaded" man. Besides being a simpleton and broke (*misio*), Eduardo's sister was well aware of what poetically she called his "triangle of flaws.": he was half blind, disposed to dishonesty and half-truths, and constantly robbing petty items from the villagers. Magdalena said she had predicted a major problem would happen the moment she saw Eduardo show up at her homestead in alarm and panic.

Upon seeing her brother, she said she muttered, "I knew this was going to happen!" As Magdalena explained, it was a tense and "delicate" (*delicado*) situation, and she did not want to complicate things by reprimanding Eduardo. Taking pity on Eduardo, Magdalena helped him escape to the *monte* just as the army brigade arrived in town. Magdalena knew her brother would be targeted by the military if he was caught since his head was shaven; he would be an easy target. The army would know he had done something wrong and perhaps suspect he was a member of the Túpac Amaru Revolutionary Movement.

When the troops arrived at Magdalena's home in search of Eduardo, she denied seeing him. Magdalena knew Eduardo had fled, but she did not expect to hear the FAL gunshot echoing through the forest so soon. It was only twenty minutes after his escape that the sound reached her ears, indicating that he had encountered mortal trouble. "My poor brother Eduardo was shot dead by the army. We found his inert body in a pool [*mancha*] of blood in the forest near the path [*trocha*] on the way toward Huicungo," continued Magdalena, with tears in her swollen, dark-brown eyes. The peaty smell of burning brush being cleared for forest gardens wafted toward us as we sat silently underneath the protection of a large *caoba* tree. There was a lull in our conversation. In a quiet gesture of human comfort, Benito placed his weather-worn hand on Magdalena's bony shoulder and softly said: "Eduardo had his flaws, but he was a good person. You are right to grieve his death. It was wrong what they did to him. But God is protecting the sunburned smiley face of Eduardo. So please, don't cry, *prima*." Tears dribbled down Magdalena's puffy face as Benito continued to soothe her, hugging his cousin's bony frame as she wept quietly on his shoulder.

How do people respond to moral outrage—that emotional state beyond distress and trauma—when they experience it? I pondered this while thinking about poor Eduardo's grieving sister. Losing her beloved brother to the clutches of the military brought into sharp focus a need in Magdalena to keep the memories of Eduardo alive. Finding traces of what had happened to him among his belongings—the copy of the funeral service, the army report, his cap—were of great importance to Magdalena. Eduardo's commemoration is enacted through manufactured items, such as a wooden box of his belongings, a watch, a religious medallion, and fading photos, including Magdalena's favorite one of him as a schoolboy before the accident that left him blinded in one eye. "I'm gradually taking out all of his priceless things and putting them back out for all to see. He is dead, yes, but these things help me stay connected to my dear brother. I know the timeline of his demise and what was happening when the cowardly military shot him in the back," she said, pointing to the creased army report.

Her face flushed—she was not finished discussing the past. Clearing her throat and wiping two streams of tears from her ruddy cheeks, she chronicled how the army never hassled her, even though her brother had been one of their innocent victims. The military came to her house only to inquire about MRTA's movements in the Caynarachi basin. She recalled how the MRTA would go around in groups of fifteen to twenty and come by her home, demanding three or four chickens at a time to eat. Like the military, the Túpac Amaru Revolutionary Movement tried to impose a new order out of the fear that permeated virtually all aspects of public life. Magdalena also told me about a nameless man from Marupa who was strung up when rumors of complicity made culpability difficult. Magdalena was not sure who denounced him to the MRTA. Some said he was a thief (*choro*), while others said he was a snitch (*soplón*) working with the *narcos* in El Porvenir. "Yes, the MRTA strung up the poor guy in the plaza. He was a young guy with fair colored hair and skin, and was only about sixteen years old. Some say he was a spy for the army, others say he was an informant for the police [*el tombo*]," Magdalena told me. She recalled hearing her neighbors accusing the young guy of passing information to the army. That is why Magdalena thought the Túpac Amaru Revolutionary Movement took him to be punished in the plaza.

Not only were traitors to the "peoples' revolution" punished, so, too, were adulterous women and men. They had their hair shaved bald (*les raparon bolanchos*).[4] Many accounts of such acts peppered people's recollections of the wartime abuses in the Caynarachi. This extreme form of symbolic violence was very much a part of the texture of daily life in the Huallaga

Valley during the internal war.[5] Diego detailed five occasions when he saw punitive hair cuttings—but given that he was in the logistics division of the MRTA, he did not participate personally in the punishments. Typically, a denunciation was made by a local resident to the MRTA, which then enforced the sentence. It was much more traumatic for women to go through this form of "popular justice" in front of the entire community for all to see. With their heads shaved, women were discriminated against more; they could not leave their homes. They were surveilled. Shaving their hair robbed them of their freedom. "It was humiliating," as Sandra noted.[6]

Sandra told me how two people from Yana Puma, a nurse Victoria* and her lover, both had their hair shaved off their heads by the guerrillas. "I remember the nurse had an affair with Nelson*, who was married to Miranda*. So, Nelson had two wives! When the *cumpas* arrived, Miranda denounced Nelson and Victoria to the MRTA command," Sandra said. "That's why Victoria and Nelson had their hair cut off," she said, and it was "horrible for poor Victoria, who was shamed by everyone for the way she looked."[7]

Concerns over policing the intimate lives of the residents of the Caynarachi took on overwhelmingly sinister overtones when the *tupachos* were in full force.[8] The MRTA had a ruthless code of ethics that justified murder as a punishment for moral violations. Whenever they deemed someone guilty of such a crime, they did not hesitate to execute them. The Túpac Amaru guerrillas called gays "undesirables" and forced other citizens to exclude them from civilian activities.[9] In the Caynarachi basin, the *tupacamaristas* told people that being gay meant they were degenerate. As the former Túpac Amaru militia member Fabiano expressed, "The party despised homosexuals [*maricones*] and transvestites [*travestis*]." In the region, gay men and cross-dressers were warned by the *tupacamaristas* that they must live as heterosexuals. Within the MRTA, there existed a distinct gender dynamic by which men adhered to a hypermilitarized, hetero-national hegemonic masculinity, emphasizing dominance and conformity to traditional masculine norms. On the other hand, women were often associated with notions of idealized motherhood and were expected to exhibit discreet sexual behavior, conforming to societal expectations. This division reinforced and perpetuated gender roles within the organization, establishing a specific framework for masculinity and femininity.

Fabiano felt that gay people had been victimized because they were a "contagious force among the men" and provided "bad examples for the boys." Sandra, Diego, and Fabiano all said there should be "no third sex." Imbricated by his faith in heterosexist Catholicism, Diego explained: "God only created man and woman. The third sex wanted to be more than a woman. It is not dignified. That is why we gave them ultimatums to leave the community."[10] Numerous members of the LGBTQ community forced from the Caynarachi basin sought refuge in relatively more tolerant urban centers like Tarapoto, Iquitos, and Lima.

However, many who escaped sexual persecution were not safe, as evidenced by the death of Hilda's gay brother-in-law Jimmy* at the nightclub Oasis* in Tarapoto*.[11] Hilda's mother-in-law and family had moved from Sauce to Tarapoto, in part to enable Jimmy to work as a hairdresser for El Moshaco Salón de Tarapot*. Clutching a faded portrait of her brother-in-law, Hilda became somber, recalling her painful recollections of him. She said he "was never a selfish person. On the contrary, Jimmy was a very good, kind, and generous guy.[12] Even though he had many friends, Jimmy constantly helped his family; they always came first for him. When I had my moped accident, he paid my clinic bills," Hilda said while rubbing her disfigured left arm. She maintained that some of Jimmy's new "friends" killed him because he was gay. Jimmy, who had previously had supper with them at a roasted chicken restaurant (pollería), was unwittingly drawn into their circle. Jimmy's new group of "friends" arrived at El Moshaco Salón where he cut hair. Hilda recalled it was on a Friday evening, during the San Juan festival, that they invited her brother-in-law to accompany them to Coco Loco, a local disco venue.[13] Hilda said that when Jimmy's new acquaintances came to the stylist shop, he was especially eager to show off a new collection of colognes that had just come in from the coast. After trying some of the new line of colognes, they all departed on motorcycles toward the nearby Coco Loco dance club, on the outskirts of Morales (Tarapoto).

"All I know is what the witnesses there reported to the police [el tombo]," Hilda said to me after a lull of haunting soundlessness. She recalled gloomily, "They shot him directly in the front of his head, between his lovely hazel brown eyes, and left him there in the grass [pasto] to die." Jimmy's murder never resulted in a conviction, Hilda said softly, her words shattered by sadness. She woefully revealed that she eventually discovered her nephew, a member of the MRTA, was the triggerman who killed Jimmy. Hilda said she often thinks of poor Jimmy, who she remembers was always "the life of the party. He was the favorite of the family."

The MRTA not only performed heinous acts of violence against the local LGBTQ population; its adherents also targeted traditional folk healers (médicos or brujos in the local vernacular). This was evident across the

Caynarachi basin. To verify reports of *brujos* or *médicos*, the Túpac Amaru Revolutionary Movement sent rebels disguised as sick people to their homes. If the alleged *brujo* diagnosed them as bewitched, they were killed. In the community of San Miguel de Achinamiza, the MRTA slaughtered two *brujos*, or shamans, Grimaldi Huansi and his wife, Brigida Sarin. The CVR's final report made passing mention of the tragedy, which took on a hauntingly personal quality after I met a former *tupacamarista* who claimed to have murdered the *bruja* Brigida Sarin.

An aged man with a scruffy beard, gamy aroma, and a few shaky teeth approached my seat in the packed village restaurant during a violent downpour and sat down facing me. He slurped his soup and started considering the past, while I methodically consumed my dish of beans, white rice, fried fish, and fried plantains (*maduro*). As I finished eating the sweet, caramelized *maduro* plantains on my now naked plate, he continued to talk about his long affiliation with the Túpac Amaru Revolutionary Movement and the historical significance of the "people's revolution," which he once thought was imminent. Rain fell from the bleak sky, bursting with pregnant clouds that shrouded the afternoon sunshine. The total stranger sitting before me recounted his life story, beginning with his birth in Moyobamba seven decades earlier. Once the rain stopped, most of the patrons had already left, but the stranger stayed and carried on his conversation. I wondered to myself why he was being so forthcoming, and then asked, "Why are you telling me all this, my friend?" The elderly man responded in a hurry, "I must speak. I'm troubled by these things" (*Tengo que hablar, estas cosas me persiguen*).[14]

In the nearly empty restaurant where only the cook and a teenage girl lingered, I changed conversation to the murder of *brujos* at the hands of Túpac Amaru Revolutionary Movement.[15] To my surprise, I learned how the old man and his Túpac Amaru *cumpas* "went off to kill a shaman and then murder his wife, who ran into the *monte*." My interlocutor nonchalantly described how he chased the *brujo*'s wife into the steep and undulating hills of San Martín and then shot her dead at close range. The old man continued with a disconnected, glassy expression, boldly declaring, "We just left them both for the buzzards to eat." And with that ghastly affirmation of culpability, the old wobbly toothed stranger stood up and said, "Adiós!" The geriatric *cumpa* slowly walked off into the sodden field across from the church, leaving me to ponder the contradictions of life. I thought aloud: "What exactly happened to the Huansis? Why were they killed? Why has their tragic history been silenced? And perhaps more importantly, would truth, let alone reconciliation, ever be possible in the Lower Huallaga Valley where the wounds are deep and lingering?"

In my discussions with several trusted senior villagers, they volunteered that Grimaldi Huansi was a powerful shamanic curer who, in fact, terrified the community. Benito confirmed Grimaldi Huansi's Hecatean prowess. He said Huansi had the unearthly capacity to beguile at will whomever he wanted. Similarly, Magdalena said she remembers constantly admonishing her children to steer clear of the Huansi couple, as they were feared *brujos*, rumored to have been responsible for various children's deaths.

In response to the sudden passing of several individuals from different families in the area, the community came together and organized an assembly. Representatives from the related but rival families participated in the assembly and expressed their strong dissatisfaction toward the couple who, like most traditional healers in the area, demanded payment for their services. Villagers complained about the Huansi couple to the local Túpac Amaru commanders. In the Caynarachi basin, informants mentioned over half a dozen suspected murders of *brujos*, including in San Miguel, Metilluyoc, Puerto Libre, Sangamayo, and Pongo del Caynarachi. Diego was quick to note that in addition to economic factors at play, those Túpac Amaru members who had Kichwa-Lamista cultural roots believed in the spiritual dangers of shamans, so the murder of traditional healers was culturally more acceptable among some.

Intersecting with the phenomenon of dark *brujería* (witchcraft), the deterioration of community well-being, and extrajudicial violence, traditional healers like Grimaldi Huansi and Brigida Sarín became vulnerable targets during the ugly times. In times of profound uncertainty, particularly when faced with the inexplicable or sudden deaths of young adults and children, certain individuals found solace in scapegoating, a tendency to indiscriminately assign blame without proper justification.[16] By denouncing geriatric couple to the MRTA, families formerly struggling with one another united against their chosen scapegoats. Former enemies became friends, rallying against the cost of paying wicked charlatan *brujos*. They took part together in the execution of violence against a specified enemy of the collective. Successfully navigating the minefield of discipline and death required skills of cunning, resilience, and courage, all of which were characteristics of Julián*, the man responsible for reporting the Huansis to the MRTA.

Two-Faced Julián and the Priest

Much like Diego, Fabiano, and Sandra, Julián, who is a sturdy and verbally nimble villager, said he saw the Túpac Amaru Revolutionary Movement with his "own eyes and lived it with [his] own flesh."[17] It was common knowledge that Julián experienced it personally as a former Túpac Amaru militant. In 1990, Julián was the president of the town's Democratic Defense Front (Frente de Defensa Democrático). The front's creation came on the heels of an order from the Túpac Amaru Revolutionary Movement's regional leadership in Tarapoto, and it was charged with locally enforcing MRTA decrees. While we both sat in the town's busy plaza one Sunday morning, awaiting the start of the weekly ritual of performative nationalism—the hoisting of the Peruvian flag and the singing of the anthem with one hand pressed over the heart while standing at erect attention—Julián said to me that "an informal pact to prevent further conflicts in town had been made between the Democratic Defense Front and the MRTA."

Julián is naturally a forgiving person. He once said to me, "Instances of insurgency and other forms of evil in a society, such as abductions, do not show the failure of [our] community. Instead, they reveal a lack of love for one another."[18] Yet Julián was resolute in commenting that "people in the community were wrong to think [they] could be decent in an indecent time."[19] As a village-level representative of the MRTA, Julián said that the Democratic Defense Front convened a secretive meeting with the town's priest; Evaristo* the judge; Roberto* the governor; and Joaquín* the town mayor; and it made a formal pact with the *cumpas* to avoid conflict. "Shit, I won't ever forget our first encounter and how Evaristo was so damned frightened of the *tupachos*," remarked Julián, who discussed how he practiced "acting with two faces" (*actuando con dos caras*) to survive the ugly times. A diplomat by nature, he was skilled at balancing competing interests and quickly adapting to volatile situations with calm, determination, and forethought. This was apparent in his strategic links to Túpac Amaru sympathizers.

As elsewhere, the ranks of the MRTA's *milicianos* comprised militant students and their teachers, as well as community representatives, such as Julián, who told me he was always indecisive about the legitimacy and viability of the *lucha armada*. He said that when Peru was gripped by internal war, he would tell his Túpac Amaru rebel contacts that the village was not primed politically to establish operations. Nevertheless, the MRTA would visit his house at two, three, or four in the morning to gather intelligence on the locals and the movements of the army or police. The most memorable for Julián was not his role in the demise of the Huansi couple, but his participation in the negotiations of several kidnapping cases conducted by the Túpac Amaru Revolutionary Movement.

To save the lives of MRTA *milicianos* who had been captured, including the instructors Tomas*, Wilbert*, and Franco*, whose connection with the insurgency was murky and inconsistent in the testimonies I recorded, two-faced Julián also described his cooperation with local authorities, especially the priest. The town's teachers were all flown off to Pampa Hermosa, another MRTA military stronghold, by an Antonov An-32B helicopter after an army convoy made an unexpected visit during the fiesta of San Rafael on October 24, 1990. The instructors, according to several town citizens, were members of an emerging MRTA cell in the Caynarachi basin. The army sought to locate the *tupacamarista* camp in Pampa Hermosa and planned to use the alleged rebel teachers as guides through the *monte*. Notwithstanding, the teachers from the Caynarachi basin were not Túpac Amaru members and ostensibly did not know the location of the rebel base in Pampa Hermosa. After an exhausting two-day march through the rainforest *selva* without footwear, proper equipment, or essential supplies, they were eventually brought back to their homes. According to Julián, the local Catholic priest's guidance and persistent intervention led to the teachers' quick and release from army custody, unscathed.

At the time, Julián was deeply involved in village politics and well aware that the locals "were afraid that there might soon be killings like those that had occurred in Yumbatos." Julián explained to me that because the MRTA was unable to establish a sizable following in town, it concentrated its efforts on the priest because he was opposed to their presence in the Caynarachi basin. They threatened him first. When the parish priest once let Túpac Amaru Revolutionary Movement rebels into the local Catholic Church on the condition that they remove their balaclava masks, Julián recalls that he discovered they were largely students. The young rebels at first could not answer the priest's query about what they wanted from him. Everyone was aware that the MRTA wanted to control the parochial radio and develop a new political base in the community by driving the church out of the Caynarachi basin.[20] The *tupacamaristas* repeated their threats and told the priest they insisted he accompany them to El Porvenir, their encampment. Unfazed, the local cleric told the young Túpac Amaru fighters that he wanted to personally speak with their comandante rather than accompany them to their rebel encampment in El Porvenir. The *tupacamaristas* were unable to free the priest from the defense of the parishioners who surrounded him in the village, so they fled without their hostage.

After a few days, a Túpac Amaru militant shot at the priest when he was on a boat traveling along the Caynarachi River near the community of Nuevo Libertad. Fortunately for the cleric, the bullet missed its target and passed right over his shoulder. As Julián recalls: "The shot didn't meet its mark and the auspicious Father escaped death." Upon the priest's return to town, *tupacamaristas* were waiting to kidnap him once more, but the villagers came out in force yet again to ensure his immediate rescue. In 1990, San Martín's peasant strike had the full support of the MRTA. Those from various communities, including villages and hamlets along the Caynarachi River, such as El Porvenir, Nuevo Libertad, Huicungo, Yana Puma, Marupa, Santa Rosa*, El Ramal*, and tiny Puerto Muyuna*, all joined in the farmer's demonstrations. After much hesitation, the residents of Julián's town finally supported the agrarian strike. The MRTA had been pressing those in his community to actively take part. "But I think each villager made their own decision whether to take part in the strike," remarked Julián, as he ruminated on the past political topography shaping life experiences for those living in the Caynarachi basin.

"The priest never told us what to do, instead he gave us his advice," Julián explained after I asked about the role the church played in political life during the ugly times. "How did the *cumpas* respond to the priest?" I asked Julián. He felt the MRTA thought the local priest was dissuading the community from supporting the general campesino strike. Therefore, Julián believed the camouflaged EPT troops arrived late one night and called the villagers to a meeting in the town's plaza. Meanwhile, the MRTA's political *mando* bellowed, "I will give you exactly ten minutes to present the priest who has been controlling this fucking village before me."

Neither the priest nor his bulky shadow materialized, so Julián said the MRTA began verbally haranguing and loudly denouncing him in the plaza. Shortly thereafter, the priest's silhouette appeared from inside the church situated across from the town square, parallel to the municipal office on one side and the health post and school on the other. As he stood upright and surveyed the gathering crowd, the uncloaked priest was told that the Túpac Amaru rebel messengers' commander, El Grillo, wanted to speak with him face-to-face at the encampment, El Porvenir, located over twelve hours of travel upriver. Julián said the priest, who had boldly moved toward the center of the plaza, valiantly shouted out to his would-be kidnappers, "No, I must gather here with my people, the villagers, I am not going with you!'"

Julián recalled that the villagers, meanwhile, surrounded the priest, like a human shield, to protect their spiritual leader as he slowly made his way to the center of main square and positioned himself in a corner of the plaza, next to the municipality and the antiquated church. Circling the priest's entourage, numerous agitated Túpac Amaru Revolutionary Movement rebels began prancing about with their red and black headbands and readied weapons on full display. Standing before them, the priest reportedly responded to the Túpac Amaru rebels in a stentorian voice: "I would prefer to die in my house. This is my village. I will never leave here." Various testimonials from various interlocutors who witnessed this event accentuate how the local priest stood firm and responded to the *tupacamaristas* with fearlessness, refusing to surrender any ground to the armed insurgents.

Julián's opinion of the priest is shared by many people I interviewed in the Caynarachi basin. Many told me the priest played a beneficial role in promoting community welfare and an end to the armed conflict. Julián's account underscored the courageous character of the priest, a man who willingly spoke directly to the MRTA leadership. Although the Catholic priest was passionately devoted to his faith and supported the principles of liberation theology, he did not endorse the MRTA's uprising or political agenda, according to Julián. However, Julián revealed the priest could still rescue many individuals: "He had a special skill. He knew how to handle people with different ways of thinking about what was right and wrong." The priest's capacity to listen gained him the trust of many in the Caynarachi. Julián shared how some MRTA rebels would even seek the priest's help in preventing the army from attacking or killing them. "Don't forget, the priest was part of the repentance process whereby some *tupachos* went to prison and others were released. He was very important during the time the fighting stopped."

In my interview with Nicolás*, the pockmarked, seventy-year-old former lieutenant governor (*teniente gobernador*) of the village of Nuevo Libertad, he described how the MRTA always wanted to enter the zone, but the priest prevented that from happening various times.[21] As Nicolás put it: "We didn't suffer massacres as they did in El Porvenir, which was a well-fortified camp, or like in Yumbatos, or even in Yana Puma or Puerto Muyuna. In our village, the church and community leaders opposed the MRTA. We didn't have anyone die here because of the subversion." Nicolás remarked how the Caynarachi basin, with its greater accessibility to the "outside world," was a place the MRTA passed through rather than permanently settled. In Nuevo

Libertad, the Túpac Amaru guerrillas got vital provisions and services and then hurried on to El Porvenir or elsewhere, like Yumbatos, Yana Puma, or Pampa Hermosa. The authorities—mayor, governor, judge, and the front under Julián's direction—also joined to resist the MRTA. "In a tense face-to-face confrontation with the *terrucos*, they told the MRTA's leadership the villagers rejected the MRTA's philosophy of violent revolution," Nicolás commented with pride. He said the Túpac Amaru Revolutionary Movement did not like this, "but they respected the town's opinion, especially the priest's courage." United against the incursions of the MRTA and its interference in communal affairs, Nuevo Libertad kept the extreme violence at bay during the height of the internal war in San Martín (1985–1995).

Julián recalled how the community was affected by continued MRTA threats. Apparently, in the late 1980s or early 1990s, an MRTA patrol came into town from El Porvenir, including an evil (*malandrín*) rebel. They told Julián, as head of the Democratic Defense Front, that the MRTA was planning to liquidate the priest—but first, they wanted to humiliate him by forcing him to exercise (*ranear*) in the Plaza de Armas. Alarmed, Julián ran off to warn the priest, and on his way, he came face-to-face with a MRTA leader, René*. In the distance, Julián said he could see the priest walking toward the insurgents, shouting at the *malandrín* MRTA member: "Coward, come directly for me. Don't send one of your soldiers to warn me!"

Accustomed to such events, Julián told me he was unnerved and dashed off to find Comrade Isula*, the Túpac Amaru commander of El Porvenir, who was in town that night. Julián questioned Commander Isula about why they were going to harm the priest when he had been so supportive of not only the community, but the MRTA as well. Julián said he reminded Commander Isula that their local priest supplied them with vital fuel and food from the parish cooperative. In a desperate voice, Julián asked Commander Isula: "How is it possible that you can treat a person who is benefiting us all in such a terrible way? To kill him?" Commander Isula relented, finally agreeing with Julián's pleas to spare the cleric's life. Julián described how he convinced the commander that killing the priest would be a poor political strategy, and he said it would immediately turn the community against the MRTA. The order to liquidate the priest was retracted, and the MRTA rebel was commanded to let the priest go unharmed.

The church was undoubtedly a bulwark against the complete establishment and acceptance of the MRTA in the village. The Túpac Amaru Revolutionary Movement and its supporters had confrontations with the priest, but Diego, Sandra, and Fabiano readily admitted that he gave them much-needed medicine, food, and even gasoline. They recalled a particular episode in which a Túpac Amaru member arrived while intoxicated and asked the priest for an extension cord, but the request was rebuffed. When Diego heard the commotion, the priest was on his knees with the barrel of a revolver pressed to his head at the hands of his inebriated MRTA companion. Diego became enraged. He told me, "I wanted to kill my *compañero* at that instant, but momentarily hesitated. Motherfucker! What are you doing?" The drunk (*huasca*) MRTA member, who also was a nurse, started dragging the priest across the main square while menacing to shoot him in the head.

Diego came running to the priest's aid, put his gun to the MRTA attacker's skull, and demanded that he release the priest unharmed.[22] The priest, as he had been in countless other events, appeared fearless throughout this dramatic encounter. He put on a "tough face" for his attacker, according to the locals. Diego was yelled at by the inebriated Túpac Amaru rebel, "Hey, why are you helping this damn priest?" One of Diego's MRTA *compañeros* who was present grabbed the intoxicated *tupacamarista*'s revolver while he wrestled the medic to the ground. The inebriated MRTA nurse was hauled off to be punished, but Mando Razor and his friends were welcomed into the priest's home. They drank some anise liquor before heading back to their rebel encampment, hidden in the shadows of the night and resounding with the symphonic sounds of the rainforest's insects and reptiles.

Anonymous Letter

The Túpac Amaru Revolutionary Movement had severe financial problems because it never established close ties to the social movements it claimed to represent, which it tried to resolve by using coercive methods like kidnapping for ransom. Although kidnapping is expressly forbidden by the international humanitarian law that the MRTA purported to uphold, the insurgent group often used extortion and abduction. This practice was employed not only for well-to-do urbanites but also for residents of the countryside. The abduction of the son of one of the influential local families by the Túpac Amaru rebels caused widespread outrage and rallied family members across the Caynarachi basin.

Besides Julián, chief of the Democratic Defense Front, the schoolteachers Franco and Wilbert (both alleged to be activists for the Túpac Amaru Revolutionary Movement), helped negotiate the return of Ángel, who had been kidnapped by the MRTA. The group departed on their first covert mission to find Ángel by boat, leaving the village's port after dark so that no one could see them leaving. The previous Sunday, Túpac Amaru rebels from El Porvenir had shown up at Julián's well-kept home. Even though he had heard various rumors about the MRTA's existence in the Huallaga Valley, Julián claimed at the time that he had never encountered this masked group.

Before being taken by Túpac Amaru Revolutionary Movement rebels, swarthy Ángel was a Tarapoto university student who, according to some, acted like an overindulged child "because of his parents' wealth." Doña Regina and her husband, Don Augustín, perceived Ángel as a *haragán*, lazy when it came time to work. He was a member of one of the most influential families in the area, who owned sizable livestock herds and vast swaths of land. One day, in 1990, a large troupe of Túpac Amaru rebels from the Caynarachi basecamp arrived in the settlement just when Ángel's parents were in Lima. People claimed that Ángel, like his father, was a notorious town gossip, constantly talking about everyone's affairs. By all accounts, the MRTA rebels had entered Ángel's parents' store to request food as "cooperation." They told Demetrio*, the dim-witted younger brother of Ángel, as they approached the well-stocked store full of food and supplies, "Compañero, collaborate by giving the MRTA fifty kilos of dried fish!" Demetrio demurred, replying that his father had left the two brothers the fish for them to sell and "not give away free."

"Damn, give these starving people [*muerto de hambre*] the dried fish. They only know how to rob; they don't know how to work!" Ángel aggressively said, interrupting his younger, less verbose brother.[23] Deeply aggrieved by Ángel's petulant and rude response, the Túpac Amaru insurgents refused to receive any of the dried salt fish from the two brothers. Within a month, twenty-five MRTA members returned to the area and forcibly removed Ángel from his bedroom before holding him hostage. Ángel's kidnappers were equipped with FN FAL weapons—*arma matapato*—according to Diego, who was involved in Ángel's kidnapping.[24] He confessed to me that Ángel "was taken away by us because he was a guy who thought he was wealthy and a big shot. He disrespected a group of MRTA *compañeros* in Nuevo Libertad so we apprehended him while he was still in his bed!"[25]

Ángel was taken prisoner by the Túpac Amaru Revolutionary Movement, who then transported him on foot through the forest to Huicungo, where Commander El Grillo was waiting to receive the rebel delegates. Ángel was informed by El Grillo that he had been abducted for disciplinary reasons and would be sent to the Túpac Amaru's rebel encampment in El Porvenir. El Grillo told Ángel that he had referred to the "people's movement" as thieves rather than working with them. Ángel was reprimanded by El Grillo for failing to acknowledge the MRTA leaders as legitimate politicians who were offering the people an alternative to the stale and corrupt politics of the past.

With the information that Ángel was still being held captive and that El Grillo had mandated his punishment, Julián and the two teachers Franco and Don Wilder returned to the village. Demetrio was watching Julián's long wooden boat approach the dock. He appealed to Julián, Wilder, and Franco and requested their help once more. Speaking for his entire family, Demetrio asked if they would return and make the difficult forest trek and lengthy river journey to secure the release of his older brother from the custody of the MRTA. His family had received an anonymous letter (*carta anónima*) demanding a sizable ransom for Ángel's release.[26]

After considering the perils of a return expedition, they reluctantly agreed. Then, Don Wilder took the rescue team by motorboat (*peque-peque*) the next morning to reach the *fundo* of Don Alberto*. That is where Julián said they encountered the Túpac Amaru platoon that had Ángel captive. It was only Julián, and the teachers, Franco and Ángel's brother-in-law Don Wilder, who were trying to bargain for his release—"the rest of the community was too frightened to try such a daring task," boasted Julián, pushing forward his chest. He said he was willing to take on this risk, "out of my lifelong friendship with the Romero family." As I heard from many in the region, Julián emphasized the importance of *communitas*. According to him, "when a friend is in difficulties, there is a moral obligation to help them," just as I had been told by Diego, Sandra, and Fabiano.

Julián described how he went with Don Wilder and Franco to El Porvenir to rescue Ángel.[27] In the rebels' clandestine encampment, the three were mistreated as soon as they arrived. According to Julián, they were all blindfolded and made to fear for their lives. He said: "It wasn't a simple question of Ángel being handed over. The *cumpas* threatened and taunted us by uttering, 'We have Ángel's head.'" "So how did you release Ángel, then?" I asked Julián, who seemed to relish his role as storyteller, judging by his inflated bodily movements. Beaming at me with pride for his friend, Julián affirmed: "Franco may have been a drunk [*borrachín*] but he was an articulate intellectual. I think he was a great leader; he had a different mentality and could negotiate the liberation of Ángel. He talked while we were blindfolded on a small river beach [*playa*]." "Then what?" I asked Julián, who was swatting at clouds of insects disrupting the still air draping the night that had enveloped us. "Our blindfolds were taken off and standing there before us was an entire platoon of uniformed *cumpas* at full attention waving a large Túpac Amaru flag," Julián divulged.

When they returned to their village, an army convoy was waiting to interrogate them all. Julián, Franco, and Wilder were taken in for questioning and locked up in the local jail (*calabozo*). During his liberator's interrogation, Ángel complained to the army commander that the community was constantly at the mercy of Túpac Amaru insurgents, who would arrive as they pleased, and then the army would come in hot pursuit. "*Jefe*," said Ángel, "it is as if we lived between two states—the MRTA and the Peruvian government." Julián, Franco, and Wilder's release was arranged after several villagers attested to their innocence, including the priest. Julián told me, "Thankfully the army commander was a good guy [*buena gente*] and understood what was going on, so he trusted us."

To uncover more about what had transpired with Ángel's kidnapping, I sought his mother, Doña Ximena Romero*, a stout and chunky eighty-year-old shopkeeper.[28] She was initially reluctant but after a bit of coaxing was willing to talk to me about the troubles that had beset her family, particularly when the MRTA took Ángel hostage.[29] At the time of Ángel's kidnapping, Doña Ximena, a severe but upstanding member of the community, was in Lima with her frail husband, Don Ignacio, who was ill with kidney failure.

During a long lull in customers, Doña Ximena told me in her shop, brimming with groceries, candy, inexpensive clothing, umbrellas, and brown bottles of Cristal beer, that she thought Ángel was kidnapped because of his association with the Liga Agraria, a peasant organization. Ángel had told her he had gone to the embouchure of the Caynarachi River to replace his father during the 1990 peasant strike. According to Doña Ximena, that is when the Túpac Amaru Revolutionary Movement punished some of those in attendance. "My dear son Ángel tried to defend them, men like Guillermo* who was punished by the MRTA for eating his food by himself. The *terrucos* thought that poor old Guillermo was incapable of sharing," said Doña Ximena. As punishment, they shaved the heads of Guillermo and two other men. Doña Ximena was convinced that her son heroically tried to defend these men during the peasant strike, so the MRTA kidnapped him for eight days.[30]

The gray-haired woman told me that the MRTA forced her family "to pay a war tax [*cupo*] of ten thousand *intis* for five months for Ángel's freedom."[31] In her recollection of the 1990 events, Ángel was released just as the military had sent troops to town to oversee the elections. She felt that this had spooked the MRTA; rebel members feared reprisals and freed Ángel.

According to Julián, the liberation of Ángel happened right when the populace was voting to determine whether the Departments of San Martín and La Libertad were to become a consolidated region (*macroregión*).[32] Most inhabitants of San Martín were not in favor of the *macroregión*, but a vote was scheduled. Julián remembers army troops were dispatched to the Caynarachi basin to oversee the integrity of the voting process. This is when Julián said that MRTA Commander El Grillo gave the order to release Ángel on a Friday, by which time the military had already arrived in Nuevo Libertad. Julián asserted that the leadership of the MRTA did not want to give the army a reason to come looking for them at their basecamp in El Porvenir, so they released Ángel, who went home to the comfort of his parents' house, where his mother was clutching her rosary beads while waiting intently for her son.

Doña Ximena had to return from Lima to deal with the crisis of her son's kidnapping, compelling her to leave behind her infirm husband in a city she remembers was under seize. "Sístero García arrived here in my patio one Sunday while I was reading my Bible. He was accompanied by several *tupachos*, including three *mandos*," recounted Doña Ximena.[33] She was appalled when García Torres refused to accept the validity of the ransom letter (*carta*) she showed him, telling her it lacked the party's stamp and that the signature was forged. Indeed, "Commander Ricardo insisted the *carta* was false [*bamba*]!" Doña Ximena exclaimed.

Doña Ximena first enumerated the amount of *cupos* charged for her son's release—two cattle and ten thousand *intis* to be paid in monthly quotas—and then told the commander of the Túpac Amaru rebels' Northeastern Front that she thought the anonymous letter originated from the El Porvenir encampment. "Ángel was blindfolded, so he never knew exactly where he was sequestered," Doña Xavier relayed to me just as her first customer in a while came into her shop. He was a young boy who bought a *chupete* (lollipop) and quickly departed. Doña Ximena continued to talk in the singsong tone characteristic of the region, telling me García Torres informed her he used only "watermarked" (*sello de agua*) paper. Doña Ximena's anonymous letter was penned on the wrong sort of paper. The elderly shopkeeper smiled, and her sullen dark eyes locked with mine. Looking directly forward, Doña Ximena said: "Only God knows why my son was saved. We were blessed."

Diego confirmed to me that the anonymous ransom letter sent to Doña Ximena was *bamba*, as it did not have the Túpac Amaru Revolutionary Movement logo imprinted on it.[34] He said, "Someone was trying to take advantage of the party's name, as they did before in Yumbatos." Like so many other impoverished peasants in town, Diego believed Ángel was a misbehaved "brat" (*malcriado*). While Ángel was with them in the rebel encampment, Diego said they treated him very well. "We made Ángel walk throughout the *monte* with us. Yes, that is true, and he was blindfolded and had no shoes," chuckled Diego. They gave him Túpac Amaru Revolutionary Movement texts to read to broaden his worldview." According to Diego, Ángel's behavior was good during the week or so he was with them at El Porvenir. The former MRTA rebel, Commander Razor, felt that Ángel acquired valuable insight from the experience: "He learned how it is to live in poverty." Perhaps the former guerrilla fighter relied on the explanation of "edification" to justify the kidnapping. In Diego's words, "We took him hostage so Ángel could learn how we suffered."

Then, with a broad, unsettling beam that revealed his asymmetrical teeth, Diego told me how he became friends with Ángel and remains close to him to this day. He referred to Ángel not as a "traitor of the people" (*traidor del pueblo*) but as a "good dude" (*buena pata*). For Diego, what occurred three decades ago has gone into a historical register that shapes the present. Remarkably, Diego insisted: "Ángel and I have forgiven each other after all of these years. What happened stays in the past [*este quedó en la historia*]."

Besides providing publicity for propaganda, kidnappings of prominent individuals generated ransom payments (*pagos de rescate*), which were an important source of scarce cash for the operational support of the MRTA. While the economic benefits derived from sequestering elites were notable, they paled compared to the rebels' deep involvement in the transnational illicit cocaine production and distribution industry. The rebels' provision of logistical support and security, and the backing of local coca growers, made them obvious allies for those working in the wildly profitable narcotics trade. Those involved in the illicit cocaine production and distribution network formed a strategic and reliable partnership by aligning themselves with the Túpac Amaru Revolutionary Movement rebels. By facilitating the movement of drugs, ensuring safety, and connecting with coca growers, the *tupacamaristas* proved themselves to be important allies. However, collaboration with key players in the drug trade underscored the MRTA's interconnectedness between political and criminal elements, blurring the fine line between insurgency and organized criminal activity. Despite these implicit challenges, the rebels could leverage significant resources and augment their influence, thanks to the alluring environment created by the profitable and widespread narcotics trade.

CHAPTER 7

White Gold

Cocaine is the atomic bomb of Latin America.

CARLOS LEHDER RIVAS

The Túpac Amaru rebels' guerrilla war coincided with drug traffickers in the Huallaga Valley, mainly Colombians and Peruvians who entered the area to establish shop with their bosses (*capos*), hitmen (*sicarios*), and small-scale traders (*traqueteros*). The state's failed agrarian policy provided ample political and economic incentives for the boom in coca leaf cultivation and cocaine production. A recent historical study of the Upper Huallaga persuasively shows that it was not the lack of the state, but its prior presence that enabled the rapid development of the region into a major hub for coca leaf cultivation, thanks in part to the "illusion of directing development according to its scientist plans."[1] In the late 1970s, the area had become a primary cocaine epicenter, with significant ties to Colombian drug cartels and the ever-expanding international cocaine market.[2] Despite stringent restrictions on human settlement and the freedom of mobility during the internal war in the Upper Huallaga, dynamic networks of connection persisted.

While mestizo campesinos continued to grow other licit crops, including rice, corn, beans, and coffee, coca leaf cultivation took off like wildfire, extending throughout the entire Upper Huallaga Valley and reaching into other areas of the Huallaga, such as Sisa, Picota, and the Caynarachi basin, where coca leaf cultivation as a commodity had been unknown.[3]

By the mid-1980s, coca leaf cultivation and processing had fully entered the region from the south, via the Upper Huallaga, and had become the primary productive activity of provinces such as Tocache, Bellavista, and other southern populated centers connected to Tingo María, which have historically been marginalized from the economic dynamics of the central and northern portions of the region.[4] At the end of the 1980s, estimates of the hectares dedicated in the Huallaga Valley to the cultivation of coca leaf for the production of cocaine ranged from 120,000 to 195,000.[5]

In the hot and humid climate of San Martín and Loreto, the yields and the alkaloid content of the coca plants are not as great as in the cooler, higher-altitude sectors of the Huallaga Valley, but the risks were far lower, especially while Alan García was in power during the late 1980s. Until the entrance of Alberto Fujimori as president, there had been no coca leaf defoliation campaigns directed by the US Drug Enforcement Agency. Fueling the booming drug trade were buyers from Tarapoto or as far away as Colombia (particularly members of the Medellín cartel), who would show up on horseback or by motorboat, and sometimes by small plane (*avioneta*) to make their clandestine purchases.[6] Increasing coca leaf cultivation, as well as coca paste (*pasta*) and cocaine hydrochloride (*clorhidrato de cocaína*) production, and the rebel activities of the Túpac Amaru Revolutionary Movement's Northeastern Front led to a strong military presence in the region of San Martín that would continue for more than a decade.

The level of social unrest and political violence in rural areas limited land clearance for a time, but as the situation stabilized, deforestation increased again following the government's routing of the MRTA from the Huallaga Valley. By the year 2000, about 1,644,577 hectares, or roughly a third of the Department of San Martín, had been deforested.[7] Licit crop prices had fallen. The high demand for workers to grow coca drove up wages for farm labor dedicated to traditional agricultural production. Compared with other legal crops, earnings from coca leaf cultivation offered much more in the way of stable earnings to local peasants. Residents in the Caynarachi basin, like Don Augustín, recall that at the outset of the 1990s, "they were only getting twenty-five *centavos* a kilo for corn, and this simply couldn't compete with the price offered by *cocaleros* for the purchase of coca leaf." Local *cocaleros* know that coca does well in the Huallaga Valley's poor soils, has markedly greater yields (up to four harvests annually), and does not need major inputs, relying on low-cost labor.[8]

In the 1980s and early to mid-1990s, proceeds from the Huallaga's booming coca economy funded both Sendero Luminoso and the Túpac Amaru

Revolutionary Movement, who ferociously battled each other, as well as state police and military forces, for control over the narcotics economy.[9] During the internal war, Sendero Luminoso partnered with *narcos* (particularly the Medellín *firma*) as "advocates" of local communities in areas of the Upper Huallaga, "protecting" them from the cruel and arbitrary abuses of both security officials and drug runners.[10] Sendero Luminoso established a dependent relationship with drug traffickers through imposing quotas and tariffs associated with the purchase, sale, and transport of coca leaves, raw basic paste, and cocaine hydrochloride. This created a marriage of convenience (*conveniencia*) between two actors—the Sendero Luminoso and the drug cartels.[11] Those cartel associates who disputed Sendero Luminoso's right to rule were slain in the central Peruvian rainforest and in the Upper Huallaga region.[12]

Amid the downpour of the rainy season in 2019, as we stood in the town's central square, our anticipation grew for a truck to ferry us to Yurimaguas. It was in this moment that Sandra imparted to me a chilling revelation from when the Upper Huallaga region had become a crucible of unparalleled violence and war. Because the road into town was in bad shape and the truck was running late, we had some time to converse. Sandra began telling a detailed, spine-tingling tale that delved into the darkness of evil. It was filled with tragedy and horror, taking me on a haunting journey to the shadowed resting place of a family victim of the internal war. Sandra's petrifying story revolved around her cousin, Fermín*, a young *tombo* sergeant who found himself stationed in the Upper Huallaga Valley's treacherous town of Tocache. The police sergeant did not know that this ordinary assignment would lead him into a deadly collision involving loyalty, greed, and human brutality.

As the appalling story unfolded, Sandra, a skilled orator, fashioned a vivid picture of the complex moral crossroads Fermín faced. The notorious Sendero Luminoso set their sights on the police sergeant and tried to seduce Fermín with the power of their lucrative financial offers. However, the *evangélico* (evangelical) Fermín stood firm in his commitment to uphold the law and to obey God's will, and refused to collaborate with the insurgent *narcocriminals*. Enraged by his defiance to assist them, members of Sendero Luminoso devised a sinister plan to eliminate Fermín and send a chilling message to others in Tocache who dared oppose them. Sandra relayed to me in a deadpan fashion that deep within the thick rainforests of the Upper Huallaga, they subjected Fermín to an unthinkable fate: they interred him alive. But this was no ordinary entombment. Sandra's words conjured a cold-blooded scene, describing how Fermín was made to strip off his clothes and beaten. He was then buried in the ground, forced to stand upright in his earthen tomb. The Sendero Luminoso's intention was obvious—-to ensure a slow and agonizing demise for the courageously defiant police sergeant.

Days turned into weeks, and weeks turned into months as Fermín languished in his subterranean prison. Sandra noted that the passage of time only amplified the horrors he must have endured, the solitude and darkness consuming his spirit. Quizzing me out aloud: "Bartuco, do you think it was hours, or days, before Fermín finally expired?" Sandra muttered. Taken aback by Sandra's inquiry, I found myself in a state of disbelief as she recounted the macabre details with an unwavering, matter-of-fact tone. With a heavy heart, I shook my head in sheer astonishment and met her gaze with a somber, melancholic expression. Tocache's police force, realizing Sargent Fermín's disappearance and suspecting foul play, relentlessly searched for their lost comrade. Sandra relayed how the police search party ventured deep into the forest's heart—Sendero Luminoso and *narco* territory—where death lurked in the shadows behind every tree and hillock. Finally, after an arduous odyssey through the impenetrable jungle, the police search party stumbled upon Fermín's discarded police uniform and rotting boots.

In close proximity, they discovered the twisted and ghastly remnants of Fermín's fingers protruding from the damp forest floor, distorted by the relentless embrace of decay. Fermín's putrid remains, teeming with writhing maggots, eerily bore witness to the unfathomable torment he had suffered. Sandra's macabre saga left me with a nasty sense of unease, a nauseating reminder of the monstrosities that can unfold in the sinister corners of the human soul. As I now rattled along in the dilapidated truck, bound for the old port city of Yurimaguas, my mind became consumed by Sandra's profoundly haunting tale of Fermín's final moments. Unearthed from the depths of memory, her cautionary tale serves as a stark reminder of the atrocities that occurred in the Huallaga Valley. It also operates as a testament to the indomitable spirit and courage exemplified by individuals like Sandra, who, despite carrying vivid memories of past misfortunes, demonstrate remarkable resilience by summoning the inner strength to give voice to their harrowing experiences. While ineffable and always incomplete, narrating human rights violations can kindle a flame of hope, guiding others to uncover the truth and seek justice.

With their novel forms of social control, rebels and *narcos* filled the space left by an absent state presence, enforcing their own laws and norms and overseeing security and communal justice in the Central and Lower Hua-llaga. According to the Túpac Amaru rebel commander Ricardo, the hamlet of Dos de Mayo (Huallabamba Valley) had two clandestine airstrips in June 1990 that were controlled by Colombian drug traffickers. To prevent interference or encroachment, the *narcos* extended provisions of sustenance, essential supplies, and clothing to the MRTA, ensuring a measure of appeasement and mutual tolerance. Until then, the MRTA had not established official quotas or fixed amounts per flight of drugs. Instead, the cocaine traffickers paid the local authorities.[13]

By allying with *narcos*, the MRTA sought not only revenue for bankrolling their armed struggle but also political legitimacy by providing armed defense against state efforts to eliminate coca leaf cultivation and seize drugs, as with the Sendero Luminoso. The Túpac Amaru Revolutionary Movement's political influence grew as it protected the underground economy from government interference. With the increasing significance of coca production in San Martín and the growing number of peasants relying on it, the MRTA got involved in providing essential precursor ingredients for cocaine manufacturing, including kerosene, lime, sulfuric acid, sodium carbonate, ammonia, diethyl ether, muriatic acid, and acetone.[14]

The MRTA intensified ties with drug traffickers by charging them with set war quotas—*cupos*—much like Sendero Luminoso had been doing for years throughout the Upper Huallaga. After learning of the clandestine airstrips for drug planes in Dos de Mayo, the Túpac Amaru Revolutionary Movement decided during its Third Central Unity Committee held in September 1990 to formally charge quotas for each *narco* flight that departed from areas controlled by the *tupacamaristas*. This measure began in November 1990, and within a year, four runways had been established in the Dos de Mayo (Huallabamba Valley), Sauce (San Martín Province), Bonilla (Pongo de Caynarachi), and Pampa Hermosa (Yurimaguas, Alto Amazonas, Loreto).[15] By this time, the Túpac Amaru Revolutionary Movement had obtained three small aircraft and formed an airline company, Aero Laser, for the transport of the wounded, armaments, and MRTA leaders. Aero Laser aircraft were subsequently involved in facilitating the transport of drugs on national flights, which reportedly netted the MRTA *cupos* as much as fifty-thousand dollars per air shipment.[16] According to informants, flights most often involved shipments of five hundred kilos of cocaine or cocaine base paste.

Covert landing strips offered the MRTA tangible leverage in dealings with drug traffickers. The practice of providing security and charging quotas per flight served to enhance the MRTA's military prowess by giving them access to cash for the purchase of weapons, provisions, and items of personal interest. Sources linked to the army estimate that the value of the *cupos* the MRTA charged to *narcos* reached several million dollars.[17] Some versions of former Túpac Amaru rebels claim that, ever since 1989, the local *tupacamarista mandos* charged quotas of between five thousand and ten thousand dollars for each plane flight full of drugs. According to these accounts, in 1990, an emissary of the military-political chief of the army's San Martín–Huánuco Front sought contact with the regional leaders of the Túpac Amaru Revolutionary Movement to coordinate mutual actions against the Sendero Luminoso. It is alleged that the delegate of the chief wanted the commander of the Northeastern Front to coordinate military actions against Sendero Luminoso in the valleys of Ponaza, Biavo, and Huayabamba. The head of the army's San Martín–Huánuco Front reportedly also requested that the MRTA coordinate its drug trafficking quotas with the army to control its own officers' involvement in the illicit cocaine economy.[18] The MRTA and the state's armed forces were not alone in their involvement with the cocaine bonanza. Sometimes, the *ronderos* of the Huallaga reportedly helped protect drug traffickers from criminal gangs, as well as collaborated with them by charging the *traqueteros cupos* for transporting *pasta* (unrefined cocaine paste) or refined cocaine hydrochloride out of the area.

An informant to the CVR stated the war bond was a paper emblazoned with the MRTA symbol and an amount that was to be paid by the *traqueteros*. The quota was designated by the Túpac Amaru Revolutionary Movement, which had various ways of collecting it, apart from charging *narcos,* abductions, and ambushes on the roads. Lucas Cachay Huamán told the informant that all the *cupos* were given to the MRTA because that was the standing order of the day. The Túpac Amaru informant noted: "The fact is everyone gave, so much so that in the end it was a disaster because everyone asked for everything. I'm sure that's where a lot of people made money. People took advantage of it."[19] When the *narcos* did not want to comply with the agreed-on quota, they were pressured to do so or coerced by lethal force. Failure to pay meant the *narcos* had no secure access to the undercover landing strips. Five thousand to ten thousand dollars were typically charged as a *cupo* for each flight. These funds were dispersed as follows: $1,500 to $3,000 went to the village authorities; $1,500 to $3,000 was destined for the "owner" of the runway; and $2,000 to $4,000 went directly to the MRTA.[20]

In the Caynarachi basin, the Túpac Amaru Revolutionary Movement offered armed protection, logistical support, and local intelligence for drug runners, which enhanced the *narcos'* access to the booming market. "The *narcos* always asked us for our support to act as watchman [*huachiman*] to protect their runways whenever they took their flights," declared Diego when I asked about their relations with *narcos* in the Caynarachi. He and his Túpac Amaru *camaradas* like Fabiano aided the *narcos* avoid ambushes with the army or police, who would often arrive impromptu by helicopter to confiscate their narcotics (*mercaderías*) and incarcerate all they found present. "Yes, they hired us so they would not be ambushed. We not only protected them, but we also acted as their spies and did little jobs [*chambitas*] for them," added Fabi. "All of us were guarding their airstrips and they had to pay a certain amount of money to the Party. And there was always plenty of cash involved. It was incredible the amounts we saw!" observed Diego with his wide smirk and perceptive eyes.[21]

The *cupo* they charged the *traqueteros* in the Caynarachi basin included the use and guarding of clandestine runways, like the one that transects the town's antiquated soccer field. The cash from the drug runners—up to five thousand dollars—then went into the "safe box" (*caja chica*) as a reserve for emergency needs. If a *tupacamarista* had an ill relative, he or she could apply for financial assistance to their superior. Fabiano explained that when *camaradas* made requests (*comunicados*) of this sort, "their *mando* would simply ask, 'Is there money or not in the box?'" When there were funds—five hundred or a thousand *intis*—they were usually given to assist a needy or ill comrade's family member(s). There was no expectation that the money be paid back; rather, it was to serve as a form of familial social security. To this end, Fabiano and Diego explained that at the Caynarachi basecamp, El Porvenir, there was a person designated in charge of accounting for the funds in the petty cash box.

When I asked Fabiano and Diego about their own experience with *narcos*, they both smirked sheepishly and said they were well versed in the black-market underbelly of cocaine production and distribution. Fabiano declared his friend Diego's involvement with Professor Edwin*, the former mayor of Puerto Muyuna who was heavily involved in the cocaine industry.[22] "Your right, Fabiano; Professor Edwin was just a teacher but a big *narcotráfico*," Diego continued. The cocaine-laden Tocache-Uchiza region was his stomping grounds, and thanks to his drug trafficking, he had international associates in Colombia, Brazil, Bolivia, and Mexico. "He is dead now, but he was my friend," Diego reflectively commented. Evidently, Edwin was accustomed to cultivating coca leaf and processing cocaine paste in the rainforest near Puerto Muyuna. Given that Diego had known the professor for many years, Edwin invited his former student to work with him. On several occasions, Diego recalls the high school teacher saying to him: "*Compañero*, I'm going to my coca fields [*cocales*] today. Let's go to work together, I need your help." To assist Edwin, Diego would get out of his MRTA duties by telling his comrades in El Porvenir: "Today I am going to town to see my girlfriend." Later on, when he was in charge of his own squad, he had greater freedom and could leave the camp as he pleased. Diego went to work for two or three days at a time with Edwin, who was shipping out his cocaine paste (*pasta básica de cocaina*, PBC) with the help of local drug traffickers. Given that Diego worked with Edwin, the migrants in the area thought he too was in the MRTA. As the cocaine industry burgeoned in the Huallaga Valley, it left an indelible mark on the lives of numerous individuals. However, Diego and Fabiano stood as exceptions to this trend. While they were familiar with the intricacies of *cocaine capitalisms*, their lives had not undergone profound alterations because of the boom in cocaine.[23] However, for many others, the situation was starkly different, as exemplified by the somber occurrence of an airplane crash that wrought profound metamorphoses upon the lives of those who beheld its descent from the heavens.

When Airplanes Crash

In the Caynarachi basin, two small-scale farmers Oli* and Antonio* made a considerable personal fortune when an *avioneta* crashed in their village of Yana Puma.[24] They became wealthy when cocaine paste (PBC) literally fell from the firmament.[25] They then purchased boats and hefty outboard motors and invested in large tracts of land with their ill-gotten gains. Both Oli and Antonio have established themselves in favorable positions within the local economy, allowing them both to relish a notable level of influence and authority typically associated with the esteemed ranks of the regional elite. They were able to "purchase" the PBC for a very low price—paying only a hundred dollars per kilo rather than the going market price, which was ten times that. To raise the loot, Oli and Antonio sold some of their cattle. They were able to sell the *pasta básica de cocaina* for the market price and made about six hundred thousand dollars, which they split down the middle.

The plane crashed approximately fifteen minutes away from the village of Yana Puma. First it made numerous circles overhead and almost hit some houses with *irapay* leaf (*Lepidocaryum tenue*) thatching as it sputtered smoke, and under the force of gravity, precipitously careened to the ground in Oli's undulating pasture (*pasto*). When they arrived at the smoldering crash site in the cattle paddock, Oli and Antonio discovered the Colombian pilots badly injured but still somewhat alive. Hearing all the commotion after the plane plummeted from the sky, several villagers soon gathered next to the wrecked fuselage, including the community nurse and an ex-marine. With noisy cries of pain coming from the cockpit and an agitated crowd demanding quick action, the former marine instructed the health post's nurse to inject the grievously wounded pilot and copilot with something to put them out of their bodily agony. "After all, we don't want these two walking around giving declarations to the police [*el tombo*] or to their *narco* bosses about what happened here," the ex-marine allegedly advised the nurse. No one in the crowd objected, and the Colombian pilots were euthanized with morphine. According to Fabiano, the villagers divided up the small quantity of cash they discovered in the burned-out cockpit. Oli and Antonio then convinced the crowd to let them take command of the *pasta básica de cocaína* in exchange for some of their cattle.

Within days, hitmen (*sicarios*) with names like Calavera (Skull) and Jergón (Bushmaster), arrived in the Caynarachi basin asking about the loss of six hundred kilos of their bosses' narcotics and the whereabouts of the *avioneta* "that had mysteriously dropped from the sky," said Diego.[26] The stolen cocaine paste had various owners, so rival henchmen and *sicarios* from several *firmas* were looking for their "product" (*mercadería*). Invariably, this triggered a confrontation and eventually a shootout in Yana Puma among the rival drug clans. Yana Puma by this time, had become an important transshipment hub for the regional drug economy. With the cover of MRTA protection, the *traqueteros* would make runs that included the transport of hard cash from neighboring Colombia, followed by a return flight from the Caynarachi with a load of cocaine paste. "The various *firmas* work like a *mafia* and always demand payment upfront," Fabiano told me. Yana Puma's townscape became twisted by the presence of mafioso figures, bodyguards, fearful campesinos, and gun-toting *tupacho* rebels.

The wildly profitable cocaine economy endorsed the development of new forms of governance and economic activity that acquired acknowledgment and backing from campesinos who approved of the provision of services that the state had failed to deliver over the previous decades.[27] By 1990, fifteen new bank branches had been established in the commercial center of Tarapoto, indicating the amount of money being "laundered."

The introduction of cable TV, the sight of individuals donning designer clothing, and luxurious new vehicles on the streets became unmistakable indicators that shed light on the remarkable purchasing power of the nouveau riche. These conspicuous displays of wealth and opulence served as tangible evidence of the thriving shadow cocaine economy that had firmly taken hold in the Central and Lower Huallaga region.[28] Despite being unevenly distributed, this wealth reached the Caynarachi basin in the form of a diverse array of consumer goods. These included high-value items such as refrigerators, electrical generators, motorcycles, chainsaws, boat motors, weapons, as well as smaller electronics like radios and cassette players. Additionally, the availability of alcohol, clothing, fuel, commercially prepared food, medicines, cologne and perfume, watches, and shoes also increased in the region.

A generation after the crash of the cocaine bonanza, Diego, like many others I interviewed, said the same people who were *cocaleros* in the ugly times continue growing coca leaves, despite the odds being heavily stacked against them. "I don't see a major improvement in their lives," Diego insisted when telling me about his cousins and uncles who have been *cocaleros* for multiple generations. "They seem worse off than I am. I don't have coca plants, but I grow cacao. San Martín has the best chocolate in the world, you know, *bróder!*" Whenever he pays his cousins and uncle a visit in Puerto Muyuna, he asks them, "What are you still doing with this way of life? You spend more time drinking alcohol than working!" Diego was told by his cousins that the only thing they had to conceal was their own genius. Through juxtaposing the notion of intellectual brilliance and the possession of illicit substances, his cousins, following in the footsteps of Oscar Wilde, injected a touch of irony and absurdity into their discourse. With a curious pride, they regaled him with accounts of the numerous kilograms of cocaine within their grasp, creating a paradoxical blend of intellectual and illicit pursuits.[29]

With the introduction of cocaine, many became addicted (*fumones*) to smoking PBC and lost hope. It became a trap to grow and consume, and as Diego was quick to observe, "Cocaine was part of the disintegration of the Túpac Amaru Revolutionary Movement, especially when Fujimori came to power and the *Gringos* helped him crush us." The shadow economy that revolved around the cultivation, processing, and transportation of coca leaf, cocaine paste, and cocaine hydrochloride provided a convenient means for the rebels to replenish their coffers. Referred to as "white gold" (*oro blanco*), the illicit trade in cocaine and its associated products (including precursor ingredients) offered a steady stream of much-needed revenue. However, the MRTA's reliance on an illegal and highly profitable industry came at a considerable cost—it corroded the rebel organization from within and eroded the integrity of its leadership structure. Despite the corrupting influence of the drug trade, a significant number of rebels steadfastly held onto their unwavering commitment to the Túpac Amaru Revolutionary Movement's political and military objectives. This was evidenced by the audacious and striking July 25, 1990, assault on Yurimaguas. The rebels demonstrated their unwavering dedication to their cause, braving great risks and deploying their forces spectacularly.

CHAPTER 8

Attack on the "Pearl of the Huallaga"

Yurimaguas

Like a limpid jewel,
in a green case,
smiling rises majestic and stately,
oh dream city,
giant's craft,
that the poets call,
the pearl of the Huallaga.

ATILIO VÁSQUEZ ALEGRÍA

As head of the Northeastern Front, Commander Ricardo contacted the Regional Directorate and informed them of the order to work on plans to storm Yurimaguas, a strategic city, that had an important river port, a bishopric, and an old neo-Gothic Catholic cathedral. Unlike the upper or middle stretches of the Huallaga Valley, which are in San Martín and Huánuco, Yurimaguas is located in the Department of Loreto (Alto Amazonas Province), in the relatively hotter and more humid lowland jungle (*selva baja*) of Peru's vast rainforested territories. Given the virtual nonexistence of terrestrial access at the time to the town of approximately forty thousand, the city was defended by a naval base, which was a key military aim of the MRTA's attack.[1]

Before the ambush, Diego was intimately involved in conducting a pre-assault study on Yurimaguas that lasted for about six or seven months. When I questioned him about the complexity of the armed incursion into

Yurimaguas, Mando Razor remarked, "Ah . . . to successfully pull that assault off—there was first a detailed study by people who came specifically to help us make a plan for the attack."[2] Beforehand, they searched for relatives or a family member working for the police to covertly gather intelligence in the area. The rebels secretly surveyed how many troops were stationed in Yurimaguas, the weaponry they possessed, and their defensive positions. In sum, the *tupacamaristas* conducted a thorough intelligence study, including detailed diagrams and maps of the town's urban layout. Security measures were well planned and strict, both within the cells and on an individual level. As Diego was quick to stress, "Bartuco, you just don't attack a certain province or district without this type of crucial, detailed information, which must be kept completely secret at all times."[3] They established more or less how many police officers were posted in Yurimaguas and how many marines were in the naval base on the Paranapura River. They determined where enemy troops were stationed and the locations of strategic entrances and viable escape routes.

The Túpac Amaru insurgents were well prepared as they made their way en masse to Yurimaguas, the "Pearl of the Huallaga."[4] Their morale was outstanding, they were heavily armed, and they had an elaborate plan of attack and retreat developed through the meticulous gathering of actionable intelligence. The rebels approached Yurimaguas with three robust columns of about 120 combatants, leaving one column in Huayabamba with roughly 60 men so that after taking Yurimaguas they could assault the city of Bellavista. Commander Ricardo thought this would oblige the army to disperse its forces and hence minimize their attacks on rebel forces. The MRTA planned to capture Yurimaguas on July 23. However, the Lima-based National Directorate informed the rebels that forty-eight comrades from the Túpac Amaru Revolutionary Movement had just escaped Miguel Castro y Castro Penitentiary, a high-security, "escape-proof" prison known as Canto Grande (Big Rock), San Juan de Lurigancho, Lima.[5] News of the July 9, 1990 escape came to the Northeastern Front rebels as they were arranging for the assault on Yurimaguas. While preparing for battle, Sístero García Torres received a call from Víctor Polay Campos, who was part of the daring prison escape. Once liberated, Commander Polay Campos ordered him to delay the attack on Yurimaguas. Polay Campos did not want a successful Northeastern Front assault on the primary town on the Lower Huallaga to garner widespread media attention and compete with news of the rebels' audacious tunnel escape from the notorious maximum-security prison.[6]

Despite Polay Campos's directives, García Torres and the other leader-ship members chose not to follow them and instead conducted the arranged attack. After a few more days of preparation, García Torres informed his soldiers that the attack on Yurimaguas had to be the most impressive pos-sible, with the potential of capturing national and perhaps even interna-tional attention. To take Yurimaguas, the Pearl of the Huallaga, the most experienced Túpac Amaru *milicianos* were asked to join the *tupacamarista* guerrilla troops.[7] The combatants arranged for motorboats to ferry the Tupacamarista People's Army troops downriver to Yarina, a small village that had an operational airfield. The rebels waited for information on the most recent intelligence reports coming in from Yurimaguas from their MRTA comrades while they were in Yarina. They also prepared for mem-bers of the Túpac Amaru Revolutionary Movement's Regional Directorate, who would bring additional ammunition, a repair part for the single MAG .30 machine gun in their possession, and money for food to feed the rebel commandos. They established attack teams and containment commandos, and they assigned people to be in charge of explosives while in Yarina. The Túpac Amaru rebels had access to their scouts' report that showed there were sixty marines, thirty members of the Technical Police (Policía Técnica), thirty men from the Republican Guard (Guardia Republicana), twenty guarding the prison, and twenty-five members of the Civil Guard (Guardia Civil).[8] While the state's armed forces had numerical strength, the surprise factor was on the side of the MRTA rebel forces.[9]

Commander Ricardo brought together the various Northeastern Front *mandos* in Yarina, where they collectively agreed on the final details of the plan to take Yurimaguas.[10] The *tupacamaristas* embarked in four motor-boats they had been commandeered from the small agrarian community. To evade detection on their way down the Huallaga River, the rebels hud-dled under plastic tarps and disguised themselves as cargo. The insurgents finally reached the larger village of Shucshuyacu (Alto Amazonas Province, Teniente César López Rojas District) at about 8 p.m. Once there, they stashed their supplies, had a meal, and coordinated a sizable rally with the inhabitants of Shucshuyacu, which is just a short motorboat ride upriver from Yurimaguas. Given its proximity to their objective target, MRTA commanders decided that their approach to the Yurimaguas port would be done with their boat's motor engines turned off. Letting their boats flow with the current prevented any suspicion from the Coast Guard.[11] While those combatants who traveled by boat met up in Shucshuyacu, Diego re-called other MRTA platoons from Juanjuí, Sauce, and Chazuta arrived in

FIGURE 13. Miguel Castro y Castro prison before the MRTA's
tunnel escape, photo by Yana-Colección Desco

Yurimaguas by road. He remembered many insurgents convened in the village of Pampa Hermosa, a rebel stronghold, before proceeding in trucks along the bumpy dirt roadway that ended at Yurimaguas.[12]

At the break of dawn on July 25, the military operation began as Commander Puma and his platoon of forty highly skilled rebel soldiers arrived at the river port via boat. Their aim was to storm the naval garrison and secure the strategic location. Commander Puma and his troops alighted from the boat and made their way toward the enemy naval base. Leading his detachment, Commander Puma and his men embarked on a Volvo truck and proceeded toward the naval facility situated approximately six kilometers away from the port. Those *tupacamaristas* in charge of attacking the Republican Guard and the prison boarded another vehicle and went toward the center of Yurimaguas, where various offices and shops surrounded the municipal square. Soon, the early morning serenity of the sleepy town was shattered by the roar of explosives, rocket-propelled grenades, Kalashnikov PKM machine-gun fire, SVD Dragunov sniper rifles, dynamite, and the frantic discharge of small firearms. All the while, billows of thick fumes obscured the tropical cerulean skyline, which soon turned murky with the impervious fog of warfare. The columns of smoke, with their dark and ominous hues, formed an eerie contrast against the lush green canvas of Yurimaguas's surrounding landscape. Video recordings of the assault reveal a thick haze obstructing the sun's power to shine its golden morning rays on the city-scape.[13] The fires that decimated parts of central Yurimaguas, according to the various accounts I gathered, started in the first block of Bolívar Street, right next to the Plaza de Armas, where the courthouse stood watch. While certain sources in Yurimaguas firmly asserted that the MRTA engaged in breaking storefront doors and played a role in facilitating the extensive plundering that occurred during the city assault, video recordings present a broader pattern of general looting.

The bombardment and shooting lasted from the time the MRTA arrived in town—from about 5 a.m. until roughly three hours later, when the MRTA conducted a political rally in the city's Plaza de Armas. Commander Ricardo reported that his *subcomandantes* were in position, but Commander Puma delayed too much—increasing the possibility of detection—and thus the MRTA lost the surprise factor in attacking the naval base.[14] Talking to Puma via walkie-talkie, Commander Ricardo learned his comrade was still in transit. Meanwhile, he heard from Ramón, the Túpac Amaru rebel tasked with taking control of the city's Policía Técnica, that he was only five meters from their post and feared being detected by the foe. Commander Ricardo told Ramón he would send Puma to his rescue. However, pinned down, Ramón communicated back to his commander, telling him in a muffled and anxious voice that two heavily armed police had just arrived.[15]

The rebels climbed to the tops of commercial and government buildings, facilitating the immobilization of the police, who barricaded themselves in their garrisons. In the middle of the gun battle in front of the police station, the MRTA yelled for the police to surrender. The police shouted back: "Let your mother surrender! And with profanity." Losing patience, Commander Ricardo ordered his explosives expert to fire a rocket-propelled grenade inside the police commissary. However, the MRTA munitions specialist told his commander he did not have the correct propellants. "I will excuse the *compañero* because maybe it was an error," said Sístero García Torres, but after talking to his colleague Commander Puma, the explosive expert's fate changed. Puma told Commander Ricardo that the marines were refusing to surrender. Rather than breaching the base with a bombardment of grenades, Commander Puma told García Torres that the explosives guy had the wrong propellants. "This is not by chance, there is an infiltrator, *gato encerrado*," said Commander Ricardo.[16] After thirty minutes of intense bombardment with grenades and gunfire, the MRTA demanded the surrender of the police, most of whom fled. The MRTA took captive six Republican Guards, two Civilian Guards, and four Technical Police.[17]

FIGURE 14. MRTA armaments decommissioned in San Martín, photo by Alarse-Colección Desco

Mando Razor was part of the first wave of Túpac Amaru Revolutionary Movement rebels to ambush the police forces in Yurimaguas.[18] His commando included eight other Túpac Amaru *compañeros*. He recalled that the armed fighting raged for over three hours in town, but the sacking of the police stations, he said, took only thirty-sixty minutes. "The entire police surrendered rapidly," Diego crowed, "perhaps thinking of their families. They came out with their hands up, waving white flags." With little experience and a lack of professional training, the *tombo* force was not militarily prepared for the lightning-bolt incursion of the MRTA. After their rapid fall and the capture of a large stash of police weapons and ammo, Diego was sent by Commander Ricardo, along with a group of fifteen Túpac Amaru comrades, at around 8 a.m., to help reinforce Commander Puma's final efforts to take the naval base.[19] Their attempt to capture the Harbor Master's Office proved futile as the insurgents faced formidable opposition from the resolute naval personnel, who valiantly withstood a barrage of extreme gunfire. During the two hours of violent confrontation, First Corporal from Peru's Coast Guard, Siomar Noriega Torres, perished in combat during the MRTA's effort to seize control of the Captaincy of the Port (Capitanía de Puerto) of Yurimaguas.[20] Nevertheless, the rebel's attempts at gaining any momentum were steadfastly repelled by the marines, who mortally wounded two of Diego's MRTA comrades.[21] Despite heavy MRTA rocket bombardment, Commander Ricardo's forces were powerless to take the heavily fortified naval base, where strong resistance resulted in at least fourteen wounded, some critically. Despite these setbacks during the assault on Yurimaguas, the Túpac Amaru Revolutionary Movement captured twelve police officers, took over two hundred weapons, and seized a large quantity of ammunition.[22]

Under Commander Ricardo's orders, Diego was tasked with reporting police activity to the various *mandos*, including his boss, Commander El Grillo. Meanwhile, Fabi had traveled from Nuevo Libertad to Yurimaguas some three or four days beforehand.[23] As a well-trained, committed *miliciano*, Fabiano helped the Túpac Amaru sympathizers distribute locally produced propaganda leaflets (*volantes*) and paint walls with *tupacamarista* symbols and political slogans such as "With the masses and the weapons, homeland or death . . . we will win!" (*Con las masas y las armas, patria o muerte . . . ¡venceremos!*). He had participated in his first taste of frontline militant work in May 1988, during the MRTA's fierce takeover of the secluded hamlet of Pucate*. While Fabiano's associates spent their time handing out food and conducting a political meeting, he and a group of six others militants spent two hours painting Túpac Amaru Revolutionary Movement graffiti with shades of bright red and black paint on the walls of Pucate, a secluded agricultural settlement located roughly five kilometers from the awe-inspiring Pucayacu waterfalls*.[24]

During the assault on Yurimaguas, Fabiano assisted in corralling stunned citizens into the historic town's main square—the Plaza de Armas—to attend a Túpac Amaru Revolutionary Movement meeting that was slated to begin commence when the cathedral clock struck 8 a.m. In the pandemonium of the assault, Fabiano remembered that "crazed people began looting the shops, including the Chinese merchants [*comerciantes*]. It was quite a spectacle. They stole all the bolts of fabric from the merchants, and the crowds burned down the Prosecutor's Office [*Fiscalía*], court [*juzgado*], and police station [*comisaría*]. Entire city blocks were on fire and the smoke filled the sky."[25] Diego said this happened after the *tupacamaristas* had attacked the prison in Yurimaguas and let out the convicts before burning the jail to the ground. "But the *cumpas* forgot to release a prisoner who was in the *calabozo* [stockade] and he was burned to death," Fabiano lamented.

The Túpac Amaru meeting was convened in the Plaza de Armas right in front of the police prisoners who were on public display before the residents, many of whom had gathered to gawk at the spectacular novelty of the events unfolding before them. Nothing like this had ever happened in the city, which was shocked by the MRTA incursion. In due course the bishop was summoned to receive the twelve police prisoners whose safe release was entrusted to the church before the expectant crowd.[26] Meanwhile, the Northeastern Front insurgents had been in communication with the MRTA's regional and national leadership and were informed that two helicopters of army commandos were on their way from Tarapoto to reinforce the marines' defense of the navy base. This prompted Sístero García Torres to promptly order his rebel troops to retreat from battle.[27]

During the military strike on Yurimaguas, eleven Túpac Amaru rebels were wounded, five seriously. One MRTA guerrilla had had his jaw blown off, three had leg or foot wounds, and one had a broken arm. The MRTA requested support from the Red Cross for the care and surgical intervention of their injured and were provided with three doctors, surgical equipment, supplies, and medicines. By around 11 a.m., the MRTA had retreated to the village of Shucshuyacu, in the nearby department of Teniente César López Rojas. The rebels remained there until night while medical attention was given to the wounded at the village's health center. The guerrilla fighters then had to contend with menacing army attack helicopters hovering over them as they made their retreat from Shucshuyacu. The fatigued rebels arrived the following day in the Caynarachi basin, where there was a landing strip used by small aircraft for the transport of the severely wounded, who were then flown to Sauce. From the town of Sauce, the wounded were sent overland to the city of Tarapoto, where they received specialized care in clandestine clinics. Sometimes, the recovery of wounded Túpac Amaru combatants took months.[28]

When recounting the Túpac Amaru rebels' assault on Yurimaguas, Diego recalled being overwhelmed by seeing so many casualties at the naval base. He spoke about two injured combatants who were first sent to Nuevo Libertad in the Caynarachi basin and then retrieved by a small airplane (*avioneta*) and flown on to Sauce for road transport to Tarapoto. He remembered them being smuggled in the back of a new Volvo truck past military checkpoints. They were admitted into the Tarpoto general hospital as transit accident victims, not as war combatants, which would have sparked unwanted questions from the police. After intently listening, Fabi added: "We were careful about that. We had medical contacts in the city [of Tarapoto] who would provide medical aid." Whenever they had a medical emergency, such as a wounded person, Diego and Fabiano said they would call on the *narcos* to transport them by airplane to Tarapoto for medical assistance. Fabiano recounted how they "would line up their injured comrades, like well-arranged bundles of firewood," in front of the *narcos'* airstrips, and the drug runners would collect the wounded in their shiny planes for transport to distant medical facilities. In San Martín and portions of Loreto, the Túpac Amaru Revolutionary Movement enjoyed the support of some doctors and surgeons. Moreover, the medical community also had family members who were active members of the MRTA and the EPT.

Retreat from the Future

The rebels' military retreat and decline began after "the taking of Yurimaguas" (*la tomada de Yurimaguas*), said Diego, when most detachments from the Caynarachi basin withdrew via the El Porvenir route because that supply line took them to Chazuta, in the tropical Andes.[29] Diego's detachment, forced into a desperate retreat along the winding river, was relentlessly pursued by the heavily armed military, their gunship helicopters hovering ominously above. In a desperate bid for survival, they eventually embarked on a treacherous escape on foot, disappearing into the unforgiving embrace of the *selva*.[30] The MRTA rebels intended to eventually make their way to the towns of Sauce, Picota, and Juanjuí—and then to disperse into smaller, mobile groups to evade detection, capture, and death. "That was our strategy, to fully retreat and disperse the Túpac Amaru platoons to evade easy detection," Mando Razor recounted. Those who were not severely wounded first forded the Yarina Stream*, made their way through the rainforest to the outskirts of the community of Marupa, and then the groups made their way across the Caynarachi River to establish a provisional camp for the night. The following morning, they were off again in the *monte*, finally making their way to the rebels' rainforest encampment at El Porvenir.

After regrouping at El Porvenir, they eagerly waited for several hours for their comrades-in-arms to join them. This included those insurgents who had been slightly injured and were able, with some help, to make the overland journey to El Porvenir. While Diego and the rest of his haggard platoon remained anxiously awaiting, an advance party of three or four MRTA members went a few hours ahead to provide the rest of the group with reconnaissance information for the retreat route. Any hostile encounter with the army would be with the much smaller advance Túpac Amaru patrol party. If the military engaged the MRTA scout unit in battle, the rest of the detachment would hear gunfire, alerting them to enemy combatants. According to Diego, Túpac Amaru foot soldiers also used gunshots as codes.

Before they traveled to the Caynarachi basin, some *tupacamaristas* first went to rendezvous with their commander, Sístero García Torres, whom they retrieved from the community of Shucshuyacu. They then retreated to Nuevo Libertad, the community in the Caynarachi where "two-faced" Julián was waiting near the landing strip for the arrival of an *avioneta* to transport the injured from the attack on Yurimaguas. "We had to support the MRTA so we could prevent a battle with the military," declared Julián.[31] According to various versions, over two hundred Túpac Amaru Revolutionary Movement rebels and *milicianos* descended on the Caynarachi basin following the takeover of Yurimaguas. "Many of the wounded were all shot up, some with badly mangled limbs and blood-soaked, long-sleeved green shirts. Then a small plane arrived and took away the most severely wounded. Where to, we don't know," Doña Regina told me.[32]

Comandante Ricardo appeared and reportedly stayed in town until almost 5:00 that afternoon. By nightfall, an army convoy had arrived in the settlement in hot pursuit of the rebels who had absconded into the Caynarachi's forests. The MRTA had brought a lot of loot with them from sacking the shops in Yurimaguas, including a scale and various medicines. Before the arrival of the army commandos from Tarapoto, assorted items were distributed by the *tupacamaristas* among the town's meager population as they frantically entered the main square. The MRTA was interested in the armaments (AKMs, pistols, revolvers, grenades, machine guns, and FALs) in Yurimaguas, all of which were transported to the jungle encampments for subsequent dispersal to *tupacamarista* columns. Diego recounted how his comrades who were not wounded took the "liberated weapons" (*armas liberadas*) to the camp at El Porvenir to hide them in various caches.[33] He recalled their leader, Commander Ricardo, and the subcommanders arriving in Huicungo with their platoon to oversee the operation and to rejoice in their triumph. While they had suffered casualties and could not take the naval base, they had stormed Yurimaguas by surprise, overtaken its police forces, and gotten substantial quantities of arms and ammo. Like his comrades, Mando Razor said he "felt the future at that point in time was theirs. The MRTA was going to build a new society. We would be victorious." I then asked Diego, "So what happened to your victory? Why was the MRTA defeated?" Looking askance, Diego reflected for a moment and then half-whispered, "Our retreat led to defeat, to the demise of the Túpac Amaru Revolutionary Movement."

CHAPTER 9

The End of the Future

El Porvenir

The military had surrounded the *cumpas*.
This made it tough for most of them to flee. They were a spent force.

DON AUGUSTÍN

"Do you like soccer, *bróder*?" asked Diego one day as we watched the local team play against a rival village. We were alone, and it was twilight. The biting insects were teeming, but the gentle breeze was helping prevent them from landing on their human prey. Nodding my head in agreement, I told him, "*Ay, amigo*. I do, but I can't play very well." The fulgid sun was in the slow process of setting, and Diego seemed quite relaxed, so I inquired about what he knew about the MRTA's confrontation in El Porvenir. "Do you know anything about that clash?" I queried, hoping to turn our exchange to what I thought years ago was the beginning of the ugly times.[1]

Slowly looking up toward me, Diego said, "Yes, there was a big confrontation at the Túpac Amaru base right after our victorious takeover of Yurimaguas back in 1990." Could Diego tell me what happened since he said he was there? Who was the confrontation with, I wondered? "Was the battle with rebels and the police, the soldiers, or between different insurgent factions?" Diego paused and then stoically answered: "It was us—the Túpac Amaru Revolutionary Movement—against the soldiers, the police, the Dirección Antidrogas de la Policía Nacional del Perú [antidrug police], and the army. It was a living hell for us. We all thought we were going to die. I thought it was the end."

"Were there casualties?" I inquired. The soccer game was wrapping up, but Diego continued to talk with his eyes glued to mine. "No, thank God not. The army only recovered some of our weaponry and ammo, but they discovered our jungle camp in the Caynarachi. A group of comrades that were still guarding the encampment was captured, and they were taken away. I'm not sure what happened to them," said Diego. It all occurred in the middle of the jungle, approximately three hours from El Porvenir's basecamp, "along a path where few could reach us in the jungle. It was near the *caserío* walking toward Yana Puma."

With renewed intensity in his voice, Diego recounted how the population of the hamlet of El Porvenir paid the human consequences. He said the army was in the mood for retaliation following the Túpac Amaru rebels' successful attack on Yurimaguas. Diego chronicled how the army went from house to house in the village of El Porvenir accusing innocent residents of being members or collaborators with the MRTA. The consequences for some were dire, and several residents from El Porvenir were never heard from again.

Don Augustín told me how the army was able to find the guerrilla basecamp. Apparently, the armed forces captured a guy from El Porvenir who eventually informed them where the *cumpas'* camp was.[2] They forced him to put on an MRTA uniform and take them to the encampment. This allowed the military to have the upper hand and to surround the Túpac Amaru rebels. They tried to escape but many could not, as they had been circled by the armed forces. The culmination of the attack came with the aerial bombardment of the encampment. While the forward operating base was vacant, the thunderous sound of the bombs rang throughout the basin, sending fear into many. No longer did the Túpac Amaru Revolutionary Movement have a secure base of operations in El Porvenir—forcing rebel soldiers like Diego to return to the hardships of life on the run in the rainforest.

Degradation

Internal conflicts within the Túpac Amaru Revolutionary Movement were exacerbated when, in August 1992, the Fujimori government enacted Decree Law No. 25666880, creating the San Martín Region.[3] This led to irreconcilable differences as to how to continue the work of the Frente de Defensa de los Intereses de la Provincia de San Martín, or FEDIPSM and that of the MRTA in the region. Lucas Cachay Huamán argued the MRTA should strengthen its active presence in civil society, but his proposal was not well received by the directorate of the MRTA, which advanced militaristic positions, opening different guerrilla fronts in the center (Junín) and south of the country (Puno). The MRTA intimidated Cachay Huamán and several FEDIPSM leaders with death threats to ensure their subordination to the new militancy of the movement. In the middle of these threats from their former comrades—not to mention from the armed forces—Lucas Cachay Huamán and Cecilia Oviedo Huapaya were forced to travel to Lima in 1992 and seek asylum at the Mexican embassy.[4]

The MRTA's conflict in San Martín with Fujimori's government unleashed state violence that served to "entrench social hierarchies and elite power."[5] The operations of the Northeastern Front were severely diminished as a result of Fujimori's intensified counterinsurgency efforts and the recapture of Víctor Polay Campos in 1992 in Huancayo, a few months before the September capture of Sendero Luminoso's supreme leader, Abimael Guzmán Reynoso. Under Fujimori's orders, countersubversive forces directly affected the continuity of the leftist social movement and organizations in the Central Huallaga. In fewer than fifteen months, leaders such as Segundo Centurión Pérez (secretary-general of the Forest Teachers Agrarian Federation—Federación Agraria Selva Maestra, FASMA), Héctor García Neira, and Javier Tuanama were all arrested and tried by military courts. Other leaders, like Lucas Cachay Huamán (secretary-general of FEDIPSM), Óscar Pinto (regional secretary of Sindicato Único de Trabajadores de San Martín, SUTESM), and Manuel Arévalo (FEDIPSM press secretary), among others, left Peru to avoid being arrested or disappeared.[6]

A testimonial collected by the Truth and Reconciliation Commission (CVR) from a resident of San José de Sisa illustrates the transformations leading to the decline of the Túpac Amaru Revolutionary Movement: "From 1990, the MRTA was no longer the same. They no longer used money or paid for what they took. They seemed like other people; at first, educated people arrived. Later on, the rebels were adolescent boys and delinquents. In my store, they stole a lot of things, and every weekend they asked [for more] and stole our products that they were going to need for their people. Thus, they made us poor."[7] Fast money was spoiling the youth and destroying the sense of community. Envy, resentment, and robbery among neighbors were on the increase. Teachers began reporting high dropout rates in secondary schools thanks to the shadow cocaine economy, addiction, and the psychosocial ravages of the internal war.

Significant disagreements emerged with the frequent change in commands from Túpac Amaru comrades from the outside, primarily Lima, with scant knowledge of the regional dynamics and different cultural understandings about how to develop the revolutionary support of the masses. When I spoke with former Túpac Amaru members or sympathizers, such as Sandra, Diego, and Fabiano, they all felt frustrated by the transformations that the Túpac Amaru Revolutionary Movement eventually heralded in the Caynarachi. "It was a period of great promise for social progress, but it ended as a failure," explained Sandra when we all had convened one late afternoon at Fabiano's home.[8] "Yes, the MRTA was an alternative to the corruption of the police and the criminal judicial system," continued Fabiano, "as well as the entire capitalist system."[9] Diego then chimed in: "We failed when the killings began. And then thieves, delinquents, and assassins entered our ranks, many of them fugitives from the law. They became refugees in the MRTA, and this mix of people did not end well." Sandra lamented that the Túpac Amaru Revolutionary Movement's plan of "wiping out all the corrupt ones failed; corruption continues to this day."

They all came to agree that the movement was destroyed when the MRTA began threatening communities, stealing, raping, and killing *brujos* (shamans) and gay people.[10] The rebels' violent practices were historically novel for the residents of the Caynarachi basin, who failed to see them in terms of purported retaliatory equivalences. Many remain steadfast in their belief that there needed to be a systematic follow-up on the human rights violations that occurred in the Central and Lower Huallaga during the internal war, including those committed against Túpac Amaru sympathizers and combatants.[11]

In the general assemblies at the province and district levels, Diego, Fabi, and Sandra confirmed people were indeed forced to march and sing Túpac Amaru Revolutionary Movement anthems—like "Himno a Túpac Amaru."[12] They readily acknowledged that numerous locals were frightened and coerced to attend political rallies. During the popular assemblies, the political commander (*mando político*) would give talks to the entire community about the party's ideology and the objectives of the MRTA.

During our conversations, Sandra, Fabiano, and Diego told me that *tupacamarista* soldiers and sympathizers were used as "peons" (*peones*) for the educated, urban-based MRTA leadership. Many were scantily educated. Most did not know how to read and write, whereas those who held higher positions within the party's hierarchy had high school, university, or technical college training. They were the ones who gave the courses or workshops (*talleres*) that comprised oral presentations to the illiterate members.

Looking at Sandra, Fabiano, and me, Diego stated that most of the rebels he knew "did not know exactly why they were fighting. They did not know the direction we were going with the *lucha armada* and what our goal was. It's sad." Gazing toward the distant, resplendent horizon, Diego uttered, "We were only kids when I think about it." Many were offered money, intoned Sandra, who said they "were all enslaved to the movement. We had to sleep in the forest, only in hammocks without homes. We suffered from cold nights and hungry days. We were nothing more than *things* to them; they didn't care about us as people." Listening patiently, Fabiano followed up by saying that the Túpac Amaru leadership became more concerned with protecting their economic interests when they promoted inequitable patterns of labor control. There were ideological differences, power struggles, arguments over the distribution of the *cupos* for the *jefes* and not them. They fought mostly over economic issues. Quarrels were common regarding the amounts of *cupos* being shared among individuals and groups. "Why are we getting less," was a common refrain among those who squabbled about money. Some wanted economic equality, while others were disturbed about the extrajudicial killings, especially in those instances where no investigation had been conducted. "We became like Sendero Luminoso, liquidating without asking what was really going on," volunteered Diego.

A relationship of servitude framed my interlocutors' commentaries regarding leaders like Comandante Rolando—not to mention regional or local commanders, such as El Grillo and Ricardo, who they noted benefited from the proceeds of ill-gotten gains, as indicated by their current wealth.[13] In the Tarapoto-based Regional Directorate, there was a group in charge of managing MRTA funds. These operatives typically lived in the city, as they supplied the guerrilla detachments with provisions: food, clothing, boots, medicine. As described by Mando Razor and Comandante Ricardo, each platoon chief had reserve money that was to be used for the purchase of food provisions and supplies. But as Comandante Ricardo noted, the MRTA rebels asked for "donations."[14] Subsequently, their practice of looting trade centers, collecting *cupos*, kidnapping, and extorting predominated.[15] Under the MRTA's watch, the distinction between public and private became scrambled, resulting in increased everyday violence associated with the accumulation of public wealth for private means. Moreover, the insurgents' close association with *narcos* undercut their ideological claims, corrupted the movement's management structure, and contributed to the failure of the rebels' Northeastern Front.

The Túpac Amaru Revolutionary Movement suffered with the shift in the quality of rebel recruits. As Fabiano perspicaciously noted: "At the outset of the armed struggle, it was easy for the teachers to convince naïve, fifteen- and sixteen-year-olds from the rural zone to follow the ideological calls of the MRTA. In those days, we didn't have access to communication, telephones, or televisions, as we do now. People lived in ignorance of the outside world." At the beginning of the armed struggle, several guerrilla recruits had just completed their military service. For many of these MRTA recruits, their time in the military had broadened their prospects beyond their natal communities, making it difficult for them to rejoin tranquil agrarian life and priming them to join the rebel brigades.[16]

Over time, many unprepared people began joining the ranks of the Túpac Amaru Revolutionary Movement "and thought with a gun they were in charge and could do as they please," remarked Sandra. Diego noted that many of the recruits to the MRTA in the latter part of the armed conflict were criminals and fugitives. This corresponds to the surge in reports of Túpac Amaru rebels abusing young women in towns and villages, damaging the reputation and moral legitimacy of the insurgency. In the Caynarachi basin, the local population did not truck with this behavior. Invariably, the rebels' erstwhile supporters began reevaluating the moral underpinnings of the MRTA. In the words of Fabiano, "The people became our enemies rather than our allies."

In addition to their intimate ties with drug trafficking, gross human rights violations alienated the regional populace from the MRTA. To wit, the murders of "undesirables," such as thieves, drug addicts, sex workers, and gay people, as well as the assassination of peasants accused of belonging to another political group, such as Sendero Luminoso or grassroots agrarian organizations, undermined popular support. Meanwhile, cleavages within the ranks of the Túpac Amaru Revolutionary Movement emerged, illustrated by the growing number of members accused of being traitors or snitches who were then summarily disappeared in unmarked graves.[17]

With the mounting conflict in the Caynarachi basin, more people turned against the *tupacamaristas*.[18] My ex-MRTA interlocutors felt that the "cleanup" (*limpieza*) period when they began meting out punishment to the "enemies of the people" in the communities of base support—traitor or informants (*traidores* or *soplones*), gay or bisexual men (*chivos, maricones, doble filos*), transvestite or transgendered people (*travesti*), thieves (*ladrones, rateros, choros*), traditional healers (*brujos, curanderos,* or *médicos*), adulterers (*saca vuelteros, daña cumbas,* and *runamulas*), and the lazy (*haraganes*)—was when things got completely out of control. Naked violence became a major driving force of an insurrectional movement whose power had begun to slip away. Hannah Arendt saw violence emerging when power is threatened. She astutely observed that when violence runs amok and is "left to its course, it ends in power's disappearance."[19] The MRTA's insurrection was the activity of an armed group of people shaped by ideologies that champion social liberation and global justice that ironically generated repression and violent persecution, leading to social fragmentation and enduring trauma. Indeed, the unchecked violence meted out by the MRTA undermined the basis of power among the rebel group's erstwhile or potential supporters.

El Grillo's Capture and Diego's Defeat

El Grillo, Diego's commander, was captured while traveling to Tarapoto to purchase medicine with his wife, who was also an active member of the Túpac Amaru Revolutionary Movement.[20] El Grillo told Diego that he and his wife were on their way back to San Miguel de Achinamiza.[21] Diego advised them that the army was patrolling in Chazuta and to be careful not to run in with the armed forces or the autonomous civil peasant patrols (*rondas campesinas*) and their members, known colloquially as *ronderos*. But El Grillo and his wife didn't heed their comrade's advice. Upon their arrival in San Miguel de Achinamiza, a village situated nearby the settlements of Shilcayo and Yanayoc in the Province of Lamas, they were promptly captured by the *ronderos*, who wanted to hand them over to the army to be disappeared. But El Grillo had heard a broadcast from Radio Tropical about the Law of Repentance (Ley de Repentimiento). By the end of the internal war, when the MRTA was under siege, numerous of its leaders availed themselves of the 1993 law.

This was Commander El Grillo's plan. He was an articulate orator and persuaded the *ronderos* not to hand them over to the military unless they reported they were repentant (*arrepentido*). He told the civil patrol watchmen they would be rewarded for turning them in to the authorities. Animated by financial gain, the *ronderos* were keen to get the reward offered for the capture of El Grillo, a *mando*—which Diego thought was set at 140,000 *intis*. Before being handed over to the military, El Grillo convinced the *ronderos* to take him and his wife to the parish church. In so doing, El Grillo guaranteed their safety. Their petitions for repentance were accepted, and the processing of their paperwork began under the auspices of the church.[22]

Diego's version of the capture of El Grillo and his wife corresponds in many respects to a local news account of his commander's capture by Achinamiza's civil patrol. Ruperto Pilco, who was an adviser to Achinamiza's

FIGURE 15. Flags, books, and belongings seized from the MRTA
in San Martín, photo by Alarse-Colección Desco

ronda campesina stated that Andrés Mendoza del Águila, a.k.a. Commander
Grillo, went to turn himself in at Pilco's home. According to Pilco's account, El Grillo had heard his mother implore her son to hand himself over
to the army. When he was captured, the local *ronderos* wanted to perform
popular justice on both Ruperto Pilco and El Grillo. They were then beaten
and El Grillo tortured. The *ronderos* apparently transferred the MRTA couple to Tarapoto to collect the financial reward offered for El Grillo's capture. First, though, they took him to San Juan del Cumbaza, where his
mother lived. She welcomed them, but in some sort of oversight, El Grillo
was then taken to the nearby military camp. Ruperto Pilco spoke with
General Bellido Mora, who let him know that El Grillo turned himself in
at his home in Achinamiza, and he wanted to collect the reward. Bellido
Mora, the political-military chief of the area, promised to review his case,
but Pilco never got a reply to his request. According to Pilco's version, he
even spoke with El Grillo himself, but he did not give importance to the
case either.[23] Diego said that the pastoral center (*centro pastoral*) was given
the reward, whereas the *ronderos* from the community of Achinamiza got
nothing for capturing Diego or Mando Razor's former boss.

Images of the pastoral center evoke recollections of the apocalyptic
night Diego heard the news broadcast on Radio Tropical that their leader,

El Grillo, had surrendered and was going to repent. At that time, Diego was in charge of the shipment of thirty Belgian made AKM weapons destined for the detachment in the Caynarachi. However, news of El Grillo's capture sank in quickly and changed the course of Diego's plans and his membership in the armed insurgency. Upon hearing the stunning news, he convened a meeting and said to his Túpac Amaru *compañeros*, "Hey, El Grillo has repented and turned himself in to the army. It seems as if he has betrayed us!" Diego's companion, Miguel Angel, a.k.a. Comrade Sapo*, turned in agreement to the group of rebels assembled. Comrade Sapo began encouraging them "to kill the traitor Grillo because he has fucking betrayed the party."

Diego recalled soothing his comrade Sapo's rage, telling him to quiet down and not be too foolish. "What can we do if he has been captured and wants to repent? Sapo, what will killing him do?" emphasized Diego. The capture gave way to demoralization for Diego and his *compañeros*. Many of the Túpac Amaru Revolutionary Movement leaders were dead or in prison, like García Torres.[24] The ferocity of Fujimori's counterinsurgency campaign had taken a heavy toll on the Túpac Amaru's leadership and rank-and-file membership. By the time Diego began noting MRTA platoon leaders' acceptance of the law of repentance, many rebels had already deserted. They were, in his words, tired and all suffering from psychosis; they were "*psicosiados*, always preparing for war." The former leader of the Northeastern Front, Sístero García Torres, announced his formal split from the Túpac Amaru Revolutionary Movement on January 22, 1992, along with approximately 120 of his guerrilla soldiers.

Life as a rebel fighter in the Huallaga Valley became increasingly difficult with declining community support and growing persecution by antisubversive forces; hunger and the dread of being captured came to predominate their existence. The ultimate psychological blow was El Grillo's capture, which led Diego to decide to lay down his gun and tell himself and his rebel companions that the MRTA's revolutionary war had failed. He confided to his comrades, "*Our forest treks have all been a waste of time!*"[25] Diego claimed that his companions initially expressed shock after hearing him announce that the *lucha armada* had ended. Comrade Sapo yelled out to the group: "How is it possible that Mando Razor is giving up?" Following a heated debate with his frustrated rebel troops, Diego told them he was simply too tired to go on fighting. "The *lucha armada* is over, we cannot win against our enemies," he stated emphatically, and he told his dispirited companions he was going to avail himself of the law of repentance promulgated by the Fujimori regime. He did not believe the army would harm them if they approached town without their AKM rifles and simultaneously volunteered to turn themselves in. After much cajoling and discussing the challenges of continued guerrilla warfare, Diego persuaded his junior comrades—including Comrade Sapo—to join him in surrendering. Renouncing the Túpac Amaru Revolutionary Movement's armed struggle allowed them to leave behind the grueling life of being a rebel fighter in the rainforest. Collectively, Mando Razor and his ten companions, nine men and one woman, accepted defeat and turned themselves into the army commandos stationed in Nuevo Libertad.[26] When he recounted the surrender of his rebel troops, Diego emphasized the personal sacrifices involved in the revolutionary struggle. With defiant confidence, he stated that "Only the person carrying the flag knows its weight."[27]

Diego revealed how the rebels had to first cross the Caynarachi River before traveling a short distance from the harbor to the heart of the town. When the rebel boat arrived into port, Doña Lola*, the village's town crier (*habladora*), was on the embankment. As the Túpac Amaru rebels traversed the waterway and approached the muddy outskirts of the settlement next to the river's edge, the portly fishmonger in her early sixties looked on. Diego remembered how his eagle-eyed aunt Lola screeched loudly: "*Asu!* God, the *terrucos* are coming [to town]. There is going to be a shooting!"[28]

In response to the mutually starling encounter, Diego told the alarmed Doña Lola, "Calm down, auntie. It's me, your nephew Diego." By this time, the counterinsurgent special force troops had spotted Mando Razor's group on the river's embankment. An army officer gruffly bellowed to them: "Who are you? What are you doing here?" From the gathering crowd came a tremulous voice, "They are the terrorists!" Another villager shouted, "They are the *tupachos* from upriver who have been attacking us! Get them before they escape or attack us. Don't trust any of them!" Diego claimed that he continued up the incline toward the priest's house in the middle of the hamlet unfazed. He was resolved to inform the parish priest that he and his fellow MRTA members had come to town to lay down their weapons, repent, and reintegrate into society. In other words, they desired to make use of the Law of Repentance.

Diego recalled that the town priest welcomed them with a smile and even ordered one of his subordinates to make mugs brimming with piping hot coffee for the starving rebels. The priest then went outside to communicate with the army commandos, who by that point had encircled the entire home and church and were assuming an aggressive position. The priest inquired of the soldiers posted outside the church who was in charge of the armed forces. Eleven members of the Túpac Amaru Revolutionary Movement, he said, were prepared to lay down their weapons and wanted to apply for the Law of Repentance.

Diego recalled a petulant lieutenant by the name of Paco* coming inside the priest's lodgings and telling them: "I am a *jefe*, but not the *máximo jefe*. The boss here is Major Pachas Quispe*—he is in charge of this counterinsurgency operation." Lieutenant Paco left to fetch his boss, who quickly showed up at the priest's sparsely furnished home. The priest's spartan living space contained a few wooden shelves full of a large collection of books and disheveled papers, a typewriter, a large electric fan, a gas-powered generator, and a crucifix obliquely fastened to the wall. Diego remembers how Major Pachas Quispe stood below the cross and asked him and his comrades if they had brought their weapons with them. "Yes, we have, but we left them on the other side of the river, hidden in the embankment," Diego said, glancing at the major in the elusive play of light reflecting from the crucifix on the wall. Mando Razor told the military that they had thirty crates of weapons and ammunition, including bullets, grenades, dynamite, handguns, revolvers, and AKMs, that they were prepared to hand over to the army commandos.

Major Pachas Quispe asked, "How do I know this isn't a trap?" and "Why should I believe you?" The major wondered aloud how many of his troops he would lose if the weapons were booby-trapped. Diego explained that he and his companions had come to reintegrate themselves into society; "otherwise, why would we have put our lives in danger?" Diego pushed the major and questioned him why he believed the rebels had not given the order to ambush the troops from the opposite side of the Caynarachi River. He reminded the army major they did "have thirty AKMs in their possession." Diego made a point of describing how Major Pachas Quispe kept asking: "Why should I believe you? How can I be sure it's not a trap?" Diego replied, "I will go with your soldiers to show them." However, the reserved major was in no hurry to change his mind. Major Pachas Quispe addressed Mando Razor and his other rebels, asking, "Why should I send my people to be bait in an MRTA trap?" Diego asked the priest to attest to his moral character. The priest knew Diego was a *mando* in the MRTA and that he was carrying firearms. When he got to the church, he told the major that he believed Diego. The priest informed the incredulous major that Diego and his comrades were prepared to lie down their weapons and make amends for their nefarious deeds as active Túpac Amaru members.

Major Pachas Quispe remained hesitant despite the priest's assurances, but he said: "OK, let's proceed in groups, in patrol formation. Two may go first, followed by four, then six." Diego told the major: "You have your war strategy. Follow what you want. For my part, we could go and get them and bring them back." Once more, Major Pachas Quispe inquired with seriousness, seeking reassurance about weapons and ammunition. Diego confirmed they did indeed have various armaments and ammunition, including five thousand rounds in thirty backpacks. The major exclaimed gleefully, "*¡A su madre!*" After the stakes had increased with the revelation of the magnitude of the arms stock, the major followed Diego. Despite his previous request, Major Pachas Quispe demanded the priest's endorsement yet again. Diego claimed that he then informed Major Pachas Quispe, somewhat angrily: "We left the weapons outside of the village to turn ourselves in first. We will go and get them. If not, they can just stay where they are and rust in the rain."

The major listened for a moment, and Diego said he could see his posture and facial expression slowly change. In a staccato voice, the commanding officer sternly barked: "All right, you fucking *terrucos*. Now pay attention to what I have to say. You have run out of time to bargain." He gave Diego and his companions fifteen minutes to gather the weapons and ammunition. Army troops would supervise them, and they would then be collected by a transport helicopter and taken to the military base at Morales in Tarapoto. Diego, who "was scared shitless" (*casi me cago de susto*), challenged the major about his assurance that the army would not drop them from the helicopter into the Huallaga River or Sauce's Laguna Azul, as they had done with so many other people they wished to erase. "We know you have disappeared many people in bags, dumping them from the helicopters to the *monte* and rivers below," Diego recalled telling his captors. Mando Razor and his ten MRTA companions were assured of their safety by the town's priest, who vouched for their security on behalf of the government. Diego recalls the army major shouting in the priest's vast chamber, with the echoes muffled by the wooden shelves of books, mountains of documents, and the creamy colored wattle and daub walls, "If you are missing, the priest will undoubtedly condemn us to the Inter-American Commission of Human Rights," retorted the major.[29] Diego said during that fleeting moment, it provided him with a semblance of security, although he recognized it to be fragile and unsubstantial.

The former logistics commander and quartermaster, Mando Razor, along with his companions, achieved their plan of trading weapons for the opportunity to reintegrate into civil society. Broken by combat, they felt compelled to take this course of action. So, Diego and his companions were escorted by an army major and his soldiers, who also recovered the guns before handing them over to the military. Diego and his comrades surrendered in July 1994, showing their belief in the Law of Repentance to grant them redemption. Despite harboring palpable fears for the future, Diego's unwavering decision to place faith in the Law of Repentance exemplified his courage, conviction, and resolute determination to seek forgiveness. As Diego remarked: "Without that law, we would have been defenseless; they could have tossed us out of those helicopters in bags. There was just no guarantee for our lives without the Repentance Law."

Diego told me his MRTA *compañeros* exemplified what he called "all the forgotten little hamlets of the Huallaga." But it was more than geography that bound the rebel fighters together; they were all united in their deep awareness of "social resentment" (*resentimiento social*). In discussing the Túpac Amaru rebels' ideology, Diego said he believed, much like the party that, "the capitalist system was a well of frustration for the Peruvian youth."[30] Diego described how his *compañeros* were people who had suffered; they had grown resentful, some with a single parent, or who had been orphaned or emotionally cast aside and left to languish in an economically unforgiving world. Many of the MRTA recruits had problems in their homes or among members of their extended family networks; they were victims of neglect, violence, abuse, sexual violation, and all sorts of depravations and traumas, which primed them to be defiant youth seeking better lives. But that was all over, said Diego, as he was put on public display in Nuevo Libertad by the army, he experienced a twisted sense of "pleasure" upon being captured, perhaps because he saw it as the conclusion of his agonizing ordeal. As he waited, with his wrists bound and his head draped in a black cloth hood, Diego said he sweated profusely while visions of Ramírez's demise filled his head. His imagined future was dominated by dread and forlorn resignation. Diego claims that these terrifying thoughts were put to rest when he heard a helicopter's distinctive resonant humming sound off in the distance. The sound grew louder and louder, its rhythmic blades slicing through the air with a rising crescendo, letting Diego and his comrades know it was coming soon. Swiftly, the helicopter descended upon the soccer field next to the town's market, sweeping up the rebels with no pomp or circumstance, all while a tempestuous flurry of leaves and market refuse swirled around them.

Once in the steel belly of the transport helicopter, Diego recalled being seated between two other *compañeros* while soldiers defended the entryway.

He said they thought that if one of them was thrown out of the helicopter, the other comrades would take the soldiers down with them. With low visibility and unsure of their location, they were all apprehensive. Diego and the others became tense as the soldiers eventually started conversing with the rebels in the middle of the flight. Upon arrival in Tarapoto, the national press was awaiting them. Once his cloth hood was taken off, Diego could see the surrounding crowds at the airport, which relieved him. He was in the public's eye again, and this finally made him feel safe after years on the run. "I no longer was gripped by the fear of being liquidated by the military or a paramilitary death squad (*matones*)," Diego recounted.

Their gamble had paid off. Diego and his small detachment from the Caynarachi basin were transported via helicopter to the army base in Morales without incident. As they deboarded, they noticed what appeared to be hundreds of *compañeros*. Perhaps this is because they were almost the very last of those to avail themselves of the Law of Repentance. In the captive group were both Túpac Amaru Revolutionary Movement and Sendero Luminoso insurgents from the Huallaga Valley. When Diego turned himself in, he had to opt to apply for repentance or go to prison. The former logistics commander opted for repentance.

Diego found himself confined at Leoncio Prado, the distinguished military institution in Lima's port of Callao, renowned for its literary portrayal by Nobel laureate Mario Vargas Llosa.[31] Diego endured an arduous eight-month period, a chapter in his life filled with vivid memories of great personal sacrifice. Amid the backdrop of learning about a "foreign way of life in Lima," he grappled with an undercurrent of monotony and a deep yearning for the comforts of home. After the first few days, the novelty of life in the Lima military barracks soon wore off. Diego and his companions became incredibly restless. They longed to return to their homes in the rainforest, but they wanted to normalize their legal situation first. They were no longer clandestine or in imminent danger for their lives. "We knew the military battles were over," Diego related, "and that was a relief." The ex-combatants went through an intensive "rehabilitation" program for their reincorporation into civilian life. Three times a week they had psychotherapy sessions with psychologists and psychiatrists assigned to the rehabilitation efforts. Social workers were designated to assist them in obtaining employment and counseled them on how to reintegrate back into civil society. Diego detailed how he and his *compañeros* "were all psychologically traumatized, and we were told that we had been brainwashed. We did not want to return to the armed struggle. And we participated in

many talks [*charlas*] and workshops [*talleres*]." Unlike the easygoing former
Túpac Amaru sympathizer Fabiano, who had put much of the past behind
him when I met him, Diego was still distressed by his exposure to the violence of guerrilla warfare. When detained at Leoncio Prado, Diego suffered
from intense confusion, anxiety, splitting headaches, and mild depression.[32]

To break the tedium of their detainment, the ex-rebels visited tourist
sites in Lima—including the National Soccer Coliseum and various armed
forces installations, like the navy base the Marina de Guerra and the Es-
cuela Técnica (the Military Technical School). These organized outings
helped shift Diego's view of the armed conflict. He said that he and his
former comrades realized that a small minority group such as the Túpac
Amaru Revolutionary Movement could never topple the Peruvian state,
with its access to incredible firepower and resources to liquidate the rebels,
such as the missiles they saw at the Grau military base. "History was not
on our side," he told me with deep resignation. Those who knew about
armaments were impressed with what they saw during their tours of the
Peruvian Armed Forces' installations. "The state was too powerful, while
the MRTA could not seek international aid like the Peruvian government
as it has with the USA," he said.

Eventually, after eight months of rehabilitation, the *procuradora anti-
terrorista* (antiterrorist attorney) ordered Diego's release, along with what
he calculated was some 2,500 ex-MRTA guerrillas. Diego remembered officials from Fujimori's government carting them around Lima in buses. Each
one of them was issued an official Certificate of Repentance for Terrorism
Crimes. He was given a civilian contractor job at the army fort—with a
low but stable wage. Despite opportunities to remain in Lima and avail
himself of employment and educational opportunities nonexistent in the
Caynarachi basin, Diego yearned to return to his village and to his community. Most importantly, he said, he had left a pregnant woman behind who
he loved, and he wanted to marry her and "return to a normal life, like before the war." Diego also had coca leaf plantations (*cocales*) in Nuevo Libertad, so he returned to the village. However, when he arrived back home,
he found all his *cocales* were dead, having been fumigated. This is precisely
why Diego switched to licit crops, most notably cacao, coffee, and plantains. "When I returned to the village, I found all of my *cocales* had dried
up and were dead. They had been fumigated by the Drug Enforcement
Agency [of the United States], which destroyed the land for twenty-five
years. That's why production has finally returned to how it was in the old
days. Things have returned to the way they were in the past," said Diego,

as he expressed trepidation about his family's future economic and social well-being in this new reality. Political violence in Peru continues because of the persistence of structural violence as a ruthless model of capitalism combined with deep ethnic inequality and classism, which has hampered the development of a national project that is truly inclusive.

Postwar Life

Diego, who has been fighting for a fair and equal society for years, expressed his disappointment that things have not improved and are in fact worse now for campesinos than when he first joined the MRTA.[33] "Others who left the MRTA became common criminals—assailants [*asaltantes*] and delinquents [*delincuentes*]. That's for those who love easy cash for the good life," Diego recounted to me in August 2019, on life after his return to the jungle following his "reeducation" in Lima. Despite his efforts to erase his troubled past, Diego said it always was following him. He was invited to take part in several illegal "jobs," as they would say, with his former MRTA *compañeros*, including road assaults and bank robberies. Diego recalled how a few years earlier he was in Yurimaguas bringing his plantains on a raft to sell when he encountered in the port a former Túpac Amaru rebel *compañero*, Manuel a.k.a. "Scorpion,"* who exclaimed, "Hey, how great is God, it's Mando Razor" (*Oye, ¿qué grande es Dios? es Mando Razor*).

Scorpion invited his pal Razor to have a *chela*, a beer with him at a nearby cantina. But first, Scorpion wanted to talk to him about a business proposition (*una chamba* or "a job") in Datem, along the lower Marañón River. Given its distant locale from the city, Diego assumed that the *chamba* had something to do with the petroleum exploration and extraction companies working in the area, or perhaps felling trees for the thriving black-market trade in valuable hardwoods. With this in mind, Diego went to Scorpion's hostel room to hear what the job entailed. "The *chamba* is next Friday. They are depositing four million soles in the National Bank [Banco de la Nación] for the monthly pay of state workers," Scorpion told his former *compañero*, who listened with incredulity. Diego learned that only nine police were stationed in the town of Datem—and the assailants would number ten. Scorpion told Diego that three police officers patrolled during the day, while the other officers rotated working the night and early morning shifts. Scorpion and his bandits were planning on using a 250-horsepower boat motor, which they felt could easily outrun the police's 150-horsepower motor.

As far as Scorpion was concerned, the scheme was straightforward and in-volved limited risk. In his words, their plan was "to assault the Banco de la Nación and get the cash! It will be easy. Have confidence in me, Razor."

"You shit, that is a bad idea," intoned Diego, who said to Scorpion: "I can't be part of your crazy plan. I have a family, a wife, and a young three-year-old son [hijito]. I am not interested in becoming a thief [choro]. I came to Yurimaguas only to sell my plantains, and that's what I have done. I'm going to leave," he stressed. "You don't want to accompany us?" growled Scorpion. "Come on. We are ten, so we would each get four hundred thou-sand soles [lucas]." But Diego demurred again: "No, I am not interested in that type of work." "Look, we have AKMs," said Scorpion, who lifted the mattress of his double bed to reveal machineguns. Scorpion urged Diego to take his pick. "No, I refuse," Diego insisted, holding his ground under the pressure of his former compañero. Scorpion began threatening Diego to be "deaf, silent, and blind [sordo, callado y ciego]." He told him, "If anything happens, we will look for you knowing you were a snitch." Disgruntled, both Diego and Scorpion left the hostel and returned to the bar-bodega and sat down to drink beer. "I have shown you all the jewels" (joyas), said Scor-pion, in code for the guns. "Are you sure you don't want to buy a jewel?"

One of the other drinkers became irate and threatened Diego drunk-enly, his eyes bulging and bloodshot. "You are thinking poorly of me, my friend," Diego said to the drunken man. "I'm mudo [literally "mute"]. Take the job if you believe it to be worthwhile," continued Diego. When he requested the beer tab [hacer chancha], Diego's MRTA companions de-murred.[34] As he departed into the darkness of the night, the would-be thieves told him they would pay for the beer. In the subsequent week, Diego received a jolting revelation through a radio news broadcast, learn-ing that the Datem bank robbery had turned into a catastrophic event. The disheartening news brought to Diego's attention the grim reality that two of his Túpac Amaru comrades had met their tragic fate during the assault, including his comrade Scorpion. "They didn't even get one sol," he re-counted in disbelief. Diego told me he would always "prefer to earn five to ten soles each day rather than robbing," despite how difficult (dura) life is. He had animals and crops in his chacra, plus there was a ton of wild game and a vast array of highly useful flora in the monte.

With a sweeping motion akin to the graceful arc of a raised sword, Diego conveyed his unyielding devotion to the majestic land of Peru. In a weighty homage to the fallen words of the leftist poet Javier Heraud Pérez, he artic-ulated his resolute commitment to "speak and defend her with my life."[35]

While vanquished, Diego insisted that his involvement with the Túpac Amaru Revolutionary Movement's struggle was noble. "Yes, we had lost the war, but I thank God I am still living. And I learned how to fight against injustice," he told me proudly. "Things will be different if the state actually did something for us," Diego said. He attributed the lack of state presence to the continued growth of a *narcoestado*, or drug state. Diego criticized the influence of global capitalists, saying they "have supplied no model of development for the small-scale farmer," which has led to an agrarian crisis during his entire adult life. "Why do we not have good roads? Schools? Health facilities?" he asked. We said our goodbyes, and he told me: "The state is just not present in the region, which is why we're forgotten and all the wealth is owned by a tiny few."

CHAPTER 10

Memory, Silence, and the Narration of Violence

Not all human distance is absence, nor is all silence oblivion.

SANDRA

The personal and collective narratives of warfare violence and life histories assembled in this book show that the followers of the Túpac Amaru Revolutionary Movement—the *tupacamaristas*—turned the Caynarachi basin into a base of secure rebel operations during the late 1980s and early 1990s. It's crucial to emphasize that "memory work" in this context should not be interpreted as straightforward reflections on "flat" chronological events, but as a much more complex type of artistry that lies at the very heart of what it is to be human. Long ago Halbwachs noted we preserve history, which improves collective memory.[1] For instance, historical sites, religious icons, and literary works all serve as reminders of earlier times and impact our memories. Yet the organization of community memory by political actors is part and parcel of the politics of memory, a partisan process through which events are recalled, noted, and/or ignored for posterity's sake.[2] The capacity for remembrance is essential for maintaining long-term social connections. This is partially because of human expectations of reciprocity, which call for a greater memory for favors or unfinished business.[3] These recollections play a significant role in determining whether someone will engage with others in the future, as they impact a person's reputation.

Talking about the deeds of the Túpac Amaru Revolutionary Movement and the Peruvian government's attempts to ruthlessly eradicate them in the

FIGURE 16. Weapons confiscated from the MRTA, including weapons with which the government palace was attacked in Lima, photo by Alarse-Colección Desco

Huallaga Valley was, to put it mildly, challenging. Most locals who were old enough to remember the internal war told me they had no interest in discussing it. They wished to steer clear of such subjects that appeared unimportant to their life. "The *cumpas* are all dead and gone. So, what does it matter now?" they would ask me. Many were silent, verbally obfuscating the convoluted echoes of the past. They simply wanted to forget the nasty memories of what some referred to as the ugly times, the *tiempos feos*, while others—rather than erasure, denial, or amnesia—sought to bracket off this period as the time of the terrorists (*tiempo de los terrucos*) when acts of heroism triumphed over maleficence, egoism, and sheer brutality. Even those who kindly agreed to talk with me about the *tiempos feos* were hesitant to do so in front of others. Many people had strong, agonizing memories of events where concealment and monitoring had taken on new, powerful connotations that frequently led to confrontation or quieter kinds of daily violence that were occasionally exposed in vulgar displays of savage behavior. Loose lips led to accusations of being a *soplón* (snitch) or an *espía* (a spy)—resulting in one's merciless departure. Certainly, the Caynarachi basin was no stranger to the impunity of injustice during the internal conflict, which, as I have shown, pitted the *cumpas* against state security forces in a perpetual and ferocious game of cat-and-mouse warfare.

As I engaged in numerous heartfelt conversations with my interlocutors, a profound realization emerged from the depths of this sublimely beautiful region of the tropics. Amid the fabric of lived experiences, the resilient individuals living in the Central and Lower Huallaga Valleys have gained a deep understanding that life, even in the face of overwhelming adversity, hardship, and heartbreak, possesses an unwavering spirit that propels them forward on their unyielding journey. The internal war shaped people's capacity for cultural persistence through forceful transformation, which is preserved in the shared memories that circulate today. Even while the stories of periods of communal sorrow, sadness, and personal loss show a certain amount of resiliency, the people who live in this part of northeastern Peru still have to handle the fact that truth and reconciliation are still phantom ideals.

In recognizing the voices of the community members who were involved in the culture of violence that brought together a wide cast of social actors with divergent interests, it would be inappropriate to interpret their narratives of trauma and violence as a simple reflection of what happened during the ugly times. Each actor had an individual perspective on the history of the MRTA in the Lower and Central Huallaga, which was influenced by a variety of things, such as identity and experiences, economic interests, status, political beliefs, spiritual convictions, and the whims of history.

For some people who were caught up in the mayhem and social death associated with the MRTA's guerrilla activities, the state security force's abusive counterinsurgency campaign, and the shadow *narco* economy, the very desire to persevere has come at the price of silence and a conscious forgetting of warfare trauma.[4] Many people in the Lower and Central Huallaga Valleys find themselves in a state of limbo, experiencing fear, and feeling socially isolated. They are trapped in a labyrinth of personal and collective pasts, unable to break free from the contradictory emotions that overwhelm them. Many find themselves stuck in the past because of memories that have caused confusion and obscured their ability to perceive meaningfully the present and clearly imagine a better future. In these situations, murkiness breeds mistrust, suspicion, and rejection—of the Peruvian state, of the official figures included in the Truth and Reconciliation Commission's final report, of the perpetrators and the victims of the indiscriminate violence and terror.[5] Most importantly—it thwarts a society's ability to uphold the restitution of rights and social harmony. After the war, "justice talk," "memory projects," "reconciliation," the confessional desires for Enlightenment-based "truths," and anticorruption campaigns all prompted a series of national dialogues—and pointed local silences—among a diverse set of stakeholders who had been affected by the armed conflict.

A review of the ethnographic work on the silence of survivors of violent trauma reveals that victims' understanding of competing, irreconcilable realms of atrocities is ineffable: they circumvent semantic fields and conscious articulation.[6] Ethnographically motivated anthropology is well adapted to the complex evidence systems of survivors, perpetrators, and the reconstruction of moral topographies. The image of pain and its ineffability draws attention to the necessary but brittle connection between the expressive vocabulary of memory and human suffering. The experience of bearing witness to human rights violations, not to mention perpetuating or being a victim of abuses, invariably seeks expression in discursive modes that frequently fail simple ethnographic translation. Perhaps not surprisingly, a deafening silence continues to characterize efforts to come to terms with the internal war in Peruvian Amazonia.

In the Caynarachi basin, there are too many acute silences associated with nonexistent demands for justice and truth for those affected by wartime violence. Muteness or defensive denials of remembering or recognizing prior relationships that individuals had with the Túpac Amaru Revolutionary Movement, or violent efforts to eradicate them, were all too common among those interviewed. There is no representative umbrella organization in the Caynarachi basin that has brought together victims and their families to act as an interlocutor with the state and to promote awareness raising among civil society about the internal war and the history of systematic human rights violations with those who are directly affected by warfare violence.

Nine testimonies gathered by the Truth and Reconciliation Commission in Tocache, San Martín, were the subject of an anthropological study that revealed how former Túpac Amaru members have kept quiet out of fear that the state or other agents could sue them.[7] This exemplifies some of the Truth and Reconciliation Commission's limitations, which include the fact that its final report is not an exhaustive examination of all the violent social phenomena that emerged throughout the war. Because the report did not include all people affected by political violence, including ex-*senderistas* and former MRTA members, there cannot be a complete national reconciliation.[8] Nor did the report try to be exhaustive, leaving large swaths of the country poorly investigated, namely Peruvian Amazonia. Similar to the Caynarachi basin, analysis of the memories of people in Tocache highlights the psychosocial effects of war violence that have materialized as disruptive experiences that harm communal and individual life and lead to suffering that transcends time. This is clear in how traumatized individuals view themselves, their culture, and—more challenging—their ability to meaningfully interact with others.[9]

Partisan Anthropology, Empathy, and Reconciliation

Too many people have decided to do without generosity to practice charity.

ALBERT CAMUS

Albert Camus's 1956 novel *The Fall*, which explores themes of innocence, social solidarity, and the purported truth of nonexistence, serves as a startling reminder of the modernist and postmodernist anxiety, alienation, and anomie that so many people in the world experience. But the individualistic and collective malaise gripping growing numbers of humanity implores engaged—or, I have argued, *partisan*—anthropologists, to join those committed to taking seriously the mandate of human liberation dedicated to imagining, as well as practicing novel forms of social relations predicated on mutuality, tolerance, and a shared sense of collective empathy.[1] To do otherwise means living in the Hobbesian world of aggression and violence that marks our times will continue ad infinitum. Fortunately, postulating a world in which cultural difference is not only respected but also actively promoted as a driving force in contemporary anthropological engagements with those traumatized by war, natural disasters, or the pathos of poverty, pestilence, and ignorance.[2]

Ethnographic fieldwork on human rights abuses in the Huallaga Valley provoke complex questions regarding ethical engagement. G. Derrick Hodge has highlighted ethical concerns, emphasizing greater methodological rigor and a more nuanced commitment toward, "the well-being of the communities with whom we work."[3] Clearly, the "well-being of the communities" I studied was and continues to be at stake, thus prompting efforts to assuage the sequelae of violent encounters. In the Huallaga Valley, my most difficult and humbling intellectual and emotional work has had little to do with violence. It has required helping those who have been labeled "terrorists," the victims of human rights abuses, or those who have been found guilty of horrible crimes feel completely alive and accepted in the world. This is a concept that is both revolutionary and optimistic. It has involved showing that each of them is deserving and that their self-respect is inherent.

As I delved deeper into my own narrow anthropological pursuits in the Huallaga Valley, I found myself irresistibly drawn into the visceral realm of dark tales depicting merciless and harrowing encounters. Along the ethnographic journey, empathy got in the way at every step. It exhorted me to express acts of kindness for the aggrieved and injured and to help others in times of need. In each case, the intention was not to harm but to understand, especially regarding the alleged offenders. Considering anthropology's intellectual legacy of primitivism and its failure to adequately address mass violence and its dreadful aftermath, I learned that one of the most significant acts of social justice one can commit is to embrace partisan, engaged, public anthropology.[4]

Kimberly Theidon, following the pioneering work of Nancy Scheper-Hughes, describes the "role of committed witness" as a requisite for those engaged anthropologists working in war and post-conflict zones.[5] Here, it is important to emphasize the role those recent humanitarian interventions—both large- and small-scale—have played in influencing how people currently understand various types of violence, including intimate, structural, and coercive. But in doing so, we raise thorny issues and ethical dilemmas regarding "humanitarian engagement" in violent conflict situations and post-conflict peacemaking initiatives. To wit, anthropologists, humanitarian aid workers, and those involved in "development work" more broadly frequently have a limited understanding of the reasons, moral economies, and emotional tendencies that underlie people's motivations for engaging in or rejecting violent encounters, let alone those who are caught in the crossfire or the hazy world of post-conflict reconciliation.

Some victims of grievous human rights abuses can be rehumanized by recounting their woeful stories of trauma, even if they are narratives of inexorable suffering and loss. This was true for Fabiano and Sandra, but not for Magdalena, whose brother Eduardo, a small-time *choro*, was brutally

FIGURE 17. Counter-Terrorist Directorate (Dirección contra el Terrorismo, DIRCOTE) photograph of presumed members of the MRTA, among them a detained journalist from the MRTA's newspaper *Semanario Cambio*, photo by Alarse-Colección Desco

murdered by the military, or for Diego, the former rebel *mando* who complains of lingering psychic scars that manifest as unpleasant dreams, intrusive thoughts about the violent past, episodic paranoia, and what he calls an emotional "hollowness" (*vacío emocional*) after the insurgents' defeat. While he participated in "reintegration" workshops in Lima, Diego noted that no such event was ever organized among the local inhabitants, illustrating the challenges facing the investigation of human rights abuses, let alone fostering communal dialogue, commemoration, and reconciliation.

Ethnography based on long-term fieldwork has persuasively provided a series of ruminations on the inevitable contradictions of Occidentalist postconflict reconciliation efforts. This is especially true for those who implore victims who find comfort in silence to publicly enunciate their stories of suffering in a rationalist effort to establish perpetrators. In the nefarious fields of grievous moral injuries, systematic corruption, and continued impunity, my research points to the limits of secular forms of reckoning, especially for stigmatized victims seeking compensatory or retributive justice rather than reconciliation.

The release of the Truth and Reconciliation Commission's final report in 2003 sparked expectations for justice on a wide range of fronts, including the likelihood of finding the missing, whose number was estimated over

8,500; the discovery of clandestine burial sites, of which over 4,600 had been acknowledged; comprehensive reparations for victims; and the prosecution of those responsible for human rights violations.[6] The publication of the report provided an ideal opportunity for the creation of associations of victims, yet with the passage of time, the investigation of human rights violations and abuses committed during the internal war simply failed to gain much traction in the Huallaga Valley. Many innocent campesinos were accused of being terrorists by the military and disappeared. For these innocent victims, there has never been any justice. Victims of military abuse have never been compensated in any way. Likewise, journalists and human rights activists who fearlessly unveiled the truth regarding Fujimori's counterinsurgency actions in the Huallaga Valley were singled out and falsely accused of being Túpac Amaru allies, thus making efforts to verify human rights claims more challenging.

The transitory nature of Peru's Truth and Reconciliation Commission and the specificity of its mandate did not provide sufficient incentives to those affected individuals or their families to band together for collective justice. As Manuel Burga Díaz, director of the Peruvian Ministry of Culture's Place of Memory, Tolerance and Social Inclusion (Lugar de la Memoria, la Tolerancia y la Inclusión Social, or LUM), has stressed, the aftermath of internal war has been difficult to come to terms with, and no national consensus exists over what happened during the tumultuous years of the internal war. To wit, the Lima-based LUM aims to appropriately portray the traumatic events by emphasizing the ones that were most significant and had the greatest influence on the broader population. In addition to chronicling the lives of the victims, insurgents and paramilitary forces, LUM has tracked the harm done to army personnel who functioned as the stewards of state law and order. In a bid to reflect on this challenging epoch and view the present and the future in a different way, LUM is committed to disclosing those events that candidly reveal that time, much like places of memory have done in other parts of the world.[7]

Despite such efforts, collective languages established by state-sponsored laws of national reconciliation have failed to render intelligible the structural and personal dimensions of everyday violence that are deeply ingrained in Peru's exclusionary national society. In the Caynarachi basin there has been a limited emergence of what has been described in postconflict Peru as a "micropolitics of reconciliation," whereby campesinos administer both retributive and restorative justice.[8] In contrast, Isaias Rojas-Pérez has described how mothers in the Peruvian Andes have reorganized their conceptions of belonging, affiliation, power, and the capacity to call the vanished back into existence through customary practices of grieving and commemoration in response to the state's failure to account for their missing dead.[9] According to Rojas-Pérez, who deftly describes how collective mourning transforms into a political diversion from the state's goal of ruling past death, the deceased can actually help secure the future of the body politic. This has not transpired in the Central or Lower Huallaga Valley, where effective coordination with other human rights victims has never emerged, perhaps due to the dispersion of localized claims and the relative isolation of those affected. Moreover, the region did not experience the same level of wartime violence as other areas of Peru, such as in Ayacucho or the Upper Huallaga, and as a result, it never established a strong civil patrol tradition. The meaning of the *rondas campesinas* in Ayacucho went far beyond their merely antirebel nature or willingness to engage with the Peruvian state.

Reconciliation and remembrance coexist under the roof of vengeance and violent retribution in postwar societies like Peru, where they are strange and occasionally contradictory bedfellows. The difficulty for public anthropologists is to mediate these shattered lines and create new social patterns that consider overlapping and occasionally opposing moral sentiments.[10] We simply cannot let neoclassical economic models rule our comprehension of the motivations and ethical nature underlying violent encounters despite the prevalence of the moral-hazard school of thought. Understanding that emotional tendencies are not just a reaction to the minimization of insecurity but are also rooted in concepts of mutuality and the cultural politics of intimacy offers a much-needed counterweight to the functional tendencies prevalent in the ethnographic study of wartime violence, vengeance, and trauma.

Various traumatic situations can happen to people during a violent conflict. As a result, there is a higher risk of developing mental health conditions like post-traumatic stress disorder, anxiety, and depression, as well as of having a worse quality of life. A wealth of ethnographic data on human rights emphasizes the significance of locally shared understandings of human solidarity, revealing the various modalities of embodiment, performance, and enactment differ depending on their contextual circumstances. By studying the implementation of rights-based approaches, ethnography can shed light on the intricacies and inconsistencies of discourse and implementation in the realm of human rights. This includes exploring both the possibilities and constraints associated with employing human rights

FIGURE 18. Contemporary Peruvian Armed Forces in Yurimaguas, photo by Bartholomew Dean

to effect societal transformations. This is illustrated by recent advances in our understanding of the intersubjectivities of suffering during times of violence.

My research on severe human rights abuses in the Huallaga Valley makes one of its most important contributions here: it acknowledges that reconciliation (the capacity for coexistence) is not equivalent to regional conceptions of justice or traditional methods of dispute resolution. The "hand of vengeance" remains barely concealed in Peru's Amazonian region, which is exacerbated by stoking resentments, crushing poverty, and long-standing social injustices that are here glossed over as corruption. "We returned [to our homes] with heavy hearts, broken by war, by what we lost, and fearful for what was yet to unfold," as my longtime confidant Diego remarked to me one steamy night over a round of sweating bottles of *chelas*.[11] Instead of "conquering the future, as we were taught by the party, *it was the end of the future*, we were defeated," Diego quipped during our lengthy rumination.[12]

While Diego's future was unknown, he admitted he was more than willing to reengage in violent encounters (vengeful and otherwise) to protect his kith and kin in the Huallaga Valley. Clearly, without reconstituting a moral community through consciously acknowledging the multiple sociocultural contours shaping overlapping epistemologies of justice, freedom, and communal well-being, efforts at lasting reconciliation will remain elusive in the Huallaga Valley.[13] As I gazed at Diego, standing contently in his horse's luxuriant paddock, I could not help but reflect on my deep conviction regarding the importance of rebuilding a moral community. To embark on this endeavor, it is essential to acknowledge the powerful historical and contemporary forces that have shaped the social and cultural framework of the Caynarachi basin. Through deliberate confrontation and active participation in these influential forces, we have the power to lay the foundation for a society that is not only equitable and harmonious but also defined by its profound compassion, empathy, and shared commitment to providing equal opportunities for every individual.

How can individuals, families, groups, and larger social networks reconcile the strain between hierarchy and equality as fellow citizens in what Benedict Anderson has famously dubbed "imagined communities"?[14] Faced with endemic warfare and violence, political citizenship is vacuous without the recognition of agentive empowerment and social citizenship, which involves all community members having access to socioeconomic and cultural capital to fully participate in national social and political life, including protection from violence. As my colleagues and I have indicated,[15] there is a strong political case for states to acknowledge not only medical and educational *pluralism*, but also different legal heterogeneities that can effectively accommodate the diversity of cultural identities (differences not only between groups, networks, and categories but also within them) and ideological orientations that envision different, inclusive *futures*.[16] By engaging with and acknowledging these heterogeneities, states can foster an environment that celebrates cultural diversity, promotes inclusivity, and enables the coexistence of multiple visions for a harmonious and equitable society.

Notes

FOREWORD

1. The public hearings organized by the Peruvian Truth and Reconciliation Commission (TRC) were of four types: case hearings, thematic hearings, institutional hearings, and public assemblies. Public hearings—Institutional Sessions of Balance and Perspective—were also presented in which members of terrorist organizations and representatives of political parties participated.
2. Luis Varese Scotto's brother Stefano penned a fascinating account of the ethnohistory of the region. See Bartholomew Dean, "Review of *Salt of the Mountain: Campa Asháninka History and Resistance in the Peruvian Jungle*," by S. Varese, *Americas* 62, no. 3 (2006): 464–66.

INTRODUCTION

Epigraph. Wilfred Own, "Mental Cases" (1918), in *Complete Poems and Fragments*, ed. Jon Stallworthy (London: Chatto and Windus, 1983).

1. Jo Ann Kawell, "The Cocaine Economy," in *The Peru Reader: History, Culture, Politics*, ed. Orin Starn, Carlos Iván Degregori, and Robin Kirk (Durham, NC: Duke University Press, 2005), 425–37. In 1990, the United States estimated that 40 percent of the world's coca leaf supply was being cultivated in San Martín and Huánuco, along the fertile Huallaga Valley.
2. The Peruvian Truth and Reconciliation Commission (TRC) identified the years between 1980 and 2000 as the "internal armed conflict." Other names, like civil war, domestic conflict, or non-international armed conflict have also been used to refer to this tumultuous and violent epoch. In this book, I opt to use the term *internal war* rather than *civil war* despite the fact that individuals from the Huallaga Valley use both terms interchangeably, causing confusion. Founded in 1985, the Uppsala Conflict Data Program (UCDP) is a renowned research project based at Uppsala University in Sweden. It aims to enhance the understanding of armed conflicts, their causes, dynamics, and consequences, as well as to facilitate conflict resolution and peacebuilding efforts. The UCDP considers the following key factors in defining a civil war: At least two parties, such as the state government and one or more non-state armed groups, must employ an organized armed force in a civil war, including civilians and combatants. Each side to the conflict must exhibit at least minimal effective resistance. This requires that the nonstate armed group(s) mount a consistent and coordinated armed uprising against the forces of the state authorities. The UCDP categorizes any conflicts that occur within a country as internal conflicts, regardless of the number of casualties, level of organization, or political aims of the par-

ticipants. Civil wars are a type of internal conflict that include intrastate battles for government control, such as the conflict in Peru.

3. Richard Mollica, *Healing Invisible Wounds Paths to Hope and Recovery in a Violent World* (Nashville, TN: Vanderbilt University Press, 2008).

4. The Caynarachi River is a tributary of the Huallaga River. Together with the Chontayacu, Tocache, Matallo, Huayabamba, Saposoa, Sisa, Mayo, Shanusi, and Caynarachi, these rivers form subbasins of diverse ecosystems. The waterways have small channels and are mostly made of rocky and stony material. On the right bank of the Huallaga are the subbasins of the rivers Biabo, Ponaza, and Chipurana. All the names of the tributaries associated with the Caynarachi basin have been altered to preserve community and individual anonymity, a point made clear to all participants in this ethnography.

5. Lima, also known as "Ciudad de los Reyes" (City of the Kings), was established by Francisco Pizarro on January 18, 1535, during the Catholic celebration of Epiphany, marking the Three Kings' visit to baby Jesus. The new Spanish Viceroyalty of Peru quickly picked Lima as its capital, replacing the former Inca city of Cuzco to the southeast, due to the coastal location's ease of contact with the metropole.

6. The phrase "revolutionary violence" refers to the use of force by a revolutionary organization or movement to bring about significant changes in governance, society, or economic relations. This type of violence involves actions such as bombings, assassinations, the distribution of propaganda, and other militant tactics aimed at establishing a new social order.

7. Antonio Gramsci, *Selections from the Prison Notebooks of Antonio Gramsci*, ed. and trans. Quintin Hoare and Geoffrey Nowell Smith (New York: International Publishers, 1971), 31. The MRTA contended that by engaging in violent confrontations, their insurgency could disrupt the prevailing order and ultimately bring about significant societal change. In short, the MRTA's understanding of history emphasized the significance of violent confrontation in shaping the trajectory of progress and paving the way for revolutionary transformation.

8. On this point, see Valérie Robin Azevedo, *Memorias y conflicto armado en Ayacucho-Perú* (Lima: La Siniestra Ensayos), 22.

9. Veena Das, *Life and Words: Violence and the Descent into the Ordinary* (Berkeley: University of California, 2005).

10. Johan Galtung, "Violence, Peace and Peace Research," *Journal of Peace Research* 6 (1969): 167–91. As Galtung argued, violence can be distinguished between that which has a clear subject-object relation and is visibly manifest as action and structural violence, which is opaque and embedded into the structure of society.

11. For further discussion of this problem, see Pierre Bourdieu and Jean Claude Passeron, *Reproduction in Education, Society and Culture* (London: Sage Publications, 1977). Symbolic violence is tantamount to internalized humiliations and legitimizations of inequality and hierarchy, which can include everything from sexism and racism to intimate manifestations of class power. Likewise, see Pierre Bourdieu and Loïc Wacquant, *An Invitation to Reflexive Sociology* (Chicago: University of Chicago Press, 1992), 167. Simply put, Bourdieu and Wacquant argue that symbolic violence is equivalent to the type of "violence which is exercised upon a social agent with his or her complicity."

12. Valérie Robin Azevedo, *Los silencios de la Guerra: Memorias y conflicto armado en Ayacucho-Perú* (Lima: La Siniestra Ensayos, 2021).

13. Mónica Espinosa Arango, "Memoria cultural y el continuo del genocidio: Lo indígena en Colombia," *Antípoda: Revista de Antropología y Arqueología* 5 (2007): 53–73.

14. According to Espinosa Arango, the political and ethical significance of these identities, consciousnesses, political subjectivities, and memories emerge from historical experiences of real violence, which gives rise to its institutionalization along a "genocidal continuum."

15. For more on the enduring history and social force of *pishtaco* beliefs, see Andrew Canessa, "Fear and Loathing on the Kharisiri Trail: Alterity and Identity in the Andes," *Journal of the Royal Anthropological Institute* 6, no. 4 (2000): 705–20; Bartholomew Dean, "From the Fat of Their Being: Vampires and Andean Modernity," review of *Gods and Vampires: Return to Chipaya, Cultural Dynamics* 9, no. 1 (1996): 111–13. Associated with ancient and diverse Andean-Amazonian mytho-historical traditions, Hilda reported that *pishtacos* are omnipresent "forest goblins responsible for stealing body fat from their victims for various cannibalistic ends."

16. Albert Camus, *Algerian Chronicles* (Cambridge, MA: Harvard University Press, 2013), 27.

17. See, e.g., Jeffrey Gamarra, *Las dificultades de la memoria, el poder y la reconciliación en los Andes: El ejemplo ayacuchano* (Ayacucho: IPAZ, 2001); Comisión de la Verdad y Reconciliación, Perú, *Informe final de la Comisión de la Verdad y Reconciliación*, 9 vols. (Lima: Comisión de la Verdad y la Reconciliación, Perú, 2003), https://www.cverdad.org.pe/ifinal/; Jo-Marie Burt, "Los usos y abusos de la memoria de María Elena Moyano," *A Contracorriente: Revista de Historia Social y Literatura en América Latina* 7, no. 2 (2010): 165–209; Mabel Moraña, "El ojo que llora: Biopolítica, nudos de la memoria y arte público en el Perú de hoy," *Latinoamérica: Revista de Estudios Latinoamericanos* 54 (2012): 183–216; Olga M. González, *Unveiling Secrets of War in the Peruvian Andes* (Chicago: University of Chicago Press, 2011); Kimberly Theidon, *Intimate Enemies: Violence and Reconciliation in Peru* (Philadelphia: University of Pennsylvania Press, 2012); Mariella Villasante Cervello, "Violencia de masas del Partido Comunista del Perú: Sendero Luminoso y campos de trabajo forzado entre los Ashaninka de la selva central," *Dossier de Memoria* 9 (2012): 1–79; Óscar Espinosa, "El terror que no termina: La persistente amenaza a la vida y seguridad de las comunidades asháninka de los ríos Ene y Tambo," *Ideele* (2013): no. 233; Cynthia Milton, "Desfigurando la memoria: (Des)atando los nudos de la memoria peruana," *Anthropologica* 33 (2015): 11–33; Miriam Encarnación Pinedo, "La memoria carcelaria en Sendero Luminoso y en el Movimiento de Liberación Nacional Tupamaro (1982-2017)," *Historia y Memoria* 21 (2020): 235–68. For a recent review of the history of political violence in the central jungle, see Mariella Villasante Cervello's *La violencia política en la selva central del Perú, 1980–2000: Los campos totalitarios senderistas y las secuelas de la guerra interna entre los Ashaninka y Nomatsiguenga: Estudio de antropología de la violencia* (Lima: Comisión de Derechos Humanos, 2019).

18. Claudia Feld and Valentina Salvi, "Cuando los perpetradores hablan: Dilemas y tensiones en torno a la voz comprometida," *Rubrica Contemporánea* 5, no. 9 (2016): 1–10.

19. As Jelin notes, discussions about witnessing have taken place in almost every academic field, from political studies to psychoanalysis, sociology, and anthropology, from literary criticism to the more general topic of cultural criticism. Elizabeth Jelin, *State Repression and the Labors of Memory*, trans. Marcial Godoy-Anativia and Judy Rein (Minneapolis: University of Minnesota Press, 2003).

20. Émile Durkheim, *Elementary Forms of the Religious Life*, trans. J. W. Swain (New York: Free Press, 1971).

21. Maurice Halbwachs, *Les cadres sociaux de la mémoire* (Paris: Librairie Félix Alcan, 1925).

22. The text draws from dozens of interviews I personally conducted primarily in the communities located in the Central and Lower Huallaga Valley (2015-2022).

23. The Truth and Reconciliation Commission's *Informe final* consists of around 4,500 printed pages and is available online at the commission's website (http://www.derechos.org/nizkor/peru/libros/cv/). For more on the commission, among others, see Ruth Elena Borja Santa Cruz, "Utilization of the Archives of the Peruvian Commission for Truth and Reconciliation (CVR)," in *Archives and Human Rights*, ed. Jens Boel, Perrine Canavaggio, and Antonio González Quintana (New York: Routledge, 2021), 277–87; Ana Claudia de Oliveira and Lilian Kanashiro, "LUM, presencias resignificantes del conflicto armado peruano," *Galáxia* 46 (2021): 1–19. For the best critical studies of the movement, see Mario Miguel Meza Bazán, "El Movimiento Revolucionario Túpac Amaru (MRTA) y las fuentes de la revolución en América Latina" (PhD diss., El Colegio de México, 2012); Miguel La Serna, *With Masses and Arms: Peru's Túpac Amaru Revolutionary Movement* (Chapel Hill: University of North Carolina Press, 2021). As Meza Bazán and La Serna both argue, the political foundations of the MRTA are best understood in terms of Peru's leftist history.

24. On the MRTA in the Central and Lower Huallaga Valley, see Bartholomew Dean, "The Túpac Amaru Revolutionary Movement (Movimiento Revolucionario Túpac Amaru) in the Central and Lower Huallaga Valley, Peruvian Amazonia," in *Oxford Research Encyclopedia of Latin American History*, edited by William H. Beezley (New York: Oxford University Press, forthcoming). For information on the Shining Path, or Sendero Luminoso, see Carlos Iván Degregori, *El surgimiento de Sendero Luminoso, 1969–1979* (Lima: IEP, 1990); Nelson Manrique, *El tiempo del miedo: Los orígenes sociales de la violencia política en el Perú, 1980–1996* (Lima: Fondo Editorial del Congreso del Perú, 2002); Instituto de Defensa Legal, *Peru hoy: En el oscuro sendero de la guerra* (Lima: Instituto de Defensa Legal, 1992). Óscar Espinosa, Silvia Romio, and Marco Ramírez Colombier's edited collection *Historias, violencias y memorias en la Amazonía* (Lima: PUCP, 2021) makes virtually no mention of the MRTA. The overwhelming majority of scholarship on this region of Peru has emphasized the Upper Huallaga Valley. Investigating the idea of legal topographies to understand how landscape interventions create territory, structure pathways, and muddle timelines, Richard Kernaghan's *Crossing the Current: Aftermaths of War along the Huallaga River* (Stanford, CA: Stanford University Press, 2022) demonstrates how prior acts of violence have subtly accumulated in the Upper Huallaga region. The Upper Huallaga has become a popular case, in particular for studies on drug trafficking and insurgency. On this point, see Maritza Paredes and Hernán Manrique insightful essay "The State's Developmentalist Illusion and the Origins of Illegal Coca Cultivation in Peru's Alto Huallaga Valley (1960–80)," *Journal of Latin American Studies* 53, no. 2 (2021): 245–67. For additional information on the Upper Huallaga, see, e.g., Manuel Bernales and Róger Rumrrill, "Narcopoder, subversión y democracia en Perú," *Nueva Sociedad* 102 (1989): 162–68; Cynthia McClintock, "Drogas-guerrilla-violencia," *Chasqui: Revista Latinoamericana de Comunicación* 29 (1989): 68–71; José E. Gonzales, "Guerrillas and Coca in the Upper Huallaga Valley," in *Shining Path of Peru*, ed. David Scott Palmer (New York: St. Martin's Press, 1992), 105–26; Steven Hendrix, "Interplay among Land Law and Policy, the Environment, the War on Drugs, Narcoterrorism, and Democratization: Perspectives on Peru's Upper Huallaga Valley" (Madison: Land Tenure Center, University of Wisconsin–Madison, 1993); Pablo Dreyfus, "When All Evils Come Together: Cocaine, Corruption and Shining Path in Peru's Upper Huallaga Valley," *Journal of Contemporary Criminal Justice* 15, no. 4 (1999): 370–96; Bruce Kay, "Violent Opportunities: The Rise and Fall of 'King Coca' and Shining Path," *Journal of Interamerican Studies and World Affairs* 41, no. 3 (1999): 97–127; F. Chamba, J. Alvarado, J. Tourrand, and M. Piketty, "Coca et violence: Le témoignage du

Alto Huallaga au Pérou," *Autrepart* 26 (2003): 157–171; Richard Kernaghan, *Coca's Gone: Of Might and Right in the Upper Huallaga Valley Post-Boom* (Stanford, CA: Stanford University Press, 2009); Mirella Van Dun, *Cocaleros: Violence, Drugs and Social Mobilization in the Post-Conflict Upper Huallaga Valley, Peru* (Amsterdam: Rozenberg Publishers, 2009); Mirella van Dun, "Narco-Territoriality and Shadow Powers in a Peruvian Cocaine Frontier," *Terrorism and Political Violence* 31, no. 5 (2019): 1026–48; Hernán Manrique López and Néstor Álvaro Pastor Armas, "Cocaína peruana: Análisis bibliográfico de la investigación sobre el tráfico ilícito de drogas cocaínicas en Perú," *Cultura y Droga* 24, no. 27 (2019): 15–38.

25. See Instituto de Defensa Legal, *Peru hoy*, 283; Robert B. Kent, "Dimensions of the Shining Path Insurgency in Peru," *Geographical Review* 83, no. 4 (1993): 441–54.

26. From September 7, 1940, to May 11, 1941, the London Blitz was a relentless series of German air raids on the United Kingdom. The attacks targeted strategic cities across Britain, but London endured the brunt of the assault. The German term *"blitzkrieg,"* meaning "lightning war," gave rise to the name "Blitz." The Luftwaffe aimed to weaken British air power and pave the way for a potential invasion. Despite inflicting substantial destruction and casualties, with over forty thousand fatalities and extensive damage to buildings, the Blitz proved unsuccessful in shattering British morale or incapacitating the nation's war economy. Germany's priorities and resources ultimately shifted toward other military endeavors, notably the invasion of the Soviet Union, diverting their attention away from Britain.

27. War is deeply intertwined in my family history, particularly the two World Wars. Among those who played significant roles was my grandfather, Eric Edwin Dean, a young man during the First World War who enlisted in the 6th Battalion of the City of London Rifles (CLR), an esteemed British Army volunteer regiment originally known as the "Printers' Battalion." Lance Corporal E. E. Dean, serving in the CLR infantry regiment, found himself amidst intense combat in the trenches shortly after joining in July 1914 and arriving at the front lines in March 1915. A year later, he suffered severe injuries shortly after the ferocious Battle of Loos, a pivotal military operation that witnessed the British military's first use of chlorine gas. Equally tragic was the fate of my paternal grandmother's brother, Lance Corporal Nelson Standish Bathurst of the London Regiment (Queen's Westminster Rifles). He perished at the front near Neuve Chapelle, France, on February 1, 1917, when he was only twenty-two. His last resting place is in the British section of the Laventie Military Cemetery in Laventie, France. In my extended family, spanning both my father's and mother's sides, several relatives were involved in World War II, with some losing their lives as combatants or innocent civilians. Additionally, my grandfather, E. E. Dean, was entangled in the infamous MS *Alfhem* incident during the Cold War period. The incident was a pivotal event in the history of Guatemala and a significant turning point in the Cold War. In 1954, amid political tensions, the Guatemalan government procured two thousand tons of weapons and ammunition from Czechoslovakia to counter US-supported opposition forces. Assisted by my grandfather, a Swedish cargo vessel named the MS *Alfhem* successfully evaded US patrols and arrived at the Guatemalan port of Puerto Barrios to unload the arms in support of the besieged Juan Jacobo Árbenz presidency (1951–1954). Despite diplomatic pressure, the United States failed to prevent the delivery, leading to it being seen as a setback for the United States and a provocation by Guatemala. See Bartholomew Dean, "MS Alfhem Affair: The Circulation of Weapons, US Empire, and the Cold War in the Americas," in *Encyclopedia of US Intelligence*, ed. D. Moore (New York: Taylor and Francis, 2015), 587–91.

28. On this point, consult W. H. R. Rivers's seminal 1917 lecture establishing the debilitating nature of psychic trauma war for combatants, "An Address on the Repression of War Experience" (delivered before the Section of Psychiatry, Royal Society of Medicine, December 4, 1917), *Lancet* 19, no. 4927 (18): 173–77.

29. Galtung, "Violence, Peace and Peace Research," 167–91. The term *structural violence* refers to those political-economic structures, such as inequitable trade agreements and structural adjustment regulations, which make life more difficult for everyone, not just the poor. The suffering and hardship associated with this form of violence is "structured" by historically rooted (and often broader socioeconomic) mechanisms and forces that operate in tandem to limit human freedom. Direct violence is an event, structural violence is a process, and cultural violence—which normalizes and makes structural violence possible—is invariable.

30. The term *slum* has been used to refer to conditions of destitution, squalor, and disease since its inception. Due to their disregard for governmental rules and regulations, poor communities are thus stigmatized as disorderly and chaotic. Bartholomew Dean, "Life in a *Callejón*: The Inner-City Poor of Lima, Perú" (MPhil thesis, Oxford University, 1987).

31. Interpersonal, domestic, and criminal violence are examples of what I have in mind when employing the term *everyday violence*.

32. MRTA, "El MRTA y las tareas en periodo pre-revolucionario," *Documento aprobado en el II Comité Central,* February 1985.

33. See Bartholomew Dean, *The State and the Awajún: Frontier Expansion in the Upper Amazon, 1541–1990* (San Diego, CA: Cognella Academic Publishing, 2020), for the tragic case of the Jivaroan-speaking Awajún of the Upper Amazon.

34. For details of the case, see Bartholomew Dean, "Machetes in Our Hands, Blood on Our Faces: Reflections on Violence and Advocacy in the Peruvian Amazon," *Anthropological Quarterly* 82, no. 4 (2009): 1069–72. See also Bartholomew Dean, "Blood in the River: Ontological Experiences and Representations of the Embodiment of Corruption in Peruvian Amazonia's Huallaga Valley," presentation at the 118th annual meeting of the American Anthropological Association and the Canadian Anthropology Society, Vancouver, BC, November 22, 2019.

35. David Maybury-Lewis, *Indigenous Peoples, Ethnic Groups and the State* (Needham, MA: Allyn and Baker, 2002), 52.

CHAPTER 1

Epigraph. Truth and Reconciliation Commission, Peru, *Hatun Willakuy: Abbreviated Version of the Final Report of the Truth and Reconciliation Commission* (Lima: Truth and Reconciliation Commission, Peru, 2014), 5.

1. When discussing campesinos, I have in mind farmers who work on small plots of land using traditional methods and tools. They rely mainly on family labor and subsistence production. Campesinos are usually part of rural communities that share common values, customs, and practices. In the Huallaga Valley, campesinos have a strong sense of identity and belonging. However, they face various challenges, such as limited access to markets, credit, technology, and education. Furthermore, they contend with a myriad of pressing concerns today, encompassing the degradation of land resources, persistent poverty, the far-reaching impacts of climate change, and the detrimental effects of social exclusion While individuals who produce food for personal consumption and the market

are known as campesinos, peasants refer to a broader group of rural people who rely on agriculture as their source of livelihood, regardless of their land tenure or market orientation. It's important to note that *campesino* and *peasant* are not interchangeable terms. Although all peasants can be considered campesinos, not all campesinos are peasants. For example, some campesinos in the Huallaga Valley have access to land through agrarian reform programs, cooperative associations, or other collective organizations that give them greater autonomy and political power compared to peasants, who may be subject to feudalistic or capitalist forms of exploitation.

2. Rafael Barrantes Segura, *Reparations and Displacement in Peru* (New York: International Center for Transitional Justice, Brookings-LSE Project on Internal Displacement, 2012); Dean, "Life in a *Callejón*." The International Center for Transitional Justice has estimated that roughly 430,000 people were forcefully displaced in Peru during the country's two-decade-long war. In "Life in a *Callejón*," I found that many of the displaced were concentrated in the shantytowns (*pueblo jovenes*) or inner-city *tugurios* of Lima, residing in zones of dire poverty and marginalized from the basic social services of the city.

3. The MRTA (1984–1996) embraced its name in honor of the quasi-mythical figure Túpac Amaru II (José Gabriel Condorcanqui), an eighteenth-century guerrilla leader who led a popular revolt against the Spanish (1780–c. 1782). He also assembled several partisans and led a rebellion in Tungasuca on November 6, 1780. Some of the oldest and most populous cities in the area—including the imperial city of Cuzco, La Paz, Puno, and Oruro—were besieged, assaulted, or occupied by the insurgent armies. Notwithstanding, Túpac Amaru II's assault on Cuzco was ultimately a failure. He was eventually captured by the Spanish and summarily executed on May 18, 1782, in Cuzco. Túpac Amaru II himself was named after his claimed forebear, Sapa Inca Túpac Amaru, the final Inca emperor who also led an unsuccessful rebellion against Spanish colonial rule, which was crushed. In 1572, Sapa Inca Túpac Amaru was also put to death by the Spanish crown.

4. Bartholomew Dean, "State Power and Indigenous Peoples in Peruvian Amazonia: A Lost Decade, 1990–2000," in *The Politics of Ethnicity: Indigenous Peoples in Latin American States*, ed. David Maybury-Lewis (Cambridge, MA: Harvard University Press, 2002), 199–238; Amnesty International, "Peru-Japan: Alberto Fujimori Must Be Brought to Justice for Human Rights Violations" (press release), July 31, 2003, https://www.amnesty.org/en/wp-content/uploads/2021/06/amr460162003en.pdf. According to Amnesty International, "The widespread and systematic nature of human rights violations committed during the government of former head of state Albert Fujimori (1990–2000) in Peru constitutes crimes against humanity under international law."

5. In 1992, Fujimori restructured the Peruvian National Police Directorate against Terrorism (Dirección contra el Terrorismo de la Policía Nacional del Perú); his government established a specialized antiterrorist police force housed in the National Directorate against Terrorism (Dirección Nacional contra el Terrorismo, DINCOTE).

6. Jeremy Bigwood, "With Guerrilla U: In the Jungle with Peru's Túpac Amaru," *Covert Action Quarterly*, no. 60 (1997). By 1997, the MRTA had been reduced to a small fragmentary group located in "the central" rainforests of Junín, Huancavelica, and Pasco.

7. Political groupings are not officially protected by either the 1998 Rome Statute or the 1948 Genocide Convention; therefore, it is simple to conflate efforts to dismantle political organizations with the assassinations of individual politicians or activists.

8. Yoon Soo Choi, "The Peruvian Hostage Crisis: Brief Review of MRTA," *International Journal of Comparative and Applied Criminal Justice* 21, no. 1 (1997): 33–49. See also Jan Lust,

Capitalism, Class and Revolution in Peru, 1980–2016 (Cham, Switzerland: Palgrave Macmillan, 2019), 176–83; Ariel Álvarez Rubio, "La toma de rehenes como acto terrorista internacional: Análisis de la operación de rescate 'Chavín de Huantar,'" *Revista de Relaciones Internacionales, Estrategia y Seguridad* 10, no. 2 (2015): 43–68; Suzie Baer, *Peru's MRTA: Tupac Amaru Revolutionary Movement* (New York: Rosen Publishing, 2003). Cerpa's original demand for the freedom of four hundred of his jailed comrades in exchange for the hostages was eventually reduced to the release of twenty imprisoned MRTA comrades in return for the captives.

9. The curly-haired and thick-glasses-wearing Hugo Avellaneda, age forty-one, became the military and political leader of the MRTA, replacing Néstor Cerpa Cartolini after his death at the Japanese ambassador's residence. M. Jaskoski, "Civilian Control of the Armed Forces in Democratic Latin America," *Armed Forces and Society* 38 (2012): 70–91.

10. In a dramatic unraveling of political events, the façade of Fujimori's authoritarian regime crumbled precipitously in 2000, triggered by the revelation of incriminating videotapes showcasing his trusted confidant, Vladimiro Montesinos, exchanging lavish bribes with influential politicians and media figures. The torrent of outrage ignited by these infamous *vladivideos* propelled Fujimori into resignation from abroad, and his self-imposed exile in Japan, the land of Fujimori's ancestors. After winning the 2001 presidential election, Alejandro Toledo swiftly approved the establishment of Peru's Truth Commission. Following the advice of spiritual authorities, Toledo added the term *Reconciliation* to the official name of the commission. For more detailed analysis of the CVR, see Lisa J. Laplante and Kimberly Theidon, "Commissioning Truth, Constructing Silences: The Peruvian Truth Commission and the Other Truths of 'Terrorists,'" *Mirrors of Justice: Law and Power in the Post–Cold War Era,* ed. Kamari Maxine Clarke and Mark Goodale (Cambridge: Cambridge University Press, 2009), 291–315; Francesca Denegri and Alexandra Hibbett, eds., *Dando cuenta: Estudios sobre el testimonio de la violencia política en el Perú (1980–2000)* (Lima: Fondo Editorial de la PUCP, 2016). The commission was tasked with investigating human rights violations during the administrations of the presidents Fernando Belaúnde Terry (1980–1985), Alan García Pérez (1985–1990), and Alberto Fujimori (1990–2000). Denegri and Hibbett provide a nuanced analysis of the nearly seventeen thousand testimonies compiled by the Truth and Reconciliation Commission (2001–2003). Their volume on archival memory and political violence in Peru is publicly available at the Information Center for Collective Memory and Human Rights of Peru's Ombudsman's Office.

11. Truth and Reconciliation Commission, *Hatun Willakuy,* 18–19; Dora Hernandez Barrientos and Adam L. Church, "Terrorism in Peru," *Prehospital and Disaster Medicine* 18, no. 2 (2003): 123–26; Patrick Ball, Jana Asher, David Sulmont, and Daniel Manrique, *How Many Peruvians Have Died? An Estimate of the Total Number of Victims Killed or Disappeared in the Armed Internal Conflict Between 1980 and 2000* (Washington, DC: American Association for the Advancement of Science, 2003). See also Silvio Rendon, "Capturing Correctly: A Reanalysis of the Indirect Capture-Recapture Methods in the Peruvian Truth and Reconciliation Commission," *Research and Politics* 6 (2019): 1–8; D. Manrique-Vallier and P. Ball, "Reality and Risk: A Refutation of S. Rendon's Analysis of the Peruvian Truth and Reconciliation Commission's Mortality Study," *Research and Politics* 6 (2019): 1–5. The commission estimated that Sendero Luminoso was responsible for 54 percent of the deaths in the conflict, the armed forces for 30 percent (6 percent of that by police), the civilian militias (*ronderos*) and paramilitary groups for 15 percent, and finally the MRTA for nearly

2 percent. Peasants made up the majority of the victims (56 percent), and most deaths occurred in rural areas (79 percent).

12. Political violence is violence that is enacted to achieve political goals. In the Huallaga River Valley, this involved violence committed by insurgent groups, such as the MRTA and Sendero Luminoso, as well as state agents. It included countless cases of coercion, abuse, and violent acts against nonstate actors (most notably cases of police and military brutality).

13. Paredes and Manrique, "The State's Developmentalist Illusion," 245–67, argue that the breakdown of state-sponsored colonization programs aided the formation of a cocaine trafficking center in the Upper Huallaga Valley.

14. Among others, see Georges Sorel, *Reflections on Violence,* ed. Jeremy Jennings (Cambridge: Cambridge University Press, 1999); Walter Benjamin, *Critique of Violence Selected Writings: 1913–1926* (Cambridge, MA: Harvard University Press, 2004), vol. 1; Hannah Arendt, *On Violence* (New York: Harcourt, Brace, Jovanovich, 1970); Frantz Fanon, *The Wretched of the Earth* (New York: Grove Press, 2004); René Girard, *Violence and the Sacred,* trans. Patrick Gregory (Baltimore: Johns Hopkins University Press, 1973). Most recently, Kimberly Theidon's *Legacies of War Violence, Ecologies, and Kin* (Raleigh, NC: Duke University Press, 2022) has persuasively shown how wartime violence in Peru and Colombia reflects the interdependency of all life.

15. William Pawlett, *Violence, Society and Radical Theory: Bataille, Baudrillard and Contemporary Society* (London: Routledge, 2013).

16. Faisal Devji, "The Return of Nonviolence," *Critical Times* 4, no. 1 (2021): 93–101, fruitfully illuminates Sorel and Fanon's approach to violence and capitalism.

17. Commander Andrés, "Light at the End of the Tunnel: Interview with an MRTA Leader, Commander Andrés," *Barricada International,* January 19, 1991.

18. In the Andes, the name is common. For example, Túpac Amaru District is one of eight districts in the Canas Province of the Region of Cuzco. Likewise, in Amazonia the name is common. Yurimaguas has a street (*calle*) Túpac Amaru; a primary informant in Picota, San Martín, resided in a home on Túpac Amaru street (*jirón*).

19. See Charlene Villaseñor Black, *Transforming Saints: From Spain to New Spain* (Nashville, TN: Vanderbilt University Press, 2022), 110.

20. Efforts are underway to highlight indigenous figures, like Micaela Bastidas and Túpac Amaru II, in the official record of national liberation, which has been dominated by leaders of European descent who came to Peru from other parts of the continent, such as Simón Bolívar and José de San Martín, or from abroad, like Thomas Cochrane, Tenth Earl of Dundonald, Marquess of Maranhão. According to the renowned historian Juan Manuel Burga Díaz, director of the Peruvian Ministry of Culture's Place of Memory, Tolerance, and Social Inclusion (Lugar de la Memoria, la Tolerancia y la Inclusión Social, LUM), overlooking the Pacific Ocean in the country's capital, Túpac Amaru II and Micaela Bastidas's eighteenth-century uprising serves as the "antecedent of independence." For Burga Díaz, Túpac Amaru II and Micaela Bastidas are part of the history "not just of the (Spanish) viceroyalty" but of the Peruvian Republic itself. See Christopher Torchia, "Long after Grisly End, Túpac Amaru Still Fascinates in Peru," Associated Press, May 18, 2021; Sara Beatriz Guardia, "Reconociendo las huellas: Micaela Bastidas y las heroinas de la independencia del Perú," in *Las mujeres en la independencia de América Latina,* ed. Sara Beatriz Guardia (Lima: CEMHAL, 2010), 31–48; Leon G. Campbell, "The Army of Peru and the Túpac Amaru Revolt, 1780–1783," *Hispanic American Historical Review* 56, no. 1 (1976): 31–57.

21. Miguel La Serna, "'I Will Return and I Will Be Millions!' The Many Lives of Túpac Amaru," *Age of Revolutions,* November 2, 2020, https://ageofrevolutions.com/2020/11/02/i-will-return-and-i-will-be-millions-the-many-lives-of-tupac-amaru/#_edn15. Likewise, see MRTA, "¡Por la causa de los pobres! ¡Con las masas y las armas! ¡Venceremos!," February 1, 1985. In their efforts to forge revolutionary nationalism, MRTA print propaganda also emphasized other historical figures, such as Manco Inca, Juan Santos Atahualpa, Túpac Amaru, Micaela Bastidas, and José Olaya.

22. In an article written by Daniele Conversi in 1995 the term appears in conjunction with the "ethno-symbolist approach." Conversi provides a mildly critical perspective: "If we focus exclusively on the power of the past and its symbols, we miss two other key features of nationalism: first, its relationship with political power, and particularly with the state; and second, its crucial border-generating function." See Daniele Conversi, "Reassessing Current Theories of Nationalism: Nationalism as Boundary Maintenance and Creation," *Nationalism and Ethnic Politics* (1995):73–85.

23. MRTA, "La situación actual y las tareas en el proceso de la guerra revolucionaria del pueblo," Comité Política, May 1984.

24. Che Guevara, *Guerrilla Warfare,* ed. Brian Loveman and Thomas M. Davies Jr. (Lanham, MD: Rowman and Littlefield, 2002), 52.

25. MRTA, "Balance y perspectivas: Campaña militar del Frente Guerrillero Nor Oriental," *Voz Rebelde,* no. 9 January 1988.

26. James Brooke, "The Rebels and the Cause: 12 Years of Peru's Turmoil," *New York Times,* December 19, 1996.

27. Gordon McCormick, *Sharp Dressed Men: Peru's Tupac Amaru Revolutionary Movement* (Santa Monica, CA: RAND Corporation, 1993), 6–7.

28. Unless otherwise indicated, no differentiation is made when using the term *police,* which represented the Republican Guard (Guardia Republicana), Civil Guard (Guardia Civil), and the Technical Police (Policía Técnica).

29. This included, among others, Héctor Delgado Parker, whose family owned Panamericana TV, José Antonio Onrubia Romero of the Romero Group, and David Armando Ballón Vera, a mining executive who was found shot dead with signs of torture after being held hostage for a year and a half.

30. Attacks on symbols of US capitalism, such as Kentucky Fried Chicken, became favored targets for the MRTA. Members set fire to a Kentucky Fried Chicken franchise on March 20, 1985, in Lima. The MRTA systematically extorted the fast-food chain for "war taxes" (*cupos*) to the tune of $50,000–$100,000. In addition to targeting US commercial establishments, the MRTA also attacked Mormon churches.

31. *La Primera,* "A 24 años de su asesinato Evocan a general López Albujar," January 9, 2014.

32. Anahí Durand Guevara, "Donde habita el olvido: Los (h)usos de la memoria y la crisis del movimiento social en San Martín" (bachelor's thesis, UNMSM, Lima, 2005), 64. The MRTA's first guerrilla activity was in 1983 in the countryside, but it resulted in disaster, much like the 1965 MIR debacle. A rebel camp established in Paucartambo, Cuzco, was discovered by the Peruvian Armed Forces, leading to the seizure of a large number of the rebels' weapons and the capture of nine of the twenty insurgents.

33. On the concept of cultural violence, see Johan Galtung, "Cultural Violence," *Journal of Peace Research* 27, no. 3 (1990): 91–305. The phrase "culture of violence" underscores the pervasiveness of specific, ingrained patterns of violence in a given social field or network. For a review of violence in Peruvian Amazonia, see Bartholomew Dean, "Ambiva-

lent Exchanges: The Violence of *Patronazgo* in the Upper Amazon," in *Cultural Construction of Violence: Victimization, Escalation, Response,* ed. M. Anderson (West Lafayette, IN: Purdue University, 2004), 214–26. On the issue of violence in the narratives of those residing in the Huallaga Valley during the internal war, see Bartholomew Dean, "Narratives, Resilience and Violence in Peruvian Amazonia: The Huallaga Valley, 1980–2015," *Anthropology: Open Journal* 1, no. 1 (2016): 1–2.

34. Law No. 201 was promulgated by President José Pardo on September 4, 1906, creating the Department of San Martín, with its capital being the historical city of Moyobamba, which had long served as the capital of the Amazonian region of Maynas. San Martín occupies the seventh place in geographical extension with an area of 51,253.31 square kilometers, and it is politically divided into ten provinces (Moyobamba, Rioja, Huallaga, Lamas, Mariscal Cáceres, San Martín, El Dorado, Bellavista, Picota, and Tocache, according to the current political demarcation) and seventy-seven districts.

35. Néstor Cerpa Cartolini, *Tomar por asalto el siglo XXI: Biografía y documentos del comandante obrero MRTA Néstor Cerpa Cartolini,* ed. Gabriel Carranza Polo (La Paz, G. Carranza 2003), 62. "Ayer éramos un puñado que teníamos como armas solamente nuestra entereza y nuestra moral, hoy somos miles, organizados en frentes guerrilleros con unidades milicianas y de autodefensa extendidas a lo largo de todo el país, pero lo más importante es que nuestra influencia crece día a día y el pueblo se suma a la lucha, y allá en el campo de la fusión de las armas y de las masas se va gestando el embrión del nuevo y futuro poder popular."

36. Herndon notes the following about the Central and Lower Huallaga: "After passing the Pongo, we entered upon a low, flat country, where the river spreads out very wide, and is obstructed by islands and sand-banks. This is the deposit from the Pongo. In the channel where we passed, I found a scant five feet of water; I suspect, but I could not find out, that more water may be had in some of the other channels. This shoal water is but for a short distance, and the soundings soon deepened to twelve and eighteen feet. Small pebbly islands are forming in the river, and much drift-wood from above lodges on them. After having stopped two hours to breakfast, we passed the mouth of the Chipurana, which is about twenty yards wide." William Lewis Herndon and Lardner Gibbon, *Exploration of the Valley of the Amazon* (Washington, DC: R. Armstrong Public Printer, 1853–1854), pt. 1, 166.

37. Located 770 kilometers from Lima in the Lambayeque region of northern Peru, Chiclayo is some 13 kilometers inland.

38. Kernaghan, *Coca's Gone,* 8; M. Menton and P. Cronkleton, "Migration and Forests in the Peruvian Amazon: A Review" (Bogor, Indonesia: Center for International Forestry Research, 2019); L. Limachi, W. de Jong, and C. Cornejo, "Models of Migration in the Peruvian Amazon and Their Impact on Tropical Forests," in *The Social Ecology of Tropical Forests: Migration; Population and Frontiers,* ed. W. de Jong, L. Tuck-Po, and A. Ken-ichi (Kyoto, Japan: Kyoto University Press, 2006), 55–78.

39. Paul Gootenberg, *Andean Cocaine: The Making of a Global Drug* (Chapel Hill: University of North Carolina Press, 2008), 292. During the late 1970s, the Upper Huallaga Valley came to produce more than half of the world's markets for coca leaf and unrefined cocaine paste. On the topic of coca leaf production, see INEI, *Compendio estadístico departamental 1996–1997* (Moyobamba: Departamento San Martín, Peru, 1997). Coca leaf was an important cash crop in San Martín during the 1980s, prompting large scale in-migration and landscape disturbances through rampant forest clearance. This lucrative illicit crop would eventually predominate Caynarachi's agricultural sector when the MRTA con-

trolled the region (1988–1993). San Martín was impacted not only by the cultivation of coca leaves but also by the artisanal transformation of the leaves into basic *pasta* (or *pasta básica de cocaína*). This was then commercialized through the so-called *traqueteros*, those individuals linked to medium-sized merchants (*capos*) and transnational narcotics cartels (*firmas*). According to the 2002 national census, the total population of the region was 757,740 inhabitants, a sixfold increase since 1940. The principal city, Tarapoto, had a population of 161,736; Moyobamba, 106,033; and Tocache, 98,265. The 2002 census found that more than 62 percent of the region's population was urban and 38 percent rural. On the radical biocultural transformation noted in the region over the past generation, see, e.g., Anne Justice, Bartholomew Dean, and Michael H. Crawford, "Molecular Consequences of Migration and Urbanization in Peruvian Amazonia," in *Causes and Consequences of Human Migration: An Evolutionary Perspective*, ed. M. H. Crawford and B. C. Campbell (New York: Cambridge University Press, 2012), 449–72; Randy David and Bartholomew Dean, "A Sociogenetic Approach to Migration and Urbanization in Peruvian Amazonia: Implications for Population Architecture," in *Human Migration: Biocultural Perspectives*, ed. M. L. Muñoz-Moreno and M. H. Crawford (Oxford: Oxford University Press, 2021), 180–96; Bartholomew Dean, "Diabetes en la Amazonia," in *Investigación* (Yurimaguas, Peru: Instituto de Educación Superior Tecnológico Público, 2019), 1–12; D. C. Robbins, B. Dean, C. Gerhold, M. J. Mosher, and J. Camargo "184-LB: Lipid and HbA1c Profiles among People with Lean and Overweight Type 2 Diabetes in the Peruvian Amazon," *Diabetes* 70 (2021): https://doi.org/10.2337/db21-184-LB; C. Gerhold, D. Robbins, M. Garcia-Touza, and B. C. Dean, "The Impact of Urbanization on the People of the Upper Amazon," *Diabetes* 72, suppl. 1 (2023): 191-LB, https://doi.org/10.2337/db23-191-LB.

40. Javier Pulgar Vidal, *Geografía del Perú: Las ocho regiones naturales del Perú* (Lima: Editorial Universo, 1972). The *selva baja* (or low forest) is located in Peruvian Amazonia between eighty and four hundred meters above sea level.

41. Pulgar Vidal.

42. Frederica Barclay, "Cambios y continuidades en el pacto colonial en la Amazonía: El caso de los indios chazutas del Huallaga Medio a finales del siglo XIX," *Bulletin de l'Institut Français d'Études Andines* 30, no. 2 (2001): 187–210, provides a useful account of the postcolonial history of the establishment of Chazuta.

43. Huimbayoc, Chipurana, Papaplaya, El Porvenir, Barranquita, Chazuta, and Caynarachi are all situated within San Martín. Notably, Huimbayoc encompasses both the province and the breathtaking Cordillera Azul National Park, sharing its northern border with Chipurana. To the south of Huimbayoc, you will find Papaplaya, and further south lies the district of El Porvenir. Renowned for its flourishing agricultural output, Barranquita is positioned adjacent to El Porvenir in the southern direction. Moving southward, Chazuta emerges, serving as a home to numerous indigenous Kichwa-Lamas communities and forming a border with Barranquita. Finally, Caynarachi district lies adjacent to Chazuta in the south.

44. Nicholas Kalmus, "Paradise Lost Is Found in the Mountains of Peru," Field Museum, October 9, 2013, https://www.fieldmuseum.org/blog/paradise-lost-found-mountains-peru. Because of its large altitudinal range, various flora types, intricate geology, and historical protection of local indigenous peoples, the Cordillera Escalera has extraordinarily diverse plant and animal groups. It is also the ancestral homeland of the indigenous Kampu Piyawi (Shawi). Their significant cultural legacy, which includes petroglyphs estimated between 1,500 and 3,000 years old, makes it a high-priority location for cultural heritage conservation.

45. Poorly documented, these small tributaries are the Mutico, Shimbillo, Panchitos, Shalluyacu, Wicungo, Pucaquebrada, Yanayacu, Palometa, Tioyacu, and Cachizapa.

46. See Durand Guevara, "Donde habita el olvido."

47. Durand Guevara, 51. Migrants from the northern highlands, mainly from the departments of Piura and Cajamarca, tended to settle in the northern provinces of San Martín, such as Rioja, Saposoa, or Moyobamba. In contrast, migrants originating from the mountainous parts of Ancash and Huanuco were more inclined to colonize the southern provinces of San Martín.

48. Peru is home to two main species of coca plants: *Erythroxylum coca* and *Erythroxylum novogranatense*. These species have different varieties that are adapted to various regions and climates. *Erythroxylum coca* var. *coca*, also known as Bolivian or Huánuco coca, grows in the eastern Andes of Peru and Bolivia, where it faces humid, tropical, and montane conditions. *Erythroxylum coca* var. *ipadu*, or Amazonian coca, is cultivated in the lowland Amazon basin of Peru and Colombia. *Erythroxylum novogranatense* var. *novogranatense* and *Erythroxylum novogranatense* var. *truxillense* are mainly found in Colombia and the northern coastal regions of Peru. The leaves of these plants contain alkaloids, such as cocaine, that have psychoactive effects when consumed. The coca leaf has a long history of traditional and cultural uses in South America, such as chewing the leaves or drinking coca tea for medicinal and stimulant purposes. However, the extraction and refinement of cocaine from the coca leaves is a relatively recent and illicit activity that involves chemical processes. Most of the coca production in Peru is illegal and sold to drug traffickers who turn it into cocaine. Coca plants themselves are not inherently illegal in Peru. Under Article 299 of the Peruvian Penal Code, possession of limited quantities of coca paste, cocaine hydrochloride, or coca leaves for personal use is legal: up to five grams of coca paste, two grams of cocaine hydrochloride, or eight grams of coca leaves. Possession of multiple types of drugs, regardless of quantity, is illegal. Cultivation of coca plants is permitted in specific regions and for cultural practices like chewing leaves or drinking coca tea. However, the majority of coca production in Peru is illegal, as it is used for cocaine production.

49. See Comité Directivo del Instituto Vial Provincial, Lamas, Perú 2009; Mejoramiento de la Cadena Productiva de Cacao y de Pijuayo.

50. Enrique Mayer, *Ugly Stories of the Peruvian Agrarian Reform* (Durham, NC: Duke University Press, 2009). Mayer demonstrates how, beginning with General Velasco Alvarado's regime (1968–1975), agrarian reform led to frustration and incredible national conflict but did break up the tyrannical *haciendas* (large estate or plantation system).

51. See Durand Guevara, "Donde habita el olvido," 51–53.

52. APRA is one of the oldest political parties in Latin America. It was founded in 1924 in Mexico City, Mexico, and in 1930 in Lima.

53. Nina Boschmann, "Coca und Guerilla in Perus Garten Eden," *TAZ*, June 5, 1990, https://taz.de/Coca-und-Guerilla-in-Perus-Garten-Eden/!1765461.

54. See Mayer, *Ugly Stories*. Ryan Brown and Lindsey Osterman, "Culture of Honor, Violence, and Homicide," in *The Oxford Handbook of Evolutionary Perspectives on Violence, Homicide, and War*, ed. Todd K. Shackelford and Viviana A. Weekes-Shackelford (Oxford: Oxford University Press, 2012), 218–32. Research suggests that cultures can encourage and permit violence to exist as a response to various environmental obstacles, such as widespread resource impoverishment.

55. See Durand Guevara, "Donde habita el olvido," 100. Cachay recalled "the massacre of March 1982 against defenseless producers of corn who demanded better prices," and

"the barbarian persecution with two hundred *sinchis* [police] against the leaders after the massacre ordered by Belaúnde and his minister Nils Ericson Correa."

CHAPTER 2

Epigraph. Albert Camus, *The Rebel: An Essay on Man in Revolt* (New York: Vintage, 2012), 15.

1. Throughout this book, an asterisk signifies a pseudonym for a person or place. Diego's interview, Caynarachi basin, 2017.

2. After three months of fighting with the MRTA in the rainforest (*selva* or *monte*), Diego became logistics commander for the Caynarachi basin.

3. "Durante operativo antidrogas en el tramo Pongo de Caynarachi y Barranquita, intervienen a dos sujetos que portaban arma de fuego hechiza," Radio Tropical, December 19, 2020, https://radiotropical.pe/durante-operativo-antidrogas-en-el-tramo-pongo-de-caynarachi-y-barranquita-intervienen-a-dos-sujetos-que-portaban-arma-de-fuego-hechiza; "San Martín: Detienen a alcalde de Caynarachi por presunta defraudación," December 18, 2018, *Andina*, https://andina.pe/agencia/noticia-san-Martín-detienen-a-alcalde-caynarachi-presunta-defraudacion-736372.aspx.

4. Interview, Caynarachi basin, 2017.

5. Quoted in Antonio López Díaz, "Los indeseables de Tarapoto," *El País*, April 4, 2016. In Peruvian Amazonia, the ideology and doctrine of the Túpac Amaru Revolutionary Movement (MRTA) were influenced by a complex blend of Marxism-Leninism, indigenous rights, and anti-imperialist ideologies. This unique amalgamation of ideologies shaped the MRTA's approach to revolutionary activism and their vision for revolutionary social change.

6. *Dicen que en las aguas / del río Amazonas se esconde la anaconda / Ya todos tienen cuidado / Dicen que en las aguas / del río Amazonas se esconde la anaconda / Ya todos tienen cuidado.*

7. *Bartuco* is the vernacular variation of my name in Spanish, Bartolomé. My editor, Katherine Faydash, kindly pointed out that *-uco* is commonly used to express fondness.

8. Menton and Cronkleton, "Migration and Forests in the Peruvian Amazon," 2. In the Amazonian lowlands, population grew in urban and rural areas in all four regions (San Martín, Loreto, Madre de Dios, and Ucayali) until the 1990s. With the 1960s colonization of Tingo María, people from Piura and Arequipa arrived in the Upper Huallaga Valley. During the 1970s, Andean migrants began emigrating to the Huallaga from Ancash, Celendín, Cajamarca, and La Libertad, a region in northwestern Peru.

9. Sístero García Torres, *Guerra en la Selva: Historia del Movimiento TUPAC AMARU en la Amazonía Peruana* (independently published, 2017), 2.

10. Alberto Gálvez Olaechea's "Prison Interview," Huacariz, Cajamarca, Peru, October 2003, cited in Durand Guevara, "Donde habita el olvido," 59. In San Martín, the MIR-VR comprised students from the agrarian university and teachers from Chiclayo, Tarapoto, and the region of Amazonas. The first MIR nucleus in Tarapoto was formed in 1975 by teachers. Within a few years, the MIR had numerous student recruits from pedagogical institutes, such as Roberto Pérez, Alcides Reátegui, and Abad Sagazeta, who became key members of the Túpac Amaru Revolutionary Movement's Northeastern Front.

11. See Durand Guevara, "Donde habita el olvido," 58. Alberto Gálvez Olaechea, leader of the MIR-VR and then the National Directorate of the MRTA, recalled in his "prison interview" that in the early 1980s, "Tarapoto was a small city, with a cultural and very precarious intellectual life. In Tarapoto and in several of the other towns, the only newspaper that

arrived was our mouthpiece, *Voz Rebelde*. The national newspapers arrived very little, VR circulated in different places and was bought mainly by the teachers."

12. Sístero García Torres, "La Pesadilla," in *La danza de la coca*, ed. Pezo Pinedo Aldinger (Tarapoto, Peru: Syndisgraf, 2001), 219–20.

13. Comisión de la Verdad y Reconciliación (Truth and Reconciliation Commission), *Informe final de la Comisión de la Verdad y Reconciliación*, vol. 4, section 3 "Los escenarios de la de la violencia,"; "La región Nororiental," chapter 1.4 (here after CVR 1.4).

14. José Carlos Mariátegui, *Seven Interpretative Essays on Peruvian Reality* (Austin: University of Texas Press, 1971).

15. García Torres, *Guerra en la Selva*, 2–3.

16. Marc Becker, *Twentieth-Century Latin American Revolutions* (Lanham, MD: Rowman and Littlefield, 2017), 7–8. Many Peruvian Marxists have emphasized the importance of the collective organization of Indigenous societies, which they assert is a forerunner to socialism, among others.

17. García Torres, "La Pesadilla," 220.

18. The Unitary Union of Workers in Education of Peru (SUTEP) is a Peruvian union that groups together teachers who work in public schools. It was founded in Cuzco on July 6, 1972. SUTEP advocated for the recognition and protection of teachers' rights, such as improved career advancement opportunities, job security, and access to professional development. They worked toward improving working conditions for teachers, including fair pay, sufficient benefits, and access to teaching resources. To address the need for better infrastructure, adequate resources for teaching and learning, and equal access to education for all, SUTEP called for increased government investment in the education sector. On the SUTEP strikes, see Philip Mauceri, "The Transition to 'Democracy' and the Failures of Institution Building," in *The Peruvian Labyrinth: Polity, Society, Economy*, ed. Maxwell A. Cameron and Philip Mauceri (University Park: Pennsylvania State University Press, 1997), 26.

19. García Torres noted that in 1985, more than a dozen MIR-VR fighters and twenty MRTA militants joined the Batallón América in Colombia.

20. The ELN, or Ejército de Liberación Nacional (National Liberation Army), started as a guerrilla group in Peru in 1962. They engaged in minor conflicts and operations, eventually leading to seven months of militant activity in 1965. It's thought that approximately fifty members of the ELN were operating in southern Peru, after receiving training in Cuba, and then entering the country via Bolivia. In December of 1965, the Peruvian Army successfully dismantled the ELN. Héctor Béjar, an ELN military commander, claimed that their goal was to forge an autonomous community of revolutionaries and to assemble an army that would bring together fighters from various political backgrounds. See Héctor Béjar, *Peru 1965: Notes on a Guerrilla Experience* (New York: Monthly Review Press, 1970).

21. García Torres, *Guerra en la Selva*, 5.

22. Meza Bazán, "El Movimiento Revolucionario Túpac Amaru," 263–64, 277; *Caretas*, no. 1397, January 18, 1997. Sixty-seven guerrillas were captured between Medellín and Manizales, including the MIR-VR follower Sístero García Torres, who spent four months in prison. García Torres subsequently returned to Peru, where he would become the commander of the Northeastern Front of the MRTA and an eventual dissident of the party.

23. García Torres, *Guerra en la Selva*, 12. The Sisa Valley is connected to the Upper Mayo, Middle Mayo, Huayabamba, and Central Huallaga. It served as an important point for transit

through the area and refuge for the EPT when it carried out its first military campaign, Túpac Amaru Vive.

24. Having spent time in Colombia and Nicaragua, the camp trained Sístero García Torres (a.k.a. Comrade Ricardo), Pedro Ojeda Zavaleta (a.k.a. Comrade Darío), and Osler Panduro Rengifo (a.k.a. Comrade Mario), who would subsequently become guerrilla leaders of the Northeastern Front. They would prepare the ground for future armed incursions carried out by the MRTA in late 1987 in San Martín.

25. CVR 1.4, 371; García Torres, "La Pesadilla," 217. The light automatic rifle, usually referred to as the *fusil automatique léger* or FAL, is a battle rifle developed in Belgium by Dieudonné Saive and manufactured by FN Herstal. SIG Sauer manufactured the SIG Pro series of semiautomatic pistols in Exeter, New Hampshire, in the United States. The SIG Pro series introduced groundbreaking features that set it apart from its predecessors and solidified its place in firearm history. Notably, it was among the earliest SIG Sauer handguns to incorporate an integrated universal accessory rail, a significant advancement that allowed users to effortlessly attach a wide range of accessories to enhance functionality and versatility. The SIG Pro series pistols had replaceable grips that let shooters alter the ergonomics to fit their unique preferences and hand sizes. It was also SIG Sauer's first polymer-frame handgun.

26. The Central Huallaga Valley spans from Cabo Leveaú and Sauce to the Ponaza and Sisa Valleys.

27. CVR 1.4, 371–372; García Torres, "La Pesadilla," 217.

28. Martín Tanaka, "Sendero Luminoso, the MRTA, and the Peruvian Paradoxes," in *Latin American Guerrilla Movements*, ed. Dirk Kruijt, Eduardo Rey Tristán, and Alberto Martín Álvarez (New York: Routledge, 2019), 183.

29. APRA Rebelde was established in 1959 following the expulsion of a number of dissident members of the APRA party during their national congress in Lima. The leader of APRA Rebelde, Luis de la Puente Uceda—nephew-in-law of Lucía Haya de la Torre, sister of Víctor Raúl Haya de la Torre—embraced the radical Marxist Left. After being militarily trained and ideologically prepared in Cuba, he helped form the Movimiento de la Izquierda Revolucionaria, or MIR, in 1962.

30. García Torres, "La Pesadilla," 200.

31. Luis de la Puente Uceda, "The Peruvian Revolution: Concepts and Perspectives," *Monthly Review* 17, no. 6 (1965): 12-28.

32. Che Guevara, *Guerrilla Warfare*. A guerrilla *foco* consists of a compact unit of revolutionaries carrying out operations in the rural regions of a country. Che Guevara's *foquismo* theory, which he referred to as the application of Marxism-Leninism to the specific conditions of Latin America, gained popularity and was later popularized by Régis Debray, *Révolution dans la révolution? Lutte armée et lutte politique en Amérique latine* (Paris: F. Maspero, 1967). As articulated by Debray, *foco* is a key theory of guerrilla warfare in which vanguardism by cadres of small, mobile paramilitary commandos acts to "focus" (*foco*) popular discord against the status quo and thereby spark a popular revolt leading to regime change.

33. José Luis Rénique, "De la traición aprista al gesto heroico—Luis de la Puente y la guerrilla del MIR," *Estudios Interdisciplinarios de América Latina y el Caribe* 15, no. 1 (2004): 89–114; Héctor Béjar, *Peru 1965: Notes on a Guerrilla Experience* (New York: Monthly Review Press, 1970); Ricardo Letts Colmenares (Pumaruna), *Peru: Revolución, insurrección, guerrillas* (Lima: Ediciones Vanguardia Revolucionaria, 1968); Stefano Varese, *Salt of the Moun-*

tain: *Campa Asháninka History and Resistance in the Peruvian Jungle* (Norman: University of Oklahoma Press, 2004), xxxii; Stefano Varese, *The Art of Memory: An Ethnographer's Journey*, trans. Margaret Randall (Chapel Hill: University of North Carolina, 2020), 116. See Michael Brown and Eduardo Fernández, *War of Shadows: The Struggle for Utopia in the Peruvian Amazon* (Berkeley: University of California Press, 1991), for a fascinating account of indigenous millenarianism and the role the Asháninka played in the MIR guerrilla campaigns of 1965–1966. Much of their book focuses on a comparison between the 1965 MIR rebel events and the Juan Santos rebellion that took place in the same region in the mid-eighteenth century. In 1965, the rebel leaders met grisly fates. Máximo Velando was thrown to his death from an army helicopter in 1965. On January 7, 1966, the last armed struggle of the Túpac Amaru rebel column took place near the Sotziquí River, where Guillermo Lobatón Milla and eight other guerrillas were killed by the army. The responsibility for their deaths has been attributed to the Asháninka leader Alejandro Calderón, who reportedly betrayed the position of the Columna Túpac Amaru and its leaders, Lobatón and Meza, and their companions (anonymous reviewer, personal communication). Their deaths marked the end of the first cycle of guerrilla warfare in Peru, a cycle that had been inspired by the Cuban Revolution and made manifest by a slew of leaders: Luis de la Puente Uceda, Guillermo Lobatón Milla and Ricardo Gadea Acosta. It was not until the 1980s reemergence of the MRTA that Guevarism was rekindled within the Peruvian radical left.

34. Héctor Béjar, *Retorno a la guerrilla* (Lima: Achebé, 2015), 328; Luis de la Puente Uceda, *El MIR histórico: Luis de la Puente y Guillermo Lobatón*, ed. Ricardo Gadea Acosta (Lima: Comisión 50 Aniversario de la Gesta Guerrillera del MIR, 2015) provides an important recent study of the MIR guerrilla movement of 1965, and the proposals of its main actors, Luis de la Puente and Guillermo Lobatón.

35. According to García Torres, "La Pesadilla," 200, this included a number of MIR factions: MIR Peru, MIR Voz Rebelde, MIR 10 de Junio, MIR Yahuarina, MIR Victoria Navarro, MIR El Militante, and MIR Cuarta Etapa.

36. The MIR-EM also participated in the electoral process for the Constituent Assembly (Asamblea Constituyente) through the People's Democratic Unity Front (Unidad Democrática Popular, or UDP).

37. MRTA, "La Comisión Política, Resoluciones del 1° de Marzo, 1982 Sobre la lucha armada." The Political Commission decided on March 1, 1982, to stop referring to the two rebel organizations as the PSR-ML and MIR-EM and to start calling them the Movimiento Revolucionario Túpac Amaru (MRTA) to indicate that they were a unified group.

38. This is reflected in the words of Comandante Andres, who argued that the MRTA put "Peruvian reality ahead of any predefined political ideology. We're proposing the building of a socialism appropriate to conditions in Peru. We don't want state centrism or the bureaucratization of Peruvian society. We should have a democratic, very participatory society; not an electoral democracy every five years, but a democracy where men and women get involved with their workplace, their community, their neighborhood, and decide their own destiny. We want our participatory democracy with the people as the actors."

39. García Torres, "La Pesadilla," 201; Tanaka, "Sendero Luminoso," 183; Lust, *Capitalism, Class and Revolution*, 176–83; La Serna, *With Masses and Arms*, 67. Graffiti, pamphlets, and leaflets served as potent communicative vehicles for expressing the MRTA's ideological mantras and objectives. In addition to others, these slogans and MRTA maxims included:

"¡El pueblo armado jamás será aplastado!" (The armed people will never be crushed!);
"¡Patria o muerte, venceremos!" (Homeland or death, we shall overcome!); "¡Revolución
o muerte!" (Revolution or death!); "¡Proletarios de todos los países, uníos!" (Proletarians
of all countries, unite!); "¡Lucha armada por la liberación!" (Armed struggle for liberation!); and "¡Contra la opresión y la explotación, lucha y revolución!" (Against oppression
and exploitation, struggle and revolution!).

40. Truth and Reconciliation Commission, *Hatun Willakuy*, 30; Cynthia Brown, *In Desperate Straits: Human Rights in Peru after a Decade of Democracy and Insurgency* (New York:
Human Rights Watch, 1990), 87–88. On December 8, 1989, the MRTA assassinated Alejandro Calderón, the Asháninka leader of the Pichis, and his son Alcides Calderón, trig-
gering a ferocious wave of ethnic violence and killings among the Yanesha, Asháninka,
and mestizos. The Asháninka reacted to the execution of Calderón and his son with the
backing of the Peruvian Army and established the Ejército Asháninka that fought the
MRTA and displaced them from the area (anonymous reviewer, personal communication). There are some indications the Yanesha were victimized because of their refusal
to join the conflict on the side of Peru's Armed Forces.

41. In the formative years of the Túpac Amaru Revolutionary Movement, Luis Varese Scotto
used his personal experience in the Sandinista National Liberation Front (FSLN) of Nicaragua to organize MRTA members. Varese Scotto helped the MRTA construct a rebel front
in Cusco's forest between 1984 until his 1986 arrest.

42. A small Quechua-speaking peasant community, Tinta is in the jurisdiction of Canchis
Province, which is located in the Region of Cuzco. The community of Tinta is situated
about fifteen miles from the provincial hub of Sicuani, a town known for its Túpac
Amaru football stadium. On the Túpac Amaru revolt, see, e.g., Lillian Estelle, *The Last
Inca Revolt, 1780–1783* (Norman: University of Oklahoma Press, 1966); Lewin Boleslao, *La
rebelión de Túpac Amaru y los orígenes de la independencia Hispanoamericana* (Buenos Aires:
Sociedad Editora Latino Americana, 1967); Daniel Valcárcel, *La rebelión de Túpac Amaru*
(Lima: Fondo de Cultura Económica, 1970); Alberto Flores Galindo, ed., *Túpac Amaru II-
1780: Sociedad colonial y sublevaciones populares* (Lima: Retablo de Papel Ediciones, 1976);
Scarlett O'Phelan Godoy, *La gran rebelión en los Andes: De Túpac Amaru a Túpac Catari*
(Cuzco, Perú: Centro de Estudios Regionales Andinos "Bartolomé de Las Casas," 1995);
Charles Walker, *The Túpac Amaru Rebellion* (Cambridge, MA: Belknap Press of Harvard
University Press, 2014). Tinta was the locale that the cacique (hereditary leader) Túpac
Amaru II (José Gabriel Condorcanqui) led a major rebellion (1780–c. 1782) against Span-
ish colonial oppression. Before his own forces being routed, Túpac Amaru II and his
family were executed by the Spanish in 1781.

43. CVR 1.4, 371; Meza Bazán, "El Movimiento Revolucionario Túpac Amaru," 277.

44. The MRTA took inspiration from the Battle of Ayacucho (also known as the Battle of
La Quinua), which took place at the Pampa de Ayacucho, near Ayacucho and Quinua,
Peru, on December 9, 1824. This key military encounter was crucial to securing the lib-
eration of Peru and other South American nations from the Spanish Crown. Although
Antonio José de Sucre's campaign in Upper Peru continued until 1825 and the fortresses
of Chiloé and Callao were besieged until 1826, Peru considers this battle the end of the
Spanish-American wars of independence. Simón Bolívar's subordinate, Lieutenant Antonio José de Sucre was in charge of the independence forces. Following the battle, the
Royalist army's second commander in chief José de Canterac, signed the final surrender
after Viceroy José de la Serna was injured. The Peruvian Army marks the anniversary of

the Battle of Ayacucho each year. On the formal integration of the two insurgent organizations, see Declaración Unitaria del Movimiento Túpac Amaru (MRTA) y del Movimiento Izquierda Revolucionaria "Voz Rebelde" (MIR-VR), I Comité Central Unitario, Lima, December 9, 1986. La Serna, *With Masses and Arms,* 65–67, notes that Gálvez and Polay met secretly in late 1985 in Sandinista-controlled Nicaragua to arrange the details of the agreement in which the MIR-VR would be included into the MRTA's organizational structure.

45. La Serna, *With Masses and Arms,* 79; CVR 1.4, 373. After leaving prison, José Ojeda Zavala, or Comandante Darío, opined on this fusion in which the *miristas* considered the *emerretistas* as petulant "*pitucos* (elites)." A number of commentators (García Torres, "La Pesadilla," 212–13; CVR 1.4, 373; Meza Bazán, "El Movimiento Revolucionario Túpac Amaru," 277) note how Comrade Darío felt that the *miristas* "are not revolutionaries; they are petty bourgeois and that can make the project fail. They have many revisionist deviations; they do not have money; they do not work; but they believe themselves to be cuckoos. They only serve to occupy positions of command."

46. CVR 1.4.

47. García Torres, "La Pesadilla," 208.

48. Durand Guevara, "Donde habita el olvido," 59.

49. Peru's Left has long struggled to capitalize on the upheaval in capitalist development for political gain. Ironically, Peru was perhaps Latin America's best chance for a prosperous Left in the 1980s. The country's reformist military government encouraged social mobilization and tolerated leftist party organizing during the late 1960s and early 1970s, when military regimes in neighboring countries like Argentina, Chile, Brazil, and Bolivia waged war on the partisan and working-class Left, while suppressing popular movements in the name of "national security." Following the transition to civilian rule, Peru had the strongest electoral Left in South America for much of the 1980s. The Left gained significant support from lower-class groups and established close ties with labor unions and grassroots movements. Peru's budding democracy stumbled in the latter part of the 1980s as political violence and increasing economic turmoil threatened to topple the state. On the thinking of Alberto Gálvez Olaechea, see his following works, Alberto Gálvez Olaechea *Con la palabra desarmada: Ensayos sobre el (pos)conflict* (Lima: Fauno, 2015); Alberto Gálvez Olaechea, "Combatiente en la batalla de ideas: Entrevista a Alberto Gálvez Olaechea por Alejandro Lavquén," *Punto Final,* October 14, 2016: "We were enthusiastic about processes such as those in Cuba or Nicaragua, and we believed that the revolution was near. And in the context of the rise of social struggles, we tried to radicalize the processes by pushing the masses toward socialism. I think there was nobility in our intentions, but the avant-garde made us think that the 'correct line' that we possessed and the consequence of our practice would be enough for the masses to follow us. We fail and pay a high price for it. History is written by the people, with their struggle, and no one can replace them." In *Con la palabra desarmada,* Gálvez Olaechea argues that his path to the MRTA insurgency was a natural journey, a product of the times, where leftist discourse considered the armed struggle a valid method to achieve the socialist revolution. He eventually renounced armed violence and began a process of reflecting on his experience in prison and his participation in this period of upheaval. By challenging his readers to try to comprehend the allure of the MRTA, Gálvez Olaechea raises crucial issues regarding the necessity of allowing for the social reintegration of those who belonged to the armed group.

50. Gálvez Olaechea, *Con la palabra desarmada*.
51. Gálvez Olaechea, *Con la palabra desarmada*. The capture of Gálvez Olaechea was a major setback for the MRTA leadership. He was arrested in 1987, escaped in 1990, and was arrested again in 1991. He remained in detention until his release in May 2015. Following incarceration, he joined leftist democratic groups. Víctor Polay Campos, "Interrogatorio a Víctor Polay, trigésima quinta sesión, June 11, 2005," in *En el banquillo: ¿Terrorista o rebelde?* ed. Víctor Polay Campos (Lima: Canta Editores, 2007), 247.
52. Interview with Víctor Polay Campos by Nina Boschmann, "Die Gesellschaft muß vom Volk neu geschaffen warden," *TAZ*, June 5, 1990, https://taz.de/!1765463.
53. Bartholomew Dean, *Urarina Society, Cosmology and History in Peruvian Amazonia* (Gainesville: University Press of Florida, 2009).
54. Similar to calling someone your brother, *bróder* is a term of social endearment in Peru, as in other areas of Latin America.
55. Julián, the Túpac Amaru rebels' chief of the Democratic Defense Front in the area, told me: "We wanted to have a regional movement so that we were no longer under the jurisdiction of Lamas. We wanted Caynarachi to be a province with its own capital, and then we could be part of Alto Amazonas since so many people had contact with Yurimaguas as there was no road at that time—only river travel. In the Caynarachi basin, most people wanted to be part of Alto Amazonas [in the Region of Loreto], but when the highway came through this political demand evaporated." Interview, Caynarachi basin, 2020.
56. Public health has been a perennial problem associated with urbanization in Peruvian Amazonia. See Bartholomew Dean, "El Dr. Máxime Kuczynski-Godard y la medicina social en la Amazonía peruana," in *La vida en la Amazonía peruana: Observaciones de un médico*, by Máxime Kuczynski-Godard (Lima: Fondo Editorial de la Universidad Nacional Mayor de San Marcos, 2004). In 1952 during his youthful journey through Loreto, Che Guevara spent time at the San Pablo Leprosarium, founded by Máxime Kuczynski-Godard.
57. Patricia Zárate Ardela, *La democracia lejos de Lima: Descentralización y política en el departamento de San Martín* (Lima: IEP Colección Mínima, 2003), covers the history of regionalism in the San Martín region. The García Pérez government's plan to unite San Martín with the coastal department of La Libertad to form an administrative *macroregión* in the name of "decentralization" met with little understanding or acceptance among the local populace.
58. Parasitic insects called botflies (*dermatobia hominis*) lay their eggs on the bodies of animals, including people. Once they have penetrated the skin, the larvae of the botfly, also known as "warbles," grow and feed on the tissues of their host, causing noticeable inflammation and discomfort. The host's body responds to the larvae by creating a tissue pocket around them in defense. After about eight weeks of growth inside the host's subcutaneous layers, the larvae emerge to pupate for at least a week, usually in the soil.
59. The term *pituco* is commonly used to talk about someone who looks or acts like they are wealthy or of elevated social standing. For an insightful perspective on the sociologically pregnant term *pituco*, see Shane Greene, "The Terruco Problem." *Editor's Forum: Hot Spots*, March 30, 2023, https://culanth.org/fieldsights/the-terruco-problem. As Greene cogently notes, "Pituco means all of the following: rich, socially ascendent, living in posh neighborhoods, white or whitish, dressed well, snobbish, showing familiarity with English." In contrast, the term *platasapa* stands for *plata* (silver) + *sapa* (the augmentative), and in the Huallaga Valley the word is used to refer to a well-to-do person.
60. MRTA, "No ha empezado ninguna revolución: A propósito de la estatización del sistema financiero," Dirección Nacional del MRTA, July 1987. See also MRTA, "¡Con las masas y

las armas por la democracia revolucionaria, la soberanía nacional, la justicia y la paz!," Nacional Dirección, December 1987. The MRTA's political platform included a long list of demands: expulsion of foreign banks; nationalization of domestic banking, financial, insurance, industrial, commercial, real estate, and food and pharmaceutical industries; suspension of foreign debt payments; annulment of oil contracts and nationalization of foreign companies operating in the country; wage increases and salaries adjustable according to cost of living; elimination of salary caps; subsidy for basic food items; price controls for food, medicines, and services; job security and respect for unions and collective bargaining; the defense of peasant and native communities; technical assistance to peasants; freezing of the price of inputs and tools; fair prices for agricultural products and marketing without intermediaries; prosecution of government officials accused of corruption; repeal of the state of emergency and the restitution of individual guarantees; elimination of the armed forces' emergency zones; prosecution and punishment of state actors who violated human rights; and freedom of political and social prisoners.

61. *¡Por la causa de los pobres! ¡Con las masas y las armas! ¡Venceremos!*

62. MRTA, *Conquistando el porvenir: Con las masas y las armas. Notas sobre la historia del MRTA* (Lima: Voz Rebelde MRTA, 1990), 312.

63. In Peruvian Amazonia, the term *florear* is commonly used to describe a type of deceit that involves trying to make everything seem positive. To *florear* involves engaging in inauthentic flattery, whitewashing, or sugarcoating, rather than simply lying.

64. Diego employed the phrase *cholo*, which can be a highly derogatory way of referring to the inhabitants of the Andes, or to those of Andean ancestry. In the past, *cholo* was an insulting term used to denigrate people of mixed descent from the Andean highlands. This phrase has evolved with time in Peru and can now have different interpretations depending on the context or area of its use. Some individuals have repurposed the term *cholo* to show their pride in their intercultural heritage and sense of self. Likewise, Diego used the derogatory term *charapa*, which people sometimes employ to refer to Amazonian peoples of indigenous or mixed ancestry. *Charapa*, which means Arrau turtle (*Podocnemis expansa*) in Quechua, is now associated with negative connotations. When used by outsiders, it implies that Amazonian peoples are uneducated, uncivilized, or outdated. Using the Quechua word for turtle emphasizes the racial and cultural bias existing between Peru's coastal, highland, and lowland areas. The perception persists that the latter is less developed in the national consciousness. To put it simply, referring to someone as *charapa* based on their ethnicity or regional background is a type of verbal aggression that further marginalizes and excludes Amazonian communities.

65. Yumbatos is situated within the administrative jurisdiction of the District of Caynarachi, which falls under the Province of Lamas in the Region of San Martín. Pampa Hermosa is a small town located in the District of Yurimaguas, which is part of the Province of Alto Amazonas, situated in the eastern region of the Department of Loreto.

66. Chirimoto District is located in the eastern part of the Amazonas Department, within the Province of Rodríguez de Mendoza.

67. Meza Bazán, "El Movimiento Revolucionario Túpac Amaru," 416n63. In general, the *emerretistas* located their permanent or transitory military camps outside of the area's villages or rural hamlets. This was to minimize civilian casualties associated with their clashes with law enforcement agencies. The MRTA also claimed to be guided by the Geneva Conventions in its armed actions and the treatment of prisoners.

68. The Northeastern Front established three military encampments in the Lower Huallaga: El Porvenir, Yumbatos, and Pampa Hermosa. El Porvenir was dedicated to directing the

armed struggle in the Caynarachi basin; the Yumbatos camp oversaw insurgent activities in the Pongo de Caynarachi Region; the base at Pampa Hermosa was focused on advancing the rebel cause in the Alto Amazonas region of Loreto.

69. Bigwood, "With Guerrilla U." Bigwood refers to the "Lima styled intellectual" Miguel Rincón Rincón as Commander Edgardo.

70. Bigwood.

71. "Hermano, los dos estamos juntos en esto."

72. As the son of a senior APRA politician and former legislator of humble origins, Víctor Polay Campos climbed quickly through the APRA ranks. He studied in Madrid and Paris in the early 1970s. While in Paris, he shared a room with the future president of Peru and fellow APRA member Alan García. Polay Campos has a law degree and is fluent in Basque and French. While in Europe, he disavowed his APRA membership and adopted a left-wing outlook that helped pave the way for the MRTA's later establishment. Polay Campos was apprehended by Peruvian authorities in Huancayo in April 1989 but escaped from jail along with forty-seven other MRTA rebels in July 1990. He was arrested again in June 1992 and condemned to life in prison in April 1993. The UN Human Rights Committee determined in 1997 that his trial and detention conditions violated articles 7, 10, and 14 of the International Covenant on Civil and Political Rights. He was subsequently sentenced to thirty-two years in prison, on March 22, 2006, after being found guilty by a Peruvian court of nearly thirty crimes committed during the late 1980s and early 1990s. He is currently imprisoned at the Callao Naval Base.

CHAPTER 3

Epigraph. Interview, Caynarachi basin, 2018.

1. Built between 1928 and 1931, the Virgin of the Snows Cathedral is located next to the Plaza Mayor, on the corner of Jaúregui and Castilla streets. The Cathedral has a central nave and two minor side naves, and an imposing central tower that is roughly forty meters high. The main altar is made of marble, artificial and simple concrete, and the side altars, the pulpit and the confessionals are fashioned from mahogany wood with ornate carved work. It plays host to Yurimaguas's *fiesta patronal*, which culminates annually on August 15. In 2000, the Peru government declared the structure part of the Cultural Patrimony of the Nation.

2. García Torres, *Guerra en la Selva*, 40. The MRTA was involved in the collection of "war quotas" (*cupos*) from drug traffickers, industrialists, and merchants. The funds were supposed to be administered nationally, but my informants paint a very different picture of their allocation.

3. CVR 1.4; Truth and Reconciliation Commission, *Hatun Willakuy*, 190. The use of strategic kidnappings, primarily for extortion, was a favored MRTA strategy. Between 1984 and 1996, the MRTA perfected this technique, turning sporadic actions into a disciplined practice.

4. Regina's niece Leonilla* worked in Yana Puma at the time and had to walk to town every day, passing by her uncle and aunt's pasture (*pasto*), where she encountered numerous groups of armed combatants. From a distance, she wasn't sure if they were *cumpas* or the army. If it was the MRTA, they would say "Buenos días, compañera." She elaborated: "we always knew, depending on how they greeted us. Everyone would agree on this. And you were required to respond in the same fashion" (interview, Caynarachi basin, 2017).

5. García Torres, *Guerra en la Selva*, 40, emphasis added.

6. Inflation had hit the *inti* hard by 1990. The *Inti millón* (I/m.) was used as a unit of account as a stopgap measure from January to July 1991. One million *intis* equaled one *Inti millón*, and hence one new sol. On July 1, 1991, the nuevo sol replaced the *inti* at an exchange rate of one million to one. Doña Ximena said that her family paid only five months of *cupos*, as the military had routed the forward operating basecamp in El Porvenir dispersing the MRTA within the Caynarachi.

7. *Choba choba* is a type of collective reciprocal labor exchange practiced among Kichwa-Lamista communities. It is the means by which kith and kin join forces to cultivate the land, assigning tasks by strength and capability. As an endogamous labor practice, *choba choba* eliminates the need for outside contractors to be paid to assist with planting and cultivation, as it is predicated on deeply held beliefs of communal reciprocity. The notion is that everyone contributes to the process and benefits from *choba choba*.

8. A number of eyewitness renditions emphasize how the army punished Augustín following his release by forcing him to do physical exercises (*ranear*), a point he never mentioned in his many hours of conversation with me. I collected anecdotal accounts in San Martín and Loreto that the army and police were responsible for unheard-of abuses by officers, and that their subordinates blackmailed the local populace by charging them money or demanding goods so as not to accuse them of being subversives. Residents also mentioned successive searches at numerous points on the highway by the armed forces or police, accompanied by the stealing of their personal belongings, livestock, or cash.

9. Interview, Caynarachi basin, 2019.

10. Interview, Lima, 2018.

11. García Torres, *Guerra en la Selva*, 2–3. This matches García Torres's descriptions of the first clandestine groups in the area, which, he says, "were made up of young people between the ages of eighteen to twenty-five years and were compartmentalized into cells of about five to six members for clandestine meetings. Everything was clandestine. Supposedly, nobody knew each other and had no reason to know the real identity of the members. They only recognized each other by their pseudonyms. They had no right to ask or know the real name of their *compañero*. If they did, they were seen as infiltrators or snitches [*soplónes*]."

12. "*Así mueren los soplones*" read the placard on the dead dog Huesito, ca. 1984–1985.

13. Ximena, the wife of Ignacio Romero, informed me "terrorists [*terrucos*] intended the warning for the entire village." She mentioned that the insurgents had used the iron window frames in her store's town center location to hang the unfortunate dog, Huesito.

14. CVR 1.4, 371. Several of my informants insisted that the MRTA was responsible for the canine's cowardly death. During the years of violence, both the Sendero Luminoso and the MRTA clashed for control over areas of coca leaf production.

15. Interview with José, Caynarachi basin, 2015.

16. Van Dun, *Cocaleros*, 77–78; García Torres, "La Pesadilla," 208. See also Dean, "Machetes in Our Hands." In general, Sendero Luminoso controlled the Upper Huallaga, whereas the MRTA dominated the Central Huallaga. Sendero Luminoso did have a fleeting presence in the Central Huallaga, first appearing in 1981 in the Shanusi Valley of San Martín. This group of *senderistas* managed to recruit a number of MIR-VR insurgents who were apparently anxious to take up arms with them. This included the president of the Producers of Corn and Sorghum, *Compañero* Velarde. In mid-1981, a group of thirty *senderistas* entered the Kocama-Kocamilla community of Lagunas, located on the Lower Huallaga River.

They attacked the town's police station, killing two officers for allegedly being corrupt. The central government responded by sending in 1,500 *sinchis* (antisubversive police) to hunt down and capture the *senderistas*. Those Sendero Luminoso insurgents who fell into the hands of the *sinchis* were imprisoned downriver in Iquitos.

17. La Serna, *With Masses and Arms*, 86. As confirmed by those ex-*tupacamarista* rebels I interviewed, Sendero Luminoso saw the MRTA as a threat to its greater political and territorial goals in the San Martín region, and hence had no desire to form any political or military alliances with MRTA.

18. While not defunct as an organization, the leader of Sendero Luminoso in the Upper Huallaga—Florindo Eleuterio Flores Hala (a.k.a. Comrade Artemio) was captured in February 2012, striking a major blow to insurgents who still relied on taxing the lucrative cocaine and *pasta básica de cocaína* markets of the region, as well as garnering funds associated with illicit logging and other contraband. Comrade Artemio was given a life sentence on June 7, 2013, along with a requirement to pay five hundred million soles in civil restitution.

19. Joseph Brown, *Force of Words: The Logic of Terrorist Threats* (New York: Columbia University Press, 2020), provides a recent analysis of the differing logistical strategies of Sendero Luminoso and the MRTA.

20. Mikhail Bakunin, *Bakunin on Anarchy: Selected Works by the Activist-Founder of World Anarchism*, ed., trans., and with introduction by Sam Dolgoff (New York: Vintage Books, 1971).

21. Polay Campos, "Interrogatorio a Víctor Polay, trigésima quinta sesión, June 11, 2005," 205–6.

22. Nina Boschmann, "Die Gesellschaft muß vom Volk neu geschaffen warden."

23. Che Guevara, "Guerra de guerrillas un método," in *Obra revolucionaria* (Mexico: Ed. Era, 1973), 551–52, 556–63. Comandante Ernesto "Che" Guevara criticized most Latin American communist parties that had renounced revolutionary warfare. Guevara developed *foquismo*, a new ideology of revolution in which the revolutionary *foco*, a tiny cell of guerrillas working from the countryside, supplanted the vanguard party. Rather than wait for the right objective conditions, revolutionaries must create the "subjective" conditions for the revolution. For Guevara, the rural peasants, not the urban workers, were the breeding ground for the popular revolution. This idea rapidly took root among sectors of Peru's left. On the region, see Tanaka, "Sendero Luminoso," 184; MRTA, *Conquistando el porvenir*, 277.

24. Durand Guevara, "Donde habita el olvido," 66.

25. Meza Bazán, "El Movimiento Revolucionario Túpac Amaru," 275. CVR 1.4; Durand Guevara, "Donde habita el olvido," 57. Between 1978 and 1979, there were road blockages and wide-scale peasant mobilizations in Chazuta, Rioja, and Moyobamba that resulted in violent confrontations and the detention of officials, along with small aircraft and heavy machinery.

26. García Torres, "La Pesadilla," 211–12. Tabalosos, a town and district located in the Province of Lamas within the Department of San Martín, sits at an elevation of six hundred meters above sea level. Positioned on the right bank of the Mayo River, which is a notable tributary of the Huallaga River, Tabalosos finds itself nestled in the *selva alta*, an elevated region of the Amazon rainforest.

27. CVR 1.4, 309–11, 371; Meza Bazán, "El Movimiento Revolucionario Túpac Amaru," 271, 276; García Torres, "La Pesadilla," 201, 218; García Torres, *Guerra en la Selva*, 13; Durand Guevara, "Donde habita el olvido," 58, MRTA, *Conquistando el porvenir*. In 1973 members

of the MIR-Voz Rebelde organized militant cells in the towns of Shapaja, Shanao, and Pucacaca. These were places where MIR-VR followers worked as teachers. From these hamlets, MIR-VR militants extended their influence to Moyobamba and Juanjuí and various localities throughout the region of San Martín.

28. Durand Guevara, "Donde habita el olvido," 58.

29. Meza Bazán, "El Movimiento Revolucionario Túpac Amaru," 362. Zárate Ardela, *La democracia lejos de Lima*, provides a useful perspective on the attitude of the elites of the region of San Martín during the regionalization process. The MRTA pursued a strategy in the Huallaga Valley that did not threaten the popular organization; rather, through its cadres and grassroots militants, it sought to infiltrate them. Despite the harsh state repression unleashed against the MRTA between 1987 and 1989, the rebel group managed to unify around the "San Martín autonomous region movement" led by FEDIPSM within the framework of *aprista* decentralization.

30. The state of emergency in the Upper Huallaga region finally ended after more than thirty years when then president Ollanta Humala lifted it in Huánuco. The state of emergency was first decreed in the Upper Huallaga during the military dictatorship of General Francisco Morales Bermúdez, then civil rights were restored in all areas during the government of Fernando Belaúnde Terry, but in mid-1984, due to the incursions of the Sendero Luminoso, the state of emergency was again decreed.

31. Durand Guevara, "Donde habita el olvido," 61, 74.

32. Meza Bazán, "El Movimiento Revolucionario Túpac Amaru," 362.

33. García Torres, *Guerra en la Selva*, 12–13.

34. La Serna, *With Masses and Arms*, 79.

35. García Torres, *Guerra en la Selva*, 14.

36. "Oficio del 28 de setiembre de 1990, dirigido al Ministro de Agricultura Carlos Amat y León," qtd. in Ricardo Soberón Garrido, "Narcotráfico, violencia y campesinado en la Selva Alta," OCR document, https://www.verdadyreconciliacionperu.com/admin/files/articulos/1598_digitalizacion.pdf. In the case of the MRTA, some peasant organizations differentiated the organization from Sendero Luminoso. The Committees of Producers of Corn and Sorghum of Shilcayo, Bajo Huallaga, Nuevo Arica, Sisa Valley, and San Martín noted: "From this time onward, groups [such as the Sendero Luminoso] took up arms in a vertical and authoritarian manner, approaching the people and their problems."

37. García Torres, *Guerra en la Selva*, 14; García Torres, "La Pesadilla," 238. MRTA raids on police stations for weapons and ammunition, coupled with sales from arms merchants, provided additional firepower.

38. Interview, Sauce, 2019.

39. In August 1986, the MRTA broke its truce with Alan García's new government and attacked the presidential palace in Lima with a grenade launcher, although the rebel attack caused only minor damage.

40. A common MRTA slogan was "With the masses and arms, Homeland or death—we will win!" ("Con las masas y las armas, Patria o muerte . . . ¡venceremos!").

41. Interview, Sauce, 2019.

42. Interview, Caynarachi basin, 2017.

43. Interview, Caynarachi basin, 2019.

44. Meza Bazán, "El Movimiento Revolucionario Túpac Amaru," 279n632; *Caretas*, no. 975, October 26, 1987. The locals' sympathies for the MRTA were noted in *Caretas*, a weekly national publication highly critical of the insurgent group.

45. Diego recalled very well the time that the *máximo jefe* Víctor Polay Campos came to the basecamp at El Porvenir. He told me how Polay Campos "arrived as if he were some sort of president. He spent a few hours speaking with the *mandos*. We coordinated, and then our *máximo jefe* left. This all happened in Sauce." Diego also had encounters with Polay Campos in Campanilla, near Juanjuí. Polay Campos had traveled to Campanilla on one occasion to assess the situation on the Northeastern Front. He met with Diego about the front's finances and logistics plans. Mando Razor's new role as a provisional MRTA quartermaster was confirmed, and he was instructed in geopolitics, with direct supervision from Polay Campos.

CHAPTER 4

Epigraph. With the masses and weapons, country or death.

1. CVR 1.4, 320.
2. Durand Guevara, "Donde habita el olvido," 67.
3. As a quartermaster, Diego was involved in arranging to pick up specially ordered uniforms sent from a textile company in Lima to Tarapoto for subsequent distribution among the detachment in El Porvenir. Enhancing corporate identity, the MRTA had their logos made for T-shirts, hats, uniforms, and backpacks.
4. García Torres, *Guerra en la Selva*, 14; MRTA, *Conquistando el porvenir*. This parallels Fabiano and Diego's claims about San Martín being ready for "armed struggle" by the late 1980s.
5. CVR 1.4, 324–25. In addition to the assaults on Tabalosos and Juanjuí, the 1987 Túpac Amaru Libertador campaign also included rebel attacks on the police garrisons of the cities of Rioja and San José de Sisa (November 7), Chazuta (November 19), Senami (December 9), Shanao (December 11), and Yorongos (December 16). On December 23, another pitched confrontation between the MRTA and state armed forces would take place in Agua Blanca, located in San Martín's El Dorado District.
6. Polay Campos, "Interrogatorio a Víctor Polay, trigésima quinta sesión, June 11, 2005," 248–63.
7. García Torres, *Guerra en la Selva*, 14; La Serna, *With Masses and Arms*, 85; MRTA, *Historia del Movimiento Revolucionario Túpac Amaru* (III Comité Central del MRTA, Documento aprobado por el III Comité Central del Movimiento Revolucionario Túpac Amaru, September 1990); Raúl González, "MRTA: La historia desconocida," *Que Hacer*, no. 51 (1988): 33–46; Raúl González, "Sendero: Los problemas del campo y de la ciudad y además el MRTA," *Que Hacer*, no. 50 (January–February 1988): 47–59; Meza Bazán, "El Movimiento Revolucionario Túpac Amaru," 278. The rebels' capture of Tabalosos took place on October 8, 1987, twenty years after Che's death in Ñancahuazú, Bolivia. In his "Sendero" essay, Raúl González hypothesizes that the MRTA was actually seeking to generate media attention because, days before, several of its leaders had been captured in Lima, including Alberto Gálvez Olaechea. According to Meza Bazán, the Tabalosos attack of October 8 coincided with the death of the founder of the MIR, Luis de la Puente Uceda. For his part, Sístero García Torres stated that the assault on Tabalosos on October 8 commemorated the death of Che Guevara. The MRTA marked November 4 as a date of significance, as it was the anniversary of the start of the 1780 initiation of Túpac Amaru II's bloody and futile rebellion against the Spaniards.
8. MRTA, *Conquistando el porvenir*, 281–82.
9. MRTA, 282.

10. MRTA, "Forjando el Ejército Tupacamarista," *Voz Rebelde*, no. 8 (November 1987); García Torres, *Guerra en la Selva*, 15.

11. Víctor Polay Campos told Boschmann in his interview while imprisoned in Canto Canto: "We [the MRTA] adhere to the Geneva Convention and respect the rights of our prisoners. We deal with criminals in a similar way: generally, they are asked to get out of the area; we only shoot a few rapists and drug dealers immediately. The training of our troops takes time. In the camps, we have our own schools where the theory and practice of guerrilla warfare are taught." See Nina Boschmann, "Die Gesellschaft muß vom Volk neu geschaffen warden."

12. Meza Bazán, "El Movimiento Revolucionario Túpac Amaru," 278, 416n63. See CVR 1.4, and La Serna, *With Masses and Arms*, 88, 104 on MRTA violations of the Geneva Conventions. In *Conquistando el Porvenir* the MRTA denies any human rights abuses. The rebels claim "the most important thing is that from the beginning, the MRTA won the affection and respect of the population. The correct behavior of the combatants, the care in their relations with the population, the humanitarian treatment with the wounded policemen, the discipline, the use of the uniform, as well as the assemblies, where the people are told why we take up arms, our objectives, as well as the accountability of the authorities, mayors, governors, before their own people. All these attitudes expressed at the same time were critical to these accomplishments" (282).

13. MRTA, "¡Con las masas y las armas por la democracia revolucionaria, la soberanía nacional, la justicia y la paz!," Nacional Dirección, December 1987; CVR 1.4, 402; Alonso Gurmendi Dunkelberg, *Conflicto armado en el Perú: La época del terrorismo bajo el derecho internacional* (Lima: Universidad del Pacífico, 2019).

14. MRTA, *Conquistando el Porvenir*, 283; Meza Bazán, "El Movimiento Revolucionario Túpac Amaru," 279.

15. CVR 1.4, 375. Former interior minister José Barsallo Burga acknowledged in a secret session of the Defense Commission of Congress that there were actually ninety-five police officers in Juanjuí, of whom fourteen were in their posts while only three attempted any defense.

16. García Torres, *Guerra en la Selva*, 15. See also La Serna, *With Masses and Arms*, 88. García Torres notes in Juanjuí that the MRTA rebels forced the surrender of four police officers and stole more than ninety rifles from three police units. In his words, this was "another great success, for us, but a lieutenant of the national police was killed." The four policemen who had surrendered were handed over to the city's parish priest.

17. MRTA, *Conquistando el porvenir*; Polay Campos, "Interrogatorio a Víctor Polay, trigésima quinta sesión, June 11, 2005," 248–63. Juanjuí's Plaza de Armas is now home to the Gran Pajatén monument, which pays tribute to the Chachapoya people who once inhabited the *selva alta* area between the Marañón and Huallaga rivers. Located in the center of Juanjuí's Plaza de Armas, the monument showcases the round stone structures of Gran Pajatén, complete with slate mosaics and reliefs. Construction of the Gran Pajatén monument commenced during the Fujimori regime and culminated in its completion in 2000. The project was a collaborative endeavor involving both regional and national entities.

18. CVR 1.4, 375. Corrupt police concocted all kinds of controls to intimidate and extort money from the populace: these included obligations to pay for the safe passage from one place to another.

19. MRTA, "El Frente guerrillero Nor-Oriental," *Voz Rebelde*, no. 11 (April–May 1988).

20. The withdrawal of the detachment was allegedly accompanied to the road by an "enthusiastic crowd." García Torres, *Guerra en la Selva*, 15. During their stay in the Sisa Valley, the

MRTA column reported displays of support and solidarity from the population. MRTA, *Conquistando el porvenir*, 284.

21. CVR 1.4, 402; García Torres, "La Pesadilla," 226.

22. MRTA, *Conquistando el porvenir*, 284. See Polay Campos, "Interrogatorio a Víctor Polay, trigésima quinta sesión, June 11, 2005," 248–63, on the San José de Sisa attack. According to the CVR 1.4, 320 (see also García Torres, "La Pesadilla," 226), villagers claim that the MRTA's armed incursion into San José de Sisa and the interview conducted by Panamericana reporter Alejandro Guerrero with Víctor Polay Campos was staged for the drama of national television.

23. García Torres, *Guerra en la Selva*, 15, 20.

24. The daily curfew throughout the region of San Martín was from 11 p.m. to 5 a.m.

25. APRODEH, *Derechos Humanos*, Boletín de Información y análisis de la Asociación Pro Derechos Humanos (Lima: APRODEH), October–December 1988.

26. *Voz Rebelde*, no. 10 (February–March 1988), 8. In response to the ferocity of the counterinsurgency campaign waged in San Martín, on February 24, 1988, a MRTA commando attacked the Lima-based Ministry of Interior with a rocket launcher, causing the destruction of a number of cars and physical damage to the building.

27. García Torres, *Guerra en la Selva*, 15, claims the number was two thousand, whereas La Serna, *With Masses and Arms*, 89, on the basis of press reports, notes that five hundred police officers were dispatched via helicopter to the conflict zone.

28. MRTA, "Forjando el Ejército Tupacamarista"; MRTA, "Balance y perspectivas." According to the MRTA report "Balance y perspectivas," this included US advisers in the region under the pretext that they were supporting Peruvian antinarcotics efforts.

29. MRTA, "Forjando el Ejército Tupacamarista"; MRTA, *Conquistando el porvenir*, 316.

30. Meza Bazán, "El Movimiento Revolucionario Túpac Amaru," 280.

31. MRTA, "Balance y perspectivas"; MRTA, *Conquistando el porvenir*, 285; CVR 1.4, 324–25. The MRTA claimed that following its capture of Chazuta and Yorongos, it attacked and destroyed a Soviet-made M1-6 helicopter with four troops inside.

32. CVR 1.4, 402.

33. García Torres, *Guerra en la Selva*, 16.

34. MRTA, *Conquistando el porvenir*.

35. Durand Guevara, "Donde habita el olvido," 119.

36. García Torres, *Guerra en la Selva*, 15. As the MRTA noted in, *Conquistando el porvenir*, 284, "these comrades fought and left their blood in this valley for the struggle. The death of these comrades hit the morale of our troops more than usual as these were our first victims. Roger López 'Cabezon' and Alcides Reátegui 'Tananta' and Lainz 'Melvin.'" See also MRTA, "Historia del Movimiento Revolucionario Túpac Amaru," III Comité Central del MRTA, document approved by III Comité Central del Movimiento Revolucionario Túpac Amaru, September 1990.

37. The CVR 1.4, 403, notes that the MRTA's high commanders (Víctor Polay Campos, Néstor Cerpa Cartolini, and Rodolfo Klein Samanez) went to Lima at this point to direct the national command of MRTA.

38. García Torres, *Guerra en la Selva*, 15–16. The MRTA accused Peruvian Army General Enrique López Albújar of responsibility for the April 1989 clash between the armed forces and the guerrillas, which resulted in sixty-two MRTA combat fatalities.

39. MRTA, *Conquistando el porvenir*; García Torres, *Guerra en la Selva*, 15. As Polay Campos claims in his interview with Nina Boschmann, "Die Gesellschaft muß vom Volk neu geschaffen warden," "in such actions, we . . . detained police officers and public charges

were brought against them. They were warned to behave properly and released."

40. MRTA, "Balance y perspectivas."

41. MRTA, *Conquistando el porvenir*, 285; CVR 1.4, 403.

42. CVR 1.4, 403.

43. CVR 1.4, 325n24. García Torres, *Guerra en la Selva*. García Torres was captured at 4 a.m. on January 23, 1988, at the home of an aunt who lived in the middle-class Suchiche neighborhood of Tarapoto. With a cloth firmly secured over his eyes, they brought him to the Morales military camp. He was tortured repeatedly and spent the next two years incarcerated until his release on January 26, 1990.

44. Meza Bazán, "El Movimiento Revolucionario Túpac Amaru," 282. No one I interviewed in the Caynarachi was aware of the details of García Torres's 1990 capture. The collective memory of his presence in the region dates to the time he was a teacher and to when he assumed command of the Northeastern Front.

45. La Serna, *With Masses and Arms*, 104.

46. La Serna, *With Masses and Arms*, 121–22; García Torres, "La Pesadilla," 227. Rodrigo Gálvez died in 1990 at the age of twenty-six in a bloody confrontation with the armed forces in Picota.

47. García Torres, "La Pesadilla," 212–13, 227, claimed that Ojeda Zavala was not in favor of the 1986 unification of the MIR-VR with the MRTA. He reportedly told García Torres that the *tupacamaristas* were petulant members of the petty bourgeoise who were taking advantage of MIR-VR's long years of political work in the region.

48. García Torres, "La Pesadilla," 227. As Commander Ricardo of the MRTA's Northeastern Front, García Torres asserted that the column had five hundred armed men, distributed in its eight control zones, with one platoon assigned to each zone.

49. Comisión de la Verdad y Reconciliación, Perú, *Informe final de la Comisión de la Verdad y Reconciliación*, Anexo 4: Casos y víctimas registradas por la CVR, 54–55; Comisión de la Verdad y Reconciliación, Perú, *Informe final de la Comisión de la Verdad y Reconciliación*, vol. 5, 2.10, 334n37; Boschmann, "Coca und Guerrilla." According to the CVR, the MRTA assassinated the mayor, governor, and judge. The three municipal authorities were murdered by the MRTA after having been accused of being involved in the illicit drug trade. The liquidation of three authorities in the village of Pilluana was controversial throughout the movement and ultimately condemned. The rebels had justified the shootings— without a public trial—by saying that the three dignitaries, members of the ruling APRA, had leaked lists with the names of UDP members to the police. Boschmann reports the villagers assessed it differently: "APRA or treason. After all, they were farmers too— which class does the MRTA defend?"

50. García Torres reports that he was released, along with thirteen comrades, after the MRTA bribed the judicial tribunal with US$7,000. Néstor Cerpa Cartolini had assumed leadership of the National Command of the MRTA following the imprisonment of Polay Campos in 1989. As an experienced trade unionist, Cerpa Cartolini participated in the famous workers' strike at Lima's Cromotex textile factory in December 1978, which was violently suppressed by the military dictatorship in February 1979, resulting in a number of workers' deaths. Cerpa Cartolini subsequently organized a sit-in in Lima's UN communications office. García Torres, "La Pesadilla," 227. The first column was located on the Middle Mayo, the second in Huayabamba, and the third on the Central Huallaga.

51. Meza Bazán, "El Movimiento Revolucionario Túpac Amaru," 364. In essence, security zones were equivalent to areas where the MRTA had effectively replaced state actors.

52. García Torres, "La Pesadilla," 227.

53. A typical meal from the Amazon region of Peru is called *juane*. It's a tamale-like dish made with rice, chicken, olives, hard-boiled eggs, and herbs and spices like cumin, turmeric, and oregano. These ingredients are mixed together, cooked, and wrapped in waxy *bijao* leaves (which resemble banana leaves). During the festival of St. John on June 24, it is widely consumed. A large influx of Chinese immigrants arrived in Peru at the end of the nineteenth century, which led to the influence of Chinese cuisine on Peruvian foods. Usually made in a wok with soy sauce and oil, *arroz chaufa* is a mixture of fried rice with vegetables, usually including scallions, eggs, and chicken.

54. Susan Lagdon, Cherie Armour, and Maurice Stringer, "Adult Experience of Mental Health Outcomes as a Result of Intimate Partner Violence Victimisation: A Systematic Review," *European Journal of Psychotraumatology* 5 (2014): https://doi.org/10.3402/ejpt.v5.24794; L. Mandelli, C. Petrelli, and A. Serretti, "The Role of Specific Early Trauma in Adult Depression: A Meta-Analysis of Published Literature, Childhood Trauma and Adult Depression," *European Psychiatry* 30, no. 6 (2015): 665–80. Lagdon, Armour, and Stringer have shown how psychological violence is a more serious form of interpersonal violence that has the potential to harm victims' mental health. Meanwhile, Mandelli, Petrelli, and Serretti have revealed an extensive body of literature indicating that early experiences with domestic violence are likely to increase an individual's potential for the development of clinical symptoms of depression.

55. Interview, Caynarachi basin, 2017.

56. Interview, Caynarachi basin, 2017.

57. Eudoxio H. Ortega, Manual de historia general del Perú; historia crítica (Lima: Fénix Latino Americana, 1968).

58. CVR, *Informe final de la Comisión de la Verdad y Reconciliación*, vol. 5, 2.10, 320. Diego and Fabiano's training experience parallels that of other former *tupacamarista* followers as described in the CVR: "Military and political instructors came from Nicaragua, Bolivia and Colombia. They did congresses, talks and schools. All that in our bases. Each zone selected its members to attend these events. Inside, we were divided between those who were indoctrinated for politics and those who were indoctrinated militarily."

59. MRTA, *Conquistando el porvenir*, 314.

60. CVR, *Informe final de la Comisión de la Verdad y Reconciliación*, vol. 5, 2.10, 319–20. To capture Saposoa, for example, the EPT assembled between three hundred and four hundred rebel combatants from two detachments: Alcides Reátegui (Central Huallaga) and Roberto Pérez (Yurimaguas).

61. Interview, Caynarachi basin, 2017.

62. García Torres, *Guerra en la Selva*, 14; Fabiano interview, Caynarachi basin, 2018.

63. Regional chief of the MRTA, Andrés Mendoza del Águila. According to Diego, El Grillo (The Cricket) was from the Upper Mayo and was an original founder of the El Porvenir rebel encampment.

64. Diego interview, Caynarachi basin, 2018. García Torres, *Guerra en la Selva*, 23. According to García Torres, the MRTA subsequently obtained firearms through weapons brokers, who at that time were beginning to proliferate.

65. Interview, Caynarachi basin, 2019.

66. Interview, Picota, 2018.

67. Interview, Picota, 2019.

68. This reminded me of what Diego had begun telling me about during our regular chats.

He once said that recounting his life story "makes his mind clear" ("aclara su mente").

69. The main component of *chicha morada*, the pre-Columbian beverage, is purple corn, or *culli*, also known as *ckolli*, which is a variety of maize native to Peru. It is widely cultivated and harvested along the Andes and is consumed throughout contemporary Peru. A milky, snowy white cheese, *queso fresco* is typically made with cow's milk and rennet. *Rosquillas de maíz* are hard, unsweetened, doughnut-shaped rolls made from corn.

70. *Pucacaca* or *Puka Qaqa* (in Quechua, *puka* means "red" and *qaqa* means "rock") is one of the ten districts of the Province of Picota.

71. Kernaghan, *Coca's Gone*, 5, has fruitfully explored the sense of danger following the Upper Huallaga Valley's coca bonanza in terms of the "sensorial atmosphere felt by some(one's) body and a sensibility or affective disposition."

72. William Donlan and Junghee Lee, "*Coraje, Nervios*, and *Susto*: Culture-Bound Syndromes and Mental Health among Mexican Migrants in the United States," *Advances in Mental Health* 9, no. 3 (2010): 288–302; D. Razzouk, B. Nogueira, and J. de Jesus Mari, "The Contribution of Latin American and Caribbean Countries on Culture Bound Syndromes Studies for the ICD-10 Revision: Key Findings from a Work in Progress," *Brazilian Journal of Psychiatry* 33, suppl. 1 (2011): 1–20. *Susto* is associated with chronic physical pain resulting from emotional trauma or witnessing other people experiencing trauma. Common throughout Latin America, *susto* is a "culture bound syndrome" of being frightened. A diverse suite of symptoms has been associated with the condition, including anxiety, insomnia, anorexia, fatigue, fever, depression, and gastrointestinal issues.

73. The Mil Mi-24 is a versatile helicopter made in Russia that can transport eight passengers and serve as a versatile gunship and attack helicopter.

74. "Está tranca, no puedo abrir este trocha. Hay muchos soldados del ejército bloqueando el camino a través del bosque." Interview, Caynarachi basin, 2018.

75. La Serna, *With Masses and Arms*, 121.

76. Interview, Picota, 2018.

77. Frightened, her husband spent the night hiding inside a large ceramic vessel (*tinaje*) used for making fermented cassava beer, or *masato*.

78. Radio Tropical 99.1 FM was established in 1961 in Tarapoto, during the golden age of radio broadcasting in the Peruvian northern Amazon. The station was founded with the assistance of Juan Pablo Morí, a wealthy Tarapoto merchant originally from Nauta Loreto. Radio Tropical 99.1 FM has a rich history in audio broadcasting and is currently still in operation.

79. "Mi mente desentierra el pasado con el propósito de nombrar a las víctimas." Interview, Picota, 2018.

80. According to Darwin*, a longtime Caynarachi resident I interviewed in 2022, the MRTA looked for adolescent recruits, whereas Sendero Luminoso tried to recruit those with military experience. Wilson had previously served in the Peruvian Army and was stationed in Uchiza in the early 1990s. He was involved in multiple armed confrontations with Sendero Luminoso. Wilson noted how this insurgent group would often use the civil populace to go first through the forest so as to protect its columns from frontal attacks. In his estimation, "the MRTA was not strong, they were a bunch of resentful [*renegados*] teachers." His perspective was presumably shaped by his experiences in the Upper Huallaga Valley, where levels of violence were relatively higher than in the Lower Huallaga, "where many people lost family members this way. They would take them off into the

forest, never to see them again." The vast majority of the people I interviewed in the Central and Lower Huallaga stated that MRTA rebel's ages typically ranged from teenage to the late twenties or early thirties.

81. Interview, Lima, 2017.

82. Likewise, Diego denied that his detachment was in any way involved in rapes in the Caynarachi basin, forcefully asserting: "We wouldn't rape our own family members. We were not monsters."

83. "Mi futuro estuvo una vez en Caynarachi, pero la guerra acabó con esa esperanza, extinguiéndola como el agua en un fuego abrasador." Interview, Lima, 2017.

CHAPTER 5

Epigraph. "En tiempos de guerra, la vida se vuelve barata y ya nada tiene gracia." Interview, Caynarachi basin, 2019.

1. Interview, Caynarachi basin, 2019.

2. Some told me that women were not typically made to do physical exercise as punishment because of their "femininity."

3. Interview, Caynarachi basin, 2018.

4. Interview, Caynarachi basin, 2019.

5. "No era tierra de nadies, no hemos tenido confianza, fue un momento de terror." Interview, Caynarachi basin, 2019.

6. Interview, Caynarachi basin, 2015.

7. Interview, Caynarachi basin, 2019.

8. Interview, Caynarachi basin, 2018. Others, such as Zacarías* and Leonila, the market woman, claimed Ramírez was an MRTA member who worked in the party's legal section and also the leader of the Agrarian League. They claimed he used this as a way to obscure his terrorist associations. Interview, Caynarachi basin, 2017.

9. On the topic of *ronderos* in central Peruvian Amazonia, see Óscar Espinosa, *Las rondas campesinas y nativas en la Amazonía peruana* (Lima: CAAAP, 1995); Beatriz Fabian Arias, *Las cosas ya no son como antes: La mujer ashaninka y los cambios socio-culturales producidos por la violencia política en la Selva Central*, Serie Documentos de trabajo (Lima: CAAAP, 1997); Leslie Villapolo, "Recursos socioculturales de los Asháninka para resistir al régimen totalitario de Sendero Luminoso y sus efectos," *Boletín del CDI* (Centro de Documentación e Investigación del Lugar de la Memoria, la Tolerancia y la Inclusión Social), 1 (2016): 8–9. For the case of the Andes, see Orin Starn, ed., *Hablan los ronderos: La búsqueda por la paz en los Andes* (Lima: IEP, 1993); Carlos Iván Degregori, "Harvesting Storms: Peasant Rondas and the Defeat of Sendero Luminoso in Ayacucho," in *Shining and Other Paths: War and Society in Peru, 1980–1995*, ed. S. J. Stern (Durham, NC: Duke University Press, 1998), 128–57; César Rodríguez Aguilar, *Justicia comunitaria y rondas campesinas en el Sur andino* (Lima: Asociación SER/ProJur, 2007). For San Martín, see Patricia Zárate Ardela, "Las rondas de la selva alta, un territorio por explorar," *Argumentos* 2, no. 15 (1994):12–14n2. The first civil patrols (*rondas campesinas*) emerged in San Martín in the town of Shapaja in 1989, following the murder of a much-loved teacher in the village by the MRTA. Immediately thereafter, Chazuta likewise created a communal paramilitary patrol comprised of local peasant *ronderos*.

10. Similarly, Alejandro said Ramírez managed to evade capture until the third time when those investigating him finally determined he was a "big pro" (*gran professional*) originally trained by the army.

11. The *varayoc*, or the civil authority in charge of the administrative government of the town, is Incaic in origin. In the Caynarachi basin, they customarily accompanied the deputy governor, or *teniente gobernador*, in taking people to be punished. They also served as guards, watching over prisoners in the community's stockade (*calabozo*).

12. Interview, Caynarachi basin, 2018.

13. Interview, Caynarachi basin, 2018.

14. George Orwell, 1984 (New York: Houghton Mifflin Harcourt, 1983), 515.

15. In the region of San Martín, many of the agricultural producers' unions had been formed as leagues (*ligas*) with the support of the National Social Mobilization Support System (Sistema Nacional de Apoyo a la Mobilización Nacional, or SINAMOS) during Velasco's regime. During the 1980s, they became increasingly autonomous, joining forces with the FASMA and, in so doing, helped summon a series of important peasant strikes that mobilized entire villages.

16. According to Diego: "The banks cater to those with [neck] ties on, not to those hunched over. Those with fine clothes are served, the rest of us without well-polished shoes can't even get in line to ask for loans. Those with patched clothes [*ropita*] are left to one side. Those who show up with a tie on are always taken care of first."

17. Julián told me how he remembered the army comandante wanted proof of Ramírez's death, "so they took his head, which was transported to Tarapoto, leaving behind a headless body."

18. Interview, Caynarachi basin, 2019.

19. Member of Sendero Luminoso.

20. In Mexico, the term *pendejo* is used to describe individuals who are considered foolish, unwise, or unpleasant, while in Peru, it is used to refer to those who are perceived as untrustworthy and cunningly selfish.

21. "A pesar de haber sido torturado y abandonado a morir, nuestro apellido salvó a Edgar de una muerte inminente." Interview, Caynarachi basin, 2019.

22. During the course of field research, I found that coordinating schedules and exchanging messages to plan a suitable time and place for a meeting can be challenging, but it highlights the significance of effective communication and shows both parties' willingness to engage in a sustained personal encounter. This aligns with the cultural norms of the Huallaga Valley, where interpersonal relationships are highly valued and continually nurtured.

23. The community of Yumbatos (Caynarachi District) is situated in the Province of Lamas, and forms part of the Region of San Martín.

24. CVR, *Informe final de la Comisión de la Verdad y Reconciliación*, vol. 5, 2.10, Testimonio 100003 Yumbatos, 387.

25. According to the *Censo nacional de población y ocupación, 1940: Departamentos: Loreto, Amazonas, San Martín, Madre de Dios* (Dirección de Estadística, 1944), 71, the 1940 census registered the town's population at fifty-seven. Interview, Yumbatos, 2017.

26. The MRTA tried to recruit Ronner many times, but he knew their claims of regular pay with a lot of money (*mucha plata*) were a lie. Mando Razor admitted to me that the MRTA did trick recruit insurgents, saying they would pay them, but the only financial help they got was when an insurgent's family member was in need, usually because of sickness. In Diego's words: "Once you were a member [of the MRTA], you couldn't ask for a wage because it would be paid with bullets. Within the party we were provided with everything—so we had no reason to ask for a wage." Some, like the "wise guy" Zacarías, the operator of a river taxi (*colectivo*), were under the impression that MRTA recruits "got a wage of thou-

sands per month, others were paid nothing but given aid when their families were sick in the health posts. The family members of the MRTA got free and preferential treatment."

27. "No había justicia." Interview, Yumbatos, 2018.

28. Silvia's husband had two sisters-in-law who willingly joined the MRTA after they were told they would work and gain a monthly wage. "That's how they first became involved—after the conflict, they returned to their lives in Yumbatos," said Silvia, who had never forgiven the two sisters-in-laws for their active role in the armed opposition.

29. CVR, *Informe final de la Comisión de la Verdad y Reconciliación*, vol. 5, 2.10, Testimonio 456682 Yumbatos, 387; see also CVR, *Informe final de la Comisión de la Verdad y Reconciliación*, vol. 5, 2.10, Testimonio 456695, 389. Felipe Tapullima was invited to a MRTA meeting but refused to attend. He replied: "I don't have time to do these things, I'm working with my dad. [My parents,] they're old and I'm working for them."

30. CVR, *Informe final de la Comisión de la Verdad y Reconciliación*, vol. 5, 2.10, Testimonio Yumbatos, 456719, 388.

31. CVR, Testimonio 456719 Yumbatos, 388.

32. CVR, *Informe final de la Comisión de la Verdad y Reconciliación*, Testimonio 456682 Yumbatos, 388–89.

33. CVR, Testimonio 456695 Yumbatos, 389. This was a common occurrence among the communities of the Caynarachi basin. The MRTA invited Julián's brother Leonardo* to participate in the radical movement just after he had finished his military service. The *cumpas* came to their house and invited Leonardo to join them in "the armed struggle." The MRTA recruiters noted how Leonardo was a former soldier in great physical shape. But Julián's brother didn't want any part in the MRTA and had to flee to Tarapoto to escape their clutches. Julián said they wanted to recruit his brother to be a spy given his military background and proven expertise on the battlefield (*campo de batalla*).

34. CVR, Testimonio 456695 Yumbatos, 389. The woman said they did not search for the remains of her relatives because they were threatened with retribution by the MRTA.

35. CVR, Testimonio 456682 Yumbatos, 389.

36. Interview, Caynarachi basin, 2017.

37. Interview, Caynarachi basin, 2022. This also happened to those "ordinary people" (*gente común*) who charged *cupos* (taxes) to the *narco* drug runners in the name of the MRTA.

38. "Los roles comenzaron a cambiar ya que la gente prefería denunciar a los ladrones y corruptos frente a las cumpas." Interview in Caynarachi basin, 2022. As I gathered accounts of corruption, I found that bribes, known as *coimas* or *sobornos*, played a major part structuring sociopolitical life in the Central and Lower Huallaga Valley.

39. Interview, Caynarachi basin, 2022. *Runamula* is feminine adultery figure in the mythology of Peruvian Amazonia. Women who are potential *runamulas* are those who engage in relationships with married men, members of the church, or are already married themselves. According to legend, the homes of disloyal women are supposedly visited by a horseman dressed entirely in black and speaking incoherently at night. After being cursed, the sexually transgressive women become half-mule hybrids known as *runamulas*.

40. Pyotr Kropotkin, "Words of a Rebel," in *The Heretic's Handbook of Quotations: Cutting Comments on Burning Issues*, ed. Charles Bufe (Tucson, AZ: Sharp Press, 1992), 26. Interview, Caynarachi basin, 2022.

41. Over the years, I have heard a number of reports of a traditional healer (*médico* or *brujo*) from Yumbatos who was killed around this time after he was denounced to the MRTA.

42. Mateo's description of justice at the outset of the Túpac Amaru rebels' presence in the

Caynarachi basin supports Diego's and Fabiano's accounts. Mateo told me how a young man who stole a cow was captured by the MRTA and brought to the village's plaza for the entire district to see. "They didn't kill him but held him captive in the stockade [*calabozo*]. During this time, things were OK. We didn't have any thieves, life was tranquil. In some ways, the village liked this. But when the military came in search of the MRTA, that's when things became *bravo*." Interview, Lima, 2015.

43. The MRTA maintained its dominance and survival among the local populace, as well as in the face of formidable adversaries like the Sendero Luminoso insurgency, by leveraging the law's provision of a monopoly over violence. This concept is connected to Walter Benjamin's perspective in his work *Critique of Violence Selected Writings: 1913–1926* (1:239). Benjamin argues that the law's insistence on monopolizing violence is not driven by the aim of safeguarding legal objectives, but rather by the imperative to uphold the very existence of the law. According to Benjamin, violence outside the control of the law poses a threat not for its particular ends but rather for its mere existence beyond legal confines.

44. García Torres, *Guerra en la Selva*, 31.

45. The nom de guerre "Chairman Gonzalo" refers to Abimael Guzmán Reynoso, who founded and led Sendero Luminoso. Guzmán Reynoso was a philosophy professor throughout the 1960s and 1970s who participated in left-wing radical politics and was heavily inspired by Marxism, Leninism, and Maoism. In 1965, at the height of the Cultural Revolution, he made his first trip to China. This dramatically influenced the way he thought about Marxism. Like Guzmán Reynoso, other Maoist rebels who traveled to China from Peru became part of the political intelligentsia rather than leaders of armed, on-the-ground combat troops. This was instrumental, rather than coincidental, as noted by Alberto Gálvez Olaechea, in "El maoísmo en dos novellas: Cuando la realidad sobrepasa la ficción," November 24, 2022, https://albertoglvezolaechea.medium.com/el-mao%C3%ADsmo-en-dos-novelas-5d70da1ce074. By 1969, Guzmán Reynoso had established the Communist Party of Peru–Shining Path (PCP-SL), and from then until his arrest by the police in September 1992, he led a revolutionary uprising against the Peruvian state. He was given a life sentence for terrorism and treason. Imprisoned at the Callao Naval Base, Guzmán Reynoso died on September 11, 2021, at the age of eighty-six. To prevent the construction of a commemorative shrine in his honor, Guzmán Reynoso's body was cremated and his ashes were scattered in a covert location(s).

46. This observation is eerily similar to Diego's 2021 admission to me: "In every conflict and every internal war, there's always a loser and a winner. That is simply the cost." García Torres, *Guerra en la Selva,* 31; CVR, *Informe final de la Comisión de la Verdad y Reconciliación*, vol. 5, 2.10, 330n31. As the CVR notes, the first recorded confrontation between Sendero Luminoso and the MRTA took place in March 1987. A group of one hundred MRTA rebels attempted to take the city of Tocache but were attacked by a Sendero Luminoso contingent who dominated the area. The MRTA was defeated, losing forty men. The clash thwarted the MRTA's plan to dominate the entire region of San Martín. The MRTA had established its territorial border by 1989, which was the left bank of the Huallaga River, affirming its dominance in the regions of the Alto Mayo and the Central and Lower Huallaga.

47. Bruce Kay, "Violent Opportunities," 103; W. Alejandro Sanchez Nieto, "Give War a Chance Revisited—The Price to Pay: The Military and Terrorism in Peru," *Defence Studies* 11, no. 3 (2011): 517–40. See S. Koc-Menard, "Fragmented Sovereignty: Why Sendero Luminoso Consolidated in Some Regions of Peru but Not in Others," *Studies in Conflict and Terrorism* 30, no. 2 (2007): 173–206.

48. Depending on whether one was addressing the armed forces or the MRTA, villagers all agreed that the rebels used the greeting *compañero* among themselves and required those they encountered to do likewise. The meanings associated with the term *compañero* varies. It usually refers to a companion, partner, coworker, comrade, buddy, or friend. Its use among the MRTA underscored unity, loyalty, and dedication to the revolutionary cause of socialism.

49. Aldo Panfichi and Jo-Marie Burt, *Peru, Caught in the Crossfire* (Jefferson City, MO: Peru Peace Network, 1992).

CHAPTER 6

1. Interview, Caynarachi basin, 2018.
2. Interview, Caynarachi basin, 2018.
3. *Minga* or *mink'a* is from the Quechua *minccacuni*, meaning "asking for help by promising something in return." Interview, Caynarachi basin, 2018.
4. Kristine Stiles, "Shaved Heads and Marked Bodies: Representations from Cultures of Trauma," *Stratégie II: Peuples Méditerranéens* 64–65 (1993): 95–117. Modern warfare has been closely associated with head shaving and sexual policing. For instance, thousands of French women had their heads shaved in front of applauding audiences during and after World War II as punishment for either cooperating with the Nazis or having sexual encounters with Nazi soldiers. Richard Evans, *The Third Reich in Power* (New York: Penguin Books, 2006), 540, notes that people accused of racial mingling were punished by the Nazis by having their heads shaved and signs hung around their necks stating their guilt.
5. Pierre Bourdieu, *On Television and Journalism* (London: Pluto Press 1998), 17, identifies symbolic violence as "wielded with [the] tacit complicity between its victims and its agents, insofar as both remain unconscious of submitting to or wielding it."
6. Interview, Caynarachi basin, 2018.
7. Associated with inflicting shame (*roche* or *vergüenza*), informants in the Caynarachi basin said that in some instances, the MRTA would charge a few hundred *intis* for each punishment of this sort.
8. For example, Rimberto* was shot for sentimental reasons by Álvaro*, a member of the MRTA El Porvenir detachment. Allegedly, Rimberto was having an affair with Álvaro's wife. With the help of two MRTA militants, Álvaro shot Rimberto, using his putative association with Sendero Luminoso as a pretext. After further investigation, it was determined that Rimberto had personal problems with his girlfriend, who happened to be married to Álvaro. Interview, Caynarachi basin, 2018.
9. García Torres, "La Pesadilla," 227. By 1989, García Torres reports, the MRTA was executing gay people and drug addicts (*fumones*) in Tarapoto. This led to denunciations on the part of the regional and national leadership, not to mention international human rights organizations.
10. Interview, Caynarachi basin, 2018.
11. Comisión de la Verdad y Reconciliación, *Informe final de la Comisión de la Verdad y Reconciliación*, vol. 4, sec. 3, 1.4.3 "Actos de terror contra minorías sexuales," 432–33; Giuliana Vidarte, "La noche de las gardenias," https://www.micromuseo.org.pe/rutas/noche-gardenias/sinopsis.html. On May 31, 1989, a group of six MRTA members violently entered a bar in Tarapoto and murdered eight transvestites. A few days later, the weekly *Cambio*,

an unofficial organ of the MRTA, claimed responsibility for the action and justified it by stating that the murdered were criminals and collaborators with the Peruvian Army. It also accused the army of protecting the existence of the "social scourges" that had "corrupted the youth." The eight people murdered, according to different sources, were César Marcelino Carvajal, Max Pérez Velásquez, Luis Mogollón, Alberto Chong Rojas, Rafael Gonzales, Carlos Piedra, Raúl Chumbe Rodríguez, and Jhony Achuy. *Cambio* also mentioned a similar murder in February 1989, when the MRTA executed a young gay man in Tarapoto.

12. Interview, Tarapoto, 2022.

13. The San John Festival, held in the Peruvian Amazon on June 24, is a crucial event that pays tribute to the patron saint of the region, San Juan Bautista (St. John the Baptist). This celebration marks two significant occasions, the winter solstice in the Southern Hemisphere and the veneration of the patron saint.

14. Interview, Caynarachi basin, 2019.

15. The active presence of the MRTA in the region encouraged many traditional healers to practice clandestinely.

16. René Girard, *Violence and the Sacred*. René Girard famously referred to the universal practice of unjustly attributing blame without adequate justification as "scapegoating." Girard reveals how this practice is tied to an ancient sacred rite in which communal sins were metaphorically inflicted upon a he-goat, which is then left in the desert, or sacrificed to the deities.

17. Interview, Caynarachi basin, 2018.

18. "Los casos de insurgencia y otras formas de maldad en una sociedad, como los secuestros, no indican el fracaso de la comunidad. En cambio, muestran claramente una falta de amor el uno por el otro." Interview, Caynarachi basin, 2018.

19. "La gente de la comunidad se equivocó al pensar que podíamos ser decentes en un momento indecente." Interview, Caynarachi basin, 2018.

20. The same thing happened to the priest when he went off to perform a mass in Yana Puma. A group of MRTA rebels from El Porvenir tried to kidnap him. They too brought him into the plaza that night so they could bring him to their base. He adamantly refused.

21. Interview, Caynarachi basin, 2018.

22. The MRTA member had been a nurse in El Porvenir, but according to Diego was an alcoholic and had been dismissed from the State Health Services for being inebriated on the job in a MRRTA dominated town called Loma Churupampa*. The party, nevertheless, accepted him as a "medic."

23. In the Caynarachi basin, to say *muerto de hambre* is a major insult indicating someone has no resources. The phrase implies social death.

24. The FN FAL was designed in 1953 by Dieudonné Saive and manufactured by FN Herstal. It was originally made to fire the intermediate .280 British (7×43 mm) caliber cartridge but was later adapted to fire the 7.62×51 mm NATO cartridge. The first FAL prototype was completed in 1946, although it was designed to fire the 7.92×33 mm Kurz cartridge used by the German Sturmgewehr 44 during World War II. During the Cold War, numerous members of the North Atlantic Treaty Organization embraced the FAL, with the exception of the United States. It has been one of the most frequently employed guns in global history, utilized by over ninety countries, with more than seven million produced.

25. Interview, Caynarachi basin, 2017.

26. The rebels used the anonymous letters (*cartas anónimos*) to demand ransom, exact extortion, and charge war taxes (*cupos*). Informants told me they had a watermark of the ham-

mer and sickle and an image of Túpac Amaru. Members of the MRTA were taught how to properly create these anonymous letters. "We were required to use tweezers to grab the paper to prevent fingerprints. And we used a cloth to prop up our wrists to cover up any fingerprints," Fabiano told me while describing his activities as a MRTA militant.

27. Interview, Caynarachi basin, 2017.

28. In the Peruvian Amazon, research has shown that women have a higher body-mass index than men, but the underlying reasons for this trend are not well understood. There are several potential explanations, including the possibility that women may have more body fat for reproductive reasons, engage in less physical activity because of domestic and caregiving duties, or have limited access to food and health care due to gender inequality. Notwithstanding, further data collection and analysis are necessary to validate these hypotheses.

29. Interview, Caynarachi basin, 2018.

30. None of the testimonials I recorded supported Doña Ximena's version of events.

31. Doña Ximena said that her family paid only five months of *cupos*, as the military had routed the basecamp in El Porvenir, dispersing the MRTA throughout the Caynarachi basin and beyond. Diego confirmed this detail of the ransom, telling me that Ángel's parents were forced to pay *cupos* for five months.

32. Interview, Caynarachi basin, 2018.

33. Comandante Ricardo, the leader of the MRTA's Northeastern Front, and his political officer (*mando político*) were going to conduct a communal meeting in town. Beforehand, they and another *mando* went to negotiate the ransom with Doña Ximena for releasing her son Ángel. According to various accounts, Comandante Ricardo wanted to ensure that the *cupo* would be paid directly to the MRTA, and not someone posing as the rebel group.

34. Interview, Caynarachi basin, 2018.

CHAPTER 7

Epigraph. "La cocaína es la bomba atómica de Latinoamérica." Qtd. in Ricardo Gutiérrez Zapata, "El Henry Ford de la cocaína," *El Spectador*, June 6, 2010. Carlos Enrique Lehder Rivas, the infamous drug trafficker who cofounded the Medellín Cartel, smuggled tons of cocaine into the United States during the 1980s. Lehder played a crucial role in the founding of Muerte a Secuestradores (MAS), a highly lethal paramilitary group whose mission was to take revenge on M-19 rebels for their kidnapping of cartel members and their loved ones. In November 1981, Lehder was targeted for ransom by the M-19 guerrilla movement, an incident that fueled his decision to join the MAS. Along with his criminal activities, he also advocated for a nationalist and anti-American movement in Colombia. Lehder Rivas, known for his admiration of Adolf Hitler and Nazism, reportedly established the National Latin Movement, a fascist-populist party aiming to abolish the 1979 extradition treaty between Colombia and the United States. However, in 1987, his deeds caught up with him as he was apprehended, extradited to the United States, and subsequently sentenced to a lifetime in prison, plus an additional 135 years. In 1991, Lehder Rivas testified against Panamanian dictator Manuel Antonio Noriega Morena, claiming that Noriega had permitted the cartel's cocaine importation activities to employ Panama as a transshipment route. In return, they reduced the sentence for Lehder to fifty-five years. After serving a thirty-three-year sentence, Lehder Rivas was released from

US incarceration in 2020 and was deported to Germany, where he possesses citizenship through his father. Since his release, he has maintained a complete silence, abstaining from any public appearances. The current whereabouts of Carlos Enrique Lehder Rivas remain unknown, fueling ongoing speculation about the possibility of his demise or seclusion in a remote location.

1. Paredes and Manrique, "The State's Developmentalist Illusion," 245–67, illustrate that the government's "developmentalist project" lured thousands of impoverished peasants from the highlands "to the Upper Huallaga through guarantees of 'open land.'" Furthermore, faulty scientific studies of the region's tropical soils worsened the difficulties faced by highland peasants arriving in a place where the Peruvian state's presence was limited and its competence restricted.

2. Gootenberg, *Andean Cocaine*, 292. At this time, the region was producing more than half of the world's markets for coca leaf and cocaine paste.

3. Arjun Appadurai, "Introduction: Commodities and the Politics of Value," in *The Social Life of Things: Commodities in a Cultural Perspective*, ed. Arjun Appadurai (Cambridge: Cambridge University Press, 1986), 3. As Appadurai observes, a commodity, at its most basic, is "anything intended for exchange," or any object of economic value.

4. Durand Guevara, "Donde habita el olvido."

5. Gootenberg, *Andean Cocaine*, 300; Edmundo Morales, "The Political Economy of Cocaine Production: An Analysis of the Peruvian Case," *Latin American Perspectives* 17, no. 4 (1990): 91–109.

6. They used spoons to carefully heat a small quantity of the unrefined cocaine paste or cocaine hydrochloride, wafted the air toward their noses, and then smelled the fumes to determine the quality of the "product."

7. See INEI, "Perú: Anuario de estadísticas ambientales 2015," in *Perú: Anuario de estadísticas ambientales* (Lima: Instituto Nacional de Estadística e Informática, 2015); Limachi, de Jong, and Cornejo, "Models of Migration," 85.

8. Eduardo Romero, *Perfil antropológico del agricultor cocalero: Historias, economías domésticas, percepciones. Un análisis comparativo de las zonas del VRAE y Aguaytía* (Lima: DEVIDA, 2011); Nicolás Zevallos, "Hoja de coca y la Estrategia Nacional de Lucha contra las Drogas 2007-2011: El problema público en el control de cultivos," *Revista de Ciencia Política y Gobierno* 1 (2014): 97–113.

9. Comisión de la Verdad y Reconciliación, *Informe final de la Comisión de la Verdad y Reconciliación*, vol. 5, 311–15; Van Dun, *Cocaleros*.

10. For a critical analysis of corruption among the Peruvian Armed Forces and their counternarcotics strategy in the Upper Huallaga, see Dreyfus, "When All Evils Come Together," 370–96.

11. Daniel Willis, The "*Testimony of Space*: Sites of Memory and Violence in Peru's Internal Armed Conflict" (PhD diss., UCL Institute of the Americas, London, 2018), 75.

12. On this issue, see Centro Amazónico de Antropológica y Aplicación Práctica, *Violencia y narcotráfico en la amazonía* (Lima: CAAAP, 1992). On Sendero Luminoso–inspired violence in the Upper Huallaga, see Gabriela Tarazona-Sevillano, "El narcoterrorismo," *Revista Occidental* 8, no. 2 (1991): 151–83. For a discussion of the shift in coca leaf production from the Upper to the Central and Lower Huallaga Valley, see Hernán Manrique López, "Las bases históricas del 'milagro de San Martín': Control territorial y estrategias estatales contra el narcotráfico y subversión (1980–1995)," *Politai* 6, no. 11 (2015): 33–51.

13. CVR, *Informe final de la Comisión de la Verdad y Reconciliación*, vol. 5, 2.10, 34.

14. This generated a booming local economy, as labor was mobilized to cultivate, tend, and harvest the coca leaves, which were then manually pressed by foot (*pisar la hoja*) into a paste and further refined chemically. Meanwhile, *narcos* paid caretakers (*cuidadores*) who were tasked with protecting their coca fields (*cocales*). Informants also mentioned the MRTA providing rubber boots and gloves for processing the coca leaves. The gloves and footwear provided a modicum of protection against the toxicity of the ingredients mixed in the "pressing pit" (*pozo*). In addition to protecting feet from exposure to chemicals and other harmful substances, rubber boots offered resistance to moisture, which is beneficial when working in damp environments commonly associated with the processing of coca leaves. Before disseminating cocaine to lower-level dealers, it was a prevalent practice among *narcos* to incorporate a myriad of adulterants into the product. These substances, including phenacetin, lidocaine, levamisole, caffeine, hydroxyzine, benzocaine, and other cutting agents, were skillfully blended to augment the quantity and alter the properties of the cocaine. Adulteration was a multifaceted practice that had various effects on the "product" and the consumers. It reduced the purity and increased the risks of the narcotic, but it also allowed the *narcos* to achieve different goals, such as enhancing profits by adding volume and improving appearance, or altering the psychoactive effects of the drug. This practice showed how strategic and rational the *narcos* were, as they tried to balance their unlawful commerce with maintaining a certain level of quality and consistency in their product.

15. CVR, *Informe final de la Comisión de la Verdad y Reconciliación*, vol. 5, 2.10, 334n38; García Torres, "La Pesadilla," 239.

16. García Torres, "La Pesadilla," 228.

17. CVR 1.4, 359.

18. García Torres, "La Pesadilla," 239. CVR 1.4, 380, cites multiple testimonies stating that some local party leaders fled after appropriating money obtained through quotas. The accounts of former members of the MRTA regarding the collection of quotas for drug trafficking and participation in the drug business coincide with the testimonies given to members of the commission in the Penal (prison) of Potracancha, Huánuco, especially EAF, captured in La Morada, although he says that it was the infiltrators in the party who charged "quotas" for drug trafficking. These statements confirm, once again, that all the primary actors in the Huallaga region's internal war were involved, to a greater or lesser extent, with the drug-trafficking networks. A different perspective is offered by Davis Fielding in his article "The Dynamics of Terror during the Peruvian Civil War," *Journal of Peace Research* 49, no. 6 (2012): 847–62. He acknowledges that the Peruvian military escalated the violence against civilians, but he also claims that counternarcotics aid reduced it. However, Fielding's argument is not very persuasive, as he does not provide sufficient evidence or analysis to support his claim regarding the reduction of violence and its linkages to the growth of counternarcotics efforts.

19. CVR, *Informe final de la Comisión de la Verdad y Reconciliación*, vol. 5, 2.10, 313n8.

20. CVR, *Informe final de la Comisión de la Verdad y Reconciliación*, vol. 5, 2.10, 334; García Torres, "La Pesadilla," 239.

21. Interview, Caynarachi basin, 2019.

22. Known locally as "Atahualpa," the secondary school teacher provided Diego with his first glimpses of large amounts of cash.

23. I use the phrase *cocaine capitalisms* to describe the economic and social structures that have emerged in Peruvian Amazonia related to the production and distribution of

cocaine and its associated "products." Typically, small-scale farmers who lack employment options cultivate coca plants, which are a key ingredient in cocaine production. Historically, rebel groups like MRTA and Sendero Luminoso protected drug producers and traffickers during the 1980s and 1990s, and the refined cocaine was then transported to markets around the globe. Cocaine paste and refined cocaine were smuggled by the MRTA from the Huallaga Valley to Colombia and Brazil.

24. As recounted by Fabiano and Diego during an interview in the Caynarachi basin in 2019.

25. Paul Gootenberg, "Between Coca and Cocaine: A Century or More of US-Peruvian Drug Paradoxes, 1860–1980," *Hispanic American Historical Review* 83, no. 1 (2003): 119–50, provides an insightful analysis of cocaine from the perspective of the "forgotten history" of the US-Peruvian axis over the past century. A general history of cocaine as a commodity is given by Patrick Clawson and Rensselaer Lee, *The Andean Cocaine Industry* (Basingstoke, UK: Macmillan, 1996).

26. Villagers disagreed over the proximate cause of the plane crash. Some asserted that the small aircraft was downed by the US Drug Enforcement Agency, others pinned the blame on the Peruvian Air Force, and still others pointed to mechanical failure. Recalling the sound of a sputtering engine, they claimed the plane had mechanical issues that caused it to fall from the sky.

27. María Méndez, "El impacto del narcotráfico en el ámbito político. La cadena narco: Amenaza para la democracia y la gobernabilidad," in *El mapa del narcotráfico en el Perú*, ed. Nicole Bernex et al. (Lima: PUCP, 2009), 43–58; Úrsula Durand Ochoa, *Coca o muerte: La radicalización del movimiento cocalero* (Lima: DESCO, 2008). Úrsula Durand Ochoa, *The Political Empowerment of the Cocaleros of Bolivia and Peru* (London: Palgrave Macmillan, 2014), is a comparative study of political empowerment among coca-leaf growers (*cocaleros*) in Peru and Bolivia.

28. Boschmann, "Coca und Guerrilla." The rise of cocaine capitalisms had a wider impact beyond just material wealth. It influenced the social dynamics and fabric of communities, shaping their aspirations and desires. The introduction of cable TV brought foreign media and entertainment into people's homes, exposing them to a dazzling new world of materialism and luxury previously unknown to most. This led to a desire for designer clothing and expensive cars, which became symbols of success and status. These items not only served practical purposes but also represented the material manifestations of wealth and success gained through involvement in the shadow economy.

29. "I have nothing to declare but my genius, and this four-kilo bag of cocaine." Oscar Wilde, *Oscar Wilde and His Wildest Quotes*, ed. C. Sreechinth (Scotts Valley, CA: CreateSpace, 2016). Although it is often claimed that Wilde made a witty comment to US customs officials in New York in 1882, purportedly saying, "I have nothing to declare except my genius," there is no evidence to verify this. A contemporary adaptation of the quote includes a four-kilogram bag of cocaine, which only increases the ridiculousness of the statement.

CHAPTER 8

Epigraph. Dr. Atilio Vásquez Alegría's unpublished song "La perla del Huallaga" has emerged as a testament to his poetic prowess and musical artistry: "Como límpida joya, / en un estuche verde, / risueña se levanta majestuosa y señorial, / oh ciudad soñada, / hechura de gigantes, / que los poetas llaman, / la perla del Huallaga."

30. The attack on Yurimaguas was led by García Torres, along with his *mandos* J. J. Tarzan, Moico, and Grillo. Diego interview, Caynarachi basin, 2019.

31. Interview, Caynarachi basin, 2017.

32. García Torres, *Guerra en la Selva*, 26. As Commander Ricardo noted, "They required plans, maps, and a sketch of the city."

33. Yurimaguas, the "Perla del Huallaga," is strategically located on the banks of the Huallaga River. With its diverse culture and economic significance, it serves as the administrative center of both the Yurimaguas District and the Alto Amazonas Province. Its vivid history as an old port city associated with the Jesuits' Mainas missions is undeniable. The reasons for its nickname are uncertain, but the beautiful location at the confluence of the Paranpura and Huallaga Rivers, surrounded by the forest and foothills of the Andes to the West and the lush rainforest all around, may have something to do with it. Yurimaguas is a crucial commercial hub for tropical produce like hardwood, oils, foodstuffs, fish, pelts, and even illegal drugs, which are transported to Iquitos via the Amazon River and the Pacific Coast via the Andes. The stunning Roman Catholic cathedral, modeled after the Cathedral of Burgos, Spain, built by the Order of the Passionists, is also a significant attraction.

34. Before dawn on July 9, 1990, forty-eight prisoners, reportedly all MRTA rebels, fled from the Miguel Castro y Castro maximum security prison in northeastern Lima. The thirty-nine men and nine women escaped through a tunnel constructed beneath the penitentiary that led to an adobe hut. According to investigators, the 333-meter-long and 14-meter-deep tunnel had been built several meters underground. It is said that it had its own ventilation and illumination system and took between six and ten months to build. Victor Polay Campos, the MRTA's commander, was one of the escaped prisoners. He had been captured in February 1989 and charged with terrorism concerning the killings of more than a hundred police officers, and was slated to go on trial at the time of his 1990 Miguel Castro y Castro prison escape.

35. García Torres, "La Pesadilla," 229; García Torres, *Guerra en la Selva*, 25–26. Daniel Willis, "Scratched from Memory: The 1986 Prison Massacres and the Limits of Acceptable Memory Discourse in Post-Conflict Peru." *Journal of Latin American Cultural Studies* 29, no. 2 (2020): 236, contends that MRTA leaders like Víctor Polay Campos took advantage of the state's failure to secure its prisons when forty-seven of its followers escaped from the Miguel Castro y Castro penitentiary. Willis argues the memories of imprisonment "represent rare moments in which party members were actually able to act out their political fantasies and self-organize, making incarceration crucial in the development of their political identities."

36. García Torres, *Guerra en la Selva*, 28, writes that the attack on Yurimaguas involved ninety-five MRTA combatants. From the El Porvenir camp, the MRTA sent thirty-five rebel troops to take Yurimaguas, according to Diego, who estimates they lost twenty comrades in total during the firefight. For him, it "was a major battle with the armed forces."

37. Before its incorporation into the Peruvian National Police (PNP) in 1991, the Investigative Police of Peru (PIP) was known as the Technical Police (Policía Técnica). It had the responsibility of conducting criminal investigations, gathering intelligence, and identifying crime in Peru. It was established in 1987 as a result of the merger of the PIP, Civil Guard, and Republican Guard. The Technical Police was based at the PNP Puente Piedra Higher Technical School, where noncommissioned officers received specialized training. In 1991, the Technical Police was replaced by the Criminal Investigation Directorate (DIRINCRI) as part of the PNP's restructuring. The Republican Guard of Peru, also

known as the Guardia Republicana del Perú, was a division of the Peruvian National Gendarmerie that operated from 1919 to 1988. It was in charge of safeguarding the offices of public institutions, overseeing prisons, and managing border security. The Republican Guard originated from the Peruvian National Gendarmerie infantry regiment which was established in 1852 to restructure the police forces. The French Republican Guard inspired its formation. Peru's Civil Guard, or Guardia Civil del Perú (GCP), was a police force in Peru with the responsibility of maintaining public order, preventing crimes and misdemeanors, protecting individuals and their possessions, ensuring free circulation on public roads, and regulating vehicular traffic. President Manuel Pardo, who modeled it after the Spanish Civil Guard, created it in 1873. Throughout its history, it underwent several reorganizations, with the most significant one being in 1919 by President Augusto B. Leguía, who modernized the force and gave it a new image. The GCP was dissolved in 1988 and merged with the Investigative Police and the Republican Guard to create the National Police of Peru.

38. García Torres, *Guerra en la Selva*, 25.
39. Diego, interview, Yurimaguas, 2021. Diego recalls that it took them about seven hours of boat travel from the Caynarachi basin to reach the city of Yurimaguas.
40. García Torres, *Guerra en la Selva*, 26.
41. Diego interview, Yurimaguas, 2021.
42. Previously, the horizon was adorned with lively tones of emerald and sapphire, but during the MRTA attack it presented a solemn scene veiled in a gloomy blanket of engulfing flames. See, for instance, video footage uploaded to the internet by Asociación de Excombatantes de la Lucha Contraterrorista, "Toma de Yurimaguas Por el MRTA" (YouTube, September 20, 2017, video, 3:25), https://www.youtube.com/watch?v=n1Q-q4O9CVY.
43. García Torres, *Guerra en la Selva*, 26.
44. García Torres, "La Pesadilla," 231.
45. García Torres, "La Pesadilla," 231–32; García Torres, *Guerra en la Selva*, 26. Orders were sent for the capture of the explosives officer, who was handcuffed and interrogated. It was then determined that he was a member of the National Police who had infiltrated their ranks.
46. García Torres, "La Pesadilla," 232.
47. Interviews were conducted in the Caynarachi basin in 2017, 2021, and 2022, as well as in Yurimaguas in 2019.
48. García Torres, "La Pesadilla," 232. By the time he called for additional MRTA reinforcements, Puma's unit had suffered seven wounded, some gravely.
49. The navy acknowledged Siomar Noriega Torres's bravery and fearlessness, awarding him posthumously the Peruvian Cross Order for Naval Merit and the Naval Medal of Honor for Merit for going above and beyond the call of duty.
50. Interview, Caynarachi basin, 2018.
51. García Torres, "La Pesadilla," 233; García Torres, *Guerra en la Selva*, 27. García Torres claimed the quantity of weapons seized in Yurimaguas was double the number obtained during the MRTA strike in 1987 on Juanjuí. He proudly noted that the MRTA was forced to acquire three more motorboats to transport the heavy weapons taken from the police stations back to their basecamps. The details of García Torres's account regarding seized armaments from Yurimaguas were confirmed by both Diego and Fabiano.
52. Interview, Caynarachi basin, 2017.
53. For mention of this incursion, see MRTA, "El Frente Guerrillero Nor-Oriental," *Voz Rebelde*, no. 11 (April–May 1988), 7.

54. García Torres, "La Pesadilla," 232–33. García Torres insists that the looting was done by the freed prisoners from the prison, the Centro de Readaptación Social (Social Readaptation Center, CRAS). Other witnesses to the events dispute this claim, asserting that the looting was more generalized among the local population.

55. García Torres, "La Pesadilla," 232.

56. García Torres, 233.

57. García Torres, *Guerra en la Selva*, 26–27.

58. Interviews conducted in the Caynarachi basin in 2017 and in Yurimaguas in 2019.

59. Interview, Caynarachi basin, 2017.

60. Interview, Caynarachi basin, 2019.

61. Interview, Caynarachi basin, 2019.

62. A portion of the weapons and ammo stolen from Yurimaguas were eventually recovered by the army in battle with the MRTA at their camp at El Porvenir.

CHAPTER 9

Epigraph. "Los militares habían rodeado a los cumpas, lo que dificultaba la huida de la mayoría de ellos. Eran una fuerza gastada." Interview, Caynarachi basin, 2018.

1. Interview, Caynarachi basin, 2018.

2. Interview, Caynarachi basin, 2018.

3. Durand Guevara, "Donde habita el olvido," 75, Diario Oficial *El Peruano*, "Decreto Ley N 2566," Lima, August 17, 1992.

4. CVR, *Informe final de la Comisión de la Verdad y Reconciliación*, vol. 5, 2.10, 336. The situation was further complicated by the crisis of the alliance between the MIR-VR and the MRTA, as leaders and militants of the MIR had been leaving the ranks of the MRTA ever since 1991. Many disagreed with the higher cadres on the continuity of the armed struggle and the possibility of political negotiation. As a result, the UDP was ruptured, and this had an impact on the North Eastern Front, where the MIR VR had a significant presence and an important ancestry among its member. For additional details, see Durand Guevara, "Donde habita el olvido," 75.

5. Willis, *Testimony of Space*, 416, persuasively shows how the MRTA's efforts to counter the policies, values, and power of the state ultimately failed and the impact of their operations was limited. In so doing, he argues that "the response by the Peruvian state, however, was a highly symbolic moment for the military constitution of the state, constructing the residence as an important symbolic space" for Fujimorism.

6. "FEDIPSM comunicado públicado," *Diario El Tarapotino*, signed by Lucas Cachay Huamán, president, and Manuel Arévalo, communications secretary, Tarapoto, December 12, 1990.

7. CVR, *Informe final de la Comisión de la Verdad y Reconciliación*, vol. 5, 2.10, 313n7.

8. Interviews, Caynarachi basin, 2019.

9. People often say, "When you have money, you get justice" (*Cuando tiene plata te hacen justicia*).

10. A local resident who had links with the MRTA allegedly killed dozens of gay men in Uchiza.

11. For his part, Diego, like Mateo, was quite adamant about the extent to which the CVR was politicized.

12. The lyrics read: "Túpac Amaru, father of thunder / your great nation is finally born / your guerrillas are finally ignited / great flames of insurrection / Túpac Amaru, condor of fire / you hear bellows in the people / you are the fire of combat / song and flag of rebellion / your children know that the lords / will no longer feed off of your poverty / the people will finally not be enslaved / nor will they be shackled by exploitation / Túpac Amaru, father of thunder / your great nation is finally born / your guerrillas are finally ignited / great flames of insurrection / Túpac Amaru, son of the sun / your blood burns, your voice flares, / the oppressed standby / Túpac Amaru, liberator / Túpac Amaru, blood of the people / you are the soul of the nation / we will advance toward socialism / with your flag of rebellion / Túpac Amaru, father of thunder / your great nation is finally born / your guerrillas are finally ignited / great flames of insurrection." MRTA, "El camino de la revolución peruana: Documentos del II C.C. del MRTA," *Cambio*, special edition, August 1988, qtd. in Miguel La Serna, "'I Will Return and I Will Be Millions!' The Many Lives of Túpac Amaru," *Age of Revolutions*, November 2, 2020, https://ageofrevolutions.com/2020/11/02/i-will-return-and-i-will-be-millions-the-many-lives-of-tupac-amaru/#_edn15.

13. Reportedly, El Grillo and other *mandos* made money by charging *cupos* from *narcos*—this left some ex-militants with hidden resources following their release from incarceration.

14. García Torres, *Guerra en la Selva*, 40.

15. For instance, the president of the Corporación de Desarrollo Socio-Económico del Departamento de San Martín (Socio-Economic Development Corporation of the Department of San Martín, CORDESAM), Demetrio Tafur, an APRA militant, was kidnapped in 1990 by the MRTA. García Torres, *Guerra en la Selva*, 40.

16. Durand Guevara, "Donde habita el olvido," 65.

17. Locals reported the existence of clandestine mass graves between Metilluyoc and Yurimaguas. They were discovered when the roadway to the Pongo de Caynarachi was being constructed. Many corpses were found in shallow graves.

18. CVR 1.4, 380.

19. Hannah Arendt thought that violence can only weaken or destroy authority, legitimacy and consent, which are the sources of true power. See Hannah Arendt, *On Violence*, 56; Fanon, *Wretched of the Earth*, 1; Sorel, "Reflections on Violence," ix–xxi . *On Violence* is Arendt's response to how Frantz Fanon's *Wretched of the Earth*, and Georges Sorel's 1908 *Reflections on Violence* comprehend the connections between politics and violence, or between violence and revolutionary struggles against neocolonialism. In the face of the master's rejection of black subjectivity, Fanon saw violence as essential to the identity formation of the colonized. Violence provides the oppressed a means for creation—for the violence of "decolonization is quite simply the substitution of one 'species' of mankind for another." Sorel saw violence in terms of its virtuous and life creating force. He argued that violent uprisings and labor strikes by the proletariat were crucial to the establishment of revolutionary syndicalism.

20. Interviews, Caynarachi basin, 2018, 2019, 2021.

21. Interviews, Caynarachi basin, 2017, 2018, 2019, 2022.

22. On May 23, 1994, El Grillo; the *jefe regional* of MRTA, Andrés Mendoza del Águila; and another thirty-one militants applied for amnesty under the Ley de Arrepentimiento.

23. Julio Quevedo Bardález, "Después de 22 años reclama recompensa por entrega de miembro del MRTA," *Voces*, June 16, 2015; "Resurrección: Historia secreta de la deserción de Andrés Mendoza 'El Grillo,'" *Sí*, September 27–October 4, 1993, 34–39.

24. García Torres, "La Pesadilla," 236. Fifteen members of the Technical Police and the National Intelligence Service (Servicio Inteligencia Nacional) captured Sístero García Torres on putative drug charges after he flew with a group of six *tupacamaristas* to the city of Iquitos. Government officials from the Dirección Nacional Contra el Terrorismo (DINCOTE) promptly ordered his transfer to Lima on charges of terrorism.

25. "Hemos caminado todo el camino del bosque *por las puras*." Interview with Diego, Caynarachi basin, 2019.

26. The female MRTA rebel lived in the area, but Diego said she was originally from a community in Leoncio Prado Province, in the Region of Huánuco. Sandra, Fabiano, and Diego all said that in the Caynarachi basin, most women who were MRTA combatants did not come from the area, although they knew of women from the nearby communities of Pampa Hermosa and Yumbatos who were former members. Most tended to be recruits from the regional cities (including Lima and Juanjuí) or surrounding Amazonian provinces, such as the Alto Mayo, who had joined the ranks of the guerrillas thanks to family ties, educational experiences, or peasant cooperative activities.

27. "El peso de la bandera solo lo conoce quien la porta." Interview, Caynarachi basin, 2022.

28. "*Asu*, Diosito, está llegando este terrucos ya va a ver una balacera." An expression of shocking surprise, *Asu* is a shortened form of *a su madre*, which is a less vulgar way of saying "to fuck one's mother."

29. The Inter-American Commission of Human Rights has the authority to issue advisory opinions on matters related to human rights, but these opinions are not legally binding on the states concerned. Hence, Diego's reference to the IACHR seems somewhat paradoxical since their advisory opinions hold no actual power, making it difficult to accept that any violator of human rights would actually fear them. Despite this, the IACHR can accept and look into particular petitions, perform site visits, release reports and recommendations, and send specific cases to the Inter-American Court of Human Rights (IACtHR), which has the authority to render legally binding decisions and award reparations.

30. MRTA, "Mensaje a la juventud," II Central Committee of the MRTA, August 1988.

31. Mario Vargas Llosa's persona was forged at the Leoncio Prado Military College in Lima, where he entered when he was a teenager. His experiences in 1950 and 1951 nurtured his first novel, *La ciudad y los perros* (*The city and the dogs*), which chronicles students enduring rigorous and at times violent discipline while undergoing austere secondary school education at the Leoncio Prado Military College. Vargas Llosa's starkly real book depicts the prevalence of corruption and violence within the military academy. *La ciudad y los perros* skillfully narrates how young cadets resort to lies, betrayal, and murder in order to survive, revealing how authoritarianism and militarism shape their brutal and dehumanizing experiences, which are emblematic of broader Peruvian society. The promotion of certain values, such as aggression, courage, manliness, and sexuality actively hinder personal growth. See Mario Vargas Llosa's classic text, *La ciudad y los perros* (Barcelona: Editorial Seix Barral, 1963).

32. After his release from detention, Diego continued to have unexplained cramps and occasionally has fainting spells and bouts of vomiting whenever the memories of his time as a guerrilla fighter come into focus.

33. "Aunque luchamos durante años para construir una sociedad más justa e igualitaria, las cosas están peor ahora que cuando luché por primera vez por el MRTA" (Although we fought for years to build a more just and equal society, things are worse now than when I first fought for the MRTA). Interview, Caynarachi basin, 2021.

34. Pooling money from several individuals to purchase something, pay a bill, or throw a

celebration is known as *hacer chancha* in Peruvian Spanish. The Spanish word *chancha* is derived from Ch'anchay, a Quechua term meaning "to join." The phrase *hacer chancha* is thought to have its roots in Peru's countryside, where people would commonly get together to get a pig (*chancha*) and divide it between them for special occasions. The idiom slowly spread throughout the Peruvian Spanish-speaking community, becoming a well-known phrase.

35. Javier Heraud Pérez, *Revolutionary Words from Three Millennia of Rebellion and Resistance*, preface Tariq Ali eds. Andrew Hsiao and Audrea Lim (New York: Verso, 2016), 226. Javier Heraud Pérez was a Peruvian poet, teacher, and guerrilla fighter born in Lima on January 19, 1942. He published three poetry books: *El río* (*The River*), *El viaje* (*The Journey*), and *Estación reunida* (*Gathered Station*), and received the Young Poet of Peru Award. In 1963, he joined the National Liberation Army (Ejército de Liberación Nacional, ELN) and took part in a rebel incursion in southern Peru. On May 15 of that year, he was killed by the police in Puerto Maldonado while navigating in a canoe on the Madre de Dios River. Heraud Pérez was a young and passionate advocate for social justice, but his life was cut short. Today, his writings and legacy are still celebrated and hold importance in a number of Peru's literary and political scenes.

CHAPTER 10

Epigraph. "No toda distancia humana es ausencia, ni todo silencio es olvido." Interview, Caynarachi basin, 2018.

1. Halbwachs, *Les cadres sociaux de la mémoire*.
2. Thus, official national or regional history is created and disseminated in accordance with memory politics.
3. See Bartholomew Dean, "Epilogue," in *Ethnography of Support Encounters*, ed. M. Schlecker and F. Fleischer (New York: Palgrave Macmillan, 2013), 195–211.
4. Michael Taussig, "Culture of Terror—Space of Death: Roger Casement's Putumayo Report and the Explanation of Torture," *Comparative Studies in Society and History* 26 (1984): 467–97. In his analysis of the early twentieth-century Putumayo rubber scandal in Amazonia, Taussig describes the "space of death" as a wide-ranging, liminal field of cultural encounter. The space of death is where hope withers to death, where the abuser needs the abused, where fantasy is made veritable, and where the incapacity to understand becomes comprehension. Ultimately, it is that space where the culture of the conqueror is bound to that of the conquered.
5. Cynthia Milton, "At the Edge of the Peruvian Truth Commission: Alternative Paths to Recounting the Past," *Radical History Review*, no. 98 (2007): 3–33. The privileged position accorded to truth commissions and their findings, like those of the CVR and its final report, as the main purveyor of truth has been persuasively called into question by Milton.
6. Alex Pillen, "Language, Translation, Trauma," *Annual Review of Anthropology* 45 (2016): 95–111.
7. Jime Padilla Cabrera, "Memoria sobre la violencia política, caso de la región San Martín (provincia de Tocache)" (bachelor's thesis, UNMSM, Lima, 2012).
8. María Lourdes Murri Benegas, "La construcción de la memoria en América Latina: Las memorias en pugna en el Perú pos conflicto armado interno," *Revista Electrónica de Estudios Latinoamericanos* 17, no. 65 (2018): 15–36.
9. Jime Padilla Cabrera, "Memoria sobre la violencia política."

CONCLUSION

Epigraph. Albert Camus, *La chute* (Paris: Gallimard, 1956).

1. Bartholomew Dean, "The Ethics of Spying," *Anthropology Today* 21, no. 4 (2005): 19–22; Bartholomew Dean, "Public Anthropology," presentation at National Applied Anthropology Congress, Andhra University, Visakhapatnam, India, December 10, 2021.

2. Ethnological interpretations of trauma and their conceptual import have long been a contested component of modern and postmodern society, particularly in social anthropology and the related area of psychiatry, which pioneered the study of psychological injuries during World War I. This is especially clear when considering the various ways that cultures and social systems have responded to the grievous effects of warfare, from blitzkrieg to low-intensity conflict.

3. G. D. Hodge, "The Problem with Ethics," *Political and Legal Anthropology Review* 36, no. 2 (2013): 286–97, at 286. Hodge observes that anthropology that is wholly detached and passive is not ethical, but that our moral engagement must be based on a substantial corpus of evidence that is evaluated using legitimate methodological and theoretical approaches. As a result, even if deontological obligations—articulated by the American Anthropological Association's Code of Ethics and institutional review boards—have been painstakingly observed, ethnographic techniques that are methodologically weak or philosophically sloppy are not ethical.

4. Bartholomew Dean, "Critical Re-vision: Clastres' *Chronicle* and the Optic of Primitivism," *Anthropology Today* 15, no. 2 (1999): 9–11.

5. Kimberly Theidon, *Intimate Enemies: Violence and Reconciliation in Peru* (Philadelphia: University of Pennsylvania Press 2012), 22); Nancy Scheper-Hughes, "The Primacy of the Ethical: Propositions for a Militant Anthropology," *Current Anthropology* 36, no. 3 (1995): 409–40. Scheper-Hughes's approach to fieldwork in "extreme conditions" places a greater emphasis on the function of the anthropologist as witness.

6. Eduardo González Cueva, "The Peruvian Truth and Reconciliation Commission and the Challenge of Impunity," in *Transitional Justice in the Twenty-First Century: Beyond Truth versus Justice*, ed. Naomi Roht-Arriaza and Javier Mariezcurrena (Cambridge: Cambridge University Press 2006), 70–93; Joanna Pietraszczyk-Sękowska, "Towards Homes and Graves: About the Returns, Desaparecidos and Exhumation Challenges in Peru at the End of the Twentieth Century," *International Studies: Interdisciplinary Political and Cultural Journal* 25, no. 1 (2020): 49–74.

7. Jorge Paredes, "Entrevista a Manuel Burga: El LUM ha sido víctima de malas interpretaciones" (Lima: APRODEH), August 20, 2018, https://www.aprodeh.org.pe/entrevista-a-manuel-burga-el-lum-ha-sido-victima-de-malas-interpretaciones/.

8. Kimberly Theidon, "Justice in Transition: The Micropolitics of Reconciliation in Postwar Peru," *Journal of Conflict Resolution* 50, no. 3 (2006): 433–57.

9. Isaias Rojas-Pérez, *Mourning Remains: State Atrocity, Exhumations, and Governing the Disappeared in Peru's Postwar Andes* (Palo Alto, CA: Stanford University Press, 2017).

10. In his classic 1748 text, *An Enquiry Concerning Human Understanding*, David Hume identified moral sentiments, such as praise and blame, as emerging from our sympathy with other human beings.

11. Interview, Yurimaguas, 2019. During my fieldwork, I found that having casual conversations over beers (known as *chupando chelas*) with key informants, both male and female, was extremely helpful in gaining valuable insight into life in the Huallaga Valley during the so-called ugly times.

12. On the futuristic aspirations of the MRTA, see *Conquistando el porvenir: Con las masas y las armas. Notas sobre la historia del MRTA* (Lima: Voz Rebelde, 1990).

13. Bartholomew Dean, "Freedom," in *Keywords of Mobility: Critical Anthropological Engagements*, ed. Noel Salazar and Kiran Jayaram (Oxford, UK: Berghahn Books, 2016), 56–74.

14. Benedict Anderson, *Imagined Communities: Reflections on the Origin and Spread of Nationalism* (London: Verso, 1983).

15. Bartholomew Dean and Jerome Levi, eds., *At the Risk of Being Heard: Identity, Indigenous Rights and Postcolonial States* (Ann Arbor: University of Michigan Press, 2003).

16. Dean and Levi; Bartholomew Dean, "Indigenous Identity and Education in Peruvian Amazonia," in *Indigenous Education: Language, Culture, and Identity*, ed. W. James Jacob, Sheng Yao Cheng, and Maureen K. Porter (Dordrecht, The Netherlands: Springer, 2015), 429–46; Bartholomew Dean, "The Value of Health and the Emerging Epidemic of Diabetes in Peruvian Amazonia" (paper presented at the "Colonialisms, Embodiment and Injustice" panel, 121st annual meeting of the Society for Medical Anthropology, American Anthropological Association, Seattle, November 10, 2022).

References

Álvarez Rubio, Ariel. "La toma de rehenes como acto terrorista internacional: Análisis de la operación de Rescate 'Chavín de Huantar.'" *Revista de Relaciones Internacionales, Estrategia y Seguridad* 10, no. 2 (2015): 43–68. https://doi.org/10.18359/ries.578.

Amnesty International. "Peru-Japan: Alberto Fujimori must be brought to justice for human rights violations." Press release, July 31, 2003. https://www.amnesty.org/en/wp-content/uploads/2021/06/amr460162003en.pdf.

Anderson, Benedict. *Imagined Communities.* London: Verso Books, 1983.

Andina. "San Martín: Detienen a alcalde de Caynarachi por presunta defraudación." December 18, 2018. *Andina.* https://andina.pe/agencia/noticia-san-Martín-detienen-a-alcalde-caynarachi-presunta-defraudacion-736372.aspx.

Appadurai, Arjun, ed. *The Social Life of Things.* Cambridge: Cambridge University Press, 1988.

Asociación Pro Derechos Humanos (APRODEH). *Derechos humanos: Boletín de información y análisis de la Asociación Pro Derechos Humanos.* Lima: APRODEH, October–December 1988.

Arendt, Hannah. *On Violence.* San Diego, CA: Harcourt Brace Jovanovich, 1970.

Azevedo, Valérie Robin. *Los silencios de la guerra: Memorias y conflicto armado en Ayacucho-Perú.* Lima: La Siniestra Ensayos, 2021.

Baer, Suzie. *Peru's MRTA: Tupac Amaru Revolutionary Movement.* New York: Rosen Publishing, 2003.

Bakunin, Mikhail. *Bakunin on Anarchy: Selected Works by the Activist-Founder of World Anarchism.* Edited, translated, and with an introduction by Sam Dolgoff. New York: Vintage Books, 1971.

Ball, Patrick, Jana Asher, David Sulmont, and Daniel Manrique. *How Many Peruvians Have Died? An Estimate of the Total Number of Victims Killed or Disappeared in the Armed Internal Conflict between 1980 and 2000.* Washington, DC: American Association for the Advancement of Science, 2003.

Barclay, Frederica. "Cambios y continuidades en el pacto colonial en la Amazonía: El caso de los indios chasutas del Huallaga medio a finales del siglo XIX." *Bulletin De l'Institut Français d'Études Andines* 30, no. 2 (2001): 187–210. https://doi.org/10.4000/bifea.6994.

Barrantes Segura, Rafael. *Reparations and Displacement in Peru.* New York: Center for Transitional Justice and the Brookings-LSE Project on Internal Displacement, International Center for Transitional Justice, 2012.

Barrientos Hernandez, Dora H., and Adam L. Church. "Terrorism in Peru." *Prehospital and Disaster Medicine* 18, no. 2 (2003): 123–26. https://doi.org/10.1017/s1049023x0000087x.

Becker, Marc. *Twentieth-Century Latin American Revolutions.* Lanham, MD: Rowman and Littlefield Publishers, 2017.

Béjar, Héctor. *Peru 1965: Notes on a Guerrilla Experience.* New York: Monthly Review Press, 1970.

———. *Retorno a la guerrilla.* Lima: Achebé, 2015.

Benjamin, Walter. "Critique of Violence." In *Selected Writings: 1913–1926*, edited by Marcus Bullock and Michael W. Jennings, vol. 1: 236–52. Cambridge, MA: Harvard University Press, 2004.

Bernales, Manuel, and Róger Rumrrill. "Narcopoder, subversión y democracia en Perú." *Nueva Sociedad* 102 (1989): 162–68.

Bigwood, Jeremy. "With Guerrilla U: In the Jungle with Peru's Tupac Amaru." *Covert Action Quarterly*, no. 60 (1997): https://www.ainfos.ca/A-Infos97/2/0135.html.

Black, Charlene Villaseñor. *Transforming Saints: From Spain to New Spain.* Nashville, TN: Vanderbilt University Press, 2022.

Boleslao, Lewin. *La rebelión de Túpac Amaru y los orígenes de la independencia hispanoamericana.* Buenos Aires: Sociedad Editora Latino Americana, 1967.

Boschmann, Nina. "Coca und Guerilla in Perus Garten Eden." *TAZ*, June 5, 1990. https://taz.de/Coca-und-Guerrilla-in-Perus-Garten-Eden/!1765461/.

———. "Die Gesellschaft muß vom Volk neu geschaffen warden." *TAZ*, June 5, 1990. https://taz.de/!1765463.

Bourdieu, Pierre. *On Television and Journalism.* Translated by Priscilla Parkhurst Ferguson. London: Pluto Press, 1998.

Bourdieu, Pierre, and Jean Claude Passeron. *Reproduction in Education, Society and Culture.* London: Sage Publications, 1977.

Brooke, James. "The Rebels and the Cause: 12 Years of Peru's Turmoil." *New York Times*, December 19, 1996.

Brown, Cynthia. *In Desperate Straits: Human Rights in Peru after a Decade of Democracy and Insurgency.* New York: Human Rights Watch, 1990.

Brown, Joseph. *Force of Words: The Logic of Terrorist Threats.* New York: Columbia University Press, 2020.

Brown, Michael, and Eduardo Fernández. *War of Shadows: The Struggle for Utopia in the Peruvian Amazon.* Berkeley: University of California Press, 1991.

Brown, Ryan, and Lindsey Osterman. "Culture of Honor, Violence, and Homicide." In *The Oxford Handbook of Evolutionary Perspectives on Violence, Homicide, and War*, edited by Todd K. Shackelford and Viviana A. Weekes-Shackelford, 218–32. Oxford: Oxford University Press, 2012.

Burt, Jo-Marie. "Los usos y abusos de la memoria de María Elena Moyano." *A Contracorriente: Revista de Historia Social y Literatura en América Latina* 7, no. 2 (2010): 165–209. https://dialnet.unirioja.es/servlet/articulo?codigo=3143367.

Campbell, Leon G. "The Army of Peru and the Túpac Amaru Revolt, 1780–1783." *Hispanic American Historical Review* 56, no. 1 (1976): 31–57.

Camus, Albert. *Algerian Chronicles.* Cambridge, MA: Harvard University Press, 2013.

———. *La chute.* Paris: Gallimard, 1956.

———. *The Rebel: An Essay on Man in Revolt.* New York: Vintage, 2012.

Canessa, Andrew. "Fear and Loathing on the Kharisiri Trail: Alterity and Identity in the Andes." *Journal of the Royal Anthropological Institute* 6, no. 4 (2000): 705–20. https://doi.org/10.1111/1467-9655.00041.

Caretas, no. 975, October 26, 1987.

———. no. 1397, January 18, 1997.

Centro Amazónico de Antropológica y Aplicación Práctica, *Violencia y narcotráfico en la Amazonía.* Lima: CAAAP, 1992.

Cerpa Cartolini, Néstor. *Tomar por asalto el siglo XXI: Biografía y documentos del comandante obrero MRTA Néstor Cerpa Cartolini.* Edited by Gabriel Carranza Polo. La Paz: G. Carranza Polo, 2003.

Choi, Yoon Soo. "The Peruvian Hostage Crisis: Brief Review of MRTA." *International Journal of Comparative and Applied Criminal Justice* 21, no. 1 (1997): 33–49. https://doi.org/10.1080 /01924036.1997.9678584.

Clawson, Patrick, and Rensselaer Lee. *The Andean Cocaine Industry.* Basingstoke, UK: Macmillan, 1996.

Comisión de la Verdad y Reconciliación. *Informe final de la Comisión de la Verdad y Reconciliación.* Lima: Comisión de la Verdad y Reconciliación, 2003.

Comité de Productores de Maíz y Sorgo. "Oficio del 28 de setiembre de 1990, dirigido al Ministro de Agricultura Carlos Amat y León." Cited in "Narcotráfico, Violencia y Campesinado en la Selva Alta" by Ricardo Soberón Garrido. *SEPIA,* 2008. https:// www.verdadyreconciliacionperu.com/admin/files/articulos/1598_digitalizacion.pdf.

Commander Andrés. "Light at the End of the Tunnel: Interview with an MRTA Leader, Commander Andrés." *Barricada International,* January 19, 1991.

Conversi, Daniele. "Reassessing Current Theories of Nationalism: Nationalism as Boundary Maintenance and Creation." *Nationalism and Ethnic Politics* 1 (1995):73–85.

Das, Veena. *Life and Words: Violence and the Descent into the Ordinary.* Berkeley: University of California Press, 2005.

David, Randy, and Bartholomew Dean. "A Sociogenetic Approach to Migration and Urbanization in Peruvian Amazonia: Implications for Population Architecture." In *Human Migration: Biocultural Perspectives,* edited by María de Lourdes Muñoz-Moreno and Michael H. Crawford, 180–96. Oxford: Oxford University Press, 2021.

Dean, Bartholomew. "Ambivalent Exchanges: The Violence of *Patronazgo* in the Upper Amazon." In *Cultural Construction of Violence: Victimization, Escalation, Response,* edited by M. Anderson, 214–26. West Lafayette, IN: Purdue University, 2004.

———. "Blood in the River: Ontological Experiences and Representations of the Embodiment of Corruption in Peruvian Amazonia's Huallaga Valley." Presentation at the joint 118th annual meeting of the American Anthropological Association and the Canadian Anthropology Society, Vancouver, BC, November 22, 2019.

———. "Critical Re-vision: Clastres' *Chronicle* and the Optic of Primitivism." *Anthropology Today* 15, no. 2 (1999): 9–11.

———. "Diabetes en la Amazonia." In *Investigación,* 1–12. Yurimaguas: Instituto de Educación Superior Tecnológico Público, 2019.

———. "El Dr. Máxime Kuczynski-Godard y la medicina social en la Amazonía peruana." In *La vida en la Amazonía peruana: Observaciones de un médico,* by Máxime Kuczynski-Godard. Lima: Fondo Editorial de la Universidad Nacional Mayor de San Marcos, 2004.

———. "Epilogue." In *Ethnography of Support Encounters,* edited by Markus Schlecker and Friederike Fleischer, 195–211. New York: Palgrave Macmillan, 2013. https://link. springer.com/chapter/10.1057/9781137330970_11.

———. "The Ethics of Spying." *Anthropology Today* 21, no. 4 (2005): 19–22. https://www.jstor. org/stable/3695071.

———. "Freedom." In *Keywords of Mobility: Critical Anthropological Engagements*, edited by Noel Salazar and Kiran Jayaram, 56–74. Oxford, UK: Berghahn Books, 2016.

———. "From the Fat of Their Being: Vampires and Andean Modernity." Review of *Gods and Vampires: Return to Chipaya. Cultural Dynamics* 9, no. 1 (1997): 111–13. https://doi.org/10.1177/092137409700900108.

———. "Identity and Intimate Violence in Peru: Commentary on 'Why Would You Marry a *Serrana?*'" *Journal of Latin American and Caribbean Anthropology* 12, no. 1 (2007): 29–32. https://doi.org/10.1525/jlat.2007.12.1.29.

———. "Indigenous Identity and Education in Peruvian Amazonia." In *Indigenous Education: Language, Culture, and Identity*, edited by W. James Jacob, Sheng Yao Cheng, and Maureen K. Porter, 429–46. Dordrecht, The Netherlands: Springer, 2015. https://link.springer.com/chapter/10.1007/978-94-017-9355-1_21.

———. "Intercambios ambivalentes en la Amazonía: Formación discursiva y la violencia del patronazgo." *Antropológica* 17 (1999): 85–115. https://revistas.pucp.edu.pe/index.php/anthropologica/article/view/1539.

———. "Life in a *Callejón*: The Inner-City Poor of Lima, Perú." MPhil thesis, Oxford University, 1987.

———. "Machetes in Our Hands, Blood on Our Faces: Reflections on Violence and Advocacy in the Peruvian Amazon." *Anthropological Quarterly* 82, no. 4 (2009): 1069–72. http://www.jstor.org/stable/20638685.

———. "MS Alfhem Affair: The Circulation of Weapons, US Empire, and Cold War in the Americas." In *Encyclopedia of US Intelligence*, edited by D. Moore, 587–91. New York: Taylor and Francis, 2015.

———. "Narratives, Resilience and Violence in Peruvian Amazonia: The Huallaga Valley, 1980–2015." *Anthropology: Open Journal* 1, no. 1 (2016): 1–2. http://dx.doi.org/10.17140/ANTPOJ-1-101.

———. "Public Anthropology." Presentation at National Applied Anthropology Congress, Andhra University, Visakhapatnam, India, India Dec. 10, 2021.

———. "*Review of Salt of the Mountain: Campa Asháninka History and Resistance in the Peruvian Jungle*," by S. Varese. *The Americas* 62, no. 3 (2006): 464–66. http://www.jstor.org/stable/4491097.

———. *The State and the Awajún: Frontier Expansion in the Upper Amazon, 1541–1990.* San Diego, CA: Cognella Academic Publishing, 2020.

———. "State Power and Indigenous Peoples in Peruvian Amazonia: A Lost Decade, 1990–2000." In *The Politics of Ethnicity: Indigenous Peoples in Latin American States*, edited by David Maybury-Lewis, 199–238. Cambridge, MA: Harvard University Press, 2002.

———. "The Transgressive Allure of White Gold in Peruvian Amazonia: Towards a Genealogy of Coca Capitalisms and Social Dread." *ID: International Dialogue, A Multidisciplinary Journal of World Affairs* 3 (2013): 150–67. https://www.unomaha.edu/college-of-arts-and-sciences/goldstein-center-for-human-rights/ID/7_reviewessay_dean2013.pdf.

———. "The Túpac Amaru Revolutionary Movement (Movimiento Revolucionario Túpac Amaru) in the Central and Lower Huallaga Valley, Peruvian Amazonia." In *Oxford Research Encyclopedia of Latin American History*, edited by William H. Beezley. New York: Oxford University Press, forthcoming.

———. *Urarina Society, Cosmology and History in Peruvian Amazonia.* Gainesville: University Press of Florida, 2009.

———. "The Value of Health and the Emerging Epidemic of Diabetes in Peruvian Amazonia." Paper presented for the "Colonialisms, Embodiment and Injustice" panel, 121st annual meeting of the Society for Medical Anthropology, American Anthropological Association, Seattle, November 10, 2022.

Dean, Bartholomew, Charles Bartles, and Timothy Berger. "Civil-Affairs Confronts the 'Weapons of the Weak': Improvised Explosive Devices in Iraq." *Small Wars Journal*, no. 3 (2009): 19–37. https://community.apan.org/wg/tradoc-g2/fmso/m/fmso-monographs/239242.

Dean, Bartholomew, and Jerome Levi, eds. *At the Risk of Being Heard: Identity, Indigenous Rights and Postcolonial States.* Ann Arbor: University of Michigan Press, 2003.

Debray, Régis. *Révolution dans la révolution? Lutte armée et lutte politique en Amérique latine.* Paris: F. Maspero, 1967.

Degregori, Carlos Iván. "Harvesting Storms: Peasant Rondas and the Defeat of Sendero Luminoso in Ayacucho." in *Shining and Other Paths: War and Society in Peru, 1980–1995*, edited by S. J. Stern, 128–57. Durham, NC: Duke University Press, 1998.

———. *El surgimiento de Sendero Luminoso 1969–1979.* Lima: IEP, 1990.

Denegri, Francesca, and Alexandra Hibbett, eds. *Dando cuenta: Estudios sobre el testimonio de la violencia política en el Perú (1980–2000).* Lima: Fondo Editorial de la PUCP, 2016.

Devji, Faisal. "The Return of Nonviolence." *Critical Times* 4, no. 1 (2021): 93–101. https://doi.org/10.1215/26410478-8855243.

Diario Oficial. *El Peruano.* "Decreto Ley No. 2566." Lima, August 17, 1992.

Dirección de Estadística. *Censo nacional de población y ocupación 1940: Departamentos: Loreto, Amazonas, San Martín, Madre de Dios.* Lima: Dirección de Estadística, 1944.

Donlan, William, and Junghee Lee. "*Coraje, Nervios*, and *Susto*: Culture-Bound Syndromes and Mental Health among Mexican Migrants in the United States." *Advances in Mental Health* 9, no. 3 (2010): 288–302. https://doi.org/10.5172/jamh.9.3.288.

Dreyfus, Pablo. "When All Evils Come Together: Cocaine, Corruption and Shining Path in Peru's Upper Huallaga Valley." *Journal of Contemporary Criminal Justice* 15, no. 4 (1999): 370–96. https://doi.org/10.1177/1043986299015004004.

Durand Guevara, Anahí. "Donde habita el olvido: Los (h)usos de la memoria y la crisis del movimiento social en San Martín." Bachelor's thesis, Universidad Nacional Mayor de San Marcos, 2005.

Durand Ochoa, Úrsula. *Coca o muerte: La radicalización del movimiento cocalero.* Lima: DESCO, 2008.

———. *The Political Empowerment of the Cocaleros of Bolivia and Peru.* London: Palgrave Macmillan, 2014.

Durkheim, Émile. *Elementary Forms of the Religious Life.* Translated by J. W. Swain. New York: Free Press, 1971.

Encarnación Pinedo, Miriam. "La memoria carcelaria en Sendero Luminoso y en el Movimiento de Liberación Nacional Tupamaro (1982–2017)." *Historia y Memoria* 21 (2020): 235–68. https://doi.org/10.19053/20275137.n21.2020.9572.

Espinosa, Óscar. "El terror que no termina: La persistente amenaza a la vida y seguridad de las comunidades asháninka de los ríos Ene y Tambo." *Ideele* (2013): 233. http://www.revistaideele.com/ideele/content/n%C3%Bamero-233.

———. *Las rondas campesinas y nativas en la Amazonía peruana.* Lima: CAAAP, 1995.

Espinosa, Óscar, Silvia Romio, and Marco Ramírez Colombier. *Historias, violencias y memorias en la Amazonía.* Lima: PUCP, 2021.

Espinosa Arango, Mónica. "Memoria cultural y el continuo del genocidio: Lo indígena en Colombia." *Antípoda: Revista de Antropología y Arqueología*, no. 5 (2007): 53–73. https://doi.org/10.7440/antipoda5.2007.03.

Estelle, Lillian. *The Last Inca Revolt, 1780–1783.* Norman: University of Oklahoma Press, 1966.

Evans, Richard. *The Third Reich in Power.* New York: Penguin Books, 2006.

Fabian Arias, Beatriz. *Las cosas ya no son como antes: La mujer ashaninka y los cambios socioculturales producidos por la violencia política en la Selva Central.* Lima: CAAAP, 1997.

Fanon, Frantz. *The Wretched of the Earth.* New York: Grove Press, 2004.

FEDIPSM. "FEDIPSM comunicado públicado." *Diario El Tarapotino.* Signed by Lucas Cachay and Manuel Arévalo, Tarapoto, December 12, 1990.

Feld, C., and V. Salvi. "Cuando los perpetradores hablan: Dilemas y tensiones en torno a la voz comprometida." *Rubrica Contemporánea* 5, no. 9 (2016): 1–10. https://revistes.uab.cat/rubrica/article/viewFile/v5-n9-feld-salvi/116-pdf-es.

Fielding, Davis. "The Dynamics of Terror during the Peruvian Civil War." *Journal of Peace Research* 49, no. 6 (2012): 847–86.

Flores Galindo, Alberto, ed. *Túpac Amaru II-1780: Sociedad colonial y sublevaciones populares.* Lima: Retablo de Papel Ediciones, 1976.

Gadea Acosta, Ricardo. *El MIR histórico.* Lima: Editorial Pueblo Unido y Ricardo Gadea, 2021.

Galtung, Johan. "Cultural Violence." *Journal of Peace Research* 27, no. 3 (1990): 291–305.

———. "Violence, Peace and Peace Research." *Journal of Peace Research* 6, no. 3 (1969): 167–91.

Gálvez Olaechea, Alberto. "Combatiente en la batalla de ideas: Entrevista a Alberto Gálvez Olaechea por Alejandro Lavquén." *Punto Final*, October 14, 2016.

———. *Con la palabra desarmada: Ensayos sobre el (pos)conflict.* Lima: Fauno, 2015.

———. "El maoísmo en dos novellas: Cuando la realidad sobrepasa la ficción." *Medium*, November 24, 2022. https://albertoglvezolaechea.medium.com/el-mao%C3%ADsmo-en-dos-novelas-5d70da1ce074.

Gamarra, Jeffrey. *Las dificultades de la memoria, el poder y la reconciliación en los Andes: El ejemplo ayacuchano.* Ayacucho, Peru: IPAZ, 2001.

García Torres, Sístero. *Guerra en la Selva: Historia del Movimiento TUPAC AMARU en la Amazonía Peruana.* N.p.: Independently published, 2017.

———. "La pesadilla." In *La danza de la coca*, edited by Aldinger Pezo. Tarapoto: Syndisgraf, 2001.

Gerhold, C., D. Robbins, M. Garcia-Touza, and B. C. Dean. "The Impact of Urbanization on the People of the Upper Amazon." *Diabetes* 72, suppl. 1 (2023): 191-LB. https://doi.org/10.2337/db23-191-LB.

Girard, René. *Violence and the Sacred.* Translated by Patrick Gregory. Baltimore: Johns Hopkins University Press, 1977.

Gonzales, José E. "Guerrillas and Coca in the Upper Huallaga Valley." In *Shining Path of Peru,* edited by David Scott Palmer, 105–26. New York: St. Martin's Press, 1992.

González, Olga M. *Unveiling Secrets of War in the Peruvian Andes.* Chicago: University of Chicago Press, 2011.

Gonzalez, Raúl. "MRTA: La historia desconocida." *Que Hacer,* no. 51 (1988): 33–46.

———. "Sendero: Los problemas del campo y de la ciudad y además el MRTA." *Que Hacer* no. 50 (1988): 47–59.

González Cueva, Eduardo. "The Peruvian Truth and Reconciliation Commission and the Challenge of Impunity." *Transitional Justice in the Twenty-First Century beyond Truth ver-*

sus Justice, edited by Naomi Roht-Arriaza and Javier Mariezcurrena, 70–93. Cambridge: Cambridge University Press, 2006.

Gootenberg, Paul. *Andean Cocaine: The Making of a Global Drug*. Chapel Hill: University of North Carolina Press, 2008.

———. "Between Coca and Cocaine: A Century or More of US-Peruvian Drug Paradoxes, 1860–1980." *Hispanic American Historical Review* 83, no. 1 (2003): 119–50.

Greene, Shane. "The Terruco Problem." *Editors' Forum: Hot Spots*, March 30, 2023. https://culanth.org/fieldsights/the-terruco-problem.

Gramsci, Antonio. *Selections from the Prison Notebooks of Antonio Gramsci*, ed. and trans. Quintin Hoare and Geoffrey Nowell Smith. New York: International Publishers, 1971.

Guardia, Sara Beatriz. "Reconociendo las huellas: Micaela Bastidas y las heroinas de la independencia del Perú." In *Las mujeres en la independencia de América Latina*, edited by Sara Beatriz Guardia, 31–48. Lima: CEMHAL, 2010.

Guevara, Ernesto Che. "Guerra de guerrillas un método." In *Obra revolucionaria*. Mexico: Ed. Era, 1973.

———. *Guerrilla Warfare*. Edited by Brian Loveman and Thomas M. Davies Jr. Lanham, MD: Rowman and Littlefield, 2002.

Gurmendi Dunkelberg, Alonso. *Conflicto armado en el Perú: La época del terrorismo bajo el derecho internacional*. Lima: Universidad del Pacífico, 2019.

Halbwachs, Maurice. *Les cadres sociaux de la mémoire*. Paris: Librairie Félix Alcan, 1925.

Hendrix, Steven E. "Interplay among Land Law and Policy, the Environment, the War on Drugs, Narcoterrorism, and Democratization: Perspectives on Peru's Upper Huallaga Valley." Madison: Land Tenure Center, University of Wisconsin 150, 1993.

Heraud Pérez, Javier. *Revolutionary Words from Three Millennia of Rebellion and Resistance*. Preface by Tariq Ali. Edited by Andrew Hsiao and Audrea Lim. New York: Verso, 2016.

Herndon, William Lewis, and Lardner Gibbon. *Exploration of the Valley of the Amazon*. Part 1 of 2, Senate document, 32nd Congress, 2nd session, no. 36. Washington, DC: R. Armstrong Public Printer, 1853–1854.

Hodge, G. D. "The Problem with Ethics." *Political and Legal Anthropology Review* 36, no. 2 (2013): 286–97.

Hume, David. *Philosophical Essays Concerning Human Understanding*. London: Printed for A. Millar, 1748.

INEI. *Compendio estadístico departamental 1996–1997*. Moyobamba, Peru: Departamento San Martín, 1997.

———. "Perú: Anuario de Estadísticas Ambientales 2015." In *Perú: Anuario de Estadísticas Ambientales 2015*. Lima: Instituto Nacional de Estadística e Informática, 2015.

Instituto de Defensa Legal. *Peru hoy: En el oscuro sendero de la guerra*. Lima: IDL, 1992.

Jaskoski, M. "Civilian Control of the Armed Forces in Democratic Latin America." *Armed Forces and Society* 38 (2012): 70–91.

Jelin, Elizabeth. *State Repression and the Labors of Memory*. Translated by Marcial Godoy-Anativia and Judy Rein. Minneapolis: University of Minnesota Press, 2003.

Justice, Anne, Bartholomew Dean, and Michael H. Crawford. "Molecular Consequences of Migration and Urbanization in Peruvian Amazonia." In *Causes and Consequences of Human Migration: An Evolutionary Perspective*, eds. Michael H. Crawford and Benjamin C. Campbell, 449–72. New York: Cambridge University Press, 2012.

Kalmus, Nicholas. "Paradise Lost Is Found in the Mountains of Peru." Field Museum, October 9, 2013. https://www.fieldmuseum.org/blog/paradise-lost-found-mountains-peru.

Kawell, Jo Ann. "The Cocaine Economy." In *The Peru Reader: History, Culture, Politics*, edited by Orin Starn, Carlos Iván Degregori, and Robin Kirk, 425–37. Durham, NC: Duke University Press.

Kay, Bruce. "Violent Opportunities: The Rise and Fall of 'King Coca' and Shining Path." *Journal of Interamerican Studies and World Affairs* 41, no. 3 (1999): 97–127.

Kent, Robert B. "Dimensions of the Shining Path Insurgency in Peru." *Geographical Review* 83, no. 4 (1993): 441–54. https://www.jstor.org/stable/215825.

Kernaghan, Richard. *Coca's Gone: Of Might and Right in the Upper Huallaga Valley Post-Boom.* Stanford, CA: Stanford University Press, 2009.

———. *Crossing the Current: Aftermaths of War along the Huallaga River.* Stanford, CA: Stanford University Press, 2022.

Koc-Menard, S. "Fragmented Sovereignty: Why Sendero Luminoso Consolidated in Some Regions of Peru but Not in Others." *Studies in Conflict and Terrorism* 30, no. 2 (2007): 173–206.

Kropotkin, Pyotr. "Words of a Rebel." In *The Heretic's Handbook of Quotations: Cutting Comments on Burning Issues*, edited by Charles Bufe, 26. Tucson, AZ: Sharp Press, 1992.

Lagdon, Susan Cherie Armour, and Maurice Stringer. "Adult Experience of Mental Health Outcomes as a Result of Intimate Partner Violence Victimisation: A Systematic Review." *European Journal of Psychotraumatology*, September 12, 2014, https://doi.org/10.3402/ejpt.v5.24794.

Laplante, Lisa J., and Kimberly Theidon. "Commissioning Truth, Constructing Silences: The Peruvian Truth Commission and the Other Truths of 'Terrorists.'" In *Mirrors of Justice: Law and Power in the Post-Cold War Era*, edited by Kamari Maxine Clarke and Mark Goodale, 291–315. Cambridge: Cambridge University Press, 2009.

La Serna, Miguel. "'I Will Return and I Will Be Millions!' The Many Lives of Túpac Amaru." *Age of Revolutions*, November 2, 2020. https://ageofrevolutions.com/2020/11/02/i-will-return-and-i-will-be-millions-the-many-lives-of-tupac-amaru/#_edn15.

———. *With masses and arms: Peru's Túpac Amaru Revolutionary Movement.* Chapel Hill: University of North Carolina Press, 2020.

Letts Colmenares, Ricardo (Pumaruna). *Peru: Revolución, insurrección, guerrillas.* Lima: Ediciones Vanguardia Revolucionaria, 1968.

Limachi, L., W. de Jong, and C. Cornejo. "Models of Migration in the Peruvian Amazon and Their Impact on Tropical Forests." In *The Social Ecology of Tropical Forests: Migration; Population and Frontiers*, edited by Will de Jong, Tuck-Po Lye, and Ken-ichi Abe, 55–78. Kyoto, Japan: Kyoto University Press, 2006.

López Díaz, Antonio. "Los indeseables de Tarapoto." *El País*, April 4, 2016.

Lust, Jan. *Capitalism, Class and Revolution in Peru, 1980–2016.* Cham, Switzerland: Palgrave Macmillan, 2019.

Mandelli, L., C. Petrelli, and A. Serretti. "The Role of Specific Early Trauma in Adult Depression: A Meta-Analysis of Published Literature, Childhood Trauma and Adult Depression." *European Psychiatry* 30, no. 6 (2015): 665–80.

Manrique, Nelson. *El tiempo del miedo: Los orígenes sociales de la violencia política en el Perú, 1980–1996.* Lima: Fondo Editorial del Congreso del Perú, 2002.

Manrique López, Hernán. "Las bases históricas del 'milagro de San Martín': Control territorial y estrategias estatales contra el narcotráfico y subversión (1980–1995)." *Politai* 6, no. 11 (2015): 33–51.

Manrique López, Hernán, and Néstor Álvaro Pastor Armas. "Cocaína peruana: Análisis bibliográfico de la investigación sobre el tráfico ilícito de drogas cocaínicas en Perú." *Cultura y Droga* 24, no. 27 (2019): 15–38.

Manrique-Vallier, D., and P. Ball. "Reality and Risk: A Refutation of S. Rendon's Analysis of the Peruvian Truth and Reconciliation Commission's Mortality Study." *Research and Politics* 6 (2019): 1–5.

Mariátegui, José Carlos. "Estudiantes y maestros." *Mundial*, March 9, 1928.

———. *Seven Interpretative Essays on Peruvian Reality*. Austin: University of Texas Press, 1971.

Mauceri, Philip. "The Transition to 'Democracy' and the Failures of Institution Building." In *The Peruvian Labyrinth: Polity, Society, Economy*, edited by Maxwell A. Cameron and Philip Mauceri, 13–36. University Park: Pennsylvania State University Press, 1997.

Maybury-Lewis, David. *Indigenous Peoples, Ethnic Groups and the State*. Needham, MA: Allyn and Bacon, 2002.

Mayer, Enrique. *Ugly Stories of the Peruvian Agrarian Reform*. Durham, NC: Duke University Press, 2009.

McClintock, Cynthia. "Drogas-guerrilla-violencia." *Chasqui: Revista Latinoamericana de Comunicación* 29 (1989): 68–71. https://doi.org/10.16921/chasqui.v0i29-30.1970.

McCormick, Gordon. *Sharp Dressed Men: Peru's Tupac Amaru Revolutionary Movement*. Santa Monica, CA: RAND Corporation, 1993.

Méndez, María. "El impacto del narcotráfico en el ámbito político. La cadena narco: Amenaza para la democracia y la gobernabilidad." In *El mapa del narcotráfico en el Perú*, edited by Nicole Bernex et al., 43–58. Lima: PUCP, 2009.

Menton, M., and P. Cronkleton. "Migration and Forests in the Peruvian Amazon: A Review." Bogor, Indonesia: Center for International Forestry Research (CIFOR), 2019. https://doi.org/10.17528/cifor/007305.

Meza Bazán, Mario Miguel. "El Movimiento Revolucionario Túpac Amaru (MRTA) y las fuentes de la revolución en América Latina." PhD diss., El Colegio de México, 2012.

Milton, Cynthia. "At the Edge of the Peruvian Truth Commission: Alternative Paths to Recounting the Past." *Radical History Review*, no. 98 (2007): 3–33.

———. "Desfigurando la memoria: (Des)atando los nudos de la memoria peruana." *Anthropologica* 33, no. 34 (2015): 11–33. https://revistas.pucp.edu.pe/index.php/anthropologica/article/view/13084/13695.

Mollica, Richard. *Healing Invisible Wounds Paths to Hope and Recovery in a Violent World*. Nashville, TN: Vanderbilt University Press, 2008.

Morales, Edmundo. "The Political Economy of Cocaine Production: An Analysis of the Peruvian Case." *Latin American Perspectives* 17, no. 4 (1990): 91–109. https://doi.org/10.1177/0094582X9001700406.

Moraña, Mabel. "El ojo que llora: Biopolítica, nudos de la memoria y arte público en el Perú de hoy." *Latinoamérica: Revista de Estudios Latinoamericanos* 1, no. 54 (2012): 183–216. http://www.scielo.org.mx/scielo.php?script=sci_arttext&pid=S1665-85742012000100008&lng=es&tlng=es.

Movimiento Revolucionario Túpac Amaru (MRTA). "Balance y perspectivas: Campaña Militar del Frente Guerrillero Nor Oriental." *Voz Rebelde*, no. 9 (January 1988).

———. "¡Con las masas y las armas por la democracia revolucionaria, la soberanía nacional, la justicia y la paz!" Dirección Nacional, Movimiento Revolucionario Túpac Amaru, December 1987.

———. *Conquistando el porvenir: Con las masas y las armas. Notas sobre la historia del MRTA.* Lima: Voz Rebelde MRTA, 1990.

———. "Declaración Unitaria del Movimiento Tupac Amaru (MRTA) y del Movimiento Izquierda Revolucionaria 'Voz Rebelde' (MIR-VR)." I Comité Central Unitario, Movimiento Revolucionario Túpac Amaru, Lima, December 9, 1986.

———. "El Frente Guerrillero Nor-Oriental." *Voz Rebelde,* no. 11 (April–May 1988).

———. "Forjando el Ejército Tupacamarista." *Voz Rebelde,* no. 8 (November 1987).

———. "Historia del Movimiento Revolucionario Túpac Amaru." III Comité Central del MRTA, Documento aprobado por el III Comité Central del Movimiento Revolucionario Túpac Amaru, September 1990.

———. "Mensaje a la juventud." II Central Committee of the Movimiento Revolucionario Túpac Amaru, August 1988.

———. "El MRTA y las tareas en periodo pre-revolucionario." Documento aprobado en el II Comité Central, Movimiento Revolucionario Túpac Amaru, February 1985.

———. "No ha empezado ninguna revolución: A propósito de la estatización del sistema financiero." Dirección Nacional del Movimiento Revolucionario Túpac Amaru, July 1987.

———. "La situación actual y las tareas en el proceso de la guerra revolucionaria del pueblo." Comité Política, Movimiento Revolucionario Túpac Amaru, May 1984.

Murri Benegas, María Lourdes. "La construcción de la memoria en América Latina: Las memorias en pugna en el Perú pos conflicto armado interno." *Revista Electrónica de Estudios Latinoamericanos* 17, no. 65 (2018): 15–36.

Oliveira, Ana Claudia de, and Lilian Kanashiro. "LUM, presencias resignificantes del conflicto armado peruano." *Galáxia* (São Paulo) 46 (2021): 1–19. https://doi.org/10.1590/198 2-2553202151951.

O'Phelan Godoy, Scarlett. *La gran rebelión en los Andes: De Túpac Amaru a Túpac Catari.* Cuzco, Perú: Centro de Estudios Regionales Andinos Bartolomé de Las Casas, 1995.

Ortega, Eudoxio H. *Manual de historia general del Perú; historia crítica.* Lima: Fénix Latino Americana, 1968.

Orwell, George. *1984.* New York: Houghton Mifflin Harcourt, 1983.

Owen, Wilfred. "Mental Cases." 1918. In *Complete Poems and Fragments,* edited by Jon Stallworthy. London: Chatto and Windus, 1983.

Padilla Cabrera, Jime. "Memoria sobre la violencia política, caso de la región San Martín (provincia de Tocache)." Bachelor's thesis, UNMSM, Lima, 2012.

Padovano, Anthony. *The Estranged God: Modern Man's Search for Belief.* Berkeley: University of California, 1966.

Panfichi, Aldo, and Jo-Marie Burt. *Peru, Caught in the Crossfire.* Jefferson City, MO: Peru Peace Network, 1992.

Paredes, Jorge. "Entrevista a Manuel Burga: El LUM ha sido víctima de malas interpretaciones." APRODEH, August 20, 2018. https://www.aprodeh.org.pe/entrevista-a-manuel-burga-el-lum-ha-sido-victima-de-malas-interpretaciones/.

Paredes, Maritza, and Hernán Manrique. "The State's Developmentalist Illusion and the Origins of Illegal Coca Cultivation in Peru's Alto Huallaga Valley (1960–80)." *Journal of Latin American Studies* 53, no. 2 (2021): 245–67. https://doi.org/10.1017/S0022216X21000225.

Pawlett, William. *Violence, Society and Radical Theory: Bataille, Baudrillard and Contemporary Society.* London: Routledge, 2013.

Pietraszczyk-Sękowska, Joanna. "Towards Homes and Graves. About the Returns, Desaparecidos and Exhumation Challenges in Peru at the End of the Twentieth Century." *International Studies: Interdisciplinary Political and Cultural Journal* 25, no. 1 (2020): 49–74. https://doi.org/10.18778/1641-4233.25.04.

Pillen, Alex. "Language, Translation, Trauma." *Annual Review of Anthropology* 45 (2016): 95–111. https://doi.org/10.1146/annurev-anthro-102215-100232.

Polay Campos, Víctor. "Interrogatorio a Víctor Polay, trigésima quinta sesión, June 11, 2005." In *En el banquillo: ¿Terrorista o rebelde?*, edited by Víctor Polay Campos. Lima: Canta Editores, 2007.

La Primera. "A 24 años de su asesinato evocan a general López Albujar." January 9, 2014.

Puente Uceda, Luis de la. *El MIR histórico: Luis de la Puente y Guillermo Lobatón.* Edited by Ricardo Gadea Acosta. Lima: Comisión 50 Aniversario de la Gesta Guerrillera del MIR, 2015.

———. "The Peruvian Revolution: Concepts and Perspectives." *Monthly Review* 17, no. 6 (1965): 12–28.

Pulgar Vidal, Javier. *Geografía del Perú: Las ocho regiones naturales del Perú.* Lima: Editorial Universo, 1972.

Quevedo Bardález, Julio. "Después de 22 años reclama recompensa por entrega de miembro del MRTA." *Voces,* June 16, 2015.

Radio Tropical. "Durante operativo antidrogas en el tramo Pongo de Caynarachi y Barranquita, intervienen a dos sujetos que portaban arma de fuego hechiza." December 19, 2020. https://radiotropical.pe/durante-operativo-antidrogas-en-el-tramo-pongo-de-caynarachi-y-barranquita-intervienen-a-dos-sujetos-que-portaban-arma-de-fuego-hechiza/.

Razzouk, Denise, Bruno Nogueira, and Jair de Jesus Mari. "The Contribution of Latin American and Caribbean Countries on Culture Bound Syndromes Studies for the ICD-10 Revision: Key Findings from a Work in Progress." *Brazilian Journal of Psychiatry* 33, suppl. 1 (2011): 1–20. https://doi.org/10.1590/S1516-44462011000500003.

Rendon, Silvio. "Capturing Correctly: A Reanalysis of the Indirect Capture-Recapture Methods in the Peruvian Truth and Reconciliation Commission." *Research and Politics* 6 (2019): 1–8. https://doi.org/10.1177/2053168018820375.

Rénique, José Luis. "De la traición aprista al gesto heroico—Luis de la Puente y la guerrilla del MIR." *Estudios Interdisciplinarios de América Latina y el Caribe* 15, no. 1 (2004): 89–114. http://eial.tau.ac.il/index.php/eial/article/view/828.

Rivers, William Halse Rivers. "The Repression of War Experience." *Proceedings of the Royal Society of Medicine* 11 (1918): 1–20.

Robbins, D. C., B. Dean, C. Gerhold, M. J. Mosher, and J. Camargo "184-LB: Lipid and HbA1c Profiles among People with Lean and Overweight Type 2 Diabetes in the Peruvian Amazon." *Diabetes* 70, suppl. 1 (2021): https://doi.org/10.2337/db21-184-LB.

Rodríguez Aguilar, César. *Justicia comunitaria y rondas campesinas en el Sur andino.* Lima: Asociación SER/ProJur, 2007.

Rojas-Pérez, Isaias. *Mourning Remains: State Atrocity, Exhumations, and Governing the Disappeared in Peru's Postwar Andes.* Palo Alto, CA: Stanford University Press, 2017.

Romero, Eduardo. *Perfil antropológico del agricultor cocalero: Historias, economías domésticas, percepciones: Un análisis comparativo de las zonas del VRAE y Aguaytía.* Lima: DEVIDA, 2011.

Sánchez Nieto, W. Alejandro. *"Give War a Chance* Revisited—The Price to Pay: The Military and Terrorism in Peru." *Defence Studies* 11, no. 3 (2011): 517-40. https://doi.org/10.1080/14 702436.2011.630178.

Santa Cruz Borja, Ruth Elena. "Utilization of the Archives of the Peruvian Commission for Truth and Reconciliation (CVR)." In *Archives and Human Rights,* edited by Jens Boel, Perrine Canavaggio, and Antonio González Quintana, 277-87. New York: Routledge, 2021.

Scheper-Hughes, Nancy. "The Primacy of the Ethical: Propositions for a Militant Anthropology." *Current Anthropology* 36, no. 3 (1995): 409-40.

Sí. "Resurrección: Historia secreta de la deserción de Andrés Mendoza 'El Grillo.'" September 27-October 4, 1993, 34-39.

Singh, M. P. *Quote Unquote: A Handbook of Famous Quotations.* New Delhi: Lotus Press, 2006.

Sorel, Georges. *Sorel: Reflections on Violence.* Edited by Jeremy Jennings. Cambridge: Cambridge University Press, 1999.

Starn, Orin, ed. *Hablan los ronderos: La búsqueda por la paz en los Andes.* Lima: IEP, 1993.

Stiles, Kristine. "Shaved Heads and Marked Bodies: Representations from Cultures of Trauma." *Stratégie II: Peuples Méditerranéens* 64-65 (1993): 95-117.

Tanaka, Martín. "Sendero Luminoso, the MRTA, and the Peruvian Paradoxes." In *Latin American Guerrilla Movements,* edited by Dirk Kruijt, Eduardo Rey Tristán, and Alberto Martín Álvarez, 181-88. New York: Routledge, 2019.

Tarazona-Sevillano, Gabriela. "El narcoterrorismo." *Revista Occidental* 8, no. 2 (1991): 151-83.

Taussig, Michael. "Culture of Terror—Space of Death: Roger Casement's Putumayo Report and the Explanation of Torture." *Comparative Studies in Society and History* 26, no. 3 (1984): 467-97. https://www.jstor.org/stable/178552.

Theidon, Kimberly. *Intimate Enemies: Violence and Reconciliation in Peru.* Philadelphia: University of Pennsylvania Press, 2012.

———. "Justice in Transition: The Micropolitics of Reconciliation in Postwar Peru." *Journal of Conflict Resolution* 50, no. 3 (2006): 433-57. https://doi.org/10.1177/0022002706286954.

———. *Legacies of War Violence, Ecologies, and Kin.* Raleigh, NC: Duke University Press, 2022.

Torchia, Christopher. "Long after Grisly End, Túpac Amaru Still Fascinates in Peru." Associated Press, May 18, 2021.

Truth and Reconciliation Commission, Peru. *Hatun Willakuy: Abbreviated Version of the Final Report of the Truth and Reconciliation Commission.* Lima: Truth and Reconciliation Commission, Peru, 2014.

Valcárcel, Daniel. *La rebelión de Túpac Amaru.* Lima: Fondo de Cultura Económica, 1970.

Valencia Chamba, Franco, J. Ríos Alvarado, Jean-François Tourrand, and M. G. Piketty. "Coca et violence: Le témoignage du Alto Huallaga au Pérou." *Autrepart* 26 (2003): 157-71.

Van Dun, Mirella. *Cocaleros: Violence, Drugs and Social Mobilization in the Post-Conflict Upper Huallaga Valley, Peru.* Amsterdam: Rozenberg Publishers, 2009.

———. "Narco-Territoriality and Shadow Powers in a Peruvian Cocaine Frontier." *Terrorism and Political Violence* 31, no. 5 (2009): 1026-48. https://doi.org/10.1080/09546553.2017.13 09392.

Varese, Stefano. *The Art of Memory: An Ethnographer's Journey.* Translated by Margaret Randall. Chapel Hill: University of North Carolina, 2020.

———. *Salt of the Mountain: Campa Asháninka History and Resistance in the Peruvian Jungle.* Norman: University of Oklahoma Press, 2004.

Vargas Llosa, Mario. *La ciudad y los perros.* Barcelona: Editorial Seix Barral, 1963.

Vidarte, Giuliana. "La noche de las gardenias." https://www.micromuseo.org.pe/rutas/ noche-gardenias/sinopsis.html.

Villapolo, Leslie. "Recursos socioculturales de los Asháninka para resistir al régimen totalitario de Sendero Luminoso y sus efectos." *Boletín del CDI* (Centro de Documentación e Investigación del Lugar de la Memoria, la Tolerancia y la Inclusión Social) 1 (2016): 8–9.

Villasante Cervello, Mariella. "Violencia de masas del Partido Comunista del Perú-Sendero Luminoso y campos de trabajo forzado entre los Ashaninka de la selva central." *Dossier de Memoria* 9 (2012): 1–79.

———. *La violencia política en la selva central del Perú, 1980–2000: Los campos totalitarios senderistas y las secuelas de la guerra interna entre los Ashaninka y Nomatsiguenga: Estudio de antropología de la violencia.* Lima: Comisión de Derechos Humanos, 2019.

Walker, Charles. *The Tupac Amaru Rebellion.* Cambridge, MA: Belknap Press of Harvard University Press, 2014.

Willis, Daniel. "Scratched from Memory: The 1986 Prison Massacres and the Limits of Acceptable Memory Discourse in Post-Conflict Peru." *Journal of Latin American Cultural Studies* 29, no. 2 (2020): 231–50.

———. "The Testimony of Space: Sites of Memory and Violence in Peru's Internal Armed Conflict." PhD diss., University College of London, Institute of the Americas, London, 2018.

Zárate, Patricia Ardela. *La democracia lejos de Lima: Descentralización y política en el departamento de San Martín.* Colección Mínima. Lima: IEP, 2003.

———. "Las rondas de la selva alta, un territorio por explorar." *Argumentos* 2, no. 15 (1994): 12–14.

Zevallos, Nicolás. "Hoja de coca y la Estrategia Nacional de Lucha contra las Drogas 2007–2011: El problema público en el control de cultivos." *Revista de Ciencia Política y Gobierno* 1 (2014): 97–113.

Acknowledgments

To give thanks in solitude is enough. Thanksgiving has wings and goes where it must go. Your prayer knows much more about it than you do.

ATTRIBUTED TO VICTOR-MARIE HUGO

I am overwhelmed with gratitude and humility for everyone who has helped me translate my ideas about the impact of postwar trauma in Peruvian Amazonia into something concrete that transcends the reductionistic level of the simple and straightforward. In fact, it's harder than it seems to write a book about trauma and the tumultuous memories of a violent battle, but it's also more rewarding than I expected. On this note, I want to thank my many wise teachers, cherished colleagues, and loyal friends for being my inspiration for starting and finishing this project. Fused through tested friendship and loving affection, the support of my wife, Luz Angélica Gómez Mendoza de Dean, saw me through all of my many setbacks and celebrated the victories. Luz Angélica's generous kindness has bestowed upon me the priceless blessing of envisioning a boundless future, instilling in me the bravery and unwavering determination to chase after my dreams. Her role was crucial to the genesis and the completion of the book. Accompanying me to the Huallaga Valley, Luz Angélica assisted in gathering vital information, helping to give a semblance of meaning to the narratives I collected and providing me with much-needed moral support, intellectual counsel, and emotional encouragement along the way. I will always be devoted to Luz Angélica, my dear Delfinita, for her creative guidance, keen judgment, and ongoing support in helping to make life worthwhile.

My beloved dog Mishkina has been a source of spiritual support and comfort for me throughout the challenging journey of writing this book, and I would like to express my wholehearted gratefulness to her. To my family, I want to thank them for always being a source of unfailing support for me during those trying and horrible moments of dark reflection, especially my parents, Warwick and Stella; my siblings, Melinda, Gregory, Adam, and Aurelia; and my children, Maxwell, Isadora, and Gideon. They gave me the vital help I required, including support I didn't even know I needed, which enabled me to finish the arduous task of writing this book.

In the same way, I owe an immeasurable debt of appreciation to everyone in the Huallaga Valley, especially in the Caynarachi River basin, who welcomed a hungry outsider into their homes when they didn't have to. My perspective of the world has been radically altered by the various people I encountered in the Huallaga Valley. These folks taught me values like reciprocity, hard love, respect, secrecy, discipline, and many other things. I am indebted to those individuals who exhibited utmost candor, bravely opening up and sharing their immensely personal experiences, even where their narratives carried the heavy weight of tragedy. Their willingness to delve into the depths of their intimate lives has given me a wealth of knowledge and a greater sense of empathy, significantly influencing my perspective on the human condition. Whether perpetrators, defenseless spectators, or victims, the valiant and the broken voices I heard and tape-recorded represented a vast spectrum of human experience and moral universes. Despite the devastation experienced by so many who I met, the ease with which many of the people I spoke with could rebuild their lives after the conflict amazed me.

I acknowledge the generous support of the University of Kansas, which, besides providing me with a stimulating intellectual home, has offered the following support for my project that spanned several years: Faculty Research Award, Center for Latin American and Caribbean Studies, Sabbatical Leave Award, KU International Programs, KU-UCR Exchange Fund Award, KU International Affairs Latin America Fund, and General Research Fund Awards. A Fulbright Scholar Award, Universidad Nacional de San Martín, Peru in 2011–2012, provided me the opportunity to conduct preliminary research on the Túpac Amaru Revolutionary Movement (MRTA). As at the University of Kansas in Lawrence, I thank my many colleagues and students at the Universidad Nacional de San Martín (Museo Regional) Tarapoto, and at the Universidad Nacional Autónoma de Alto Amazonas, Yurimaguas, Peru, who have all helped shape my thinking on the impact of the internal war and the MRTA in the Lower Huallaga Valley. I appreciate the efforts of Manuel Burga Díaz, director of the Peruvian Ministry of Culture's Place of Memory, Tolerance, and Social Inclusion (Lugar de la Memoria, la Tolerancia y la Inclusión Social, LUM) for providing access to photographic images appearing in the text. Unless otherwise noted, the photographs are part of the collection of the Centro de Estudios y Promoción del Desarrollo, Lima, housed at LUM, and were taken by several journalists during the period covered in this book.

Allow me to express my deepest thanks to the remarkable individuals of the Vanderbilt University Press staff, whose unwavering help has been an indispensable source of guidance and support throughout my endeavors. I extend my recognition to Zachary Gresham, a paragon of unwavering support, who served as my acquisitions editor. Zach's generosity and the exceptional external peer reviewers who so kindly gave me their invaluable suggestions deserve my sincere gratitude. Their expert advice has fortified the arguments, augmenting the text with additional vital references and helping to sharpen my arguments. Likewise, I am beholden to Katherine Faydash for her discerning evaluation of my manuscript and the immeasurable contributions she has made throughout the editorial process. Katherine's dedication and unparalleled expertise have unequivocally enriched the essence of my book. I would like to express my sincere gratitude to Brady Cullen of the University Press of Kansas for her meticulous work in creating the book's index. Her dedication and expertise have resulted in an invaluable tool for navigating the book's content. Additionally, I extend my thanks to Joell Smith-Borne, who serves as the managing production editor at Vanderbilt University Press. Her careful oversight of the project has significantly contributed to the book's quality. Lastly, I would like to acknowledge Gianna Mosser, the director of Vanderbilt University Press, for her unwavering support throughout the project. Her guidance and endorsement have played a pivotal role in bringing this work to fruition. ¡Gracias a todos!

In my role as an ethnographer, I humbly recognize that I bear full responsibility for any inaccuracies, errors, or misinterpretations that may exist within the contents of this book. It is essential for me to emphasize the utmost importance of respecting and preserving the privacy and well-being of the individuals who have generously shared their life stories with me. To honor their trust and maintain their anonymity, I have conscientiously employed various measures, such as using pseudonyms or obscuring specific place-names whenever circumstances have permitted. When you see an asterisk next to a person's name in the book, it signifies the adoption of a pseudonym. I have taken these deliberate actions intending to provide a protective shield that safeguards their identities and affirms their fundamental right to confidentiality. By creating such a secure environment, I aim to cultivate a space that encourages open and honest sharing, fostering an atmosphere of trust and enabling the genuine expression of personal experiences.

Index

Page references in *italic* refer to figures.

Achinamiza, 82, 127, 168–69
Agua Blanca, 74
AKM (assault rifles), 61, 89, 99, 171–72,
    178
  Belgian, 170
  flaunting of, 65
  supplied by National Directorate, 86
  Yurimaguas, 161
  See also Túpac Amaru Revolutionary
    Movement (MRTA); weapons
Alianza, 21, 58
American Popular Revolutionary Alliance
    (APRA), 34, 40, 59, 63
Anderson, Benedict, 191
aniquilación (annihilation), 116–17
Aoki, Morihisa, 12
Arendt, Hannah, 167
Arévalo, Manuel, 164
armed front, 16, 35, 37
armed struggle
  accounts of, 24, 27, 44, 54, 166–67,
    175–76
  historical causes of, 21
  in Northeastern Front, 15–16
  and political legitimacy, 145
  reactivation of, 35
  See also Túpac Amaru Revolutionary
    Movement (MRTA)

assassination
  of General Enrique López Albujar
    Trint, 16
  of peasants, 167
asustada (scared), 102. *See also* fear
asymmetric warfare, 10
Aucayacu, 56
avioneta (small airplane), 75, 142, 148–49,
    159, 161
Ayacucho, 4, 9, 189
Azevedo, Valérie Robin, 4

Bakunin, Mikhail, 57
Banco de Credito, *17*
Bastidas, Micaela, 14
Battle of Angamos, 69
Battle of Ayacucho, 36
Belaúnde Terry, Fernando, 18, 34, 40
Bellavista, 58, 72, 93
  airstrips in, 116
  coca leaf processing in, 142
  guerrilla assaults on, 77
  and Túpac Amaru, 102, 153
Bellido Mora, Eduardo, 169
Bigwood, Jeremy, 45
Black, Charlene 14. *See also* Catholic
    Church
Blanco Galdós, Hugo, 34

bombings, 16, 74
Bonilla, 145
bourgeoisie, 27, 31, 43
brujería (witchcraft), 128
brujos (shamans), 126–28, 165, 167
Burga Díaz, Manuel, 188

Cacatachi, 58
Cachay Huamán, Lucas, 21, 68, 146
  and FEDIPSM, 59, 77
  and MRTA, 163–64
  as policy secretary, 31
  and Revolutionary Left Movement, 29
  and Unitary Fighting Command, 58
cago de susto ("scared shitless"), 173. *See also* fear
calabozo (jail), 137, 158
Campanilla, 36
Campesino Confederation of Peru
  (Confederación Campesina del Perú
  [CCP]), 57
Camus, Albert, 5, 185
capitalism, 14, 177
Cárdenas Schulte, Peter David Peabody
  (a.k.a., Comrade Alejandro or "El
  Siciliano"), 36, 37
Carlos Mariátegui, José, 8, 29, 30, 31
Carretera Marginal de la Selva (Marginal
  Highway of the Jungle), 18, 58, 70–71
Castro y Castro Penitentiary, 153, 155
Cathedral of the Virgin of the Snows
  (Templo de la Virgen de las Nieves),
  48
Catholic Church
  censorship of, 14
  and El Grillo, 168
  and political life, 131–33
  priests, 51, 94, 106, 107, 129–31, 132–
  34, 137, 171–73
  and Túpac Amaru Revolutionary
  Movement, 130
Centurión Pérez, Segundo, 58, 164
Cerpa Cartolini, Néstor Fortunato (a.k.a.,
  Comrade Evaristo), 12, 17, 35,

36, 68, 77. *See also* Túpac Amaru
  Revolutionary Movement (MRTA)
chacra (small farm), 51, 62–63, 66, 78, 94,
  178
  and MRTA, 54, 92, 98, 104, 113–14
Chazuta, 7, 78, 82, 160
  army patrol in, 168
  Kichwa-Lamista community in, 19
  platoons in, 154
  raids in, 74
Chiclayo, 18, 32, 38
choba choba (reciprocal labor), 51
choro (thief), 122, 124, 167 178, 186
civil peasant patrols, 168. *See also rondas*
  campesinas; ronderos
colaborar (collaborate), 49
cocaine
  alliance of MRTA and narcos, 145–46,
  148–49, 150
  bonanza, 146
  capitalisms, 148
  effects of, 164
  failed agrarian policy, 141–42, 143
  transnational distribution network, 139,
  141
cocaleros (coca growers), 4, 142, 150
  and drug cartels, 61
  and the Túpac Amaru Revolutionary
  Movement, 53–54
colectivos (cargo and passenger boats), 101,
  102
colgado (strung up as punishment), 122
collaboration, 49, 139
  dangers of, 52, 53, 103
  as protection, 102
  transport, 103
Colombia, 4, 16, 36, 60, 75, 86
  guerrilla training in, 50, 61, 66–67
  MIR-VR and, 31–33
  National Liberation Army, 36
  drug traffickers, 141–42, 145, 147
Comisión de la Verdad y Reconciliación
  (CVR), 8, 33, 127, 146, 164
  accounts of torture, 95

limitations, 183–84
mission of, 13
report of, 95–96
testimonies by, 111–12, 114–16, 164
Commander Ricardo. *See* Sístero García
   Torres
Committee of the Producers of Corn and
   Sorghum (Comité de Productores de
   Maíz y Sorgo), 38
communal life, violence of, 16
concealment, 7, 86
Cordillera Escalera, 18, 19, 112
counterinsurgency
   and Túpac Amaru Revolutionary
      Movement, 5, 49, 52, 73–74, 95, 164,
      170, 182
   in Huallaga Valley, 11, 108
Counter-Terrorist Directorate (Dirección
   contra el Terrorismo, DIRCOTE),
   187
Cumapa, Marcial, 38
Cuñumbuque, *71*
cupos (war taxes), 53, 65–66, 145–46
   collection of, 49–50, 116–17, 120, 138,
   166
Cusco, 35

Das, Veena, 3
deforestation, 142
Democratic Defense Front (Frente de
   Defensa Democrático), 129, 133, 134
Dirección Antidrogas de la Policía
   Nacional del Perú (antidrug police),
   162
disappearances, 13, 73
drug trafficking. *See* narcos
Durkheim, Émile 6

economic crisis, 9, 40
1821 War of Independence, 14
Ejército Popular Tupacamarista (EPT), 36,
   131, 160
   and MRTA, 68–70, 84
Espinosa Arango, Mónica, 4

executions, 13, 122, 115
extrajudicial killings, 13, 166

Fanon, Frantz, 14
fear
   of army convoys, 85
   of checkpoints, 93
   of Commander Ricardo, 62
   of *cumpas*, 49
   of encampments, 61
   impact of living in, 64–66, 87, 91, 96,
      114–15
   of lethal retribution, 49
   physical effects of, 88, 109, 136
   and social isolation, 182
   social organizations, 59
   MRTA use of, 118–19, 128
   See also memory; trauma
firmas (drug cartels), 51, 61, 149
flag
   of MRTA, 64, 72
   of Túpac Amaru, 65, 137
FN FAL weapons (*arma matapato*), 135
focos ("focuses"), 57
foquismo, 57
Forest Teachers Agrarian Federation
   (Federación Agraria Selva Maestra
   [FASMA]), 58, 164
Front for the Defense of the Interests
   of the Province of San Martín
   (Frente de Defensa de los Intereses
   de la Provincia de San Martín
   [FEDIPSM]), 59, 77, 163, 164
Fujimori Inomoto, Alberto, 164, 170, 176,
   188
   and cocaine, 142, 150
   and creation of San Martín Region, 163
   as president, 11–12
   US support of, 11
fumones (addicted). *See* substance abusers
fundo (farm), 48–49
   of Don Alberto, 136
   of Don Wilder, 43
   of Don Xavier, 26

Gabriel Condorcanqui, José, 14, 15, 65, 69
Gálvez, Rodrigo (a.k.a., Comrade
  Roberto), 77, 90
Gálvez Olaechea, Alberto (a.k.a.,
  Comrade Guillermo), 33, 38, 60,
  68–69
García, Trigoso, 88, 90. *See also* Túpac
  Amaru Revolutionary Movement
  (MRTA)
García Neira, Héctor, 164
García Pérez, Alan, 9, 40
  faltering government of, 63
  first government of, 21
  in San Martín, 73
  See also American Popular
    Revolutionary Alliance (APRA)
garitas policiales (police checkpoints), 93
gay people
  exclusion of, 125–26
  murder of, 11, 165, 167
General Velasco, 20, 34
Geneva Conventions, 70
gente humilde (humble people), 23–25
González Prada, Manuel, 81
Grau, 111
Guerrero, Alejandro, and Panamericana's
  Channel 5, 72
guerrilla front, 17
  in civil society, 163–64
  formation of, 75
  in San Martín, 57, 60
guerrilla warfare
  campaign of, 36
  manual on, 30
  reliance on, 11, 15
  training, 32–33, 61, 81–82
  urban, 16
  violence of, 171, 176
Guevara, Che (Ernesto Rafael Guevara de
  la Serna), 29–30, 39
Guzmán, Abimael, 12, 63. *See also* Sendero
  Luminoso (the Shining Path)

Halbwachs, Maurice, 6, 180
Heraud Pérez, Javier, 178

Herndon, Commander William Lewis,
  17–18
hitmen
  MRTA use of, 61, 141, 149
  of Ramírez, 106
Hodge, Derrick G., 186
hostages, 131
  crisis, 12
  trauma of, 135, 137, 139
huachiman (watchman), 147
Huancapi. *See* Ayacucho
Huancavelica, 9
Huánuco, 152
Huayabamba, 76, 83, 146, 153
huerta (backyard garden), 40, 89, 122–23
human rights violations, 9, 10, 13, 95, 116,
  144, 165, 167
hyperinflation, 63

imperialism, 9, 15, 16, 31, 42
inflation, 21
insurgents, 16
insurrection
  armed, 36, 42
  forced, 112, 167–68
  initiation of, 61, 69
  politics of, 21
  of 1780–1782, 14
internal war
  critics of, 95
  daily life during, 20, 74, 98, 101, 113,
    124–25, 129–30
  effect on community, 133, 143, 164
  and popular justice, 103
  retreat during, 89
  See also fear; trauma
internationalism, 15
interrogation
  as torture, 106, 137
  abuse by interrogators, 51, 110
Iquitos, 20, 67, 73, 126

jail (*calabozo*), 137, 158
Jelin, Elizabeth, 5, 195
Juan Guerra, 30, 33, 58

Juanjuí, 19, 76, 82–83, 160
   assault on, 69, 72–73, 74–75, 93
   military cells in, 38
   and MRTA, 57–58, 154
Junín, 34, 75, 164
justice, 4, 21, 77, 144–45, 168, 169, 183,
   186–88, 190–91
   for past, 112–13, 114
   of peace, 20
   popular, 104, 117–18, 119, 125
   social, 53
   by state, 44, 77

Kalashnikov PKM machine-gun, 155. *See
   also* weapons
Kichwa-Lamista, 28, 38
   in Caynarachi basin, 28
   memories of, 38, 52
   and MIR-VR, 38
   Túpac Amaru members, 128
kidnapping, 16, 130, 134–35, 137–39,
   166. *See also* fear; trauma
Klein Samanez, Rodolfo (a.k.a., Comrade
   Dimas), 37, 68
Kokama-Kokamilla and Sendero
   Luminoso, 9
Kropotkin, Peter, 118

Laguna Azul, 66, 173
La Libertad and Departments of San
   Martín, 138
Lamas, 82, 115, 168
   arrival of MRTA in, 18–19
   bombing of, 74
   capture of, 67
   military bases in, 73
Larco Cox, Guillermo, 73
La Shinao, 74
Law of Repentance
   and El Grillo, 168
   and Fujimori regime, 172
   MRTA's use of, 171, 174–75
Lenin, Vladimir, 29, 31
   and MIR-VR, 30–31, 38
Leoncio, Prado, 175

LGBTQ community, 11, 126. *See also* gay
   people
liberation theology, 132
Lima, *17*, 30, 32–36, 38–39, 44, 55, 67,
   81, 135, 137–38, 153, 164–65, 175–
   77, 181, 187
   central government, 2, 40, 63
   elites, 42
   migration to, 76, 96, 115, 126
   and MRTA, 15–16, 73, 93
   poverty in, 9, 20–21
   weapons from, 86
Lobatón Milla, Guillermo, 34
López, Roger (a.k.a., Comrade Cabezón),
   75–76
López Albujar Trint, Enrique, 16. *See also*
   American Popular Revolutionary
   Alliance (APRA); García Pérez, Alan
López y Lainz, Roger (a.k.a., Comrade
   Melvin), 76
Los Aguanos, 72
lucha armada, la (the armed struggle), 35.
   See also Túpac Amaru Revolutionary
   Movement (MRTA)

mafia, 149
Maoism, 8, 9, 57
mapacho (Nicotiana rustica cigar), 42, 43,
   78
Marañón River, 19, 177
Marginal Highway of the Jungle
   (Carretera Marginal de la Selva), 18,
   58, 70–71
martyrs, 7, 75, 76
masses, 15, 17, 27, 31, 43, 58, 61, 78, 158,
   165
Maybury-Lewis, David, 9
Medellín cartel, 142–43
memory, 1, 4, 5, 8, 103, 109, 113, 144
   collective, 180
   fading, 27
   narrativized, 2, 6
   regimes, 6
   of violence, 1–2, 183
   See also fear; trauma

Mendoza del Águila, Andrés (a.k.a.,
    Commander Grillo) 86, 90, 135–36,
    138, 158, 166, 169–70
mestizo campesinos, 19, 141
Metilluyoc, 126
Meza Bravo, Antonio, 35
miliciano (MRTA sympathizer or militant),
    45, 52, 79, 84, 129–30, 154, 158, 161
MIR-VR. *See* Revolutionary Left
    Movement (Movimiento de
    Izquierda Revolucionaria [MIR])
Mollica, Richard, 2
monte (rainforest), 42, 54, 123, 139, 173
    ambushes in, 63, 66, 113, 127, 160
    flora in, 178
    rebel teachers in, 130
    training in, 61, 77
    weapon stashes in, 85–86
Morales (Tarapoto), 58, 73, 126
    army base in, 173, 175
Morales Bermúdez, Francisco, 58
moral outrage, 124
Moral Rengifo, Rafael, 73
Moyobamba, 18, 82, 88, 101, 127
    military cells in, 38
    students from, 27
MRTA. *See* Túpac Amaru Revolutionary
    Movement (MRTA)

narcocriminals, 143
narcos, 5, 51–52, 61, 117, 159, 166
    in El Porvenir, 124
    and MRTA, 117, 144–45, 146–47, 149
    and Sendero Luminoso, 143
    See also cocaine; *cocaleros* (coca growers)
narrative modes, 7
National Directorate, 86, 153
    in lower Huallaga area, 44
    in training camps, 75
    See also Túpac Amaru Revolutionary
    Movement (MRTA)
National Executive Committee (Comité
    Ejecutivo Nacional [CEN]), 36
national liberation, 15, 41

National Social Mobilization Support
    System (Sistema Nacional de
    Apoyo a la Mobilización Nacional
    [SINAMOS]), 58
National University of San Marcos
    (Universidad Nacional Mayor de San
    Marcos), 39
neocolonialism, 14, 15
nervios (nerves). *See* fear
noncombatants, 11
Noriega Torres, Siomar, 157

Ocros. *See* Huamanga
Ojeda Zavaleta, Pedro (a.k.a., Comrade
    Darío), 77
Ortega, Eudoxio, 81
Orwell, George, 106
Oviedo Huapaya, Cecilia (a.k.a.,
    Comrade Tía), 37, 164

Pampa Hermosa, 7, 58
Partido Socialista Revolucionario–
    Leónidas Rodríguez Figueroa, 35
Partido Socialista Revolucionario
    Marxista-Leninista (PSR-ML), 34–
    35. *See also* Lenin, Vladimir
partisan anthropology, 185
pasta básica de cocaina, 148. *See* cocaine
Pawlett, William, 14
peasant strike, 21, 58, 131, 137
People's Revolutionary War, 13, 15, 17
Perú Posile government, 12
Picota, 141, 160
    1990 attack on, 87–88, 90–91, 92–93
    police station attack in, 77
Pinto, Óscar, 164
Pintoyacu, 115
Place of Memory, Tolerance, and Social
    Inclusion (Lugar de la Memoria,
    la Tolerancia y la Inclusión Social
    [LUM]), 188
Polay Campos, Víctor, 12, 35–36, 38, *46*,
    64, 67, 68–69, 119–20
    in countryside, 57

recapture of, 164
well-educated leader, 37, 72, 75, 153–54
See also Túpac Amaru Revolutionary
Movement (MRTA)
political violence, 13, 21, 94
against women, 11
limiting deforestation, 142
and nonaction of government, 59
Ponaza Valley, 120
Pongo de Caynarachi (Motico Hill), 19,
52, 58, 109
highway near, 45
routes to, 82, 97
runaways in, 145
Popular Action Party, 18
post-traumatic stress disorder, 8. *See also*
torture; trauma
prison, 144, 158, 170, 175
escape, 153–54, 155
executions, 110
MRTA members in, 88–89, 132
Sístero García Torres's release from, 87
propaganda, 7, 43, 50, 85, 139, 158
as acts of sabotage, 16
goal of, 76
performances, 116
revolutionary action, 35–36
See also Túpac Amaru Revolutionary
Movement (MRTA)
psychosis, 170. *See also* torture; trauma
Pucacaca, 38, 58, 88
Puente Uceda, Luis Felipe de la, 34
Puerto Libre, 128
purma (secondary rainforest), 26, 28, 80

racialized violence, 21
radio, 130, 178
fear of, 63, 87
use of, by MRTA, 16, 35, 86
Radio Tropical, 92, 168, 169
ranear (forced physical exercises), 98, 133.
See also torture
ransom, 136
and financial problems of MRTA, 134

letter, 138–39
See also kidnapping; trauma
rapar (shaving hair), 121–25, 137. *See also*
torture
rape, 13, 53, 95, 115. *See also* kidnapping;
trauma
Reátegui, Alcides (a.k.a., Comrade
Tananta), 75–76, 77
reconciliation, 128, 190–91
failures of, 188
idea of, 182
Occidentalist, 187
post-war, 186
See also Comisión de la Verdad y
Reconciliación (CVR)
reconstruction of moral topographies, 183.
See also reconciliation
"rehabilitation" program for ex-
combatants, 175–76
remapping, 6
repression, 59, 167–68
resistance, 59, 70, 72, 158
revolutionary government, 14
Revolutionary Left Movement
(Movimiento de Izquierda
Revolucionaria [MIR])
column reconstitution, 77
and community effort, 37–38
fronts of, 34
leftist network of, 58–59
MIR-EM, 35
MIR-VR, 60–61, 68–69
and MRTA, 36–37
supporters, 29–30, 62
preparation for combat, 31–32
Revolutionary Vanguard (Vanguardia
Revolucionaria), 35. *See also* Cerpa
Cartolini, Néstor Fortunato (a.k.a.,
Comrade Evaristo); Rincón Rincón,
Manuel (a.k.a., Comrade Francisco)
revolutionary war, 14, 15, 27, 170
Rincón Rincón, Manuel (a.k.a., Comrade
Francisco), 35–36, 45, 68, 75
Rioja, 77, 82

Ríos, Velarde, 38
Rivero, Francisco, and Caretas, 71–72
Robin Azevedo, Valérie, 4
Rojas-Pérez, Isaias, 188–89
rondas campesinas, 11, 120, 189
ronderos (self-defense committees), 51,
    104, 146, 168–69
Rubén Abimael Guzmán Reynoso,
    Manuel, 12. *See also* Sendero
    Luminoso (the Shining Path)
runamula (adulterer), 117, 167, 226n39

Sandinista National Liberation Front
    (Frente Sandinista de Liberación
    Nacional [FSLN]), 33
Sangamayo, 128
San José de Sisa, 72, 76–77, 164
San Juan del Cumbaza, 169
San Miguel de Achinamiza. *See*
    Achinamiza
Saposoa, 74–75, 77, 92
scapegoating, 128
Scheper-Hughes, Nancy, 186
self-defense committee. *See ronderos*
selva alta (high-jungle), 18, 101
selva baja (lowland rainforest), 18, 19, 39,
    84, 152
Senami, 74
Sendero Luminoso (the Shining Path)
    in Caynarachi basin, 56–57
    and coca economy, 142–43, 145–46
    government initiative against, 11
    and MRTA, 11–12, 31, 70, 72, 109,
        117–19
    and narcos, 51
    and Néstor Cerpa Cartolini, 35
    recruitment of, 55
    and *tupacamaristas*, 36, 40, 120
    in Yumbatos, 119–20
sensory ethnography, 5
sexual assault, 11
sexualized abuse, 11
sexual violence
    against members of the LGBTQ
        community, 117, 125–26

against MRTA recruits, 174
    against sex workers, 167
    against women 11, 116, 165
sex workers, 11, 167
shamans, 11, 127, 128, 165
Shanao, 38, 74
Shanusi
    combat school in, 31, 33, 82
    MIR-VR and MRTA in, 68, 75–76, 119
    rebels in, 119
Shapaja, 33, 38, 77
shapshico, 64
Shawi, in Caynarachi basin, 19, 98
Shilcayo, 168
Shucshuyacu, 154, 159
SIG Pro pistols, 33. *See also* weapons
Silva, Migdoño (a.k.a., "The Puma"), 61
Sisa Valley, 33, 75–76
    and MRTA, 71–72, 74
Sístero García Torres, 42–43, 44–45, 81,
    85–87, 90, 103, 119, 153, 156, 159–
    70
    as comandante general, 60–63
    and community, 64–65, 75–77
    creation of Peasant Vanguard, 50
    reemergence as commander, 66–67
    stand against neocolonialism, 21–22
    and teaching, 29–31, 32–33
    See also Túpac Amaru Revolutionary
        Movement (MRTA)
slogans
    of MRTA, 15, 93, 158
    of Sendero Luminoso, 9
social
    fragmentation, 168
    misery, 2
    resentment (*resentimiento social*) and
        MRTA, 174
    spectatorship, 4
    suffering, 9
Socialist Revolutionary Party (PSR), 34
soplón (snitch), 55, 98, 114, 124, 167, 178,
    182
Sorel, Georges, 14
Soritor, 70, 71, 73, 76

spectacle, 105, 108, 158
state of emergency, 59, 71, 95
  in San Martín, 73–74
strategic silencing, 6
strikes
  campesino strike of 1982, 58
  forty-eight-hour strike in 1987, 73
  indefinite regional strike in 1990, 59
  rural and urban workers in 1984, 59
structural violence, 3, 177
substance abusers, 11, 150
suffering, 170
  avoidance of, 55
  and hunger, 78
  imposed by MRTA, 24, 84, 93–94
  See also trauma
surveillance, 45, 73, 108
susto (fright). *See* fear
SVD Dragunov sniper rifle, 155. *See also*
  weaponry
symbolic violence, 3, 16, 124

Tabalosos, 58, 69–71, 73, 76,
Tarapoto, 33, 43–45, 62–63, 66, 92–93,
  101, 110–11, 115–16, 126, 129, 135,
  142, 149, 159–61, 166, 168–69, 173,
  175
  highway in, 58, 60, 87, 88–89
  Marxist-Leninist literature of, 30
  Military-Political Command
    headquarters in, 73
  MRTA meeting in, 73–74
  passage to, 18
  police in, 51
  recruits from, 38
  university of, 78, 80–81
terror, 23, 61, 89, 102, 109. *See also* fear;
  trauma
terrorism, 9, 11, 66. *See also terruco*
  (terrorists)
terruco (terrorists), 15, 42, 55, 62–63, 88,
  95, 105, 171, 181, 186, 188
  clandestine meetings of, 56–57
  interrogation of, 51–52
  support of, 64–65

testimonies, 5, 13, 111, 130, 183. *See
  also* Comisión de la Verdad y
  Reconciliación (CVR)
Theidon, Kimberly, "role of committed
  witness," 186–87
thieves, 117, 178
  and MRTA, 121–22, 136, 165, 167
tiempos feos (ugly times), 3, 24–25, 97–98,
  111, 162
  and Catholic Church, 131
  and cocaleros, 150
  in Picota, 87
  reconciling with, 54–55, 95, 181–82
  and trauma, 52–53, 54–55, 88, 93, 104–
    5, 128–29
Tingo María, 18, 108, 111, 142
Tocache, 19
  coca leaf cultivation in, 142–43,
    147
  militants from, 68
  military base in, 73
  MRTA and Sendero Luminoso in,
    56–57, 120, 143
  police force, 144
  road connecting, 18
  Truth and Reconciliation Commission
    in, 183–84
Toledo Manrique, Alejandro, 13
Tolstoy, Leo, 40
toma de carreteran (road block) by militia
  members, 93
tombo (police), 11, 45, 89, 102, 124, 126,
  143, 149, 157
  abuse by, 51–52, 88
  and *emerretistas*, 49
  public trials of, 118
torture, 11, 13, 52
  by army, 106
  of civilians by MRTA, 95, 109–10, 121
  of El Grillo, 169
  mental, 13
transgender people, 167
traqueteros (drug dealers), 61, 80, 149
  airstrips, 50
  alliance with MRTA, 50–51, 141, 146–47

traqueteros (*continued*)
  and Central Intelligence Agency, 80
  and community, 61, 116
  See also cocaine
trauma, 24, 87, 109, 124, 168, 182, 183,
  186, 189
  and chaos, 93
  explaining, 43–44
  interpreting, 6–7
  migration, 96
  See also fear; memory
Trigoso García, Jaime, 88, 90
Trotsky, Leon 29, 31. *See also*
  Revolutionary Left Movement
  (Movimiento de Izquierda
  Revolucionaria [MIR])
Trujillo, 73
Truth and Reconciliation Commission, 8,
  33, 127, 146, 164
Tuanama, Javier, 164
tugurios (slums), 9
tunche (spirits), 93, 108
Tupacamarista Popular Army (Ejército
  Popular Tupacamarista [EPT]), 36, 68
Túpac Amaru Libertador campaign, 69,
  72, 74–75
Túpac Amaru Revolutionary Movement
  (MRTA)
  and AKM, 47, 61, 65, 86, 89, 99, 170,
    171
  armed struggle, 35
  colonial rule, 14
  detention of, 9, 110
  distinction between public and private,
    165
  gender ideals of, 125, 167
  Gramscian approach of, 2
  and Guevarism, 57
  militarization of social life, 11
  militia, 17, 39, 93, 125
  multinational financial institutions, 15
  and murder, 11, 106, 126, 127, 128,
    224, 229, 238
  stealing weaponry, 11

Túpac Amaru II. *See* Gabriel
  Condorcanqui, José
tupacho (MRTA militants), 16, 51–52, 102,
  104, 129, 138, 171
  effect on family, 78
  imprisonment of, 132
  as law enforcement, 117, 121–22, 125,
    149
tushpa (cooking fire), 48, 89

Uchiza, 49, 56, 73, 147
unfaithful partners, 11
Unitary Fighting Command (Comando
  Unitario de Lucha [CUL]), 58
Unitary Union of Education Workers
  of Peru (Sindicato Unitario de
  Trabajadores en la Educación del
  Perú [SUTEP]), 32
Urarina, 39
urbanization, 18, 20
US Drug Enforcement Agency, 142. *See
  also* cocaine
utopian liberation, 15

Vanguardia Campesina (the Peasants'
  Vanguard), 50, 74
varayocs (guards), 104. *See also* prison
Varese Scotto, Luis (pseud., Comrade
  Louis), 35. *See also* Socialist
  Revolutionary Party (PSR)
Vargas Llosa, Mario, 175
Velando, Máximo, 34
Velasco Alvarado, Juan, 14, 20, 106
victims, 5, 13, 111–12, 159, 183, 186–87,
  188–89
  naming, 93
  remembering, 110, 124, 174
  of Yumbatos massacre, 114–15
Villanueva del Campo, Armando, 59
violence, 22, 24, 40, 43, 57, 59, 78, 88, 94,
  101, 105, 109, 119, 126, 128, 143,
  164, 167–68, 174, 182
  conflict, 4, 13, 52, 62, 186
  counter, 14

encounters of, 6
gendered, 11
revolution, 35, 133
systemic, 14
warfare, 1, 2, 88, 180, 183–84
witnessing, 8, 185–86, 189–90

walkie-talkie, 91, 156
War of the Pacific, 69
weapons, 77, 87–89, 92, 105–6, *107*,
    120–21, 146, 150, *157*, 161, 172,
    181
  AKM rifle, 61, 170–71
  fear of, 49, 118, 132
  FN FAL, 135
  hiding, 85–86
  masses and, 43, 158
  of police stations, 70, 75, 158
  rocket-propelled grenade, 156
  seizure of, 72
  as strength, 17
  trading, 173
white gold. *See* cocaine

Wilde, Oscar, 150
witness testimony, 2

Yanayoc, 168
Yánesha, 35
Yorongos, 74
Yumbatos, 7, 44, 111, 117, 119–20, 130,
    132–33, 139
  combatants from, 82
  massacres in, 112–13, 114, 115–16
  support of rebels, 67
Yurimaguas, 7, 18, 19–20, 41, 47, 55, 60,
    94, 101, 102, 143, 144, 152–53, 163,
    177–78, *190*
  Catholic Cathedral in, 48
  guerrilla assault on, 77, 82–83, 88–89,
    151
  "Pearl of the Huallaga," 154–55, 156,
    157, 158, 159, 160–61, 162
  release of prisoners in, 89
  runaways in, 145
  seizure of, 67
  unpaved roads in, 58

Printed in the USA
CPSIA information can be obtained
at www.ICGtesting.com
LVHW051211041223
765471LV00004B/308